THE
NAKED
PUBLIC
SQUARE

Religion and Democracy in America

by

Richard John Neuhaus

WILLIAM B. EERDMANS PUBLISHING COMPANY
GRAND RAPIDS, MICHIGAN

for

The Community of Christ in the City

Ann   Larry
Casey   Mandy
Jeff   Tom

Library of Congress Cataloging in Publication Data

Neuhaus, Richard John.
The naked public square.

Includes index.
1. United States—Religion—1960-   . 2. United
States—Moral conditions. 3. Religion and politics—
United States. I. Title.
BL2525.N48 1984   261.7   84-6017
ISBN 0-8028-3588-0

CONTENTS

SOME DEBTS

THE FOLLOWING PEOPLE ARE NOT MORALLY RESPONSIBLE FOR the views set forth here, and some of them will no doubt be grateful for that. I am grateful to each of them for generously discussing the questions raised and thus contributing to my understanding, such as it is, of religion in American life: James Armstrong, Larry Bailey, Brigitte and Peter Berger, Charles Bergstrom, Margaret Boeth, Allan Carlson, Donald Cutler, Jerry Falwell, James Finn, Stanley Hauerwas, Bryan Hehir, George Higgins, John Howard, Dean Kelley, Norman Lear, Ernest Lefever, Robert Myers, Bruce Nichols, Michael Novak, Arthur Simon, Richard Stith, Glenn Stone, Marc Tanenbaum, Richard Viguerie, George Weigel, Paul Weyrich, and Elliott Wright.

A WORD
TO THE READER

THIS IS A BOOK ABOUT RELIGIOUS POLITICS AND POLITICAL religion. Politics and religion are different enterprises, and it is understandable that many people would like to keep them as separate as possible. But they are constantly coupling and getting quite mixed up with one another. There is nothing new about this. It seems likely that it has always been the case in all societies.

What is relatively new is the naked public square. The naked public square is the result of political doctrine and practice that would exclude religion and religiously grounded values from the conduct of public business. The doctrine is that America is a secular society. It finds dogmatic expression in the ideology of secularism. I will argue that the doctrine is demonstrably false and the dogma exceedingly dangerous.

In the late 1970s, and especially in connection with the 1980 presidential election, pundits religious and secular expressed surprise and alarm at the emergence of moral majoritarianism. I will argue that politically militant evangelical and fundamentalist protest against the naked public square has been building for decades. More important, it will be with us for years to come. Most important, it alerts us to a widespread pattern of thought and practice that has distorted and threatens to discredit the American democratic experiment.

The moral majoritarians would claim that the naked public square is the product of a conspiracy by secular humanists. There is limited merit to this claim, very limited. Another factor of great significance is the abdication or final disestablishment of mainline Protestantism. We are witnessing today a contention between religious groups—evangelical, fundamentalist, Catholic—to succeed mainline Protestantism as the culture-shaping force that provides moral legitimacy for democracy in America. The telling of our story employs the theory of "the circulation of elites" propounded by Italian social theorist Vilfredo Pareto (d. 1923). Central to the story is the claim that the public square will not and cannot remain naked. If it is not clothed with the "meanings" borne by religion, new "meanings" will be imposed by virtue of the ambitions of the modern state.

The bias of the author is not concealed. I am a Lutheran whose understanding of the Christian reality is best described as catholic and ecumen-

vii

ical. I am economically pragmatic, culturally conservative, and politically devoted to what used to be, and may be again, the "vital center" of liberal democracy. In the present climate of suspiciousness about the purposes of anyone addressing questions of religion and politics, it is essential that these biases and commitments be stated with candor.

As will become evident, I am skeptical about the alarums and crisis-mongering that mark so much writing about American society and America's role in the world. It is therefore with reluctance, joined by modest hope, that I set forth the reasons for believing that ours is indeed a period of crisis throwing into severe jeopardy the future of religion and democracy in America.

Richard John Neuhaus

THE
NAKED
PUBLIC
SQUARE

CHAPTER ONE

MISREADING THE SIGNS OF THE TIMES

THE STORY IS TOLD OF A PREACHER WHO IN A SUNDAY SER-
vice began the prayers this way: "O Lord, have you read this morning's
New York Times?" The Lord has seen the comings and goings of many
things that at the time impressed his creatures as being of inordinate moment. We are all susceptible to the imperiousness of the present. I say "all"
advisedly, even though many of us try to resist the claims of immediacy
by, as we say, keeping things in historical perspective. The proposition is
nonetheless compelling that the past is past and the future is not yet and
therefore the present is all that we have. On the Christian view of things,
that is a highly dubious proposition. In truth, it is false. It is false, that is,
if God is the Power of the Future who lovingly holds close to himself every
past moment as he leads us through the present to the promise of what is
to be.

In a *New Yorker* cartoon the directors are seated around a boardroom
table on which sits a box of breakfast cereal emblazoned with the word
"New!" The chairman says to a director: "What do you mean, 'What's
new about it?' The 'New!' on the box is what's new." Despite our doubts
about the onward-and-upward view of historical progress, habits of mind
persist in thinking that what is new is better, or at least more important.
In the communications media "news" is big business. An all-news radio
station where I live repeatedly asserts, "Something is happening right now,
and the sooner you know about it the better." That too is not true. Two
children were killed in a South Bronx fire this morning, Miss Connecticut
has been deprived of her crown because of fiscal irregularities, and Nigeria
has again denounced South Africa at the United Nations. About these
matters most of us have, as they say in the intelligence community, no
need to know. On this score our sanity is restored by vacations far from
newspapers, radio, and television. Returning after a week or three, we pick
up the newspaper and discover how very little we have missed.

We are neophyliacs, lovers of the new who are titillated by the news.
It gives us an illusory sense of involvement in our times. We fear being
left out of what is happening. The imperative of participation, carried to
excess, becomes frenetic and compulsive. Oscar Wilde somewhere said
that the trouble with socialism is that it leaves one with no free evenings.
Failing to participate fully in our own lives, we seek participation in real-

ities constructed by others. To the extent a person has a life of her own, it is a life defined by limits. With respect to innumerable things that are happening we are "out of it," thank God. Engagement in everything that is happening is an impossible imperative. That is why it has been attended to by God and is not our job. Our job, our vocation, if you will, is to attend to that to which we have been called. Readers of this book presumably are of the opinion that they are called—in one way or another, to a greater or lesser degree—to attend to what is happening in American religion, politics, and culture.

This book does not pretend to discuss, or even to touch upon, everything that is happening in these fields of near-infinite complexity. At the same time, I would not exaggerate the modesty of the intent. The intent is to set out an analysis and argument that, if convincing, might significantly change our understanding of America and of religion's role in our public life. As what is happening is not entirely new, so neither the analysis nor the argument is entirely new. Indeed, if a statement were entirely new, it would be unintelligible. To be intelligible, to make sense, requires that what we say be in continuity with past perceptions, thoughts, and language. To the neophyliac mind, the admission that something is not entirely new is fatal. Experts of all sorts have a vested interest in the allegedly new. If the situation is not new, who needs experts to research, lecture, and write books in order to explain the situation? I am persuaded, however, that bringing together what we know or think we know is both challenging and important. It is in examining the taken-for-granted truths that our errors are unearthed. And in this critical bringing together I am at least as impressed by the continuities as I am by the discontinuities in the story of American religion and culture. (It will become apparent that that story is, in turn, composed of several quite different stories. The intriguing thing is that those sometimes conflicting stories are today being told in unusual and often disturbing ways.)

Having emphasized the continuities, I do believe there is something new and important happening in American religion, especially in what might be called public religion. That is more than a tentative hunch. It is a belief derived from Christian teaching about history itself. That what is happening is *important* is implicit in the assertion that the project we call history was not created for nothing. That it is *new* is implicit in the truth that God is not repeating himself; he is not going around in circles. From the earliest times of Christian reflection upon history, the basic posture has wavered between two biblical perspectives on change. The first is Ecclesiastes 1:9-10: "What has been is what will be, and what has been done is what will be done; and there is nothing new under the sun. Is there a thing of which it is said, 'See, this is new'? It has been already, in the ages before us." The second is Isaiah 43:18-19: "Remember not the

4

former things, nor consider the things of old. Behold, I am doing a new thing; now it springs forth, do you not perceive it?"

One is inclined to say that those statements are equally true, but the second is more true than the first. To explore the new in the knowledge of the sameness of things is to be wise; to let the sameness of things obscure the new is to be jaded. Nothing is as new as it is cracked up to be; nothing is quite the same as anything else. "Behold, I am doing a new thing." Ours is not the definitive time in which that new thing is happening (that time was the resurrection of Jesus, which is in mysterious truth our past, present, and promised future); but neither is our time any other time. Times past and present are littered with talk about revolutions— *new* politics, *new* religious movements, *new* cultural crises. The poignancy of innocents caught up in the latest novelty is matched by the tragedy of the fatigued who deny the possibility of the new. Santayana was only partly right: Whether or not we remember the past, we are not given the chance to repeat it.

In the eighth decade of this century a new thing happened that portends, I believe, major changes in American religion and politics. To be precise, it did not just happen in the late seventies; it had been happening long before that, or perhaps it is better to say that it had been building for a long time, getting ready to happen. In any case, with a suddenness that shocked most observers, it came to public attention in the year prior to the 1980 elections. The new thing was the religious new right. Reflection on the phenomenon has already produced a literature of considerable size and uneven merit.[1] This is not another book on the religious new right, its organizations, personalities, and tactics. My purpose, rather, is to address some of the major questions raised by the phenomenon and by the reactions to it. Some of the questions are perennials; in different forms they have been debated in decades and centuries past. They are not likely to—nor should they—go away any time soon. It is possible that five years from now the personalities and campaigns of the religious new right will largely be forgotten. The questions will remain.

I should say something about the term "religious new right." Among other terms used are the new religious right or just the new Christian right. From the start we should stipulate, as the lawyers say, that the "new" will soon be made obsolete by the sheer passage of time. A decade ago there was a new left that wanted to distinguish itself from the Stalinist left of the 1930s and the liberal left of the post-World War II period. Of course each of those lefts was, in its time, the new left. So also the new right today wants to distinguish itself from the old right of the past. Among the chief personalities of the old right was William Buckley, founder of *National Review* and premier publicist of conservative viewpoints. Before that, its champion was acknowledged to be the late Senator Robert Taft. The new right is represented by Richard Viguerie, mogul of direct mail politics, and people such as Phyllis Schlafly, Jesse Helms, Howard Phillips, and Paul Weyrich, who have built an organizational network of interlocking directorates. They speak about the old right of the northeasternestablishment (one word) in tones of deepest disdain.

When discussing the religious new right, then, one begins with the new right. "Religious" is the modifier of "new right." In the beginning was the new right. The usage "new religious right" is in danger of getting things backward. Defined in terms of the cardinal points of fundamentalism, there has for almost a century been a religious right. Religiously speaking, the new religious right is not new. The argument can be made that the new thing is the political activism of the religious right. But even that is only partially accurate. The religious right, as we shall see, has been politically activistic in the past. The difference now is its apparent political effectiveness. "New religious right" is also misleading because it implies that the whole of the religious right, the many worlds of fundamentalism, is engaged in that newly effective political activism. That is definitely not true. Talk about the "new Christian right" compounds the problem by suggesting a limitation that does not exist. Groups such as the moral majority insist that they are not Christian in any limiting sense. They reach out to Jews and, at least in theory, even to nonbelievers, so long as these people agree on the "moral agenda" of the new right.

The new right is the base phenomenon and the religious new right is its division in charge of marshaling the troops around what are defined as the moral issues. In many hours of conversation with the religious and secular leaders of the new right, this way of stating the division of labor is not challenged. It is usually declared quite explicitly and without embarrassment. An objection sometimes raised to the term "religious new right" is that it is not really right. In, for example, its populist passions in pitting ordinary people (The People) against the several establishments, it very much resembles what used to be called the left. The gyrations of the left-right metaphor are especially fevered today. But the metaphor has almost never been stable. Going back several centuries, as it does, to where representatives sat in a French assembly, it is hardly capable of accommodating the ever shifting alignments of quite different political worlds. Nonetheless, the new right calls itself that and, for reasons of courtesy if not accuracy, we go along with it.

Describing the religious new right as a division of the new right carries the odious implication that religion is being "used" for partisan purposes. That is undoubtedly the case. Similarly, it is charged that, for instance, the National Council of Churches is "used" for the partisan purposes of the left. Generally speaking, that too is the case. Viewed from within these different worlds of politicized religion, however, the accusation is not so odious. It does not call into question the motives or sincerity of the actors. There are obviously different agendas for social and political change in America. If committed believers favor one agenda over another—as publicly concerned folks inevitably do—then they marshal whatever resources they have, including religious resources, to advance that agenda. They are criticized for employing religion to give their agenda the character of a holy crusade. They respond that their agenda does in fact engage questions of ultimate right and wrong and therefore warrants a panache of holiness. The issue is not one of religion "being used" for politics, but of whether one thinks the left or the right is right. It is not a matter of being used but of being of service. What to one person is exploitation of religion is to another the exercise of responsibility.

Of course this is not a very satisfying explanation. We persist in believing that the public engagement of religion should be more than a matter of placing your money and making your choice. It should not be as arbitrary and divisive as that. Surely God's purpose—which, after all, is to have priority in Christian thinking—cannot converge so conveniently with *any* political agenda. Religion should not be capturable by *any* partisan program. The transcendent dimensions of religious faith should provide, even make mandatory, a critical distancing from all temporal movements. So we persist in believing, and not without reason. And yet, as with the injunction to be in the world but not of the world, the mastery of critical engagement is forever eluding us. Just when we think we have gotten the hang of it in one situation, the situation changes and we have to start all over again. This is not only true of Christianity and politics in America; it has been true everywhere for two millennia now. And, of course, it is not only true of Christian religion.

Wherever in the world there is freedom for political engagement, the Christian community will provide a constellation of engagement models. In America that constellation is being moved dramatically by the emergence of the religious new right. Already the religious new right as an identifiable movement may have peaked. Clearly there are many who hope that is the case, and some have hastened to write its obituary. Reports of its death are, I believe, greatly exaggerated. At most we are witnessing an end of the beginning. Even if the initial surge is over, the impact of the religious new right will be echoing around the corridors of American religion for years to come. Among both those who have cheered it and those who have jeered it, the emergence of the religious new right is forcing a first-principle reexamination of the role of religion in American life. Perhaps more important, it is forcing to the forefront the question of "religious America"—the ways in which the American experiment is appropriately conceived as a sacred enterprise. Of direct importance to electoral politics, the religious new right has given entrance to the political arena to millions of people who, correctly or not, thought they had been excluded heretofore.

For those who do not share its vision, the religious new right has been both new and frightening. Like true believers of other movements, its leaders are possessed by a crusading mentality that invokes the fear of fanaticisms once presumed to be past. Several years before the phenomenon came to general attention, H. Edward Rowe set forth its vision in *Save America!*[2] With eerie prescience that little book foretold much of what has come to pass. It is prefaced by this passage from I Samuel:

> Jonathan said to the young man who bore his armor, "Come, let us cross over to the garrison of these uncircumcised; perhaps the Lord will work for us; for nothing can hinder the Lord from saving by many or by few." ... And there was a trembling in the camp of the Philistines, in the field, and among all the people. Even the garrison and the raiders trembled, and the earth quaked so that it became a great trembling.

The great trembling, or at least profound misgiving, is upon us. To those who cherish the democratic process, the model of politics as warfare cannot help but seem threatening. To be sure, politicians such as Alfred Smith and Hubert Humphrey exulted in being called "happy warrior," but the note of happiness is absent in Rowe's vision of the battle. There was of course a kind of happiness, bordering on smugness, in the religious new right's declarations about its initial electoral successes. But it is not the democratic happiness of being immersed in a political process of give-and-take, of gamelike confidence that the rules will survive momentary wins and losses, of knowing today's opponents may be tomorrow's allies. When it is the Lord's battle you are fighting, politics takes on an aura of deadly earnestness.

Fanaticism is contagious. It tends to evoke a similar response from opponents not ordinarily given to being fanatical. When this happens, it becomes almost impossible to blunt the do-or-die edge of politics. Nothing so sharply hones that edge as the frictions of religious passion. Pascal said it more than three centuries ago: "Men never do evil so completely and cheerfully as when they do it from religious conviction." Little wonder that modern societies have tried to keep religion at one remove from the public square. History throws up too many instances in which the perfervid mix of religion and politics has destroyed the possibilities of civil discourse. That happened during the wars of religion in seventeenth-century Europe, and the memory of that devastation was a major factor in shaping the secularist doctrines of the eighteenth-century Enlightenment. When politics is conflicted by putatively divine revelations, there is little room for reasonable argument and compromise.

The case can be made that the great social and political devastations of our century have been perpetrated by regimes of militant secularism, notably those of Hitler, Stalin, and Mao. That is true, and it suggests that the naked public square is a dangerous place. When religious transcendence is excluded, when the public square has been swept clean of divisive sectarianisms, the space is opened to seven demons aspiring to transcendent authority. As with a person so also with a society, the last condition is worse than the first. Nonetheless, the awareness of this truth does not alleviate our anxiety about forces that, no matter how much they deny it, seem bent upon establishing something like a theocracy.

If the myths of secularism are collapsing, and if there is a resurgence of publicly potent religion, we need to look for quite unprecedented ways of relating politics and religion. Our question can certainly not be the old one of whether religion and politics should be mixed. They inescapably do mix, like it or not. The question is whether we can devise forms for that interaction which can revive rather than destroy the liberal democracy that is required by a society that would be pluralistic and free. The prospect of our achieving this is not encouraging. One reason for this is that in all our institutions, including the churches, there is pervasive confusion about what is meant by references such as "liberal democracy," "pluralism," and "freedom."

In our time we see a growing understanding that the future of liberal democracy cannot be equated with the fortunes of a political agenda that we once called "liberal." Most people who bother to think about these things are familiar with the difference between the classical, almost libertarian, liberalism of the nineteenth century and the later liberalism of expanding government responsibility and power. The differences that emerged in the permutations of liberalism should not, however, obscure the continuities. The main continuity is the understood connection between liberalism and liberty. If democratic liberties are reasonably secured, the political process is kept open to change, including a return to some of the concerns that have been borne in recent decades by the agenda called liberal. Unlike those who think they are waging the definitive battle of the Lord against the uncircumcised, we are not committed to conclusive, final, solutions. In the ebb and flow of partisan fortunes, a larger movement is evolving new political formations, the shapes of which we can only vaguely discern. I do not suggest that we can occupy some lofty ground far from the battles that convulse the madding crowd. But we can remember that liberalism and conservatism mean something different from what they meant a hundred or even ten years ago. We can remember that our deeper stake is not in the policy specifics of liberalism or of conservatism but in the larger movement of liberal democracy that makes both possible and necessary the continuing redefinition of partisan positions and postures.

For the politically engaged there is surely a connection between policy specifics and the democratic process. It is not easy to keep the distinction clear, to be somewhat dispassionate about the policies while deeply committed to the process. In our recent history the response to opponents by those who call themselves liberal is marked by a deplorable failure even to try to sustain that distinction. As a result, it has been more reaction than response. If liberalism's opponents are reactionary, then mere reaction to them is reactionary twice over. Politically liberal religious forces in particular have demonstrated a rigidity and confrontational posture that have at times made them appear to be the mirror image of their opponents.

Some of the hysteria in the liberal reaction could at first be attributed to sheer surprise. In many circles the rightist victories of the eighties were greeted with a mix of shock and incredulity. It was suggested that the nation had gone crazy, that the people "out there" had abandoned both conscience and common sense. With special reference to the religious component of the conservative juggernaut, it was implied, and sometimes said, that the animals had been let out of their cages and now the job is to get them back in. We need to recall how in the months immediately before the 1980 elections the media exploded with stories on the newly discovered religious new right. Some critics claimed that the phenomenon was really a media creation, brought into being by the attention bestowed upon it. Certainly people like Jerry Falwell did not seem to be shying away from the publicity. Others criticized the media for being taken by surprise. Yet there were few in the "mainline" religious communities who were prepared for what happened.

Among the curious reactions, few were so curious as the protest that the political activities of the religious new right "violated the separation of church and state." Within a few short years, within what seemed but a flash, the tables were turned on religious political activism. A set piece in our understanding of American religion and culture had been that a key difference between religious liberals and conservatives is that liberals favored and conservatives opposed the mixing of religion and politics. In March of 1965 Jerry Falwell preached a sermon that by 1980 was no longer on his list of things to write in for. "Ministers and Marchers" chastised clergy for their involvement in civil rights at Selma, Alabama, and elsewhere. "Believing the Bible as I do," declared Falwell, "I would find it impossible to stop preaching the pure saving gospel of Jesus Christ, and begin doing anything else—including fighting communism, or participating in civil rights reforms. . . . Preachers are not called to be politicians but to be soul winners. . . . Nowhere are we commissioned to reform the externals. The gospel does not clean up the outside but rather regenerates the inside."[3] By 1980, 1965 seemed like a very long time ago.

Voting rights, anti-war protest, welfare reform, feminist and homosexual advocacy—these were the causes of the liberal Protestant and Catholic forces in the public arena. To be sure, the connection between religion and putative progress goes back much further than the civil rights movement of the 1950s. Historians have argued that the roots of America's struggle for independence from Britain are to be found in the Great Awakening, the religious revival of the eighteenth century. A hundred years later, the movement for the abolition of slavery was empowered, and often resisted, by religious forces. This century's prohibition of alcoholic drink was motored by evangelical Protestants. (It is sometimes forgotten that prohibition was clearly seen at the time as a progressive cause and was powerfully supported by an earlier feminist movement.) In those days, indeed until very recently, all Protestants called themselves "evangelical."

To be evangelical meant simply that one was not Roman Catholic (or "Papist," as many preferred to call Catholics). The term "evangelical" was withdrawn from circulation for a time, only to come back in the 1950s as the polite word for fundamentalist. Rhetoric is almost never *mere* rhetoric. Terminological disputes bear upon substance and power, as witness arguments over "pro-life" and "pro-choice" in the abortion debate. Having preempted the term "evangelical," a sector of American religion may now be preempting the culture-forming role once associated with that term. Evangelical is a full-blooded word, beside which "liberal" and "mainline" look anemic. "Liberal" speaks of tolerance and "mainline" is a synonym for conventional. It is a limp rhetoric. True, mainliners also describe themselves as "ecumenical," a term of some theological dignity and even of stirring vision to those familiar with it. But not very many are familiar with it. "Evangelical" signals a position that is gospel based and inspired. Some of the more bellicose political activists today are so self-confident that they no longer feel the need to disguise their convictions by the polite terminology. They come right out and call themselves fundamentalist. There is no doubt an element of propriety-defying exhilaration in this. It is like the person who no longer calls himself a democratic socialist but flatly declares he is a Marxist. The rhetoric of democratic socialism has, one suspects, a better chance of influencing the political shape of things to come. So also those who call themselves evangelical (upper or lower case) are more likely to play a part in the reconstruction of American public life. That is not because, being more respectable, they are better able to influence what is thought of as the religious and cultural mainline. It is because they bid fair to become the mainline. Capturing the emphatically mainline appellation "evangelical" was a good beginning.

In our world-weary moments we may agree with the observation (attributed to Elbert Hubbard) that history is just one damned thing after another. While history contains much that is eminently damnable, however, that view hardly accords with a Christian understanding of God's intent in time. An awkward consequence of the Christian view, it must be admitted, is that we are frequently unsure what that intent is with respect to specifics at hand. We are not disinterested observers, we are not an audience, but, however large or small our role (and we can never know that for sure either), we are both the subjects and the objects of our inquiry into what may be happening. Our Lord cautions us in no uncertain terms about unwarranted certainty. We are not to say, "Lo here! or, Lo there!" Yet we cannot help but say, "Maybe here, and, Maybe there." And then we must act in the courage of our uncertainties.

Historical changes that in retrospect seem major are sometimes worked out over a long period of time by subtle transformations that largely escaped the notice of those who were living through them. As with an individual life so also with periods of history, it is only at the end, only in retrospect, that we can say what it was all about, that we can put a name on the phenomenon. The Christians at Corinth in A.D. 75 did not tell one another, "We are the New Testament church of the earliest Christian era." Nor did the people of a later time think of themselves as actors in what we call the Middle Ages.

True, there are other times when the actors of the time put a name on their time and that name has stood up in retrospect. In the sixteenth century some Christians saw their moment as one of great spiritual reformation, and many of us still see it that way today. In 1850 many Englishmen thought they were living through something like an industrial revolution, and we today do not disagree. In other instances, people did not so much look around and see great historical change afoot but rather worked deductively from some grand scheme of historical change and then found their place within that scheme. In Greek antiquity and regularly in Christian thought, people have schematized history in terms of stages moving toward a preordained *telos* or divinely appointed purpose. Sometimes the transitions from stage to stage are tidy and progressive, sometimes they involve apocalyptic eruptions.[4] The Puritan preachers of seventeenth-century America were possessed of such a grand scheme in their "figural" reading of the Bible. Declared one, "*Prophecie* is Historie *antedated* and Historie is *Postdated Prophecie*: the same thing is told in both. Therefore the Historie of the Old Testament is Example to us. . . . Such accommodations will be easy to New England; seeing there is such considerable similitude and agreement in the circumstances."[5] Again today, many Christians are being caught up in varieties of "Bible prophecy" that give them a powerful certitude about the meaning of these times.

Our observations are not derived from such certitude. On the other hand, the choice need not be between such certitude and viewing history as one damned thing after another. The deductive approach is unwarranted, I believe. In addition, the variety of such grand schemes, plus the indifference to supporting evidence, make such deductive approaches implausible, if not incomprehensible. It does not follow that there is no purpose at all in history, that the particular events of our time have no meaning in relation to the big picture, so to speak. To suggest that the specific happenings of which we are part are sheer accident or the product of natural forces bereft of purpose is reductive. The deductive approach is implausible, demanding a suspension of our critical faculties. The reductive is trivializing and debasing. It enervates commitment to the moment that is ours. It is the enemy of that faith-filled modesty by which Christians seek to apprehend, however tentatively, the meaning of the penultimate

12

present in relation to the ultimate future. An alternative to both the deductive and the reductive is the inductive.

In this context, inductive method should not be confused with a narrow, vulgarized, and now discredited notion of the scientific method. In that notion, largely derived from the natural sciences, nothing is considered true and nothing is to be taken into account in searching for the truth unless it can be "proved" by empirical evidence. Such a restrictive version of the inductive method is of limited use in the laboratory and of no use at all in life. By history we mean the experience of life, including our reflection upon that experience. In that reflection we look for evidences that may suggest that the experience has meaning, that there is something like a coherent story. Such evidences include not only the things that we think up by ourselves, so to speak, but all the stories and ways of explaining things that we receive from elsewhere. We weigh stories and explanatory devices in order to determine their power in making sense of things. For Christians the normative story and explanation is of course the biblical story centered in the gospel of Jesus the Christ.[6]

This brief excursus on an inductive approach to history may seem excessively abstract, suggesting a level of tentativeness that is not appropriate to a robust Christian faith. Surely, it might be objected, with respect to the final meaning of our lives we Christians do have a certainty that is derived—even deductively, if you will—from the gospel. Yes, and to live in that confidence is to live in faith. The questions at hand, however, are not about our personal salvation, which we may understand to be assured. Nor are they about God's final vindication of his promise that history will be fulfilled in the coming of the kingdom of God. In that too we may trust, and indeed our personal salvation is inseparable from that vindication. We are living on this side of that ultimate fulfillment, however. In this preliminary moment we ask what God might be doing and therefore what his servants ought to be doing.

Our efforts to read "the signs of the times" are filled with risk. That is why such efforts must be faith-filled. Faith is our trusting response to risk. In relation to the imponderables of the future, faith takes the form of hope. Faith is not a backstop for reason. It is not as though we "know" a certain number of things by rational calculation based upon evidence and then add to that other things that we "know" by faith. It is rather that, as reasonable actors, we "know" a few things with a fair degree of certainty. Faith is not an additional quantity of knowledge, so to speak, but the quality of a life lived in trust toward the unknown. The faith-filled life is a life premised upon the promise that beyond all the unknowns is a love that is ultimately trustworthy, worthy of trust. The trustworthiness of that love has already been demonstrated in time by the raising of Jesus from the dead. He is raised by the ultimate love that *is* God (I John 4).

Such is the Christian truth claim that make us bold to read the signs of the times. To talk about the signs of the times assumes that the times have meaning, that time itself is possessed of a *telos.* Signs are pointless unless they point to something beyond themselves. History, which is composed of times and time, is *public* in character. Believers and nonbelievers alike participate in the same history. What Christians say about history, if it is true, is true for everybody, whether they know it or not. All humanity shares the same history, premised upon the same promise. Christians are distinguished from others by their knowing about the promise and by their entrusting themselves to that promise. In apprehending that promise by faith, we already now experience the promised future. In Christ the kingdom of God has appeared ahead of time. By faith in the rule of God that has appeared in Christ, Christians are living ahead of time. The kingdom of God is already in our midst (Luke 17).

Yet this kingdom which we anticipate by faith is still to be consummated in the promised end time. What we personally and communally anticipate is the future of all; the promise is a *public* promise. It is God's purpose that in the end time "at the name of Jesus every knee should bow, in heaven and on earth and under the earth, and every tongue confess that Jesus Christ is Lord, to the glory of God the Father" (Phil. 2:10-11). The question for every human being now, the question of salvation, is whether she is living a life in anticipation of, or in resistance to, that coming kingdom. But *that* the kingdom is coming is true for everybody or it is true for nobody. The difference between those who believe and those who do not believe is the difference between those who will see the kingdom's coming as joyful vindication of their hope and those who will see it as tragic repudiation of the lives they lived.

Within the Christian community there has been a great divide between those who understand salvation in essentially private or essentially public terms. In the privatized version, salvation is essentially a matter of my getting my soul into heaven, while the rest of the reality we call history can, quite literally, go to hell. This is the stereotype of a certain kind of fundamentalist and revivalistic Protestantism. In this version of the Christian message, the world is condemned, and the most urgent question, indeed the only question, is, "Are you saved?" Christians outside the fundamentalist camp have been generally critical of this understanding of salvation. They have insisted that the gospel is of public significance, that it provides a context of meaning that illuminates human experience within actual history. Thus it has been thought that fundamentalism, with its focus upon privatized salvation, is indifferent to history, while liberal Christianity takes history seriously but shortchanges the quest for private, or personal, salvation. This way of understanding our differences is, I believe, no longer adequate.

In a curious way, fundamentalism today is most assertive about the public meaning of the gospel. That is, the proponents of sundry forms of

"Bible prophecy" are advancing a reading of historical change that is in competition with, for example, the reading one might get from the pages of *The New York Times*. They are not saying that certain things are happening, and are going to happen, *if* you happen to believe. Rather, they read the signs of the times and assert what is happening and what is going to happen, whether you believe it or not. Their interpretation of prophecy does not shy away from specifics. They are quite prepared to match Bible passages with historical particularities as specific as Israel's occupation of the West Bank, Soviet rearmament, and the incidence of drug addiction in America. Many of these predictive prophecies strike us as arbitrary, contradictory, and, not to put too fine a point on it, bizarre. These hustlers of competing lo-heres-and-lo-theres are often deserving of the ridicule they receive. Too often lost in the ridicule, however, is the recognition that they are asserting a *public* story that purports to explain the meaning of historical change. No matter how crude their style and how different their rendition of the story, they are in this respect in the company of Eusebius, the fourth-century "father of church history," of Joachim of Fiore, the twelfth-century prophet of apocalypse, and of Cotton Mather, who espied God's intent in the founding of New England.

I must try to be quite precise about the point being made. One does not wish to give aid and comfort to the proponents of currently prevalent forms of Bible prophecy. The point is that they dare to assert the public meaning of the biblical message. The way in which that assertion is made is profoundly disturbing on several scores. The intention of the assertion seems usually to be *against* rather than *for* the enterprise we call history. That is, their gospel is only gospel (good news) for the relatively small minority that will be rescued from the tribulations to come. Most of history and of the people who are the object of God's creative and redemptive love are to be consigned to perdition.

In addition, the assertion is authoritarian and arbitrary. While their message is public in import, it is not public in the sense of being accountable to public reason. While they invoke the authority of an infallible and inerrant Bible, the authority of the specific readings of history rests upon trust in individual readers of the texts. This in turn not only encourages but requires the cultivation of personality cults, which sometimes come close to the cultivation of idolatry. The stature of "prophetic" leaders, magnified by communications technology of all kinds, is not unlike that of those who in other cultures forecast future events by reading the entrails of doves and rats. Bible study is reduced to a kind of reading of entrails. To be fair to entrail reading, those forecasters were held accountable and were discredited or even killed when subsequent events did not bear out their predictions. Today's Bible seers run no such risks. If they even acknowledge their errors, which they usually do not, it is simply to find corrective nuances in the text that only further demonstrate the inerrancy of the

Scriptures—an inerrancy indistinguishable from that of the interpreter. And to be fair to the schools of Bible prophecy, let it be noted that not all of the practitioners are as crude or dishonest as this description suggests. But all are deductively authoritarian in their method. They work within a closed circle of supposedly revealed truth that is neither accountable to nor accessible to those outside that circle. Thus while the message, if true, has public import, there is no way in which the truth of it can be publicly weighed and tested. Also their reasoning, such as it is, is circular: first accept the truth and then you will know it is true. Fundamentalist Bible prophecy is in accord with a classic Christian tradition in asserting that the gospel is a statement about public and universal reality. It is alien to that tradition in its refusal to engage the Christian message in conversation with public and universal discourse outside the circle of true believers.

The popularity of fundamentalist and authoritarian religion today is frequently explained (explained away?) by saying that it is a refuge of certainty in an uncertain world. The implication, often made explicit, is that its followers lack the maturity or the nerve to live with ambiguity in the face of changes that are beyond our control. Like little children, these people latch onto clear and comprehensive answers that brook no critical examination. As I have indicated, I believe there is considerable merit to this explanation. The true believer is peculiarly susceptible to fanaticism. Fanaticism is from the Latin word *fanum*, meaning temple; the true believer refuses to move beyond the temple precincts of certain sacred meanings, lest those meanings be questioned through engagement with alternative truth claims. Yet this search for security in an uncertain world is, I suspect, only part of the reason for the fundamentalist renascence. It may describe the patterns promoted by some fundamentalist leaders and subscribed to by their hard-core followers, but it does not tell us why millions of other Christians are so receptive to their message.

In principle, we should be suspicious of explanations for other people's beliefs and behavior when those explanations imply that they would believe and behave as we do, if only they were as mature and enlightened as we are. Far too much of what has been written and said about the fundamentalist phenomenon has been marked by a reductionism that is tinged with contempt.[7] One result of that is that fundamentalists are reinforced in their belief that other Christians are joined in a conspiracy to demean and discredit them and the truth they believe they have found. Another result is that those who indulge in reductionist explanations are themselves reduced in their understanding of alternative ways of being Christian and in their appreciation of the spiritual dynamics of our time. Not least important, reductionist and dismissive explanations are profoundly anti-ecumenical. Whether or not the proponents of politicized fundamentalism recognize us as sisters and brothers in Christ, we must recognize them as such. No matter how convenient it would be or how strong the temptation to do so, we cannot write them off. The imperative to take them seriously is underscored, quite apart from theological considerations, by the fact that Christianity ranged along the conservative evangelical-fundamentalist spectrum may well become the largest and most vital constellation of religious forces in American life. An ecumenical movement that holds back from entering into conversation with millions of fellow believers has become pitifully sectarian.

It is not possible to enter fully into the experience and beliefs of others. When the subject is religion—what others believe to be ultimately true—the difficulties are magnified. Whether we are dealing with alternative ways of being Christian or with other world religions, our approach must be marked by modesty and respect. Even if we take a rigorously phenomenological tack that is careful to attend to the described experience of others, we can attain only a tentative and approximate understanding of what is going on in the sphere in which others believe they encounter the divine. If we are at all reflective, we know how uncertain is our understanding of our own religious experience and how little we really know about the experience of those who share our own way of articulating and living out the Christian faith. It is a curious conceit that leads us to claim greater confidence about the religious dynamics experienced by others than we would claim for our knowledge of our own spiritual journeyings. We are especially tempted to that conceit when the "others" in question take a critical or even hostile stance toward our way of being Christian.

While the elements of authoritarianism in fundamentalist religion are evident enough, we cannot be content to dismiss its appeal as mere pandering to what is scornfully termed "the authoritarian personality."[8] Until now the "authoritarian" and the "autonomous" have been set in contrast, indeed in opposition, to one another. In religion, psychology, politics, and almost every other field of behavior, it was suggested that personal growth means moving from childlike dependence upon authority to adultlike independence and "thinking for oneself." Instead of thinking only about the authoritarian and autonomous, we should pay attention to yet another kind of personality, namely, the person who recognizes what is authoritative. If we are to describe this in terms of a line of growth or life projectory, the movement is from the authoritarian, through the autonomous, to the acknowledgment of the authoritative. As freedom from authoritarian oppression, autonomy is a kind of liberation. But autonomy alone, thought of as unqualified fulfillment of self, is a new oppression. Religious geniuses such as Paul, Augustine, and Luther viewed such autonomy as *the* oppression of the imperial self, the source and shape of our alienation from God. Beyond autonomy is the *free* acknowledgment of that by which we are bound. We are bound to be free. We are bound to be free in the sense of being called or destined to freedom. And we are bound

17

to be free in the sense that our freedom is only actualized in the free acceptance of that which authoritatively claims our assent and obedience.

This movement toward the authoritative takes place at all levels of life. Morally, for example, we acknowledge familial and friendship claims that are not necessarily of our individualistic devising nor always in accord with our inclination. Cognitively, the movement is away from all varieties of solipsism and toward the acknowledgment of truth that is external to ourselves. Whatever may be the elements of authoritarianism in fundamentalism's appeal, many no doubt discover in it a welcome claim to authoritative truth. It does not detract from the claim to note that the claim is made in a confused world where everything seems to be up for grabs. That simply helps explain why the claim is so welcome.

Two ships, both without a compass, are drifting on a night as dark as pitch. The one captain is resigned to having lost his way. The other searches, perhaps desperately, for a glimpse of the North Star. The second is looking for an authoritative point of reference, while the first assumes there is none. The merits of their behavior cannot be determined by reference to different personality types. One is not autonomous and mature while the other is dependent and authoritarian. Our judgment of their different attitudes depends on whether we believe that, in fact, there is such a star that can provide an authoritative point of reference and direction.

An appeal of fundamentalism is its claim to have sighted the star and to have a sure sense of its leading. Fundamentalist preachers routinely assert that nonfundamentalist Christians have resigned themselves to an abject relativism of perpetual drift. Those of us in the other churches— whether mainline Protestant, Lutheran, or Roman Catholic—know the assertion is unfair. Within these churches are enormous resources of vital and confident Christian faith. And yet, as Dean Kelley wrote more than a decade ago in *Why Conservative Churches are Growing,*[9] many of our churches have made themselves unnecessarily vulnerable to exploitation by fundamentalist proselytizers. We have given the impression of confusing virtue and necessity; we have seemed to suggest that uncertainty is not the condition but the goal of our pilgrimage. Kelley's argument is not, as some critics have claimed, that we should imitate the strictness and dogmatism of reactionary religious groups. He does urge that we rethink the ways in which discipline is essential to Christian freedom. He does point to the need for dogma that can provide authoritative communal referents by which we can weigh the authoritarian claims of both fundamentalist religion and secular culture.

For the spiritual life and, increasingly, for political activity, fundamentalism in its several varieties is providing a comprehensive public world view for many Americans. As a religious phenomenon, fundamentalist growth is not a matter of public interest. American tolerance can and does accommodate myriad ways in which individuals and commu-

18

nities work out their relationship to the transcendent. By asserting the public nature of its truth claims, however, fundamentalism serves notice that it is not content to confine itself to the privatized sphere of religion. Those of us in the ecumenical churches who have traditionally railed against the bifurcation of the sacred from the secular and who have insisted that religion cannot remain captive to the personal or private sphere should not now reverse field and charge that fundamentalism's public assertiveness is an assault upon democratic pluralism. Such a reversal would put us in subordinate alliance with secularist proponents of the very privatization of religion that we have rightly criticized.

Our quarrel with politicized fundamentalism is not that it has broken the rules of the game by "going public" with Christian truth claims. Christian truth, if it is true, is public truth. It is accessible to public reason. It impinges upon public space. At some critical points of morality and ethics it speaks to public policy. Our quarrel with politicized fundamentalism is not so much over the form of religion's role in society but over the substance of the claims made. To put it differently, our quarrel is primarily theological. Unless that quarrel is transformed into an engagement that moves toward dialogue, we will continue to collaborate, knowingly or not, in discrediting the public responsibility of religion. We will discredit it by finding ourselves in awkward support of those who would exclude religion from the public square. And we will discredit it by giving a monopoly on religiously informed political action to the most strident moral majoritarians who show few signs of understanding the problems and promises inherent in the American experiment. The political triumph of that monopoly would, among those who care about liberal democracy, make anathema the idea of public religion for a long time to come.

CHAPTER TWO

PUBLIC RELIGION
AND PUBLIC REASON

THE IDEA OF PUBLIC RELIGION IS THE SUBJECT OF GREAT PUB-
lic confusion. The idea is widely accepted that religion is something
between an individual and his God. Each person is free to worship the God
of her choice. Religion is the business of church and home and has no place
in public space. These and other axioms are, it is commonly said, part of
the American way. Legally and politically, they are supported by a notion
of the "separation of church and state" that is understood to mean the
separation of religion and religiously based morality from the public realm.

A competing set of ideas gravitates around the insistent intuition
that America is in some significant sense a "Christian nation." Today that
is generally thought to be a conservative sentiment. Christians in mainline
churches of a liberal political disposition, however, also insist that Christian faith is in some necessary way "relevant" to public policy. Christians,
as Christians (and not simply as people of goodwill), have a responsibility
to advance a social vision derived from biblical teaching.

In the late sixties another way of talking about public religion was
revived. Taking a leaf from Rousseau, the conversation turned to "civil
religion." Some scholars preferred to talk about "public virtue" or "public
piety," referring to the operative values by which, more or less, American
life is ordered.[1] That discussion was carried on chiefly among academics
in social science and religious studies departments. For the most part, they
did not dissent from the conventional and essentially liberal agenda for
social progress. Certainly they lived and wrote in a world far removed from
the constituencies of what was to become the religious new right.

The current discussion is in continuity with these earlier ways of
thinking about public religion. But the discussion has also been changed
dramatically by the power and prominence of politicized Christian conservatism. It might appear that there is another discussion within the
Christian community itself. It is in many respects a new and politically
escalated discussion along the fundamentalist-modernist lines of sixty and
more years ago. In truth, it is more confrontation than discussion, at least
to date. The earlier fundamentalist-modernist confrontation was a theological dispute. But contrary readings of social and political change were
never far from the surface and sometimes dominated the argument. Therefore to say that an earlier theological dispute has now been politicized is

20

only part of the story. As already indicated, the basic questions joined today are more properly seen as theological than as questions of political alignment. Of course it is often easier—also, oddly enough, easier for theologians—to talk about politics.

Perhaps Christians should, if they have the ecumenical nerve for it, first try to resolve the disputes among themselves before they attempt to articulate the implications of what they believe for the society at large. This proposal has a distinct appeal. Two thousand years of Christian history, however, offer little reason to believe that such a comprehensive ecumenical resolution is likely or even possible. In addition, committed Christians with distinctly different agendas for political and social change are not going to hold themselves back from the public arena pending such an ecumenical agreement. (Nor can we overlook the fact that many of the most aggressive among fundamentalist political actors are persuaded that such an ecumenical rapprochement is undesirable. The Christians with whom they disagree are seen as being marginally Christian, if they are Christians at all. Ecumenical initiatives will, for the most part, have to come from those who have traditionally deemed ecumenism a virtue.)

Those who would keep the public square naked of religious symbol and substance are often motivated by a not unreasonable fear. The frequently expressed fear is that politics could degenerate into religious warfare. When one speaks of religion influencing public policy, the immediate question is, *Whose* religion? If one subscribes to the notion that this is in some sense a Christian society, then the question becomes, *Whose* Christianity? Without some basic agreement religiously, the entrance of religion into the public arena would seem to be a formula for open-ended conflict and possible anarchy.

Yet, in the absence of a public ethic, we arrive at that point where, in Alisdair MacIntyre's arresting phrase, "politics becomes civil war carried on by other means."[2] MacIntyre believes that we have already reached that point, and he may be right. A major problem, however, is that a public ethic cannot be reestablished unless it is informed by religiously grounded values. That is, without such an engagement of religion, it cannot be reestablished in a way that would be viewed as democratically legitimate. The reason for this is that, in sociological fact, the values of the American people are deeply rooted in religion.

That sociological reality is not necessarily something to be cheered. It simply is. There are other, perhaps more attractive, ways to go about constructing a public ethic. A long and in many respects admirable history of moral philosophy has worked at establishing such an ethic that would be based upon "objective" reason and in no way dependent upon particular religious beliefs. This enterprise, while usually self-consciously secular, is not necessarily hostile to religion. To the contrary, major figures such as Immanuel Kant were at pains to assert that their ethical reasoning was

21

perfectly consonant with Christian faith. In American thought there is ample evidence that the founding fathers—Jefferson, the Adamses, Madison, et al.—had the deepest appreciation of the need for a public ethic and the cultivation of what were called republican virtues. They would also have protested vigorously the suggestion that they shortchanged the importance of particular religions. In their view, a public and universal ethic is to be supported in its observance by the teachings of a variety of faiths. The confidence was frequently expressed that, when it comes to public morality, the sundry sects were, despite their conflicts of doctrine, in essential agreement upon the ethical basics. Still in this century that confidence was reflected in Protestant ecumenical efforts which declared that doctrines divide while ethics and service unite.

Religious belief was seen as a reinforcement, a backstop, if you will, to the public ethic. Religion, especially in its insistence upon ultimate rewards and punishments, was the motivating force for good behavior. But the agreed upon understanding of what constitutes "good" behavior was not to be derived from religious belief. In other words, religion was to motivate and sanction but not to inform or shape the public ethic. The definitions of right and wrong were to be constructed from other building materials. It is important to note that, unlike Rousseau, for example, the founders thought the conventional religions could manage this role of ancillary reinforcement. They did not think it necessary to construct a new "civil religion" for the maintenance of republican virtue.

Thinking about public ethics in the American experiment has not been all of a piece. There was, on the one hand, the belief that, if all religions were reduced to their moral essentials, they were really saying the same thing. In this sense, the public ethic was seen to be derived from a religious common denominator. On the other hand, and this is a more recent development, the articulation of a public ethic has been conscientiously divorced from religious belief. The approach that assumed a religious common denominator, although at times painfully contrived, worked passably well for a long time. It worked as long as it could be safely assumed by the country's several establishments that America is essentially white Anglo-Saxon Protestant. This was the regularly declared assumption in the great common school movement of the nineteenth century.[3] Today's debates about how or whether values are to be taught in public schools would have been inconceivable a hundred years ago. Then it was a matter of course that the public school was to inculcate a Christian and Protestant ethic.

That taken-for-granted assumption was early contested by Roman Catholics, Lutherans, and others who had a different understanding of the relationship between belief and ethics. Instead of working through the problematic of a public ethic, the American polity at that time allowed these dissidents to spin off their deviant view into separately supported parochial school systems. This allowance, it should be noted, was not made readily. Indeed it was not until 1925 (*Pierce v. Society of Sisters*) that the Supreme Court made it clear that government schools could not exercise a coercive monopoly over education. In any case, having made exception for deviations from the norm, the public school continued to advance what was taken to be (and to a large extent was) the mainline moral consensus.

The idea of a religiously based moral common denominator was soon to come in for hard times, however. The alternative to the common denominator of the American "melting pot" is often described in terms of the rise of pluralism. (Pluralism, as we will have occasion to consider in greater detail, is frequently a synonym for pervasive confusion.) In moments of candor public educators had recognized that the common denominator was somewhat artificial and contrived; too much of what people *really* believed most deeply had to be swept under the carpet in order to maintain the putative consensus. At the same time, there were new and aggressive forces in American cultural and political life that did not go along even with the minimal belief system. The much assailed *Humanist Manifesto* of 1933 was a particularly strident dissent from the consensus. The signers, including John Dewey, the high priest of American public philosophy, must be credited with honesty in their pointing out what might be described as the bootlegging of religion into the public arena, and especially into government schools. That is, the complaint is warranted if one is serious, as the signers of the manifesto were, in believing that America is or should be a secular society.

H. Edward Rowe is typical of the critics of secular humanism: "There are only two movements in history—God's and man's. *God's movement* has been revealed in the Holy Scriptures, which tell us about salvation through Christ, freedom, morality, justice, and the life of service. It is theocentric: God is at the center. *Man's movement* is humanism. It is based on the denial of God's existence. It is anthropocentric: Man is at the center."[4] Among the signers of the manifesto, Paul Blanshard outdid most in his stridency. Writing in *The Humanist,* the magazine of the movement, he declares: "We have an obligation to expose and attack the world of religious miracles, magic, Bible-worship, salvationism, heaven, hell, and all the mythical deities. We should be particularly specific and energetic in attacking such quack millennialists as Billy Graham and such embattled reactionaries as [the pope] because they represent the two greatest anti-humanist aggregates in our society."[5]

Rowe's distinction between "God's movement" and "man's movement" is simplistic but nonetheless revealing. A great change had in fact been worked in American public thought. A century and more ago, Horace Mann, the father of the common school movement, would have had little, if any, difficulty in accepting Rowe's idea of "God's movement" as being congenial to the purposes of public education. He would have been considerably less definite about scriptural revelation and salvation through Christ, but the rest of the definition was unquestionably entrenched in the WASP consensus. Today, needless to say, the proposal that public education should inculcate such an understanding of "God's movement" would be deemed an egregious violation of the constitutional stricture against the "establishment" of religion. Those who today express puzzlement at the fury of the religious new right sometimes suggest that the changes have not been that dramatic, that these reactionaries are making it all up. As historian Robert Handy has argued in his *Christian America*, however, the idea that ours is a secular society is of amazingly recent provenance.[6]

Of course the change was not effected simply by the *Humanist Manifesto* and those who signed it. It is likely that in 1933—and this is also true today—relatively few people shared the manifesto's robust confidence that a vital public ethic could be maintained without the taint, so to speak, of religion. Even fewer would assault religion with the passionate intensity that came naturally to the Paul Blanshards. Forty years later, when a memorial version, as it were, of the manifesto was issued, that confidence and that animus seemed to have declined even further. The signers of *Humanist Manifesto II* made up a reunion of survivors against this century's assaults upon unbelief. Those under seventy were in a distinct minority. From the geriatric wards of America, academics emeritus gathered to unfold the grand old banner one last time. Religionists who rage against the "secular humanist conspiracy" appear to be beating up on old people who might more kindly be left to their dreams of a brave new world that was not to be.

There may, however, be another reason why few of today's leaders thought it worthwhile forty years later to sign up with the movement for secular humanism. It may be that the movement is passé only because a movement is no longer needed. Nobody today would sign a petition calling on the United States to match German rearmament. That hot issue of 1933 was settled by World War II. In truth, short of war ending in unconditional surrender, no movement for change is ever completely or securely triumphant. The new right exaggerates the victories of secular humanism. It does so for understandable strategic reasons. Focusing on the *Humanist Manifesto* lifts up an abrasive and doctrinaire world view that is abhorrent to most Americans. Almost every movement depicts its opponents in the least attractive light. The *Humanist Manifesto*, with its vulgar apotheosis of supposedly rational man and its dogmatic dismissal of religion as superstition, is not likely to fare well in a public referendum.

Exaggerations aside, however, those who attack secular humanism are not so wide of the mark as some of their critics suggest. True, in the face of these attacks it must be responded that there is a venerable tradition

24

of humanism, also Christian humanism, that is not secularistic. Christians especially should affirm humanism. After all, we are the ones who say that God became a human being, and you cannot get any more humanistic than that. Nonetheless, it cannot be denied that the variant called *secular humanism* has had a pervasive and debilitating effect upon our public life. Without ever having to put them to a vote, without even subjecting them to democratic debate, some of the key arguments of what is properly called *secularism* have prevailed. There need not be a conspiracy in any coherent or calculated sense for ideas and prejudices to insinuate themselves into our thinking and acting. They are part of the conceptual air we breathe.

One idea that has been insinuated and legally rooted is a peculiar reading of what the First Amendment means for "the separation of church and state." It is not, as some fundamentalists complain, that God has been taken out of our public schools or out of our public life. God, being God, cannot be "taken out" of anything. It is the case that truth claims and normative ethics that have specific reference to God or religion have been, at least in theory, excluded. One says "at least in theory" because, in uncounted classrooms and forums where the business of the *polis* is debated, religiously grounded beliefs continue to play a vigorous part. In everyday fact, people do not and cannot bifurcate themselves so at one moment they are thinking religiously and at another secularly, so to speak. But specific reference to religion, specific claims "tainted" by religious belief, are always subject to challenge. The challengers can usually call in the law on their side.

Thus religion in public space became increasingly surreptitious and suspect. There are remnants in public oaths, prayers in legislatures, and the like. Determined secularists view these as residual inconsistencies that they have not yet got around to extirpating and that may not be worth bothering about. A few belligerent atheists might excite themselves about these matters, but they are not taken seriously and their legal protests are dismissed as nuisance suits. (On the other hand, in the 1950s not many people took seriously the proposal that prayer in public schools might be unconstitutional.) From the secularist perspective it may be that the essential battles have been won and excessive zeal in pressing a final mopping-up operation might only excite further public hostility. Residual religion in public poses no threat. Something of this reasoning is reflected in a recent state court ruling that tolerated even some prayer in a public classroom. The prayer, said the court in effect, should be seen as a morale-boosting folk custom and not significantly religious in nature. When religion has been tamed and its triumph no longer threatens, it can be tolerated as cultural trivia. Secularists with some appreciation of cultural continuities might actually fight the removal of, for example, inscriptions on courtroom walls that refer to God. Such things are, after all, quite harmless; at most they are piquant reminders of how America used to be.

The separation of church and state is an issue to which we will return in these pages. It is an issue that should not be, that cannot be, resolved short of the coming of the kingdom of God. In recent decades, separationism has provided the legal rationale for the sanitizing of the public square. As we have seen, this sanitizing of public space, while programmatic in nature, has not been subjected to democratic debate or vote. Leo Pfeffer, a grand old warhorse of strict separationism who has to his credit several important Supreme Court rulings, is quite candid on this score:

> The nine judges on the Supreme Court, being immune to political reprisal since they serve for life, may be performing a significant though quite controversial function; they may be compelling the people to accept what the judges think is good for them but which they would not accept from elected legislators.[7]

At times the courts have been called upon to resolve questions that resist political resolution. Even on some relatively minor but divisive questions, politicians prefer not to stand up and be counted and they therefore toss "hot potatoes" to the courts. When this happens, it does not necessarily constitute a failure of democratic governance. The courts too are part of the democratic process. Nor do we forget that, as Mr. Dooley observed, the Supreme Court, for all its august majesty, also follows the election returns.

Thus the courts venture where politicians fear to tread. An outstanding instance of this was the Dred Scott decision of 1857, excluding slaves from the protection of the Constitution. That decision did not "take" democratically; it did not resolve but only exacerbated the issue it intended to settle. In that case, the issue was only resolved by civil war carried on by means of civil war. In more recent history, notably in the *Brown* decision of 1954 on school segregation, the court has moved in to break up logjams created by the absence and apparent unattainability of political consensus. In the instance of *Brown*, societal forces ratified the court's direction, although not without much pain and continuing confusions. Today our public life is not significantly influenced by the few holdouts against the proposition that legally mandated racial segregation is wrong and should be forbidden.

Yet more recently, the court rushed in where politicians had been tromping all over the issue. In *Roe v. Wade* (1973) the court "settled" the debate over abortion law by the apparently simple expedient of suspending all law relative to the protection of the unborn. As John Noonan, professor of jurisprudence at the University of California, has noted, this is an audacious experiment without precedent in the law of any Western nation.[8] As many others have noted, the failure of *Roe v. Wade* to be ratified by public consensus invokes the memory of the Dred Scott decision.[9] Mr. Pfeffer and those who cheered the abortion ruling deplore the fact that Americans (a majority of Americans?) have refused to "accept what the

26

judges think is good for them." It is said that the court may have been too far ahead of popular opinion and prejudice. It seems more likely, however, that this is not an instance of aheadness or behindness but of fundamental disagreement with the court's decision. One suspects that the most fundamental disagreement is with the court's stated assumption that religious belief can have no bearing upon the determination of which human life has a claim and which human life does not have a claim upon societal protection.

In American public life today, abortion law is the single most fevered and volatile question that inescapably joins religion and politics. It is far from being the only such question, but those on all sides of the debate insist that it is not merely one question among others. I believe they are right. Some political theorists talk about questions that are pre-political or meta-political. Abortion may be such a question. That is, it may be prior to, or it may transcend, what is ordinarily meant by the political. As a result, it will never be resolved to the satisfaction of all, and quite possibly no resolution will ever be supported by a stable consensus. (It should be remembered, however, that until the early 1960s there had been a more or less stable consensus for more than a century, a consensus that supported minor state-by-state exceptions to the blanket protection of the unborn. The immediate point is not that abortion was not a problem then but only that we should not preclude the possibility of a reconstituted and relatively enduring consensus in the future.)

Abortion poses the most basic, indeed conundrum-like, of problems regarding the individual and community. From the "pro-choice" viewpoint it asks about the meaning of privacy and the limits of individual freedom. From the "pro-life" viewpoint, it is a matter of how we define the human community for which we accept collective responsibility. We will not go into further detail at the moment regarding the merits of the conflicting arguments in this debate. The reader would be making no mistake, however, in sensing the presence of that debate throughout these pages. No other dispute so clearly and painfully illustrates the problematic of the naked public square.

Through specific policy disputes underlying assumptions erupt. It is the underlying assumptions, the cultural postures, if you will, that concern us here. Our own underlying assumption, which needs to be brought to the surface and exposed to examination, is that politics is in large part a function of culture. Beyond that, it is our assumption that at the heart of culture is religion. In this connection "religion" is meant comprehensively. It includes not just those ideas and activities and attitudes that we ordinarily call religious, but all the ways we think and act and interact with respect to what we believe is ultimately true and important. There is nothing frightfully original in this way of connecting politics, culture, and religion. A host of thinkers, including Tillich, Hegel, and Plato, have made the connection in a similar way. With astonishing frequency, however, the connection is neglected in writing about religion and politics today. In American history, of course, the understanding of ultimacies was publicly articulated with specific reference to biblical, Judeo-Christian religion. It is the relatively recent exclusion of that specificity which is now being so vigorously protested by many Americans. They feel that they were not consulted by whoever decided that this is a secular society. And they resent that; they resent it very much.

Among the most important truths about politics is the truth about the limits of politics. As Doctor Johnson put it:

> How small, of all that human hearts endure,
> That part which laws or kings can cause or cure!
> Still to ourselves in every place consign'd,
> Our own felicity we make or find.

Just because "our own felicity" is not, at least for most of us, in the realm of politics, that does not mean that we are preoccupied exclusively with private rather than public affairs. There is a great deal that is public but not in the ordinary sense of the term political.[10] Family life, work, learning, and entertainment all have public dimensions of interaction, not only interaction with other individuals but also with other communities. For those of us who are not professional politicians or political junkies, what matters to us most does not take place in the political arena as such. The things that matter most happen in the "mediating structures" of our personal and communal existence.[11] These structures—family, neighborhood, church, voluntary association—are the people-sized, face-to-face institutions where we work day by day at our felicities and our fears. The public square is not limited to Government Square. At the same time—and for reasons that may be nearly unavoidable—government impinges upon all public squares.

This impingement is no great problem if there is a large degree of cultural harmony between the private and the public, and between the public and the political. As Daniel Bell has brilliantly analyzed, however, that degree of harmony seems to be sharply diminished in post-industrial society.[12] There are jarring dysjunctions between the spheres of activity and sensibility in which we live. Especially the political and its impingement on public spaces seems to be "out of synch" with the way we believe the world is or should be. We speak of ourselves as being forced to live schizophrenically in several different worlds. Moving between worlds, we take off and put on different selves, until we are no longer sure which is the true "self." We do not feel "at home" anywhere, least of all in unrelieved privacy when we are most completely by our self, whoever that may be. Nor are we at home in the public arena where, in order to gain admittance, we are told to check our deepest beliefs at the door. The result of this is, in sociological jargon, the delegitimation of the political dimen-

28

sion of our public life. This makes it possible for not a few politicians to build political careers upon being anti-politics. Even governments are formed on the platform of being anti-government. It is all very curious.

The foregoing description of what it feels like to be alienated from the public and the political will doubtless have many heads nodding agreement. Other heads are perhaps nodding in inattention, for the description is so very familiar. But do people, in fact, really feel that alienation? The evidence seems incontrovertible that it is felt powerfully by the forces that make up the new right. The populist premise of that movement is that "they"—the government and whoever else is in charge of the culture—are not simply alien but are contemptuous of "us"—the little people, the real people. As the title of one book has it, *Harvard Hates America*. This sensation is not limited to the right, however. The very term "alienation"—derived as it is from Marxist theory—has a distinctly leftist cast. Not surprisingly, many on the left today who call themselves social democrats or democratic socialists seem to be as suspicious as the new right about government's unlimited embrace of public space.[13] Having learned something from the collectivist catastrophes of socialism in our time, they too seek forms of community fit for people who do not possess exchangeable selves.

Such communities would be more whole, less dysjunctional. The communities that are candidates for meeting that felt need are, for the most part, outside the sphere of laws and kings. There is, across the spectrum of political viewpoints, a resurgent yearning for communities that are, as we say, authentic. At its best, this yearning can revivify the diversity of communities in which felicities can be made and found. That revival can, in turn, check the imperiousness of the political that would change all public space into political space.

The same yearning, however, can result in retreat from the political. The problem with that is not that people who retreat from the political are living smaller lives. Largeness of life has little to do with the size of the space engaged. The person watching the evening political news about budget battles in Washington and bloodier battles in Beirut is not necessarily living more largely. Larger horizons on life's possibilities might more likely be disclosed by listening to a Mozart concerto or taking the dog for a walk around the neighborhood.

We hear it said, also in the churches, that every question is finally a political question. We can be very grateful that that is not true. If one means that the gospel of the coming kingdom is about the coming of the ultimate New Politics—the new and right ordering of all things—then, in that sense, everything is political. From the Christian perspective, to live in the presence of that final promise is to know that there is nothing that is not engaged by the promise's fulfillment. But that is not what is ordinarily meant by politics, and it is not the meaning of politics in the present discussion. Politics is the business (more art than science) of governing. It has to do most essentially with power—getting, keeping, and exercising it. I am aware that this is not a very elevated view of politics. Politics can involve nobler works and even visions. But they are not essentially what politics is about. We should resist being taken in by inflated and romantic views of politics. It is in the interest of politicians and the hordes of people who make their living by talking about what politicians do to disguise the stark and simple truth that they are engaged in getting and keeping power. Power, in turn, is the ability to get other people to do what you want, and not to do what you do not want. People who make their living doing that are said to govern.

Every system of government, no matter what it is called, is a system by which some people rule over other people. In every political system, political legerdemain, which is to say political success, requires that people be kept from recognizing the elementary fact that in any society there are the rulers and there are the ruled. In the most fetching evasion of this reality, the rulers insist upon being called public servants. For some who have the peculiar taste for it, politics is the highest enterprise they can imagine. It is said that Thomas Jefferson envisioned heaven as the U.S. Senate in never ending session. In fairness to Jefferson, it should be remembered that the gentlemen's debating society that he knew is related to national politics today in much the way that an elegant dinner at the Four Seasons is related to an army mess hall. And, of course, Jefferson in fact preferred to retire to Monticello where he could nurture his felicities with his philosophical theories, his science, and his slaves.

Nonetheless, attention must be paid to the political; not because everything is political but because, if attention is not paid, the political threatens to encompass everything. The proper word for the state of affairs in which the political encompasses, or aspires to encompass, everything is totalitarianism. Critics have suggested that totalitarianism is a bogeyman employed by "neo-conservatives" and "neo-liberals" to scare voters away from leftist politics.[14] In the century of Hitler, Stalin, and Mao, however, it is hard to understand how anyone could think the threat of totalitarianism to be bogus. One remembers too that *democratic* totalitarianism is also quite possible. Majority rule is no sure guarantee of freedom. The Grand Inquisitor in Dostoyevsky's *The Brothers Karamazov* had a keen appreciation of humanity's limited appetite for freedom. He was correct in having little doubt that his banishment of Jesus, who talked so recklessly about freedom, would have been supported by democratic referendum.

Attention must be paid the political, then, not because politics bestows meaning upon our lives but because, if we do not, others will pay attention. Almost invariably they will claim to offer an alternative to a society of the rulers and the ruled. When others rule, the system is op-

30

pressive; when they come to rule, the society is liberated. This is not to say that some governments are not more oppressive and others more liberating. It is to say that, paraphrasing Spinoza, power abhors a vacuum. Biblical people should not be surprised by this view of government. We have been instructed to have no illusions about the principalities and powers short of the kingdom of God. At the deepest level, our feeling of alienation is not disease but sign of health. Our eyes and hearts are fixed on another liberation movement.

On this side of eschatological fulfillment, however, there are degrees of political alienation that may portend significant change. While those who are called conservative and those who are called liberal or radical may be alienated equally from the political process, it is the conservatives who seem to have the fire in their bellies to "turn the country around." They have the advantage of feeling they are the party that has survived long assault and is now in a position to launch a counterattack. Of course there is a simple time factor involved here. After a while, the "new" right, or the "new" anything else, is not so new. After a lengthy period of what is perceived as conservative government, its opponents may also be ready to launch a counterattack. That said, it is hard to imagine Christians of a liberal political persuasion counterattacking with the intensity and cohesiveness that conservatives have displayed. A religious new left of high political potency does not seem likely anytime soon.

One reason for this, it might be suggested, is that liberals are basically nice people with a deep respect for civility. They do not go in for the nasty confrontational politics that is the specialty of the right. That might be suggested, but the suggestion is not very plausible. Anyone who has worked for long in liberal politics, including liberal politics in the churches, knows better than that. A more believable reason why the left is not likely to raise an effective holy crusade for political change has to do with the intensity of actions and reactions. That is, under a conservative government left-of-center Christians do not feel themselves assaulted in the way that right-of-center Christians feel they are assaulted under a liberal government. From a liberal viewpoint, the faults of a conservative government are more passive than active, more sins of omission than sins of commission. The liberal complaint against conservative government is that it does not take care of the domestic poor, or advance foreign aid, or expand environmental protection, or press for the extension of minority rights, or a host of other things that liberals think it the business of government to do.

In conservative eyes, however, the sins of liberal government are sins of commission: government does many things they think it should not do and forbids them to do things they think they should be free to do. They are notably outraged by governments that, they believe, advance changes in sexual and family mores—areas that could hardly be more value-laden.

31

While accepting the prohibition of mandatory race segregation, they resent deeply programs such as school busing and "affirmative action" aimed at mandatory racial integration. They react vociferously to government actions that get in the way of praying in schools, owning handguns, hiring whom they want, and living where they please. In sum, in very everyday ways they feel assaulted by liberal government as liberals do not feel assaulted by conservative government.

True, a liberal may feel deeply offended and outraged by the failure of the government to maintain, say, the food stamp program at the level he thinks desirable. Unless he is on food stamps, however, the issue does not immediately affect his way of living. If a government were to expand food stamps and similar programs, the middle-class liberal voter knows he may pay more taxes somewhere along the way but chiefly he feels better because "something is being done" for the poor. Although he may not be on speaking terms with any poor people, he feels obliged to "speak up for" the poor. Even if he does not actually see any, the poor are ever in his moral line of vision. All of this is in many respects admirable and, indeed, morally imperative. But the issue here is that the action or nonaction of government does not immediately or significantly change anything in *his* life or in the communities that constitute his daily reality.

Admittedly, it is impossible to measure degrees of felt offense. What to one person may be a slight disappointment is to another a catastrophe. Liberal offense at conservative politics might, in some cases, fall into the latter category. In trying to explain how prophets are different from the rest of us, Rabbi Abraham Joshua Heschel wrote: "To us a single act of injustice—cheating in business, exploitation of the poor—is slight; to the prophets, a disaster. To us injustice is injurious to the welfare of the people; to the prophets it is a deathblow to existence: to us, an episode; to them, a catastrophe, a threat to the world."[15] Churches have offices and task forces to churn out "prophetic" pronouncements. The political air today is filled with "prophecy" from the right and the left. But in truth, prophets are so rare as to be history's most long-standing endangered species. They do not form political majorities, moral or otherwise, and that may be just as well.

The argument at hand is that, except for a few rare souls, the sense of liberal outrage is somewhat abstract and intermittent. Between liberals and conservatives there is a significant difference in what might be called "experienced assault level" when their opponents are in power. The implications of this go beyond specific policy disputes. There are different biases about the nature of government. Liberalism, at least since the New Deal, has been marked by the belief, quite simply, that government should *do* more. The analogy is to Samuel Gomper's one-word statement of purpose for the American labor movement: "More!" Or, as Gary Wills somewhere remarks, the most visible difference between liberals and conservatives today is that liberals think government should spend more and conservatives think government should spend less—on everything but defense. In any case, a government that does more is going to be seen as more intrusive and is therefore more likely to generate politically effective resentment.

Once again the abortion debate is persistently pertinent to our subject. In this debate liberal/conservative postures seem to be reversed. It is liberals who seem to resent the government's "doing something" about the protection of the unborn. If not for themselves, at least for others they want no limits on the freedom to abort. Conservatives, on the other hand, not only welcome but demand governmental "intrusion" in a most intimate sphere of life. This apparent reversal of attitudes toward government action deserves careful attention and we will be returning to it. At the moment, suffice it that there is considerable dispute over whether the abortion debate does in fact fall into the left/right imagery. The case can be made that the pro-life position is in fact the liberal one, since it has been characteristic of liberalism to enlarge the circle of communal and governmental care. At the same time, it has also been characteristic of some liberalisms to accentuate above all individual freedom of choice, thus making liberalism pro-choice with respect to abortion. Survey research suggests that the pro-life/pro-choice divide cuts fairly evenly through the population regardless of how people identify themselves politically.[16]

Categorizing the pro-life position as conservative makes sense in that it involves the proposal that we return to the policy of a prior time. The proposed return is hardly to an ancient past; it has been little more than a decade since *Roe v. Wade.* To be sure, pro-life advocates insist that laws protecting the unborn now would not mean a simple return. For one thing, there has been significant development in medical technology. (Ironically, these developments are largely the result of financial incentives produced by a greatly expanded abortion industry.) As a result, whatever might be the incidence of illegal abortion after a change in the law, it would be as medically safe as legal abortions are today. In addition, at its best the pro-life movement advocates a quite new and caring attitude toward babies and mothers in difficult circumstances—an attitude that was not typically evident prior to 1973.

Nonetheless, there remains an element of "return" in the pro-life posture and therefore it is understandably viewed as conservative by many. Reinforcing this is the strong insistence upon individual and familial responsibility. Behavior, including sexual behavior, has consequences. It can be debated whether concern for moral responsibility in matters related to sex and family is a conservative monopoly. One would like to think that is not the case. Then too, there are those who contend that what conservatives call concern for moral responsibility is really vindictiveness toward pregnant women. Be that as it may, it becomes obvious that placing the abortion debate within left/right imagery becomes more problematic the more we think about it. The issue clearly does not fit the mode of "experienced assault level" that otherwise helps us understand the political potency of conservative reaction. More than that, abortion likely cannot be fitted into any political construct. It is a classically pre-political question of our attitude toward the fact that so many people are killing their sons and daughters. Lest that seem to be stating it too sharply, one might say that each year since 1973 in America about 1.5 million lives have been terminated that, if not terminated, would have resulted in sons and daughters. Whether one thinks that is alright, or an unavoidable evil, or an eminently avoidable moral outrage is a pre-political question. Certainly it is not inherently liberal or conservative.

On a broad range of issues conservatives react to *a high level of experienced assault*. The issues are not always coherently related, or at least so it seems to the outsider. A large part of the resentment, as we have seen, can be attributed to different attitudes toward government. Behind that difference, however, is a difference yet more deeply grounded. Christians entertain profoundly different ways of thinking about the American experiment in relation to religion. Liberals and all their ways and all their works are viewed by millions of others as being allied with forces that are hostile, or at least indifferent, to religious teaching and values. Politically liberal Christians are understandably outraged by this allegation. They protest that their political views and actions are clearly motivated by Christian commitment, and the protest is no doubt sincere. Their critics, however, assert that Christianity doesn't seem to make much difference in being liberal. They note that liberals, whether they be believers or militantly unbelieving, seem to end up at the same point on issue after issue.

"Our side" always looks more coherent to our opponents than it does to us. Especially is this true if said opponents have a natural proclivity for conspiracy theories. To them, our stumbling ragtag defensive action has all the appearances of a juggernaut. Liberal activism and the way liberals are aligned on specific issues may in fact be no more coherent or consistent than is apparently the case with conservatives. But there is a perceptible pattern in the postures of politically liberal Christians. The pattern involves political agreement with secularists who make no secret of their contempt for religion. To take an obvious example, the official social and political positions of the United Methodist Church are not discernibly different from those of the more leftward planks of the Democratic party platform. We will be looking at the history of how this came about, not only with respect to the Methodists but also other "mainline" Protestant churches. Allowing for the moment that it is the case, it is worth asking what it might mean.

We know that conservative critics explain the phenomenon by saying

34

that these liberals cannot be significantly Christian since they so consistently agree with those who have no use for the faith. To which it might be responded that, in the marvelous ways of God, the left side of the Democratic party just happens to take positions that are also mandated by Christian faith. After all, there is a common morality—some call it natural law—that is consonant with, although not explicitly derived from, Christian teaching. The God who is the Father of Jesus is also the universal God of all creation. A liberal who is accused of conforming to the values of the world can respond that it is God's world, isn't it? If so, it is not so surprising that others who follow worldly wisdom will arrive at what Christians believe are the morally correct conclusions. We do not have, nor do we need to have, Bible study in Democratic caucuses.

This is a doctrine of happy convergence between Christianity and culture. Those who subscribe to it risk sounding silly when they call their view prophetic, but such convergence is not entirely implausible. While the fit between Christian truth and secular partisanship seems too neat, all things are possible with God. Eusebius, the father of church history, thought such a convergence of Christ and culture had been divinely effected under the Roman empire. That those who condemn "Constantinianism" should themselves be affirming a new form of the same is not the first, although it would be among the more exquisite, of the ironies resulting from the marriage of politics and religion. We cannot determine here whether the typical alignment of religious and political liberalism is an instance of happy convergence or of cultural captivity. Unless, in sectarian fashion, one pits Christianity against culture, agreement between Christians and non-Christians on social and political issues is cause for celebration rather than suspicion. Suspicion may be justified, however, when a program that is said to be shaped by a specifically Christian vision parallels *tout cort* the programs of secular parties that are at least indifferent to that vision. That is a degree of happy convergence that one might have thought is reserved for the kingdom of God.

With respect to suspiciously happy convergences of Christian morality and partisan politics, conservatives are hardly above criticism. The alliance between the religious new right and the Republican party has not gone unnoticed. Conservative leaders claim that that alliance is temporary and tentative. Indeed the whole new right to which they have attached their fortunes frequently flexes its muscles of putative independence, threatening to go elsewhere if Republicans do not toe their line. It may or may not be an idle threat. Perhaps a Democratic party that is in search of a "third way" could provide an alternative for advancing the populist passions of the new right, including its religion-based battalions. Such a development would seem to require a Democratic party that proposes a vision other than New Deal nostalgia or rightist reaction. Most particularly, it would require a Democratic seizure of the "social and moral issues" that motor the new right. Such a Democratic turn seems improbable. That does not mean the new right has only the Republicans. In American politics there is strong precedent for populist movements to express themselves independently of both major parties.

The power of the new right, especially in its religious dimensions, is that it represents a movable constituency. For example, the majority of its white, Southern, evangelical constituency was, until recently, reliably Democratic. They have followed their issues into the Republican column. Being "issues oriented" in politics is usually thought of as a liberal virtue. Seldom, however, have we been witness to a more issues-oriented constituency than that of the new right. For the moment its leaders believe that, at least at the national level, its issues are more effectively carried by the Republican party. Because, they say, the constituency is movable, they will not become Republican captives in the way that, say, liberals and blacks are Democratic captives.

A fringe of the religious new right would prefer a party that comes right out and says that America is a Christian society. For several decades there has been a proposed constitutional amendment knocking about that says just that. The effective leadership, however, in deference to pluralism, has learned to mute the talk about Christian America. They feel they can work within a party that permits the dream of Christian America to be expressed *sotto voce*. This basis of Republican alliance is strengthened by a Democratic alternative that they perceive as militantly secularist. When they enter the public arena, new right leaders do not insist that everyone there must pass a test of Judeo-Christian moral orthodoxy. They do insist that they will not check their own beliefs in the cloakroom before entering. No longer content to be smugglers, they are in open rebellion against the border patrols that would maintain and even intensify the line between sacred and secular. In the Republican party they find greater sympathy for relaxing the border patrol.

This chapter began by suggesting that the issues joined are more theological than political. A dilemma, both political and theological, facing the religious new right is simply this: *it wants to enter the political arena making public claims on the basis of private truths.* The integrity of politics itself requires that such a proposal be resisted. Public decisions must be made by arguments that are public in character. A public argument is transsubjective. It is not derived from sources of revelation or disposition that are essentially private and arbitrary. The perplexity of fundamentalism in public is that its self-understanding is premised upon a view of religion that is emphatically not public in character. Fundamentalism is the religious variant of what Alisdair MacIntyre calls "modern emotivism." By emotivism is meant that state of affairs in which every moral statement is simply a statement of private preference. It has no inherently normative or public force. Of course it can have great force in public effect if those who agree with it can marshal a majority to their side and thus impose it upon those who do not agree. That is what MacIntyre means when he says that politics becomes civil war carried on by other means.

Fundamentalist leaders rail against secular humanists for creating what I have called the naked public square. In fact, fundamentalism is an indispensable collaborator in that creation. By separating public argument from private belief, by building a wall of strict separationism between faith and reason, fundamentalist religion ratifies and reinforces the conclusions of militant secularism. In order to counter this unwelcome result, the religious new right takes a leaf from the manual of an earlier Christian liberalism: the claim is made that, despite differences in religious belief, there is a core consensus on what is moral. This is the much discussed "moral agenda" on which, presumably, Christians of all stripes and even nonbelievers can come together. That approach will not wash now, however, just as it did not wash for long when employed by earlier religious actors in the public arena. The issues facing our society engage ultimacies. The issues themselves may be penultimate or less, but their resolution requires a publicly discussable sense of more ultimate truths that serve as points of reference in guiding our agreements and disagreements. Such resolution requires a public ethic that we do not now possess.

Groups such as Moral Majority kicked a tripwire alerting us to a pervasive contradiction in our culture and politics. We insist that we are a democratic society, yet we have in recent decades systematically excluded from policy consideration the operatives values of the American people, values that are overwhelmingly grounded in religious belief. We may acknowledge our indebtedness to those who have kicked the tripwire while, at the same time, recognizing that they may be the least helpful in addressing the contradiction they have illuminated. Those who have set off the alarm are at the heart of what is alarming. Fundamentalist morality, which is derived from beliefs that cannot be submitted to examination by public reason, is essentially a private morality. If enough people who share that morality are mobilized, it can score victories in the public arena. But every such victory is a setback in the search for a public ethic.

A serviceable public ethic is not somewhere in our past, just waiting to be found and reinstalled. From the past, however, there may be clues to the reconstruction of such an ethic for our time. In exploring this possibility we should at least entertain the hope that those who kicked, or perhaps merely stumbled over, the tripwire may become partners in that reconstruction.

CHAPTER THREE

"TURNING AMERICA AROUND"

POLITICALLY LIBERAL CHRISTIANS STAND ACCUSED OF EXCES-sive accommodation to cultural trends. They, we are told, are the trendy ones; adoring in their approval of whatever is thought to be new, terrified by the prospect of being left behind. In the late 1960s a local church in San Francisco reportedly styled itself The Church of What Is Happening Now. Critics of religious fashions got a good deal of mileage out of that one. The caricature of trendy liberalism has considerable foundation in fact. But it is a conceit of critics to think they are immune to what they criticize. The conservative religionists of new-found political potency are also shaped by, and perhaps captive to, larger trends to which they have attached themselves. In a society as large and diverse as ours, the public thoroughfares are cluttered with bandwagons large and small, moving in every imaginable direction. At a certain moment one band's music may attract more jumpers-on than another's, but every movement has its band and its wagon. Only the prophet, that rare soul, stands aside. Certainly he does not climb aboard any wagon oom-pah-pahing prophecy—whether it be called Bible prophecy or prophetic social criticism.

The religious new right has its wagon. It is called the new right. That does not mean it was simply a question of getting aboard something that was already moving. Its emergence also depended upon a larger trend. That larger trend had to do with religious demographics. The sheer numerical growth of conservative churches in recent decades would, it now seems inevitable, find some way to make its influence felt beyond the confines of what is narrowly defined as the religious. One need not be cynical to suppose that leaders who had attracted so very many people and so very much money would begin to think it a shame to let such potential power go to waste. It is, after all, a matter of good stewardship. Surely such influence should be devoted to the Lord's work. And if the Lord's work includes working out a scenario of world-historical change that requires an America reconstituted in righteousness, then the political tasks become both manifest and urgent.

Trends converge. The growing awareness of the size and potential power of evangelicaldom was not, in the first instance, brought about by the new right. A large part of the credit for that goes to Jimmy Carter, no friend of the new right. In the campaign of 1976 there was a burst of

38

excited interest in, and puzzlement over, "born-again Christianity." It was 1976, not 1980, that George Gallup dubbed "The Year of the Evangelical." In the world of religion, nonfundamentalist evangelicals had been preparing the way for an evangelical renascence since the 1950s. Where they had sown, others reaped. The reapers were fundamentalists who muted their fundamentalism under the evangelical banner for a time. They were different from others gathered around the banner, however, in that they had a quite explicit political agenda, an agenda fashioned by the new right but eminently adaptable to conservative religious sensibilities. More respectable evangelicals were demonstrating their respectability by embracing social concerns respectably defined by nonevangelicals. According to his conservative critics, this was most maddeningly the case with Jimmy Carter who, in deference to "liberal, feminist, anti-family" lobbies, seemed pathetically eager to prove that his faith did not make him a redneck reactionary. In the curious ways of such things, President Carter was perceived as abandoning his natural religious constituency, but the fact remains that it was a Democratic president who gave impetus to the religionized politics that were later to benefit Republican purposes.

Cultural and political trends interact with advances in technology. What came to be called the "electronic church" may not have been created by technology. After all, the electronic church had arrived earlier with the appearance of radio. It has even been suggested that the audiences of radio preachers in the thirties and forties were, when added up, larger than those of television evangelists today.[1] It is not necessary to understand Marshall McLuhan, however, to sense that television is in some significant way "different." Beyond whatever that difference may be, a large part of the electronic church of the seventies smelled a moment of political opportunity that had not been there before. True, Father Coughlin in the 1930s had for a time considerable clout; or so it seemed until he broke with Roosevelt and tried to lead his radio millions into electoral politics under his own banner. Today's prime time preachers are less individualistic; they joined their forces to a new right that calculated—with reason, as it turned out—the takeover of one of the two major parties. In addition to the convergence of trends, there are more timeless factors in the rise of politicized religious conservatism. Ambition is such a factor, and it becomes a very potent factor when combined with an apocalyptic vision of historical urgency. It is no doubt a heady thing to have hundreds of thousands of supporters agree with your conviction that you are called by God to lead the hosts of righteousness in crossing over to slay the uncircumcised.

Trends ebb and flow. Bandwagons break down or are commandeered by other factions. Movements, like shooting stars, disappear into the void. So also the religious new right is not a permanent fixture in American life. The background commotion from which it came, however, is more permanent, insofar as anything can be permanent in the context of social change. It came from the explosion of evangelical-fundamentalist vitalities in recent years. The religious new right in no way represents all fundamentalists or evangelicals. As we have noted, small but significant sectors of evangelicaldom are devoted to a politics we would ordinarily describe as liberal or radical. The grouping around *Sojourners* magazine is conventionally mentioned in this connection. Then too, while a majority of evangelicals and fundamentalists may be conservative politically, that same majority continues to believe that a "wall of separation" should be maintained between religion and politics. Baptists in particular have a lively allegiance to the tradition of Roger Williams and are primarily concerned about religious freedom.

In 1982 the Southern Baptist Convention supported the call to allow voluntary prayer in government schools. They were roundly criticized by some for abandoning their previous adherence to strict separationism between church and state. The criticism is formally correct, but the change may have less to do with a change of mind than with a change of sociological circumstance. A religious community that no longer understands itself as an embattled minority begins to think more about influence than about tolerance. Nonetheless, the impression remains that most Baptists still shy away from signing up their churches for crusades aimed at social and political change. As for the variety of fundamentalists, they believe in the imminent fulfillment of Bible prophecy and the political preachers have not yet persuaded all of them that it makes sense to become politically involved in the short time remaining before Jesus' return. Whatever their reasons, most evangelicals and fundamentalists probably believe that Jerry Falwell was right in 1965 and wrong in 1980; that is, he was right when he proclaimed that a choice had to be made between preaching and marching.

The fact that most conservative Protestants do not endorse the activities of the religious new right, however, should not be misunderstood. Polls are regularly produced indicating that most evangelicals are not very familiar with organizations such as Moral Majority, and that many who are familiar with them do not approve of them. The religious new right does not need majority approval, however. It is not running for office, at least not directly. The critical distinction is between a numerical majority and a politically effective majority. Given the alternatives thrown up by the electoral process, a minority becomes the politically effective majority when it is able to tip the balance in the direction it favors. And that is what the religious new right has been able to do with a frequency that is disconcerting to its opponents.

As there is no uniformity among evangelicals and fundamentalists on political engagement, so the ecumenical or liberal churches are not of one piece. There is a sometimes awesome distance between the positions of national church leaderships on the one hand, and the local churches on the other. There is also a gap between the political views of clergy, who are somewhat closer to the national leaders, and the views of the laity.[2] In 1969 sociologist Jeffrey K. Hadden analyzed these distancings in *The Gathering Storm in the Churches.*[3] Almost fifteen years later the thrust of his argument has been vindicated with a force that even his most convinced readers might not have anticipated.

Like a volcanic eruption, the new form of politicized religion results from deep shiftings of religious and cultural formations. These slow but inexorable movements are imperceptible even to many who live on or near the volcanic mountain. Thus the eruption of 1980 took so many by surprise. In liberal leadership circles, both mainline Protestant and Roman Catholic, the immediate reaction was simply that—reaction. In 1981, when a freshly inaugurated President Reagan had just begun to set out his program, the Governing Board of the National Council of Churches issued what was tantamount to an anathema against all his works and all his ways. "In the new administration's philosophy, the nation confronts a crossroads choice between alternative visions of the meaning and purpose of America," the council declared. "In [the Reagan] vision of America the fittest survive and prosper, and there is little room for public purpose since it interferes with private gain. Compassion is a weakness in the competitive struggle of each against all." Against the administration, the council proposed its "alternative vision," which, it said, "has deep roots in religious faith and biblical images of divine intent and human possibility."[4] In this way the coordinating center of mainline Protestantism seemed to be announcing that it was going into exile for the duration of the conservative unpleasantness.

Unimaginative reaction, however, has not been the only posture of mainline leadership. A minority in the mainline recognizes that there is no going back to "the good old days" of the New Deal coalition. Neither is "The Movement" of the sixties likely to be revived. Others persist in believing, nonetheless, that what happened in 1980 and everything represented by the Reagan years are but a momentary interruption in the inexorable march toward liberalism's version of social justice. If we simply keep the faith and wait out the barbarians, the country will return to its senses and resume the interrupted march.

It seems at times that almost anything can happen, and usually does. Revolutions, it has been observed, are declared impossible before they happen and inevitable after they happen. Yet the notion of liberalism's temporarily interrupted march seems implausible in the extreme. There are many reasons why this is so. By its economic and other policies the Reagan administration has made structural changes that cannot easily be undone. It would not be a matter of a simple vote to restore the New Deal or the Great Society. It would take a thousand battles and a thousand votes to replace piece by piece the programs that together constituted liberal

41

policy. With a speed that astonished many (but was not nearly fast enough for the new right), the Reagan government has not simply dismantled many liberal policies but has put into place formidable obstacles to their restoration. In addition, the idea of a temporarily interrupted march, the posture of waiting-them-out, is improbable because on the so-called social and moral issues the old liberal assumptions about modernity and secularization have few convinced or convincing defenders. Also of importance is the fact that the specific policies and programs of an older liberalism are widely, whether or not correctly, perceived to have failed. Especially with regard to the poor, it is thought that such approaches did not do what they were supposed to do. The purpose, it should be remembered, was not to make it easier to be poor but to help the poor become no longer poor. As a result of all these factors, the idea of the temporarily interrupted march is not very persuasive. The policy content of what we would go back to in order to resume the course of progress is, to put it kindly, very unclear.

In the churches there is no evident constituency demand for such a return to the past. The conflict between leadership direction and church membership, so perceptively described by Hadden and others, is now exposed for all to see. Leaders may strike a posture of prophetic protest for a time. They can and do rail against the political forces of darkness that have for a time, they believe, eclipsed the vision of Christian caring. But leaders who intend to remain in positions of believable leadership must after a while move toward their constituencies. Otherwise they will be viewed not as leaders but as leftovers, not as prophetic but as stubbornly wrongheaded.

In all the churches, fortunately, there are those who are not content with reacting to the reactionaries. Looking for new paths and postures, they recognize that it will no longer do to claim a divine sanction for a particular social and political direction because it has, in the words of the National Council, "deep roots in religious faith and biblical images of divine intent and human possibility." It will not do for a number of reasons, not least because there is another and probably more potent religious grouping that makes the same claim for its social and political direction. That is a new factor and its importance should not be underestimated. As noted earlier, for longer than most of us can remember there was an undoubted division between religionists who espoused political engagement and social relevance and those who did not. The political directions of the "relevancy party" were not usually argued on their own merits. The argument was over whether or not the churches should be relevant to what was thought to be "the real world." The direction of the engagement was more or less taken for granted. With gradations, the direction was almost uniformly left of center on the political spectrum. Now, however, the debate within and between the churches is no longer over *whether* religion

42

should be politically relevant. Across the board, there is an emerging consensus that religion must be critical of societal patterns and must be engaged in advancing alternatives. The question is no longer about relevance but about relevance to what and toward what end.

After their half-century in exile, the fundamentalists have returned to the public arena. Their return forces a new situation in which dramatically different concepts of the common good are proposed for Christian action. Ideological agendas can no longer be hidden under the rhetoric of relevance, concern, compassion, prophetic criticism, and so forth. This could mean we are entering a time of greater candor. It is certainly a time in which decisions become more difficult. It is no longer enough to *be* concerned, for instance, about the poor and marginal at home or abroad; now choices must be made between alternative ways of making that concern effective. Through a more up-front debate about different political means toward moral ends, it may turn out that the credibility and, yes, relevance of liberal religious leadership will be strengthened. That may be yet another ironic consequence of the eruption of the religious new right.

Those who for so long enjoyed a monopoly on the language of Christian social engagement have been forced to distinguish their engagement from that of other Christian forces in the public arena. Frequently attempts to make that distinction do not face up to the fact that there are substantive differences in the analysis of what is wrong with the world and what ought to be done to set things right. For instance, it is suggested that the difference between "us" and "them" is that they are arrogant and judgmental while we are tolerant and open. We believe in pluralism, while they would impose their values upon everybody else. We recognize that politics is complex and requires compromise, while they promote the crusading spirit of "one-issue politics." These ways of drawing the lines of difference are of very limited usefulness and of even more limited truth.

It is hard to listen, really listen, to others; it is sometimes just as hard to hear ourselves. One group may declare that a certain program should be supported by all Christians. What the opposing group hears being said is that anyone who does not support that program is not a Christian. What we mean to say is that there are reasons we find compelling, reasons informed by Christian morality, for favoring policy X. What others hear us saying is that X is *the* Christian position. And sometimes the reason they hear us saying that is because that is in fact what we said. We did not say what we meant to say, or at least what, when challenged, we say we meant to say. There is carelessness in all this, but not necessarily moral culpability. When you are trying to mobilize people for a definite course of action, you are not inclined to offer a carefully nuanced reflection that is scrupulously fair to the arguments against that course of action.

Politics, especially in the give-and-take of the democratic process, is impassioned. That is one reason why the facile invocation of the deity can be dangerous to politics and can, at the same time, devalue the currency of moral discourse. In 1969 an antiwar group with which I was involved was planning to take out a full-page advertisement in major newspapers. The message was quite simple: "Stop!" It was a religiously based organization and some of the leaders proposed the heading, "God says, 'Stop!' " Others thought that somewhat presumptuous. The advertisement finally read, " 'Stop!' in the name of God." Admittedly, the distinction is a fine one, but there is a difference between presuming to announce God's position on U.S. foreign policy and pleading—in the name of God but not necessarily on behalf of God—for a change of policy. In the mix of politics and religion that fine distinction is often lost. With equal vehemence the political right and left in American religion denounce one another for pretending to speak God's mind on everything from arms control to prayer in government schools.

Whether the politics be left or right, or somewhere outside the limits of the left-right metaphor, religionists are involved in the same problematic when it comes to relating religiously based morality to public affairs. One part of the problematic is the debasing of religion, making it an appendage to partisan purpose. Those on all sides can cite ample instances of their opponents' seeming to do just that. Such "using" of religion is, by any serious definition of the term, blasphemy. Too many criticisms of the new political activism are formal or stylistic in nature. That is, it is charged that "they" do certain kinds of things in certain ways that the rest of us find abhorrent. But almost all such charges can be turned upon the critics themselves. The religious new right has not been seriously engaged until we move from the stylistic to the substantive. In other words, the main thing is not that they are people who pursue their ends in a way that we deem objectionable; rather, there is a deep-seated disagreement about the ends to be pursued. What has been called the "back to basics" movement sets forth goals—in areas as various as education, criminal justice, and foreign policy—which are in conflict with the goals pursued by the several American elites of recent decades.[5]

The traditionalist resurgence has a substantive quarrel with most everything that has in our lifetimes been called liberal or progressive. In part, the resurgence is motored by disillusioned liberals, now called neo-conservatives or neo-liberals. In larger part, its forces are made up of people who have disagreed all along with the diagnoses and prescriptions of liberalism. Until recently their attitude was one of angry moping and muttering about the directions of the society. Many of their preachers and seers unrestrainedly exulted in the perceived madnesses of our time, pointing to them as sure signs that the last days are upon us. The coming of the religious new right marked a change of perspective. The new perspective is not that the world is any less mad or immoral but that the "forces of righteousness" can do something about changing directions. With some imaginative retuning, the same apocalyptic rhetoric could be used to suggest that doing something about societal directions could either delay the day of reckoning or, alternatively, set the divinely willed eschatological scenario back on course. In any case, if this analysis has any merit, the country did not change its mind in "going conservative" in the late seventies. Rather, millions of people who had disagreed with societal directions all along found new ways to make their disagreement politically effective. Most particularly, millions of fundamentalists and conservative evangelicals came in from the political cold. Having forced a degree of recognition as participants in the public arena, they are not about to return to the wilderness.

In saying that the disagreements between traditionalists and liberal innovationists are substantive I do not mean to suggest that the question of style is unimportant. For most Americans blessed or blighted by higher education, everything associated with fundamentalism has been indelibly poisoned by the acid brilliance of H. L. Mencken and his innumerable imitators. Fundamentalism, and indeed conservative religion in general, represents all the bigotry, know-nothingness, and legalistic repression that have ever afflicted humankind. Liberalism and the very progress of civilization consist in liberation from the sway of fundamentalism of every stripe. And of course this way of understanding progress is not limited to the Protestant world. Roman Catholics have had and continue to have their own wars with traditionalism. Roman Catholic traditionalism has often had a more aristocratic cast, represented by figures such as Chesterton, Belloc, Evelyn Waugh, and, in our day, William Buckley. A surprising number of leaders in the new right, such as Richard Viguerie and Paul Weyrich, are devout Catholics. They represent a potentially significant merging of a Catholic conservative strain, urban and often urbane, with its more rustic and sweated Protestant counterpart. In both, grumbling resentment against modernity is being transformed into unbridled rebellion. Their meeting point is in the passion for authority and, therefore, in the necessity of challenging, or even overthrowing, the authorities that have allegedly undermined legitimate authority in the modern world.

While contempt for conservative Catholicism is cultivated in the higher culture and scarcely disguised in the popular media, contempt for Protestant fundamentalism is both more long-standing and pervasive. It should not be thought that this contempt is motivated entirely by social or intellectual snobbishness. There are fundamentalist vulgarizations of religion that are criticized also by people who are deeply concerned about the integrity of religion in a secularistic age. The Bible-pounding, apocalyptic, clergy crusaders come in for criticism. But, equally, there is concern about a style of religion that may be less abrasive, that is in fact all too smooth. It disturbs none of the presuppositions of a secular culture, contenting itself with offering religiously coated pills for the promotion of

45

health and happiness. This is the style of religion that seems to make a good mix with mass communications. Samuel Hux offers a description of what we have in mind:

> This remains a predominantly secular culture that we live in. The television spectacular—a kind of liturgical Lawrence Welk Show, presided over by the showman-clergyman of the Saint Carnegie Temple of Positive Christianity with his delivery and substance half pitchman, half undergraduate sociology C student, and attended by a congregation of smiling, self-satisfied faces one thinks he's seen already in an audience of "Let's Make a Deal"—is more dramatic than quiet worship at the local church; but this mawkishness hardly signals a challenge to the secularism of our age.[6]

Note that Hux's outrage is not against a conservative religion that is out of step with the modern world. To the contrary, his problem is with a religion that is all too much in step with the most fatuous and least elevating dimensions of what we call the modern world. Hux is not a clergyman; in fact he writes about the hard time he's having in being a Christian believer at all. The most blistering assaults on television evangelism typically come from other religious leaders, the professional believers, so to speak. Those who are the objects of such criticism sometimes express the suspicion that their colleagues are simply envious. While acknowledging that that is not very nice, it would be impious to claim that any group of people is immune to the sin of envy.

Apart from such impugning of motives, it is important to note that the mainline religious critique of televised religious spectaculars is purportedly concerned about the integrity of religion. It is in large part a critique based upon questions of style. Against the politicized preachers who would supposedly lead mobs in burning books and imposing their repressive rules upon the rest of us, the criticism is that they are philistines, enemies of progress, and a threat to civil liberties. Against the preachers of the "Saint Carnegie Temple of Positive Christianity," the criticism is that they exploit a blasphemous oversimplification of the faith in their pandering to the masses' itch for success and security. In our American past these two strains of criticism were found, in the first instance, in Mencken-like caricatures of fundamentalism and, in the second, in the roasting of the spiritual utilitarianism of Norman Vincent Peale. The first can be traced back to what appeared to be the definitive defeat of fundamentalism in the 1920s and the second to the "religious boom" of the 1950s. In the 1920s the alarm was over religious oppression, in the 1950s over religious pandering. Today these two much-criticized forms of popular religion are joined. The highly politicized preachers are, as often as not, also the promoters of a Christianity that promises guaranteed payoffs in terms of individual success and fulfillment. The conflictual language of crusading to "turn America around" is uneasily joined to the

46

language of happy convergence between divine intent and personal benefit. At stake is the form, or the style, in which the Christian message is presented. The current merger of positive thinking and Christian crusade invites a doubling of the criticism directed at popular religion in the past since it brings together the two chief styles criticized.

Opponents of the religious new right usually couch their criticism in terms of styles that presumably separate "them" from "us." One reason for this, quite possibly, is that it is easier to criticize ways in which people try to advance their viewpoints than it is to challenge those viewpoints directly. Especially is this true if one suspects that the opposition's viewpoints may command a broader agreement than our own. I believe that those who now identify themselves as conservative and call for a return to basics are at heart exercised over the ramifications of the naked public square. There is nothing inherently liberal or conservative in that concern. The concern has gravitated to the right, so to speak, because it has been thoughtlessly neglected by others. The understanding that public discourse, especially public moral discourse, must be shaped by and rooted in tradition is neither liberal nor conservative. If liberal and ecumenical Christians of the so-called mainstream are to appreciate the meaning of this, it is necessary to move beyond excoriating the religious new right's style of behavior and enter into conversation about that movement's substantive claims. Before we can return to that project, however, we must try to place into perspective some of the other objections raised on the grounds of style.

One of the more frequent charges lodged against conservative activists is that they engage in "one-issue politics." They sometimes do. There is no denying that. Especially is this true with regard to abortion, although it is again necessary to remind ourselves that numerous pro-life advocates insist that their cause is not conservative but a genuinely liberal concern for the protection of the weak and helpless. We also recall that the agenda of the religious new right is hardly composed of one issue. Almost as often as these forces are accused of practicing one-issue politics, they are accused of promiscuity in attaching such a variety of issues to their version of "the Christian agenda." Thus it is pointed out that legislators are given moral ratings on issues as diverse as support for international treaties and funding for selected programs of the Department of Health and Human Services. The result is that the same people are attacked for practicing one-issue and too-many-issues politics. In most instances it would clear the air were it more frankly admitted that the reason for the attack has little to do with the broadness or narrowness of the agenda. They are attacked because they are promoting *their* issues.

Uneasiness over what is called one-issue politics is legitimate, indeed necessary. The cliches that are invoked in this connection have become cliches because they are confirmed by common experience: politics is a multifaceted, complex process that requires a weighing of concerns and interests in the hope of mutually tolerable compromise. And so forth. Nonetheless, various interests and concerns are kept in play only because particular groups in the political process give highest priority, even exclusive attention, to narrow agendas. We can and should aspire to advance a comprehensive concern for the common weal. But every individual and every group is shaped by a world that is but a slice of the whole. Within those worlds particular hopes and discontents assume an urgency that may not be felt by others. In addition to the inevitable partiality of our experience, there are times in which we deliberately choose to accent one concern that otherwise might be neglected in the larger mix we call the political process. Democracy depends upon countervailing forces, and those who place what we think is an inordinate accent on one issue are essential to sustaining the democratic enterprise. Their hope may be to prevail but their contribution is to countervail.

In any discussion of one-issue politics it should not be forgotten that civil rights and, later, Vietnam were not so long ago the one-issue politics of liberalism. In 1968, Hubert Humphrey, that liberal stalwart, was defeated by Richard Nixon in part because many liberals asserted that, no matter how splendid Humphrey's record on a host of other issues, he must be punished for supporting the war when he was Lyndon Johnson's Vice President. John Searle, in his analysis of the student radicalisms of the 1960s, speaks about the role of "sacred topics."[7] Vietnam and race were two such sacred topics. Other issues gained legitimacy only as they could somehow be related to a sacred topic. The churches today, as is almost always the case, reflect the spectrum of views prevalent in the society, and on that spectrum are located the various sacred topics of the left and the right.

The list of the left includes South Africa, the Pinochet government in Chile, American support for anti-Communist regimes generally, multinational corporations, military spending, and the now lamented Equal Rights Amendment. Anyone who deviates from proper opinion on these and other questions is thought to be suspect, if not beyond the pale of moral discourse. On most of the left's sacred topics, the positions of the right are not so much a mirror image as they are reflective of a sharply different understanding of what the right believes to be at stake in view of the overwhelming threat of Communism. In addition to the Communist threat, and often related to it in the view from the right, is a host of issues connected with sexuality and standards of "public decency" (it is a comment on our times that references to decency should be put in quotation marks). What the left sees as movements of liberation the right views as degeneration. In addition, the moral majoritarians claim, the advocates of these movements have, through law and mass media, been imposing their values on Americans who find those values repugnant. The possibility of a new and more civil exchange about our differences requires an understanding that the "imposition question" cuts both ways.

Closely tied to the question of one-issue politics are the various rating systems employed by the religious right. They are accused of issuing "moral hit lists" which imply that their opponents are morally disqualified from participating in the political process. The claim is made that this violates the democratic "rules of the game." In fact, however, such rating systems have for many years been a stock-in-trade of interest groups. Since 1947 the Americans for Democratic Action has used a 0 to 100 scale to assign officeholders a "Liberal Quotient." And, of course, those on the low side of the scale are deemed deficient in compassion or intelligence, particularly on issues affecting the poor, minorities, and the interests of labor. Ralph Nader's lobby, Congress Watch, puts out a similar rating that tags those with whom it disagrees as anti-consumer. Thus a congressman's attitude toward a waterway running from Tennessee to the Gulf Coast is a "consumer" issue. In its rating system, the National Education Association determines "support for education" in part upon support for a paid federal holiday on the birthday of Martin Luther King, Jr. Ecological groups publicize a list of the congressional "dirty dozen" who haven't seen the light on selected environmental issues. Bread for the World, a "Christian citizens lobby" on world hunger with which I have long been involved, issues "bread" and "crust" awards to senators and congressmen who agree or disagree with its positions.[8] Are all these "hit lists" that violate the rules of democratic politics? I think not.

If the religious new right is different from these other political protagonists, one difference is precisely that its way of measuring is not one-issue but so maddeningly multifaceted. Consider, for instance, Moral Majority's *Ninety-Five Theses For the 1980's,* put out in May 1980. It promotes the American flag, the free enterprise system, strong support for Israel, bigger defense budgets, limited federal power, tougher treatment of criminals, and opposition to "anti-family" issues ranging from communal living, homosexuality, abortion, child or wife abuse, pornography, and government harassment of "Christian schools." Clearly, if your goal is to "turn the country around," you can hardly limit your concern to one or even to a dozen issues.

The religious new right is not distinguished from its opponents in the *form* of its engagement in the political process. Further, many of its issues do not differ from the issues of the opposition; it is only that the several sides have conflicting ideas about how those issues should be addressed and resolved. With respect to organized religious engagement in politics, the temptation is great to invoke a pox on all the houses, left and right. But, unless one believes that Christian integrity calls for an enprincipled opposition to political engagement as such, that is not a choice available to us. Since democracy is a raucous enterprise, we must be prepared for the impassioned oversimplifications by which partisans attempt to mobilize their several constituencies. What we are prepared for is not necessarily what we find acceptable. There is a responsibility to resist oversimplifications, to think clearly, to speak the truth in love. One would like to think it is part of the mission of the churches to temper falsifying excesses. In fact, however, one does not expect mobilizers to view truth-telling as their primary responsibility. There is an inescapable tension between truth and power, and the mark of moral stature in an activist is that she acknowledges that tension. It is less than truthful, for instance, to condemn as unfair the methods that we employ when they are employed to greater success by our opponents.

Our response to rightist activism will be more honest, mature, and, possibly, effective as we move beyond criticism of form and style in order to engage their arguments. Among the earliest and least helpful of reactions to the religious new right was People for the American Way, an organization formed by television producer Norman Lear. In a widely distributed television commercial, it may be remembered, actors declared their preferences as to how eggs should be done. One liked them scrambled, another poached, and another fried. The punch line—aimed at the moral majoritarians who allegedly would impose one way on everybody—is that everybody should be free to do his own thing: "That's the American way!" But, of course, this is a fatuous trivialization of the questions exercising so many Americans. Disputes over what forms of "meaningful human life" are entitled to constitutional protection, over the role of punishment in criminal justice, over parental authority in education—these and other disputes are not comparable to differences over how to fix eggs for breakfast. Given his trivialization of religiously based moral concerns, it is extraordinary that Mr. Lear was able to gain the endorsement of some of the country's most prominent religious leaders. The explanation likely is that initial alarm over the threat of conservative reactionaries overwhelmed a liberal sense of obligation to public civility or basic truth-telling.

A few years later, some of the same religious leaders were having second thoughts. Not surprisingly, this return to critical reflection was most evident among Roman Catholics. Catholics have not inherited the genes of visceral reaction to Protestant fundamentalism. They did not go through the Protestant version of the modernist-fundamentalist battles that began in the last century and climaxed in the 1920s. Catholics of a liberal bent are unevenly yoked with liberal Protestants, for the thoughtful Catholic does not forget that, in tone and substance, much of the liberal animus against the religious new right was once directed against Catholics. In addition, on specific public issues most Catholics find themselves in sympathy with planks of the fundamentalist platform. This is notably the case with abortion and government aid to nongovernmental schools. In a more far-reaching way, the Catholic spirit is not amenable to the "strict separationist" program that would elevate to the level of dogma the proposition that America is a secular society.

Few people so embody the Catholic strain of liberalism on issues of social justice and labor as does Monsignor George Higgins. He served as research director for the U.S. Catholic Conference and was early recruited by Norman Lear for the advisory board of People for the American Way. In August 1982 he resigned from the board, protesting the "letter and spirit" of some of the organization's activities. He said he was influenced by editorial statements in the liberal Catholic magazine *Commonweal*. The editors of *Commonweal* had written, "Norman Lear is to politics pretty much what [Moral Majority leader] Jerry Falwell is to theology. They are both television personalities with a natural capacity for packaging the pieties of their separate worlds." Lear's advertisements, *Commonweal* said, "combine tabloid style headlines and a few shocking examples or quotations [that are] much like the technique that the religious right employs against 'secular humanists' or 'atheistic liberals.' " Higgins noted that much of the leftist reaction to the rightist reactionaries reveals "a deep-seated and almost fanatical abhorrence of any and all forms of religious fundamentalism. ... Their bias extends to almost any religion, whether fundamentalist or not, which has a domestic and international missionary outreach and which claims the right to try to influence public policy on the abortion issue, for example." Higgins called upon liberals to take seriously the religious right's concern about "the breakdown of moral values in American society."[9]

Catholics are not alone among liberals who have had second thoughts about the initial reactions to the religious new right. One thinks, for example, of some of the more determinedly Calvinist thinkers who are instrumental in the current renascence of scholarly reflection about public religion in a pluralistic society. Rockne McCarthy and Gordon Spykman are among those doing fresh thinking about the relationship between state, society, and education.[10] James Skillen heads up an Association for Public Justice that addresses from an unabashedly Christian viewpoint the full range of questions on the public agenda. In addition, Jewish scholars such as Daniel Bell and Nathan Glazer are raising sharp challenges to the secularist vision of a naked public square. All of these voices are from within the commodious house of liberalism and all are sympathetic to the core intuition that is shared also by the religious new right—namely, that the American experiment is severely and unnaturally crippled if the religiously grounded values of the American people are ruled out of order in public discourse.

Sharing that intuition does not mean agreement with all who share that intuition. For some of us that intuition calls for a delicate exploration into what may have gone wrong and how things, just maybe, might be set to rights. Intuitions are jarringly violated when they are turned into high-decibel propaganda. Yet most who share the intuition that the dogma that ours is a secular society is at best a dangerous half-truth recognize that the screaming outrage of the moral majoritarians may be a necessary alert and perhaps a corrective. The more intellectually fastidious are dependent upon the vulgarians to bring their reflections to public attention. Recall the story of the Arkansas farmer who trained mules by methods of sweetness and light but hit them over the head with a two-by-four "in order to get their attention." The religious new right focused more serious intellectual effort on questions that will, I expect, be preoccupying us for years to come. Whatever may be the alternatives to secularistic views of American society, they cannot be permitted to violate the imperatives of pluralism or to undo the great constitutional achievement represented by the "free exercise" and "no establishment" clauses of the First Amendment. If the alternative to the naked public square means a return to a polity in which those who do not share a particular religious covenant are excluded from the civil covenant of common citizenship, it is not acceptable. The exploration of shared intuitions cannot proceed except in the hope that this is not the only alternative.

What we might call the imposition question is at the center of today's disputes about morality and public policy. Who is imposing whose values on whom? (With apologies to Leninists who have customarily claimed that every issue finally comes down to the question of who-whom.) It would seem that those who have been in a position to impose have likely done the most imposing. Consider, for instance, the changing fortunes of forces in the religious communities. Until recently the National Council of Churches, say, received a much more respectful hearing from politicians and the press than did, say, the National Association of Evangelicals. When President Eisenhower presided at the dedication of the National Council headquarters in New York, nobody complained, except perhaps some disgruntled fundamentalists. When, however, President Reagan addresses fundamentalist preachers at The Roundtable or solicits Jerry Falwell's support for a Supreme Court nominee, there are mainline protests against government's captivity to religious fanatics. The two situations are not identical, but the analogy points up the way in which, depending upon one's alliances, an association can seem either normal or sinister. Only now is it beginning to occur to mainline religious leadership that the forces that entered the arena under the banners of the religious new right are part of the new normality.

Millions of Americans have for a long time felt put upon. Theirs is a powerful resentment against values that they believe have been imposed upon them, and an equally powerful sense of outrage at the suggestion that they are the ones who pose the threat of undemocratically imposing values upon others. As they begin to feel more secure about their place in the new normality, the sense of resentment, and thus of belligerence, may decline. It is far from clear that the religious new right, as a politically mobilizable force, could survive such success. This is true of any movement that begins with strong feelings about being excluded from what are viewed as the magic circles of power. Herbert Marcuse, the Marxist guru of certain radicalisms of the sixties, lamented the "repressive tolerance" by which American society neutralizes and incorporates its critics. The process was more commonly called co-optation. The co-optation and possible demise of the religious new right begins as its opponents modify their unqualified confrontation with the religious new right. The moral majoritarians thrive on confrontation. Their opponents assure their own defeat by challenging the moral majoritarians to the confrontational games at which they have achieved mastery. The spirit and tactics of confrontational populism are on the other side. Not only the spirit and tactics, but also the numbers. The survey research on the subject is indecisive, but it seems quite possible that the Moral Majority is right in claiming that, on a majority of its issues, the majority of Americans agree with Moral Majority.[11]

Admittedly, co-optation is an unsatisfactory course. Especially must it seem unsatisfactory to the most rigid opponents of the "back to basics" movement. In their eyes co-optation is tantamount to betrayal, to selling out. There is no doubt that co-optation does require a degree of accommodation. Those who refuse to accommodate have other choices. They can bank on some dramatic turn in cultural and political tides, or they can enjoy the sweet satisfactions of maintaining their purity in isolation. It is the genius of democracy, however, to know that every accommodation is not a compromise of principle. This is not to trot out the tired saw that politics is the art of the possible. Politics is the art of exploring what may be possible. But the democratic spirit recognizes that that exploration is being pressed by different parties toward different, sometimes conflicting, goals.

Democratic discourse, as Reinhold Niebuhr tirelessly insisted, depends not so much upon our agreement about righteousness as upon our agreement about sin—our own sin, and thus our own fallibility, as well as the sin and fallibility of others. Democratic discourse requires that no party fashion itself as the moral majority in order to imply that others belong to an immoral minority. Nor should groups style themselves as People for the American Way, thus suggesting that their opponents are unAmerican. (The reintroduction of the category "unAmerican" by liberals was especially curious since "unAmerican" was the favored epithet during the hated years of "McCarthyism.") Democratic discourse requires also that religious activists not claim, as some do, that they speak for "the constituency of conscience." It requires an acknowledgment that God has distributed conscience a good deal more liberally, so to speak, than we have sometimes allowed. Finally, a reconstructed democratic discourse depends upon retiring the wearied and futile polemics about style, form, and motive. Today quite different understandings of the American experiment invite our disciplined reflection. That the differences do not conform to categories of left and right is both disturbing and promising.

CHAPTER FOUR

CRITICAL PATRIOTISM
AND THE CIVIL COMMUNITY

CIVILITY IS HIGHLY PRIZED BY THE UNCERTAIN. IT NEEDS most to be exercised by the certain. But civility, which has to do with how we handle our disputes, can become a code word that exacerbates our disputes. Donald, as I shall call him, is a young man who works for Moral Majority in Washington. He is clean-cut, fashionably dressed, well educated, well spoken, and, taken all together, the kind of person who prompts the question about what a nice fellow like him is doing in an outfit like this. We are seated together in a meeting being addressed by Jerry Falwell in his typically straightforward manner. The speaker concludes his jeremiad on America's decline with a thorough excoriation of pornographers, poverty pimps, liberal do-gooders, and friends of the enemies of freedom. "He's a very great man," says Donald, "and often he's very vulgar. I would be more hopeful about America if we had more vulgarity like his." Donald allows that, at least in the abstract, civility is a virtue. But, paraphrasing a statement attributed to Hitler's propaganda minister, Joseph Goebbels, he says, "When I hear the word civility I reach for my gun." He says it with a smile but his meaning is serious. Civility, he explains, has become a synonym for fudging. More than that, those who talk most about civility usually define it in terms of their accustomed way of doing things: "Their way of doing things means they continue to be in control. We mean to take over—nicely, if possible; but, if that's not possible, well, civility is not the highest of the virtues." Fifteen years earlier the sentiment would have come from a leftist militant of "The Movement" aimed at "getting America on the right side of the revolution."

Of course he is right about the possible uses of civility. It often does translate into tactics of evasion. It can also be a synonym for snobbery. There is a streak of desperation in this way of trying to discredit the new activists of the right. It has aptly been described as bigotry with clean fingernails. Prejudice is in bad odor today, but a few prejudices are still respectable. It is frequently noted that, among secular intellectuals, anti-Catholic bigotry routinely goes uncensured. And in some circles it is not only respectable but a veritable duty to despise fundamentalists, especially if they have about them a whiff of the rural South. I have discovered that this bigotry is sometimes most pronounced in mainline religionists who come from a fundamentalist background. They feel they have been liberated from the religious and moral oppression of their childhood. Often it has required hard struggle and a painful breaking of ties. They are not entirely certain that they are free from it. They are the products of a narrow escape, and therefore forever fearful of being drawn back into the world they have determinedly put behind. Even a moment's sympathetic consideration of the fundamentalist alternative is a sign of weakening that jeopardizes their fragile liberation. The line between today's "we" and yesteryear's "them" is indelible and must never be compromised. It is a most uncivil attitude and those who adopt it talk much about civility. Civil is what we are. Those on the other side of the line are uncivil, which, among civil people, is recognized as being not too far from uncivilized.

It is implied, and sometimes asserted, that the American people are intelligent enough to see, in time, the difference between enlightened mainline leadership and the bumpkins of the religious new right. And, if the people do not wake up and see the difference between bad guys and good guys, then the worst that we ever suspected about America is confirmed and the country will get the leadership it deserves. In a public discussion of the current troubles a prominent liberal rabbi in New York declared, "Look, you people are making this too complicated. They're Yahoos and rednecks and racists and Ku Kluxers and we're not, and that's the difference. That's all there is to it. All we have to do is make the difference clear to the American people." But of course that is not all there is to it. In the camp of "them" are Ph.D.s wearing three-piece suits, operating from the executive suites of major corporations, persuaded of the need for racial equality, and convinced that they are the last defenders of the constitutional rights of majorities and minorities alike. True, some of the most visible of them keep in business the manufacturers of plaid double-knit suits, wear white shiny-buckled loafers, and do not see what is wrong with telling a really good and perfectly "clean" racial joke. In their entourage they might well have a "colored" aid who assures them he takes no offense. "So there, you see?" But the difference of style is not "all there is to it." The meaning of civility is not summed up in attitudes toward double-knit suits. This despite a theological colleague who assures me that all sound ethical judgments are essentially aesthetic judgments. He condemns the religious new right, he says, for the same reason the Bonhoeffer family despised the Nazis: "They were in such very bad taste." I persist in believing that there was more to Dietrich Bonhoeffer's witness than a question of taste.

Religious folks join secular journalists in looking for additional ways to be excused from taking seriously the challenge of conservative activists. Secular journalism is obsessed with the Elmer Gantry syndrome. It is assumed that professional publicists of righteousness must be hiding some very juicy wickedness. Thus, for example, critics of the moral majoritarians make no secret of their devout hope to discover that the leaders of the movement are sleeping around with loose women. Better yet, with little boys and, best of all, with little black boys. Of course it will turn out that they have been lavishing vast amounts of embezzled funds upon their partners in corruption. There have in fact been ripples of scandal, especially fiscal scandal, and there will no doubt be others. But so far the religious new right has not cooperated with these more desperate hopes of manicured bigotry. In general, its leaders have maintained a posture of powerful, frequently insufferable, personal rectitude.

When we have exhausted the ploys of exposing and debunking we edge up to the recognition that the forces represented by the religious new right are here to stay. They will suffer defeats from time to time; they are not the unstoppable juggernaut of their own advertisements and of some liberal fears. They may even be momentarily routed and thrown into disarray. But they will not disappear. Millions of Americans have half marched, half stumbled, into the public space we mistakenly thought was ours. They make no apologies for breaking down the door, since they think it should not have been locked in the first place. To put it differently, at the family reunion of American religion, the disreputable side of the family has for the first time shown up in force. Not only that, but they show every sign of wanting to take over, for now they are the ones raising questions about the pedigree of their cousins. It is most disconcerting to those who were always assumed to be the mainliners. The mainliners boast of being ecumenical, but do not want to carry ecumenism too far. Dialogue with gentle Buddhists and ungentle Marxists is clearly required. But to enter into conversation with Bible-banging pushers of blood-bought salvation and bullishness on capitalism is simply to ask too much.

Religious leadership that does not want to take fundamentalism's former place in the wilderness will, it may be assumed, enter into that conversation. On the other hand, the wilderness is not necessarily the wrong place for true religion to find itself. Exile may, in some circumstances, be the mark of fidelity. There is a venerable Christian tradition of choosing the "sectarian" rather than the "churchly" model of discipleship. The churchly model is inclusive, catholic, eager to influence the social order. The sectarian model defines itself against that order. It speaks truth to power from outside the circle of power, and is frankly skeptical about influencing that power for good. In the sectarian view, there can be no legitimate commerce between Christ and Caesar. Sectarianism for the sake of the integrity of the gospel has at times been an honorable and indeed necessary choice.

The leadership of the mainline churches is not sectarian. This is manifestly true of Roman Catholicism and will likely continue to be true, despite those who expect and cheer Catholicism's becoming a "peace church" in the manner of, for instance, the Mennonites. Occasional rhetorical flights aside, the leadership of the mainline Protestant churches is also not at home with the sectarian model. Their ingrained ethical and theological habits are based upon the mandate to relate Christian faith to the public order. If this group goes into exile, it will not be a sectarian choice for the sake of the integrity of their theology. Their theology can countenance being driven into exile, but it cannot countenance *choosing* exile from the public square. Exile may not be a sectarian choice but simply something that happens to leaders who do not recognize the new shape of American religion and politics. Or it may be deliberately chosen by those who prefer exile to the distasteful prospect of dialogue with Christians who are so utterly and threateningly different.

The refusal to talk with these strange cousins will not likely be permanent. As it becomes evident that these *arrivistes* are not going to go back to where they came from, the futility of the refusal is more clearly recognized. In addition, leaders of whatever persuasion are alike in some respects. The leaders of the traditionalist rebellion are no doubt motivated in part by dreams of power and glory, protestations to the contrary. These are very human dynamics, and the churches are nothing if not human. Leaders want to be where the action is, as it used to be said. The difference is that mainliners are more or less accustomed to being there. The taste for power, or at least proximity to power, is not easily abandoned. Those who have been in command of the temple precincts do not readily take up the role of John the Baptist in the desert. Especially are they disinclined to do so when they recognize that their exile would have less to do with gospel fidelity than with disagreements over "supply-side economics" and a clutch of other controversies over issues that should not qualify as ultimate concerns.

Admittedly, a modest degree of influence, of purely derivative influence, can be exercised in exile. It is not nothing to be the most visible critics of the parties in power. But neither is it very much. In any case, mainline leaders are by their own definition "responsible" leaders. Being responsible in this context means not permitting oneself to be marginalized. The reasonable expectation, therefore, is that the bulk of mainline leadership will—slowly, reluctantly, erratically—move toward what has become, by virtue of uncivil invasion, the center. If the term "mainline" means anything, it means the place at the center. The center is usually not a viewpoint but an expedient place to be in the absence of viewpoints. It is standing between viewpoints. It is responsible. It is mainline.

I do not suggest that mainline religious leadership merely bends with prevailing winds. A degree of flexibility on questions of penultimate moment or less is not a vice. Nor is a propensity for final, nonnegotiable position-taking necessarily a virtue. Joseph Conrad somewhere observes that we all have a fear of finality that prevents so many heroisms, and so many crimes. One does not, generally speaking, become a bishop or general secretary of matters that matter by being heroic. The dynamics of religious

58

leadership are not all that different from those that mark electoral or corporate politics. The churches rightly resist resigning themselves to that reality. They believe that spiritual excellences and even divine guidance should somehow make a difference, and they should. Usually the difference is marvelously obscured, visible only, as it were, to the eyes of faith.

A few heroic souls offer a kind of leadership by standing in solitary witness against great evil. Sometimes a significant sector of the church may assume this posture of isolation for the sake of the truth. The most commonly cited instance is that of the "confessing church" in Nazi Germany. There are in fact some voices declaring that the ascendancy of the religious and political right in America is comparable to the rise of Nazism. They are few and are thought to be extreme. More moderate leaders who wish to be viewed as responsible are nonetheless worried, and with good reason. What appears to be happening does not fit in with what the experts—political, sociological, and politico-socio-theological—led us to expect from the future. However, because the business of leadership is to lead, it must engage what is happening in order to influence what might happen.

Several years after the debut of the moral majoritarians, such engagement was only beginning. Political and religious keepers of the liberal flame were still preoccupied in denying the presence or potency of the newcomers. Many still question the legitimacy of those who are questioning the legitimacy of the old order. Thus certain styles of liberalism bid fair to become the new conservatism. A perverse civility divides the *civitas* into parties beyond the reach of conversation, not to mention reconciliation. The left becomes the party of aristocratic taste, hoping to endure the siege and consoling itself with assurances of its superiorities of tone and moral vision. The distinction between us and them, however, is not essentially one of tone nor of our presumed moral superiority. It is a fundamental difference in the understanding of the world, of religion's role in society, and of what God might be up to in history. If we merely marshal our forces behind our respective "sacred topics," the outlook is not encouraging.

There is no reason to welcome a head-on political contest between the social platform of the mainline churches and that of the moral majoritarians. But even if the political balance were different from what it probably is, it is degrading for religion to divide its influence by providing little more than moralizing appendages to the right wing of the Republican party and the left wing of the Democratic. Such a division defeats what is, at best, the intention of all involved. That intention is to restore the role of religion in helping to give moral definition and direction to American public life and policy. On this view, the 1980s are a time neither for conservative triumphalism nor for liberal defeatism, although these are the prevalent temptations. Needed now is the asking of elementary questions about how we arrived at this moment of confrontation and how we move beyond it, if not toward consensus, at least toward a less debilitating polarization.

The public role of religion will not be decided by a few defeats or victories in specific elections or policy disputes. It will be decided in large part by the capacity of various religious leaderships to liberate themselves from their captivity to political partisanships. It will be decided by religion's ability to help reconstruct a "sacred canopy" for the American experiment. Such a moral legitimation does not mean declaring that the way things are is legitimate. (When it comes to criticizing the way things are, incidentally, it is hard to tell whether the left or the right is today more radical.) Moral legitimation means providing a meaning and a purpose, and therefore a framework within which the violation of that meaning and purpose can be criticized. The vision that is required cannot be produced by the political process itself. Politics derives its directions from the ethos, from the cultural sensibilities that are the context of political action. The cultural context is shaped by our moral judgments and intuitions about how the world is and how it ought to be. Again, for the great majority of Americans such moral judgments and intuitions are inseparable from religious belief. Perhaps this is true not just of the majority but of all of us, whether or not we call our ultimate values religious. In any event, whether it is called the Judeo-Christian ethic, or Christianity, or the operative social values, or a civil religion, it is the dynamic of religion that holds the promise of binding together (*religare*) a nation in a way that may more nearly approximate *civitas*. Conseqently, while the years ahead may be described politically as liberal, conservative, or something else, the religious forces that will have greatest public influence are those that are seen to contribute most to the moral redefinition of the American future.

Moral redefinition is itself not easy to define. It touches upon what, in sociological jargon, is termed legitimation theory, and legitimation theories can become exceedingly complex. For our present purposes, moral redefinition has to do with the "meaning business." Religion is in the meaning business. That is not the only function of religion, of course, but it is perhaps the most distinctive function. Religion responds to the inescapable human question, What does this mean? The "what" in question may be something so inclusive as the meaning of history, or it may be the meaning of a sickness or a death in the family. For something to "mean" something means that is related to a larger reality, a context that makes it intelligible. The most obvious meaning of talk about meaning is related to language. Sounds that are not related to some ordered pattern of language are mere gibberish. They are meaning*less*, incoherent. Even emotive sounds or expletives find their meaning, if they have meaning, within order. Sometimes the order is marvelously flexible, but we usually think we understand when "Ouch!" or "Wow!" are appropriate or inappropriate

60

responses to a situation. The meanings of "Oh" can vary with the numerous variations of tone employed, but it has meaning nonetheless.

What seems self-evident with respect to language becomes a problem when religion addresses other meanings. Preachers with a modicum of orthodoxy have no difficulty in addressing the ultimate meaning of history. That is, history is presumably the unfolding story of God's purposes, culminating in the vindication that is the kingdom of God. Even less orthodox Christians can assert some kind of cosmic order—maybe even divine order—to which human affairs ought to be accountable.[1] Short of such encompassing assertions, most Christians find it eminently "meaningful" to talk about the meaning of their individual lives. (Admittedly, too often today talk about meaning degenerates into the solipsisms of self-fulfillment and self-actualization. Self-fulfillment is, of course, meaningless unless it is based upon a purposeful definition of the self that is to be fulfilled.) But many of us have a much more difficult time speaking about the meaning of historical communities such as, say, America. We become tongue-tied, defensive, and embarrassed. Talk about the meaning of America is uncomfortably reminiscent of an antique and discredited language about the destiny, even the manifest destiny, of America.

Civility is more than politeness or courtesy, although, to be sure, the importance of politeness and courtesy should not be underestimated. Politeness and courtesy come from an acknowledgment of the need for restraint and deference, especially in the face of disagreement and the disagreeable. But restraint remains an anemic virtue unless it is restraint exercised for the sake of sustaining and advancing something more vibrant. Vision gives vibrancy to civility. True civility speaks not merely about limits but about a vision of the *civitas*. Historically, mainline Protestantism in America provided that kind of vision of an experimental and exemplary America. However it was expressed, the confidence was that America had a meaning within the larger purposes of God in world-historical change. One way of expressing it was to say that America has been "elected" by God. Abraham Lincoln, who has rightly been celebrated as the foremost theologian of the American experiment, talked about America as an "almost chosen" people. Today most of us eschew the notion of chosenness or election altogether. Such language is condemned as reflecting an unseemly and dangerous hubris—an overweening historical pride that, if acted upon, invites certain destruction. The "lessons of history" have presumably taught us that there is nothing all that special about America. Sometimes this insight is pressed and twisted into what might be called a reverse election. That is, it is argued that America is indeed singular, but singular in the sense of being the prime source of the world's sundry miseries.

The language of communal meaning, based upon a sense of purpose, does not necessarily imply superiority or inferiority, righteousness or wickedness. Rather, to talk about the meaning of America, even the election of America, is to say something about historical opportunity, responsibility, and judgment.[2] Consider the case of a swimmer who stands on the shore and does nothing while thirty feet away a ten-year-old girl drowns. We would not hesitate to say that he was responsible for trying to save her. We might even say he was elected to that task. In saying this we do not imply anything about his superiority or inferiority in comparison with innumerable other swimmers in the world. It is simply that he was at that time and in that place, and others were not. He had the opportunity and the ability, which is to say he had the response-ability. His failure to act as he ought to have acted brings him under judgment. It brings him under *our* judgment, to be sure. But many of us would want to say more than that. Within the total ordering of reality—which is not finally accidental or capricious—his is a moment of responsibility grievously missed.

It is not a simple matter to transfer such moral reasoning from the individual case to the case of communities and nations. Ideas about collective guilt and collective righteousness are in ill repute, and deservedly so. Not all Germans are collectively guilty for the crimes of the Nazis, nor all Russians for the crimes of Stalin, nor all white Americans for the crime of slavery. Curiously, the negative side of the notion of election—namely, judgment—occurs with routine frequency in current religious language. Whether the subject is land abuse, child abuse, or the neglect of the aged, we have little difficulty in saying that we as a society are guilty. No one is surprised, and perhaps they do not even think twice, about church pronouncements declaring Americans guilty of world hunger and myriad oppressions in the third world. Conservatives conventionally charge that liberals love to wallow in guilt. Like drug addicts, they get a high from "guilt trips." In the face of whatever horror, they mistake therapeutic breast-beating and self-condemnation for having "done something about it." The additional charge is that the condemnation is not really *self*-condemnation. Rather, the condemnation is aimed at others who presumably are responsible for the systemic evils and oppressive structures of American society.

There is considerable merit to these charges, as anyone knows who has worked within the "peace and justice" bureaus of American religion. We should not, however, permit the condemnation of injustices to be dismissed as indulgence in self-flagellation or the flagellation of others. The corrective is to be more precise about evil, virtue, and the nature of responsibility. A few years ago a German theologian friend had occasion to spend a day observing a conference of Methodist pastors in California. Their deliberations, he reported, were marked by an edifying note of urgency as they addressed a host of social issues. He confessed his initial confusion, however, about their frequent statements to the effect that "we" are guilty of doing this or not doing that, and "we" are called by God to do something else. His confusion was that he did not know who they meant by "we." We Methodists, we Christians, we Americans, or we whatever? Finally it dawned upon him: "I realized that all the 'wes' were interchangeable." But of course the "wes" are not interchangeable. As it is said, if everyone is guilty no one is guilty. During the Vietnam War years, Abraham Joshua Heschel often reminded us, "Some are guilty; all are responsible."

The indictment of wrongs depends on a revived understanding of what ought to be and can be. Failure bespeaks possibility. The several communities to which we each belong require discriminations in moral judgment. True, it can be argued that the idea of America as a community is problematic to the point of being meaningless. Church, family, friendships, professional associations, neighborhood, maybe even town or city— these are real communities, made up of touchable face-to-face connections. In these communities one can accept specific responsibility for specific purposes. But America—from Sacramento to Orlando, from Cisco to Minneapolis, and points between—is altogether too various and amorphous. This argument should not be brushed aside as an evasion of responsibility. In fact most of us are "elected" to our chief responsibilities within what Edmund Burke called the "little platoons" of everyday life. Not everybody, thank God, has a vocation to politics, whether in the affairs of the nation or our own neighborhood. And of course many who are in a state of sustained commotion about affairs national and international grievously evade the responsibilities that are theirs closer to home. Nor is it true, as some theorists of social contract would have it, that we are bound to one another by solemn societal agreements. Some of us may feel that we were just born here; we never signed on for the American experiment or anything else quite so ambitious.

Nonetheless. There is this notion of democracy. However qualified, it suggests that government is by the people, and each of us is unavoidably part of whatever is meant by the people. Where there is the opportunity for such participation in governance, Christian teaching has generally indicated that there is an accompanying responsibility. The nature and extent of that participation may depend upon our station in life, to use an old-fashioned term. It certainly does not require the intensities of "participatory democracy" in which we take part in every decision affecting our lives. Such a degree of participation is neither possible nor desirable. I will not go to next week's public hearings at which the transit authority will decide whether to raise subway fares, although it will certainly affect my life. Again, we remember Oscar Wilde's jibe that the problem with socialism is that it leaves you with no free evenings.

In addition to irrefragable limits of time, energy, and circumstance, the objection can also be raised that all such democratic participation is illusory; that, in fact, all the important decisions are made by elites who only go through the motions of democracy in order to disguise their power with the appearance of democratic legitimacy. Some who think they have seen through the game simply refuse to play their assigned role. They are mistakenly called apathetic. It is merely that they have come to Mr. Dooley's conclusion about politics and politicians: "Don't vote. It only encourages them." Others who refuse to be taken in by illusory democracy, however, are exceedingly active democrats, exercising their responsibility to denounce the charade and—not always, but sometimes—proposing alternatives to it.

I have earlier suggested that a sober view of politics begins with the subject of power. Every form of governance requires that there be governors and governed. There is a significant difference, nonetheless, when a society professes and to some degree approximates democratic governance. In a way that is not true of Nazi Germany, nor of the Soviet Union, nor, sad to say, of the great majority of nations today, the concept of collective responsibility has some warrant in American life. The case can be made that democracy is among our "useful fictions." On this view, which easily slides into cynicism, it is admitted that the governance of our society is not really democratic but it is useful, even necessary, to pretend it is. People who spend all their free evenings in party caucuses may sustain a sense of sharing in the society's governance. If they did not have that sense they would likely not spend their energies as they do. At the same time, behaving as they do no doubt reinforces the sense of participation. For many more Americans, however, democratic participation consists in being able to identify major political figures and issues projected by the evening news and in winding up democracy's wheels by pulling the lever in a ballot box every two or four years. Regardless of the level of participation, however, we recognize that, unless one holds a very major position in government, we are more ruled than ruling. Even then, those who presumably held power, including American presidents, talk much about the illusion of power. The feeling of being ruled is reflected in our everyday talk about what "they" are likely to do about this issue or that. The result of this need not be the cynicism that declares democracy to be a fiction. Rather, we reach a tempered notion of democracy that accents the representative and indirect nature of popular participation.

And yet a sense of shared responsibility is required. It is required for the maintenance of liberal democracy. In view of the historically available alternatives to liberal democracy, that is no little consideration. In addition it is morally required. That is because, in the Christian understanding, our historical placement is not merely accidental. Where we have the opportunity to do so, we are "called" to exercise influence to the glory of God and the welfare of our neighbor. Again, this does not mean that everyone has a full-time vocation to politics. We should not condemn as sinfully "privatizing" those who focus their exercise of loving obedience in smaller

64

communities of family, friendship, and other associations of interest and loyalty. They may be relatively indifferent to politics yet living lives of both greater fulfillment and greater obedience. Having said that, the churches are nonetheless right in constantly challenging Christians to political responsibility. The purpose is not to give people a bad conscience if they choose to devote energies to "private" rather than "public" matters. The purpose is, by critically challenging our choices, to refine our thinking about our vocations, to help assure that we have really accepted responsibility for the choices we make. An additional and important purpose is, quite simply, to increase public participation and therefore the plausibility of the democratic process. This is necessary because, in a society where political participation is voluntary, most sensible people would otherwise conclude that the chief satisfactions—and opportunities to help others— are not in the sphere of the political.

Even if we are persuaded of the urgency of political participation, Christians may have difficulties in defining the *civitas* for which they are to accept responsibility. As we have seen, these difficulties arise when we speak of the United States of America as a community of responsibility. The problems in "identifying" with America are in some respects peculiar to our experience of this society. In other ways, however, Christians would have the same difficulties in identifying any particular community as their sphere of responsibility, whether the community in question be Tanzania, Norway, or China. In the Christian view it would seem there are only two communities for which we are morally accountable, the community of believers and humankind itself. Even then, the community of believers, the church, claims our loyalty only because it is the sign of the ultimate unity of humankind in Christ. To the extent that Christians might depart from this universalistic vision, it would likely be in favor of particular communities such as family and friends. But surely it is difficult to assign moral status to a construct so artificial as a nation-state and a "community" so indeterminate as America. In fact, to do so would seem to be a betrayal of the universal love to which we are called. We are, after all, "citizens of the world." And, if we speak of Christians possessing "dual citizenship," the other citizenship is not in America but in the kingdom of God. If we do not accept with moral earnestness our citizenship in America, however, we will have no part in redefining the American experiment. In that case, the task of societal redirection will not go unattended, it will be attended to by others. Today it is the moral majoritarians who bring moral earnestness and theological authority to the task of redefining America and its role in God's purposes.[3]

The apparent conflict between universal and particular loves is not new. In the Greek city-state, which was a much more specifiable community than is America, the philosophers pondered the difficulties in reconciling love for the state, love for humanity, and love for friends.[4] With the coming of Christianity the difficulties were sharpened. After all, Christians worshiped a Lord who had been killed by the state. It would have been surprising had there *not* been a powerful impulse to withhold allegiance from all earthly communities and governments that are under the sway of the "principalities and powers" of the time before the end time. That most Christians did finally make a kind of peace, perhaps just a truce, with temporal powers is frequently condemned still today as a form of betrayal, as a "fall" from the purity of the primitive church. An alternative and more favorable interpretation is that Christians came to understand that a universal ethic of love required the exercise of love with respect to the particularities of our historical placement.

In his treatise *On Christian Doctrine* (I.xxviii) St. Augustine pondered the connection between universal love and the loves of particular placement.

> All men are to be loved equally. But since you cannot do good to all, you are to pay special regard to those who, by the accidents of time, or place, or circumstance, are brought into closer connection with you. For, suppose that you had a great deal of some commodity, and felt bound to give it away to somebody who had none, and that it could not be given to more than one person; if two persons presented themselves, neither of whom had either from need or relationship a greater claim upon you than the other, you could do nothing fairer than choose by lot to which you would give what could not be given to both. Just so among men, since you cannot consult for the good of them all, you must take the matter as decided for you by a sort of lot, according as each man happens for the time being to be more closely connected with you.

Gilbert Meilaender describes Augustine's notion as a kind of "divine lottery," for Augustine "suggests that within the finite, historical realm these 'accidents' are God's doing." Meilaender adds, "We cannot in this finite life 'consult for the good of them all,' nor achieve a love which is truly universal. The particular loves are the means God uses to lead his creatures toward the universal love of *caritas*, but they are still the means God has chosen."[5] Meilaender is talking not about nations but about the love appropriate to friendship. And Augustine certainly was not promoting the idea that Christians should "identify" with the collapsing Roman empire of his time. But in our "time, place, and circumstance" the moral reasoning is relevant also to our thinking about what it means to be an American. Of all the ties by which we are "closely connected" to others, our American citizenship is by no means the most compelling. Yet it is there as an obligation and an opportunity. The more compelling we feel this community's claim upon us, the more likely will we have a part in forging a compelling vision of the community's future.

The civility that is necessary to redefining America, then, has to come to terms with the universalistic thrust of the Christian ethic. It is not always easy to resign ourselves to Augustine's assertion that we "cannot consult for the good of all." We persist in believing that we must take into account the good of all. Augustine and other Christian thinkers who have wrestled with the problems of universal and particular loves are not indifferent to that persistent belief. Thomas, Luther, Calvin, and a host of others join Augustine in suggesting that it is precisely by doing our duty by the particular that we best serve the universal. We may be doubtful today about whether the universe is so well ordered by God as they sometimes seemed to imply. As we have our doubts about an "invisible hand" in economics that transforms private greeds to the meeting of public needs, so we may doubt that duty to the *civitas* is service to *humanitas*. Early Puritan thinking did not, however, place its simple confidence in an invisible hand working all things for the best in a fine-tuned universe. People like Jonathan Edwards and Cotton Mather were quite prepared to read "the signs of the times" and point to the evidences that commitment to the American experiment would advance the universal purposes of God in history.

Many Christians today are more troubled by the choice of particularities than they are by the problematic connection between the universal and the particular. That is, they now read "the signs of the times" and identify some other *civitas* with which they would be joined in advancing a universal hope. Thus we talk about standing in "solidarity with the poor and the oppressed." The language of solidarity is in our time much used and much abused.

It is abused when employed for narrow partisan purposes. This abuse is manifest in certain radical forms of sleight of mind in which it is proposed that our "identification" with the poor somehow brings about solidarity with a new community of history's victims. Such "identification" is achieved through a process of "consciousness raising" that may well result in (to borrow a term from our Marxist friends) false consciousness. The solidarity that we should affirm is a prior fact, a given, that is not of our creation. We cannot leap out of our historical circumstance in order to stand in the shoes, so to speak, of others. Of course we can and should exercise our imaginations and capacities for empathy in order to try to understand (to stand under) the circumstances of others, especially of others who are less privileged than ourselves. But it is false consciousness to think that even the most intensive empathy can create a solidarity of identity and experience. Such false consciousness has two unhappy consequences.

First, it distorts the circumstance of "the other" with whom we would identify. It violates the respect, even the reverence, that we should render the singularity of every other person and life experience. We fail to defer to that singularity when we cast great numbers of persons into generalized categories such as "the poor and oppressed." Not incidentally, those who are most facile in category-casting are often the same people who think they are in a position to know what is best for those whom they have categorized. In this way, what begins with empathy, compassion, and imagination ends up with the advancement of totalist solutions. Since we are in solidarity with the oppressed, it is thought, we have the right to advance such solutions and our solutions must be benign. Thus for the more powerful, "identifying" with the victim becomes a disguise for what is only another establishment of the governors and the governed.

A second unhappy consequence of this false consciousness is that we abdicate responsibility for the historical placement that is in fact our own. I am American, white, male, educated, middle class and—on the scale of contemporary human circumstances—part of an immensely privileged elite. The response to this life circumstance is not one of guilt but of responsibility. In my case, and I assume in the case of most of the readers of this book, whatever modest achievements and successes we have are not knowingly at the price of failure or deprivation for others. "Knowingly" is the important qualifier. Most of us would claim, correctly, that we have not deliberately or calculatedly deprived others in order to benefit ourselves. Nobody else would be better off were we worse off. That having been said, it remains the case that we may have benefited from arrangements—social, economic, political—that are unfair to others who are less favorably situated. In that sense, is not our advantage at the price of their disadvantage?

The last question is urgently important and, for those who are aware of the gross disparities of well-being in our society and in our world, it may be an exceedingly painful one. We can only deal with it, however, if we are unflinchingly honest about the community to which we belong. One "arrangement" of which we are part is the entity called the United States of America. Given the embarrassment that the sensitive rich tend to feel in the presence of the misery of others, there is an understandable desire to "identify with" the others. Such identification, however, can be a form of evasion. We tell ourselves that we do not really belong to the community of which we are part; in fact we condemn that community; we are one with the putative victims of that community's privilege. As I say, the sleight of mind involved is perfectly understandable. But it is nonetheless destructive of intelligent moral response. For those who are greatly impressed by the putative evils of American society and of America's role in the world, the identification with America can become emotionally unbearable. By various devices we seek to be shed of that identity and clothed in another that is less ambiguous, that may even betoken a certain moral dignity, such as identification with the poor and oppressed. Such devices, however, preclude the link of civility that is required to move from confrontation to a beginning of conversation between the right and the left. The reason is that civility assumes, if not a consensus about, at least a search for a reconstituted vision of the *civitas.*

No people will knowingly accept the leadership of their declared enemies. Nonetheless vocal sectors in the mainline churches today are perceived as declaring themselves to be the enemies of the American experiment. Such a perception is sharply disputed by those who are accused of being anti-American. We are not anti-American but pro-American, they say. They merely want radically to transform America in order to get it "on the right side of the revolution." A problem with this variety of pro-Americanism, however, is that its proposals are in dramatic discontinuity with anything that is historically identifiable as America. Historical identity requires more or less fixed characteristics that are enduring referents through time. Characteristics of the project we call America would include, for examples, a devotion to liberal democracy, a near obsession with civil liberties, a relatively open market economy, the aspiration toward equality of opportunity, a commitment to an institutionalized balancing of powers and countervailing forces, and a readiness to defend this kind of social experiment, if necessary, by military force. For those who are deeply alienated from the American project, each of the characteristics mentioned should be described quite differently. Liberal democracy is a charade that disguises "bourgeois" liberties by which corporate power increases inequalities in order to ensure the continuance of an exploited mass of laborers who are necessary to capitalism's goal of global expansion with the aid of militaristic imperialism. These are two quite different ways of describing the American phenomenon. The choice between them is not a clear-cut either/or. But one, it would seem, is likely to be more accurate than the other. Those who think the second is more accurate than the first are improbable participants in the search for a more vibrant civility.

Some currents of social witness in the churches, especially those associated with various "liberation theologies," are closer to the second than the first description of the American reality. Let it be said that the second description may in fact be more accurate, although I do not think so. That is not the immediate point. The immediate point is that any putative pro-Americanism based upon the second description is inevitably going to be perceived by most Americans as anti-American. Not long ago I was in South Africa doing research on social and political change there. An Afrikaner political leader told me privately that he was in favor of the liberation of blacks in South Africa. In fact he declared himself prepared to sit down and negotiate with the African National Congress, which is the main organization devoted to revolutionary armed struggle. He was not anti-ANC, he said; rather, he was in favor of the purposes of ANC. The problem with the ANC, according to him, is that it is on the wrong side of advancing the interests of blacks in South Africa. His hope was that the revolutionaries would come to recognize that true black liberation lies in the direction of cooperating with the white regime in reconstructing South Africa along lines of separate but fair divisions of economic and political power. This is what is meant by sleight of mind. It is hard to take seriously such an argument. It is little short of fatuous to declare ourselves in favor of something only when we have redefined that something into something it obviously is not. When I say that I love you on condition that you become somebody else, I am saying that I do not love you.

But is this not perilously close to the "love it or leave it" reaction of many Americans to the protestors against the Vietnam War? It would be easy to say that the present argument is totally unrelated to that reaction. It would not be accurate, however. Beneath the vulgarity of "love it or leave it," there is a deeper truth. Those who shouted or muttered that slogan with the intent of repressing dissent were probably not aware of the deeper truth. Nor were the dissenters at whom the slogan was aimed. The deeper truth is that reform, if it is real reform, is an exercise of love. Prophecy, if it is real prophecy, is an exercise of love. Amos, Hosea, and Jeremiah employed such harsh language in criticizing the children of Israel precisely because they thought more of the people than the people thought of themselves. The prophets were in love with, were possessed by, a vision of the dignity and destiny of those they addressed. The outrageousness of sin and failure was in direct proportion to the greatness of God's intent for his people. Prophecy was always an exercise of love, never of contempt, for those to whom the prophet addressed his criticism.

One can love the American promise and be repulsed by all that at present contradicts that promise. That is not the same thing as being repulsed by the America that is. Effective criticism makes clear that the promise is in continuity with the present and the past, that what is participates in what might be. In a curious way that many observers of America have thought to be singular, the American continuity is change. It is, however, change along an identifiable trajectory that at each point bears the marks of being American. Those marks include the characteristics of liberal democracy mentioned earlier. Of course there are alternatives to effective criticism. There is, for example, the alternative of withdrawal from political concern or action. And there is the alternative of revolutionary change.

Christians who accept the proposition that there can be justifiable violence in warfare should also be able to accept, however reluctantly, the justification of revolutionary violence. I have written elsewhere about the moral requirements for justifiable revolution in America and will not elaborate on that here.[6] The strange development today is that many Christians make revolutionary statements about America but deny that they favor revolution. "Capitalism is inherently incompatible with Christianity." "American corporate imperialism is the primary cause of the oppression of the poor in today's world." "An emphasis on civil and political rights is maintained at the cost of depriving the poor of their economic rights." In recent years such statements have proliferated in religious social pronouncements, so much so that, more often than not, they do not even occasion comment. Such statements are counter-propositions to what the late John Courtney Murray called "the American proposition."[7] Again, the counter-propositions may be correct. They are certainly revolutionary.

Those who advance such propositions would, if they acted upon them, be advancing revolution. Of course they may not act upon them. They may believe that these propositions are statements of tragic fact about which little can be done. Or they may believe that it is not Americans but forces external to America that will bring about the required revolution. Or they may devote themselves to activist communities of nonviolent revolutionary change. Whatever one decides to do or not do about it, subscription to these counter-propositions puts one outside the circle of discourse in which the future of the *civitas* is to be re-envisioned. Embracing the American proposition or its counter-propositions is not necessarily a question of moral superiority or inferiority. In fact the difference may not be one of value judgment at all. It is a difference in our understanding of the fact-condition, if you will, in our reading of the "signs of the times."

During the "popular front" period of the anti-Vietnam War movement the differences were there but were strategically suppressed, for the most part. Sometimes they would break out into the open. Remember the instances in which the American flag was burned at anti-war rallies. Such actions were regularly condemned by the "responsible" leadership of the movement. Remember also how in the late sixties support for the war was signaled simply by wearing an American flag in one's lapel. All the symbols of the *civitas*, of communal identity, of patriotism, if you will, were permitted to gravitate to the right. Figures such as Bob Hope and Billy Graham led "I Love America" rallies. The inference to be drawn was that dissenters did not love America. Most of us vigorously protested that propaganda ploy, insisting that our dissent was for and not against America. A very visible minority on "our side," however, proclaimed that the inference was all too accurate. They wanted it to be known that they did indeed hate "Amerika." Many of these professed revolutionaries are now working in brokerage houses or teaching English literature. Still in the 1980s residual elements of the revolution-that-was-to-be come out of hiding from time to time and are briefly the focus of nostalgic media attention. Those who overtly repudiated the symbols of American identity were, to be sure, always in the minority. The moderates who were tactically allied with them, however, never succeeded in convincingly embracing those symbols. Through the 1970s and still today the sacred symbols are perceived to be the property of the right.

Still today many of us are not sure about the meaning of Vietnam.[8] Among those who protested administration policy, the line then and now

71

is drawn between those who saw Vietnam as the distortion and those who saw it as the revelation of America's role in the world. Was it the moment of truth about American power or an instance of its tragic falsification? My purpose here is not to attempt to settle the many questions remaining about Vietnam. It is to emphasize that that period—remember that the American participation in the war lasted for twelve years—is indelibly impressed upon the posture of the left in America, including the political left in religious leadership. Before Vietnam, in what seemed the ebullient years following World War II, the "liberal" left triumphed over the "old left" that had been in basic sympathy with Stalinism. Today few people anywhere—including, most particularly, people in the Soviet Union—have much good to say for Stalin or Stalinism. Now the new "old left" has seen the future in the sundry liberation struggles of "the third world." Church delegations from America visit Cuba, Vietnam, and other Marxist states, returning to report their discovery that socialism works, that it alone is compatible with Christian morality, and that America should get on the right side of the revolution.[9]

I take the following to be a carefully nuanced proposition: *On balance and considering the alternatives, the influence of the United States is a force for good in the world.* Influence in this connection means political, cultural, economic, and, yes, military. In short, it means all those ways in which any country might have influence beyond its borders. It does not mean that all such American influences are good nor that any good influence is good all the time. "On balance and considering the alternatives"—the qualifiers are important. Among the 160 nations of the world, the nation that is the chief alternative influence is, of course, the Soviet Union. In some minds the suspicion immediately arises that such a statement is aimed at reviving a "cold war" mentality. Quite apart from the fact that a cold war is immeasurably preferable to the other kind, the suspicion is unwarranted. To say that the chief alternative influence is the Soviet Union is a simple statement of fact. The Soviet Union says it is so, and has persisted in saying so for decades. Not, to be sure, that we should believe everything that the Soviet leadership says. But, when someone declares himself to be your enemy and that someone has the ability to make life unpleasant for you, it is not prudent to discount entirely what he says. What we should do about this "simple fact" calls for thoughtful debate in which differences are respectfully explored. Those who do not acknowledge the simple fact, however, are not likely to contribute to that debate.

Once again the proposition: On balance and considering the alternatives, the influence of the United States is a force for good in the world. Research indicates that the response of mainline religious leadership to that proposition is, at best, equivocal. Such research is joined to my own impressions gathered over more than twenty years and is reinforced by a

continued reading of the effluent from numerous church-and-society bu-
reaucracies in the American churches.[10] Especially among those with chief
responsibility for relating religion to social and political questions, I believe
a minority of perhaps not more than twenty-five percent would clearly
affirm the proposition about American influence as a force for good. A
group of similar size would unqualifiedly deny it, and the remainder would
add so many additional qualifications that its meaning would be quite
hopelessly vitiated.

The assertion about America's being an influence for good is a kind
of litmus test. Litmus tests have their limitations. We resist sharp demar-
cations between the good guys and bad guys, the children of light and the
children of darkness. Such resistance is not without reason. E. M. Forster
is supposed to have remarked that there are two kinds of people in the
world—those who say there are two kinds of people in the world and those
who do not say that. Invoking a litmus test seems to be "simplistic."
Those who dismiss any hard question as simplistic, however, often evidence a compulsion to complexify that ends up obscuring the obvious.
The influence of America is indeed a very big and multifaceted subject.
Our feelings about it are confused by myriad and passionate political disputes. And yet it should not be so difficult to respond yes or no to the
assertion about the nature of its influence. Consider the same assertion
made about a different historical phenomenon: On balance and considering
the alternatives, the influence of the Roman Catholic Church is a force
for good in the world. Surely this is not a "meaningless" assertion. Why
should the assertion be meaningless when made with respect to America?
In place of the Roman Catholic Church, put the United Methodist Church
or the Democratic party. About these and other identifiable groupings
most of us have formed more or less definite opinions.

To say that the influence of X is a force for good does not mean that
all the alternatives to X are evil. Nor does it imply uncritical affirmation
of X. On the contrary, it is the presupposition of effective criticism. That
is, the affirmation of loyalty to a community is the ticket that grants
admission to the critical debate about the meaning of that community.
The alternative to loyalty is disloyalty. No community knowingly takes
its directions from the avowedly disloyal. We are speaking of course about
patriotism. The tragedy is that patriotism has become a negative, or at
least a shadowed, concept in the view from the left. Effective criticism,
however, depends upon rejoining protest to patriotism. There is no doubt
that a debased patriotism can be the last resort of the scoundrel. And
uncritical forms of patriotism have been employed to suppress dissent and
promote unjustifiable wars. But the same can be said of religion or any
other sphere of intense human behavior. We do well to keep in mind the
theological principle that the abuse of a thing does not abolish its legitimate use. All powerful ideas and emotions are dangerous, but the security

that is found by seeking refuge in emotional and intellectual sterility is neither secure nor fulfilling.

Patriotism is a species of piety. Wherever patriotism has been at all reflective it has transcended mere tribal attachment. Patriotism assumes a sense of placement, a context within which political responsibilities can be examined. The investigation of politics is not an abstract and value-free enterprise. Politics, according to Aristotle, is the investigation of "instances of morally fine and just conduct."[11] Conduct is of necessity in an historical context. Also in the spirit of Aristotle is our assertion of both tentativeness and urgency about the positive influence of America. In his *Ethics* Aristotle writes, "In discussing subjects, and arguing from evidence, conditioned in this way, we must be satisfied with a broad outline of the truth; that is, in arguing about what is for the most part so from premises which are for the most part true we must be content to draw conclusions that are similarly qualified."[12] We must insist that patriotism is not the highest virtue, nor is it to be affirmed in isolation from other virtues and communities of commitment. Again, Christians know that priority must be given to their membership in the community of believers, the church. And, as has been noted, that commitment to the church is mandated only because the church is the bearer of the universal promise that is for all humankind. Our ultimate loyalty is to God, who is the God of all or else he is God not at all. As patriotism speaks of the context of our particular political responsibilities, so biblical faith in the universal purposes of God sets the context and limits of patriotism. As in Christian belief the infinite does not destroy the finite, so also the universal does not abolish the particular.

We are right to reject the slogan, "Love it or leave it!" when it is advanced in order to exclude criticism and dissent. In recent years another and closely related slogan has been much condemned: "My country right or wrong." Stephen Decatur raised that call in Norfolk, 1816: "Our country! In her intercourse with foreign nations may she always be in the right; but our country, right or wrong." More than eighty years later, addressing an Anti-Imperialistic Conference in Chicago, Carl Schurz sharpened the meaning of those words: "Our country, right or wrong. When right, to be kept right; when wrong, to be put right." Note that in both instances it is not the country that *determines* what is right or wrong. Right and wrong are determined by a context of higher reference. This tension between moral judgment and political allegiance makes possible critical patriotism.

Since membership in the *civitas* cannot be given highest priority, there can be conflicts between allegiances. E. M. Forster again: "If I had to choose between betraying my country and betraying my friend I hope I should have the guts to betray my country. Such a choice may scandalize the modern reader. . . . It would not have shocked Dante, though. Dante places Brutus and Cassius in the lowest circle of Hell because they had chosen to betray their friend Julius Caesar rather than their country Rome."[13] Whether one agrees with Forster's choice or not, the seriousness of the choice consists in his knowing that he would in that instance be *betraying* his country. What many modern readers today would think scandalous is that anyone should be scandalized by such a choice.

Most of us would likely agree that it is, as Aristotle might say, "for the most part so" that there has been a sharp falling off in the seriousness of promise-making and promise-keeping in our society. The most cited evidence of this is the casual acceptance of divorce. Corporate and university managers deplore a similar decline in institutional loyalty. The notion that one should be "loyal" to a business or educational institution is in some circles thought to be little more than quaint. Similarly, the concept of honor is almost totally exorcised from contemporary writing and conversation. General Douglas MacArthur's famous West Point speech about "duty, honor, country" is viewed as the last hurrah of antique virtues. Not so incidentally, it is assumed that an antique virtue must be a discredited virtue.

It is easy to lapse into a lament about the old verities being scorned, nothing is sacred anymore, and so forth. Yet some of the more reflective minds of our times are uneasily suspicious that something along those lines is in fact the case. Civility has become form without substance. The bonds of public belonging have been dissolved. We find it hard to enter into the spirit of confident hope sounded by Lincoln in his First Inaugural:

> We are not enemies, but friends. We must not be enemies. Though passion may have strained, it must not break, our bonds of affection. The mystic chords of memory, stretching from every battlefield and patriot grave to every living heart and hearthstone all over this broad land, will yet swell the chorus of the Union when again touched, as surely they will be, by the better angels of our nature.

At the heart of our communal discontent is that which is most aptly described as decadence. Decadence is the decay that results from the hollowing out of meanings. When decadence is in full swing, meanings are not simply hollow but we exult in the gutting of them. This we call autonomy, liberation, freedom. We are liberated from duty, from honor, from country. It is the freedom of the naked public square. If we are determined to keep the public square naked, we do well to resist the idea of patriotism. In the naked public square, patriotism poses a great threat; it cannot be checked or kept within limits because there is no transcendent reference by which to hold it in critical tension. Patriotism *alone* cannot help but lead to nationalistic hubris.

Loyalty to the *civitas* can safely be nurtured only if the *civitas* is not the object of highest loyalty. The piety of patriotism must be ordered by a more encompassing piety. Jonathan Edwards, the greatest of Puritan divines, spoke of religious affections being grounded in a "consent to being," a consent to God.[14] In that consent is an attitude and a disposition. Attitude has to do with the cognitive and intellectual. Our attitude toward statements about the good or evil of American influences will be shaped by our reading of the facts. Disposition is more emotive; it is our readiness to act with and on behalf of the community. It is a posture of sympathy, a readiness to embrace the reality by which we are embraced. Attitude and disposition may not always live together in harmony, but they are covenanted in a conversation made necessary also by disagreement. Together they consent to participation in the project that is America. Such consent connotes faithfulness, a readiness to play our part in the project of which we are part. It is the freedom that has moved beyond authoritarianism but also beyond autonomy. It has moved to the acknowledgment of what is authoritative. On this view of patriotism, we accept from others the claims of the community upon ourselves while, at the same time, critically turning those same claims back upon others. To be sure, the precise nature of those claims is always subject to discussion. The nature of the discussion, in turn, is enlivened and limited by constitutional procedure that precludes some possible conclusions. Most basically, it is agreed in advance that we will never bring the discussion to a definitive end. And, although it is not written down as such, it is understood that the discussion will be limited to those who have consented to the community and its constituting vision.

As late as 1954, at the height of the McCarthy era, the words "under God" were placed into the pledge of allegiance. "One nation, under God." The insertion is still today deplored by those who think it suggests that America is somehow the chosen people, immune to the sins that afflict other nations and possessed of a right to claim blessings that others are denied. However dubious the reasons for inserting the words in the first place, we should, I believe, understand "under God" to mean under the judgment of God. Under judgment does not signify that God is angry with America, although I should suppose he is indeed angry with much that is done by Americans and in the name of America. Rather, under judgment means most importantly that there is a transcendent point of reference to which we as a people are accountable. It means there is an acknowledged framework within which criticism does not destroy community and protest is not the enemy of patriotism. In the naked public square there is no agreed-upon authority that is higher than the community itself. There is no publicly recognizable source for such criticism nor check upon such patriotism. Therefore criticism becomes impossible and patriotism unsafe.

Civility as good manners is always in short supply. We should be grateful for any signs of its revival. But the burden of this chapter is that our much talk about civility will, with some justice, be looked upon as evasion unless we go beyond questions of style to substantive affirmation of the *civitas*. Those forces in American religion that are best able to articulate an American future that holds together prophecy and patriotism, love and criticism, will, I believe, play the dominant role in giving moral definition to the nation. Such articulation is, of course, more than a matter of manipulating language. It is more than a matter of saying the same old things, except with more frequent and respectful references to the flag. As it is not a matter of saying the same old things, neither can we say something entirely new. We are not starting from scratch. The mystic chords bind the living but are also communion with the dead; we sense their watching what we do with the experiment that was and is theirs as well as ours. We can consent to the finite claims made upon us by the living and the dead because we have first consented to a claim that is infinite. We can consent to the *civitas* because we know it is not our ultimate home. We can consent to this conversation because, in the promise of both forgiveness and vindication, the conversation is to be continued.

CHAPTER FIVE

THE VULNERABILITY
OF THE NAKED SQUARE

MARTIN LUTHER KING, JR. AND JERRY FALWELL. FRIENDS OF both would likely be offended by the suggestion that they are in any way similar. And yet they are, I believe. Of course they are also strikingly different figures, with quite different analyses of what is wrong with America and what ought to be done about it. They were on opposite sides of the civil rights struggle in the fifties and sixties. (Without going so far as to say that King was right, the Falwells regularly acknowledge that they were wrong on race.) There is the sharpest contrast between King's enprincipled nonviolence and Falwell's advocacy of bellicose toughness in dealing with the Communists. Numerous other differences, political and theological, could be itemized. But in this they are similar: both Martin Luther King and Jerry Falwell disrupt the business of secular America by an appeal to religiously based public values.

Although in quite different ways, both are profoundly patriotic figures. Dr. King's dream was of America as an exemplar of racial and social justice, an anticipation of that "beloved community" promised by God. The patriotic fervor with which Dr. King invoked an American promise is often forgotten. But the March on Washington, for instance, can never be forgotten by those who were there, nor, one hopes, by the millions who have watched its replay on television documentaries. On that oppressively hot Wednesday afternoon of August 28, 1963, before the Lincoln Memorial, a baritone trumpet sought to recall America to its better self. "Five score years ago, a great American, in whose symbolic shadow we stand, signed the Emancipation Proclamation," Dr. King began. He then described the ways in which the promise had not been kept and rhetorically etched the shape of its fulfillment. "This will be the day when all God's children will be able to sing with new meaning 'My country 'tis of thee, sweet land of liberty, of thee I sing. Land where my fathers died, land of the pilgrim's pride, from every mountain side, let freedom ring.' " Lest we succumb to the prejudice that patriotic rhetoric is by definition ignoble, the peroration deserves to be committed to memory:

> When we let freedom ring, when we let it ring from every village and every hamlet, from every state and every city, we will be able to speed up that day when all God's children, black men and white men, Jews and Gentiles, Protestants and Catholics, will be able to join hands

and sing in the words of that old Negro spiritual, "Free at last! Free at last! Thank God almighty, we are free at last!"

A biographer of King, who had learned in the school of economic determinism that moral appeals are but the instrumental disguise of class conflict, says of the March on Washington speech: "This was rhetoric almost without content, but this was, after all, a day of heroic fantasy."[1] Such a comment suggests that the impingement of religious vision upon the public square can be permitted from time to time—if it is employed in the right causes, and if it is not taken too seriously. Thus also today's discharge of religious language in public space is assumed to hide narrow partisan interests. Although immeasurably less eloquent or persuasive than Dr. King's, contemporary religious rhetoric of populist patriotism deserves to be treated as seriously. To treat it seriously does not, of course, mean that one agrees. But when today's political preachers lift up a vision of a morally rejuvenated America serving as the base for global evangelism and as the defense against atheistic totalitarianism, there is no good reason to doubt that they are—to use that much overworked word—sincere. That is, it is not necessarily suspect language, language employed to advance some purpose other than the purpose indicated by the language itself.

To be sure, activists in whatever cause employ—and even, in the negative sense of the term, exploit—language in order to conceal loyalties and heighten emotional commitment. Activism is inescapably concerned not for disinterested truth but for *effective* truth, truth that is effective in advancing the purpose at hand. From this reality derives the pervasive mendacity that distorts all political engagement, to a greater or lesser degree. That being said, it remains important to note which rhetoric is chosen to advance the cause. Few leaders are so false to the core as to choose a rhetoric for its manipulative effect alone. As skeptical as we may rightly be about appeals to moral ideals, it is reasonable to believe that the ideals by which leaders would call others to judgment are the ideals by which, at least in their more reflective moments, they believe they are themselves judged. This observation is not invalidated by La Rochefoucauld's famous maxim, "Hypocrisy is the homage that vice pays to virtue." The truth of the maxim does not allow even the greatest cynic to be dismissive about moral ideals in public discourse. On the contrary, the hypocrisies by which we know ourselves to fail are of decisive importance. Be they hypocrisies or be they truths nobly adhered to, they are the moral points of reference by which communities are called to accountability. My point is not to suggest that either Dr. King or current political preachers are hypocritical. It is to emphasize that they are alike in proposing a vision of public virtue, and that that vision is religiously based.

The assertion that binds together otherwise different causes is the claim that only a transcendent, a religious, vision can turn this society from certain disaster and toward the fulfillment of its destiny. In this connection "destiny" is but another word for purpose. From whatever point on the political spectrum such an assertion is made, it challenges the conventional wisdom that America is a secular society. In recent decades we have become accustomed to believe that *of course* America is a secular society. That, in the minds of many, is what is meant by the separation of church and state. But this way of thinking is of relatively recent vintage. As late as 1931 the Supreme Court could assert without fear of contradiction, "We are a Christian people, according to one another the equal right of religious freedom, and acknowledging with reverence the duty of obedience to the will of God." The 1931 case had to do with whether a conscientious objector to war could become a citizen. After the above statement about obedience to God, the court concluded, "But, also, we are a nation with the duty to survive." Citizenship was denied *(US v. Macintosh).*

In 1952, in a dispute over students getting off from public schools in released time for religious instruction, Justice Douglas, hardly a religiously observant man, wrote, "We are a religious people whose institutions presuppose a Supreme Being" *(Zorach v. Clauson).* As time went on, however, the court's references to religion had less and less to do with what is usually meant by religion. That is, religion no longer referred to those communal traditions of ultimate beliefs and practices ordinarily called religion. Religion, in the court's meaning, became radically individualized and privatized. Religion became a synonym for conscience. For instance, in cases again related to conscientious objection, exemption from the military draft was to be allowed on the "registrant's moral, ethical, or religious beliefs about what is right and wrong [provided] those beliefs be held with the strength of traditional religious convictions" *(Welsh v. U.S.,* 1970). Thus religion is no longer a matter of content but of sincerity. It is no longer a matter of communal values but of individual conviction. In short, it is no longer a public reality and therefore cannot interfere with public business.

Such a religious evacuation of the public square cannot be sustained, either in concept or in practice. When religion in any traditional or recognizable form is excluded from the public square, it does not mean that the public square is in fact naked. This is the other side of the "naked public square" metaphor. When recognizable religion is excluded, the vacuum will be filled by *ersatz* religion, by religion bootlegged into public space under other names. Again, to paraphrase Spinoza: transcendence abhors a vacuum. The reason why the naked public square cannot, in fact, remain naked is in the very nature of law and laws. If law and laws are not seen to be coherently related to basic presuppositions about right and wrong, good and evil, they will be condemned as illegitimate. After having excluded traditional religion, then, the legal and political trick is to address questions of right and wrong in a way that is not "contaminated" by the label "religious." This relatively new sleight-of-hand results in what many have called "civil religion." It places a burden upon the law to act religiously without being suspected of committing religion. While social theorists might talk about "civil religion," the courts dare not do so, for that too would be an unconstitutional "establishment" of religion.

Admittedly, it is all very confusing. The late Alexander Bickel of Yale recognized more clearly than most that law inevitably engages ultimate beliefs about right and wrong. If law is to be viewed as legitimate, it must be backed by moral judgment. But, it is argued, in a society where moral judgments differ in source and conclusion, the final grounding of moral judgment must be disguised so as not to give democratic offense. It must be grounded so *generally* so as to obscure the particularities of religious disagreement in a pluralistic society. Bickel proposes a way in which this might be done:

> The function of the Justices ... is to immerse themselves in the tradition of our society and of kindred societies that have gone before, in history and in the sediment of history which is law, and in the thought and the vision of the philosophers and the poets. The Justices will then be fit to extract "fundamental presuppositions" from their deepest selves, but in fact from the evolving morality of our tradition. ... The search for the deepest controlling sources, for the precise "how" and the final "whence" of the judgment may, after all, end in the attempt to express the inexpressible. This is not to say that the duty to judge the judgment might as well be abandoned. The inexpressible can be recognized, even though one is unable to parse it.[2]

This is an elegantly convoluted way of thinking about right and wrong in a democratic society that in fact understands its morality to be derived from the Judeo-Christian tradition. Bickel's proposal is for a semi-sanitized public square, for a legal process that is religious in function but dare not speak the name of religion. ("Philosophers and poets" are admitted, be it noted, but not prophets or religious ethicists and teachers.) The tortured reasoning required by the exclusion of identifiable religion is surely a puzzle to many, perhaps most, Americans. It may be that they are puzzled because they do not understand the requirements of a pluralistic society. Or they may be puzzled because they are more impressed by the claim that this is a democratic society. In a democratic society, presumably, the public business is carried on in conversation with the actual values of people who *are* the society. In a survey of North Carolinians in the 1970s, seventy-four percent agree with the statement: "Human rights come from God and not merely from laws." Seventy-eight percent claim the U.S. flag is "sacred." And, despite Vietnam and all that, a third assent to the proposition, "America is God's chosen nation today."[3] North Carolinians may be more "traditional" than other Americans on these scores, although there is no reason to assume that. One suspects, rather, that there is among Americans a deep and widespread uneasiness about the denial of the obvious. The obvious is that, in some significant sense, this is, as the Supreme Court said in 1931, a Christian people. The popular intuition is that this fact ought, somehow, to make a difference. It is not an embarrassment to be denied or disguised. It is an inescapable part of what Bickel calls the "tradition of our society and of kindred societies that have gone before." Not only is it tradition in the sense of historic past; it is demonstrably the present source of moral vitalities by which we measure our virtues and hypocrisies.

The notion that this is a secular society is relatively new. It might be proposed that, while the society is incorrigibly religious, the state is secular. But such a dysjunction between society and state is a formula for governmental delegitimation. In a democratic society, state and society must draw from the same moral well. In addition, because transcendence abhors a vacuum, the state that styles itself as secular will almost certainly succumb to secularism. Because government cannot help but make moral judgments of an ultimate nature, it must, if it has in principle excluded identifiable religion, make those judgments by "secular" reasoning that is given the force of religion. Because this process is already advanced in the spheres of law and public education, there is a measure of justice in the complaints about "secular humanism." Secular humanism, in this case, is simply the term unhappily chosen for *ersatz* religion.

More than that, the notion of the secular state can become the prelude to totalitarianism. That is, once religion is reduced to nothing more than privatized conscience, the public square has only two actors in it— the state and the individual. Religion as a mediating structure—a community that generates and transmits moral values—is no longer available as a countervailing force to the ambitions of the state. Whether in Hitler's Third Reich or in today's sundry states professing Marxist-Leninism, the chief attack is not upon individual religious belief. Individual religious belief can be dismissed scornfully as superstition, for it finally poses little threat to the power of the state. No, the chief attack is upon the *institutions* that bear and promulgate belief in a transcendent reality by which the state can be called to judgment. Such institutions threaten the totalitarian proposition that everything is to be within the state, nothing is to be outside the state.

It is to be expected that the move in this discussion from the naked public square to the dangers of totalitarianism will be resisted by some readers. It may seem too abrupt and even extreme. We will be coming back to the subject in order to fill in some of the intermediate steps. At the moment, suffice it to register a degree of sympathy with those who resist talk about the dangers of totalitarianism. They object, quite rightly, that many discussions of the threat of totalitarianism are only thinly veiled attacks upon Communism. A one-sided attack upon Communism, they protest, tends to overlook the many forms of authoritarian government that also violate our understandings of democratic freedom. Authoritarian, sometimes brutally authoritarian, regimes with which the United States is allied end up being tolerated or even lauded in order to maintain a common front against the Communist adversary. There is considerable merit to this critique, unfortunately. Anti-Communism is a necessary but hardly a sufficient basis for understanding the perils of our day. In this light, then, one can sympathize with those who resist much contemporary talk about the threat of totalitarianism.

A less admirable component in that resistance, however, is the naive notion that "it can't happen here." Those who subscribe to this notion are too often oblivious of the novelty and fragility of liberal democracy as a political system. They are inadequately sensitive to the distinctly minority status of such an order in our world. It is thought that liberal democracy and the freedoms associated with it are somehow "normal," part of the "establishment." The new and exciting thing, in this view, is the proposal of alternatives to liberal democracy. In the longer reaches of history, however, liberal democracy appears as a curious exception to the various tyrannies under which human beings have suffered. Of the 160 member nations of the United Nations, probably less than thirty qualify as democracies in the sense that we tend to take for granted. This historical and contemporary perspective is essential. Without such a perspective, it is impossible to understand what Americans from Jefferson to Lincoln to John F. Kennedy intended when they spoke of America as an "experiment" launched and sustained in defiance of the "normal" course of history.

Those who think all talk about a totalitarian threat to be exaggerated also evidence an insouciance, sometimes a willful ignorance, with respect to the fact that liberal democracy does have declared adversaries. There are adversaries such as the authoritarian regimes of South America, South Africa, and the Philippines. In a significant way, however, these authoritarian regimes are not adversaries. That is, they do not *claim* to be adversaries, they do not oppose liberal democracy in principle; rather, they often claim to aspire to liberal democracy, asserting that their denial of democratic freedoms is only a temporary expedient on the way to that goal. And in fact we are not without recent examples of authoritarian societies that have been moved toward democracy; Spain, Portugal, and Nigeria are cases in point. In both the long and short term, the more ominous adversaries of liberal democracy are those forces that are totalitarian *in principle*. The only global, systematic movement of this kind today is Marxist-Leninism. In the 1930s, Mussolini's Fascism and Hitler's National Socialism represented another such movement. After World War II, and despite loose talk that equates any repressive regime with "fascism," only Marxist-Leninism is left as a theoretically comprehensive and, to many, morally compelling global adversary of liberal democracy.

In such a world it is not extreme but elementary common sense to be concerned about the threat of totalitarianism. "It can't happen here" is but a form of whistling in the dark. It is strange that among the foremost whistlers are some civil libertarians who are otherwise always reminding us of how precarious are the constitutional freedoms that we are too inclined to take for granted. The threat of totalitarianism is not posed chiefly by the prospect of defeat as a result of nuclear war. Nor is the main anxiety that the Soviet Union will launch a victorious march across Alaska and down through Canada. The chief threat comes from a collapse of the idea of freedom and of the social arrangements necessary to sustaining liberal democracy. Crucial to such a democratic order is a public square in which there are many actors. The state is one actor among others. Indispensable to this arrangement are the institutional actors, such as the institutions of religion, that make claims of ultimate or transcendent meaning. The several actors in the public square—government, corporations, education, communications, religion—are there to challenge, check, and compete with one another. They also cooperate with one another, or sometimes one will cooperate with an other in competition with the others. In a democracy the role of cooperation is not to be deemed morally superior to the roles of checking and competing. Giving consistent priority to the virtue of cooperation, as some Christians do, is the formula for the death of democracy.

There is an inherent and necessary relationship between democracy and pluralism. Pluralism, in this connection, does not mean simply that there are many different kinds of people and institutions in societal play. More radically than that, it means that there are contenders striving with one another to define what the play is about—what are the rules and what the goal. The democratic soul is steeled to resist the allure of a "cooperation" that would bring that contention to a premature closure. Indeed, within the bond of civility, the democratic soul exults in that contention. He exults not because contention is a good in itself, although there is a legitimate joy in contending, but because it is a necessary provisional good short of the coming of the kingdom of God. He strives to sustain the contention within the bond of civility, also, because he recognizes the totalitarianism that is the presently available alternative to such democratic contention.

John Courtney Murray, the great Jesuit analyst of American democracy, understood the nature of the contest in which we are engaged. For many years his work was viewed as suspect by church authorities but he was soundly vindicated by Vatican Council II. Christian thinkers such as Murray and Reinhold Niebuhr are frequently discounted today as old hat. Such mindless dismissal results in part from a desire to espouse the latest thing. It is a bias of the superficially educated that books written thirty years ago, not to say three hundred years ago, are passé. In Christian circles this dismissal takes the curious twist of being conducted in the name of the most current version of "true Christianity," based upon bib-

84

lical books written two thousand and more years ago. Murray, a deeply educated man, understood that epochs are not demarcated by publishers' seasons. The test of our epoch, he understood, is to sustain the democratic "proposition" in the face of the human yearning for monism. Monism is another word for totalitarianism, and Murray described it this way:

> [The] cardinal assertion is a thorough-going monism, political, social, juridical, religious: there is only one Sovereign, one society, one law, one faith. And the cardinal denial is of the Christian dualism of powers, societies, and laws—spiritual and temporal, divine and human. Upon this denial follows the absorption of the Church in the community, the absorption of the community in the state, the absorption of the state in the party, and the assertion that the party-state is the supreme spiritual and moral, as well as political authority and reality. It has its own absolutely autonomous ideological substance and its own absolutely independent purpose: it is the ultimate bearer of human destiny. Outside of this One Sovereign there is nothing. Or rather, what presumes to stand outside is "the enemy."[4]

The prelude to this totalitarian monism is the notion that society can be ordered according to secular technological reason without reference to religious grounded meaning. Murray again:

> And if this country is to be overthrown from within or from without, I would suggest that it will not be overthrown by Communism. It will be overthrown because it will have made an impossible experiment. It will have undertaken to establish a technological order of most marvelous intricacy, which will have been constructed and will operate without relations to true political ends: and this technological order will hang, as it were, suspended over a moral confusion; and this moral confusion will itself be suspended over a spiritual vacuum. This would be the real danger resulting from a type of fallacious, fictitious, fragile unity that could be created among us.[5]

This "vacuum" with respect to political and spiritual truth is the naked public square. If we are "overthrown," the root cause of the defeat would lie in the "impossible" effort to sustain that vacuum. Murray is right: not Communism, but the effort to establish and maintain the naked public square would be the source of the collapse. Totalitarian monism would be the consequence of such a collapse. Because it is the only totalitarian ideology in play today, the consequence would likely be Marxist-Leninist; which is to say it would be, in one form or another, Communism. The probability that it would be a distinctively American form of Communism will not vindicate those who now say "It can't happen here." Americans may, with a little help from their adversaries, find their own distinctive way to terminate the democratic experiment to which they gave birth. The fact that democracy's demise bears the marking "Made in America" will console only national chauvinists. It will be little comfort to those whose devotion to America was derived from their devotion to the democratic idea.

85

The naked public square is, as Murray suggests, an "impossible" project. That, however, does not deter people from attempting it. In the minds of some secularists the naked public square is a desirable goal. They subscribe to the dogma of the secular Enlightenment that, as people become more enlightened (educated), religion will wither away; or, if it does not wither away, it can be safely sealed off from public consideration, reduced to a private eccentricity. Our argument is that the naked public square is not desirable, even if it were possible. It is not desirable in the view of believers because they are inescapably entangled in the belief that the moral truths of religion have a universal and public validity. The Ten Commandments, to take an obvious example, have a normative status. They are not, as it has been said, Ten Suggestions or Ten Significant Moral Insights to be more or less appreciated according to one's subjective disposition. Even if one is not a believer, the divorce of public business from the moral vitalities of the society is not desirable if one is committed to the democratic idea. In addition to not being desirable, however, we have argued that the naked public square is not possible. It is an illusion, for the public square cannot and does not remain naked. When particularist religious values and the institutions that bear them are excluded, the inescapable need to make public moral judgments will result in an elite construction of a normative morality from sources and principles not democratically recognized by the society.

The truly naked public square is at best a transitional phenomenon. It is a vacuum begging to be filled. When the democratically affirmed institutions that generate and transmit values are excluded, the vacuum will be filled by the agent left in control of the public square, the state. In this manner, a perverse notion of the disestablishment of religion leads to the establishment of the state as church. Not without reason, religion is viewed by some as a repressive imposition upon the public square. They would cast out the devil of particularist religion and thus put the public square in proper secular order. Having cast out the one devil, as noted earlier, they unavoidably invite the entrance of seven devils worse than the first.

The totalitarian alternative edges in from the wings, waiting impatiently for the stage to be cleared of competing actors. Most important is that the stage be cleared of those religious actors that presume to assert absolute values and thus pose such a troublesome check upon the pretensions of the state. The state is not waiting with a set of absolute values of its own or with a ready-made religion. Far from waiting with a package of absolutes, in a society where the remnants of procedural democracy survive the state may be absolutely committed only to the relativization of all values. In that instance, however, the relativity of all things becomes the absolute. Without the counter-claims of "meaning-bestowing" institutions of religion, there is not an absence of religion but, rather, the triumph of the religion of relativity. It is a religion that must in principle deny that it is religious. It is the religion that dare not speak its name. In its triumph there is no contender that can, in Peter Berger's phrase, "relativize the relativizers."[6]

The entrance of the seven devils that take over the cleansed public square is not an alarmist scenario. Conceptually there is no alternative to it, unless of course one believes that a society can get along without a normative ethic. Admittedly, there are those who do believe this. They are, as Alisdair MacIntyre contends, the barbarians. "This time," writes MacIntyre, "the barbarians are not waiting beyond the frontiers; they have already been governing us for quite some time."[7] That the barbarians are composed of the most sophisticated and educated elites of our society makes them no less barbarian. The barbarians are those who in principle refuse to recognize a normative ethic or the reality of public virtue.

The barbarians are the party of emancipation from the truths civilized people consider self-evident. The founding fathers of the American experiment declared certain truths to be self-evident and moved on from that premise. It is a measure of our decline into what may be the new dark ages that today we are compelled to produce evidence for the self-evident. Not that it does much good to produce such evidence, however, for such evidences are ruled to be inadmissible since, again in principle, it is asserted that every moral judgment is simply an instance of emotivism, a statement of subjective preference that cannot be "imposed" upon others. MacIntyre's dismal reading of our times is no doubt an accurate description of the *logic* of contemporary philosophical, moral, and legal reasoning. Fortunately, the real world is not terribly logical. The vitalities of democracy protest that dour logic. Populist resentment against the logic of the naked public square is a source of hope. That resentment is premised upon an alternative vision that calls for a new articulation. When it finds its voice, it will likely sound very much like the voice of Christian America. That voice will not be heard and thus will not prevail in the public square, however, unless it is a voice that aims to reassure those who dissent from the vision.

We have said that conceptually there is no alternative to a *de facto* state religion once traditional religion is driven from the public square. Even if some were to argue that an alternative could be hypothetically conceived, we must attend to actual historical experience. We have witnessed again and again the entrance of the seven devils worse than the first. In every instance except that of the Third Reich, in this century they have entered under the banner of Communism. We who embrace the liberal tradition have suffered from a debilitating obtuseness on this score. It has too often been left to conservatives and reactionaries to point out that the emperor carries a very nasty club. Afraid to be thought anti-Communist, a species of liberalism has degenerated to fevered anti-anti-Communism.

This is the unpopular truth underscored by Susan Sontag in the dramatic 1982 confrontation at Town Hall in New York City. The meeting, the reader will recall, was for the purpose of expressing solidarity with Solidarity, the Polish labor movement that had been brutally repressed under martial law. The meeting was sponsored in part by the *Nation*, a magazine of self-consciously liberal orthodoxy. An impressive lineup of literary and entertainment celebrities were expected to say nice things about the revolutionary proletariat in Poland and the dangers of fascist repression in the United States. Ms. Sontag went beyond expectations. She pointed out that the repression in Poland was not an aberration but inherent in the theory and practice of Marxist-Leninism. She noted that the left routinely railed against the threat of fascism.

> We had identified the enemy as fascism. We heard the demonic language of fascism. We believed in, or at least applied a double standard to, the angelic language of communism. . . . The emigres from communist countries we didn't listen to, who found it far easier to get published in the *Reader's Digest* than in *The Nation* or the *New Statesman*, were telling the truth. Now we hear them. Why didn't we hear them before? . . . The result was that many of us, and I include myself, did not understand the nature of the communist tyranny. . . . What the recent Polish events illustrate is a truth that we should have understood a very long time ago: that communism *is* fascism. . . . Not only is fascism the probable destiny of all communist societies, but communism is in itself a variant of fascism. Fascism with a human face.[8]

The conclusion to be drawn is not that the *Reader's Digest* is the oracle of truth. Anti-Communism combined with American boosterism is not a sufficient political philosophy. But, as Ms. Sontag would argue, neither is anti-anti-Communism sufficient. Alexander Solzhenitsyn comes closer to being an oracle on these questions. Commenting on the Polish developments following the emergence of Solidarity in 1981, he notes the ways in which sundry socialists of a Marxist bent attempt to dissociate themselves from what is happening in that tortured land, or even try to claim Solidarity as a representative of "true socialism" in protest against socialism's Communist distortion. "It is the Communist ideology that, with its heavy steps, is crushing Poland," writes Solzhenitsyn, "and let us admit it is not entirely alien to the socialists, though they are protesting vehemently: The ideology of any communism is based on the coercive power of the state. Let's not be mistaken: Solidarity inspired itself not by socialism but by Christianity."[9] Beyond reasonable doubt, it is the presence of the Catholic Church in the Polish public square that prevents the regime from realizing its ambition for total control.

A literal example of the consistently denuded public square is, of course, Red Square in Moscow. Because it is in the nature of public squares not to remain naked, there is the sacred shrine of Lenin's tomb where thousands are transported each day to stand in line, waiting their turn to pay homage. Within this circumscribed space the maxim, "All within the state, nothing outside the state," is fulfilled. On several occasions in the early eighties a few bold Soviet citizens attempted to unfold banners appealing for peace and disarmament. They were promptly arrested and hustled off to psychiatric clinics. As Murray tried to help us understand, in such a society opposition to the will of the party is by definition a sign of insanity, or worse. *Tass*, the official newspaper (there being, of course, no other kind), described the dissident "Committee to Establish Trust Between the U.S.S.R. and the U.S.A." as an "act of provocation of Western secret services." According to *The New York Times* report, the protestors were condemned as "anti-Sovieteers, renegades and criminals . . . a handful of swindlers who do not represent anyone in the Soviet Union."[10]

In our society the proponents of the naked public square do not describe themselves as proponents of the naked public square. Some are technocratic liberals, some are secular pragmatists, some are libertarians of either the leftist or rightist sort. Some are socialists who insist that we need to establish "rational control" of political, economic, and cultural forces in order to forge something like a national purpose and plan. Whatever the rationale or intention, however, the presupposition is the naked public square, the exclusion of particularist religious and moral belief from public discourse. And whatever the intention, because the naked square cannot remain naked, the direction is toward the state-as-church, toward totalitarianism. And again, the available form of totalitarianism—an aggressively available form, so to speak—is Marxist-Leninism.

In one of his less felicitous statements, President Carter in a major foreign policy address cautioned against our "inordinate fear of Communism." He did not make clear what measure of fear might be ordinate. Similarly, those who now underscore the dangers of Communism caution us against an inordinate fear of McCarthyism. Presumably, in this respect too there is a measure of fear that is ordinate. The present argument suggests that both fears are legitimate and necessary. Of the two, McCarthyism as a form of what Richard Hofstadter called "the paranoid style" in American politics is the more immediate possibility. We have been through that and the scars are still touchable. In the longer term—say, the next twenty to sixty years—totalitarianism is the more ominous prospect. This does not mean we should risk "just a little" McCarthyism in order to ward off that prospect. It does mean that we should stop calling a sensible anxiety about that prospect "McCarthyism." It does mean we should stop telling ourselves and others that the choice is between McCarthyism, which truncates liberal democracy, and totalitarianism, which terminates liberal democracy. An open-eyed awareness of the fragility of liberal democracy, and of the alternatives to it, is the best insurance against being reduced to such a dismal choice. As that awareness is heightened, we will as a society be more resistant both to the totalitarian temptation and to the illusion that democracy can be saved by becoming less democratic.

In 1981 the Institute on Religion and Democracy was established in Washington, D.C. Its declared purpose was to lift up the public significance of religion in the democratic process, to promote democratic ideals within the religious communities, and, as a necessary correlate of that, to oppose those dynamics in the churches that seem inclined toward the totalitarian temptation. "Christianity and Democracy" is the Institute's manifesto-like assertion of what it means by democracy:

> Democratic government is limited government. It is limited in the claims it makes and in the power it seeks to exercise. Democratic government understands itself to be accountable to values and to truth which transcend any regime or party. Thus in the United States of America we declare ours to be a nation "under God," which means, first of all, a nation under judgment. In addition, limited government means that a clear distinction is made between the state and the society. The state is not the whole of the society, but is one important actor in the society. Other institutions—notably the family, the Church, educational, economic and cultural enterprises—are at least equally important actors in the society. They do not exist or act by sufferance of the state. Rather, these spheres have their own peculiar sovereignty which must be respected by the state.[11]

The statement goes on to affirm the importance of participation, equality, and fairness in a democratic society. Without dwelling on the point, it notes that "as a matter of historical fact democratic governance exists only where the free market plays a large part in a society's economy." The statement and the Institute received widespread (some would say inordinate) attention in the general media and in the churches. They were the object of a formal debate sponsored by the National Council of Churches and of numerous critiques by theologians and social philosophers on all points of the political spectrum.[12]

The debate produced around groups such as the Institute on Religion and Democracy gives some reason to believe that this decade could be remembered as a time of reinvigorated appreciation of the democratic idea among Christians in America. The intuition of the connection between democracy and religion was until recently part of the foundational consensus supporting what Murray called "the American proposition." It was a constitutive element of the vital center in American thought. The vital center, it will be recalled, was the title Arthur M. Schlesinger, Jr., chose for his 1949 manifesto in favor of democratic freedom. *The Vital Center* is in the tradition of Walter Lippmann's "public philosophy" and John Dewey's "common faith." If one did not know that *The Vital Center* was written thirty-five years ago, she would suspect it was written by one of those who today are called neo-conservative. It is a curiosity of our time that the mainstream liberalism of a few decades ago—and nobody has more assiduously attended to his credentials as a mainstream liberal than Arthur M. Schlesinger, Jr.—is the neo-conservatism of today. The mainstream liberal argument then was, quite rightly, viewed as a radical proposition on the screen of world-historical change. Schlesinger wrote:

> Our problem is not resources or leadership. It is primarily one of faith and time: faith in the value of our own freedoms, and time to do the necessary things to save them. To achieve the fullness of faith, we must renew the traditional sources of American radicalism and seek out ways to maintain our belief at a high pitch of vibration. To achieve a sufficiency of time, we must ward off the totalitarian threat to free society—and do so without permitting ourselves to become the slaves of Stalinism, as any man may become the slave of the things he hates.[13]

Schlesinger and those like him then viewed with approval, indeed the highest hope, the role of the "affirmative" or "positive" state. They knew there were dangers in the self-aggrandizement of the state, but the acknowledgment of the importance of other public actors is almost an aside:

> In the short run, the failure of voluntary initiative invites the spread of state power. In the long run, the disappearance of voluntary association paves the way for the pulverization of the social structure essential to totalitarianism. By the revitalization of voluntary associations, we can siphon off emotions which might otherwise be driven to the solutions of despair. We can create strong bulwarks against the totalitarianization of society.[14]

But this nod to what we have called the mediating structures of society is almost cancelled out by the emphasis upon state power. To be sure, Schlesinger observed then, "We have strayed too far from the insights of Burke and de Maistre; we have forgotten that constitutions work only as they reflect an actual sense of community."[15] He also warned against "arrogant forms of individualism." "It is only so far as ... individualism derives freely from community, that democracy will be immune to the virus of totalitarianism."[16] The reiterated "we" in Schlesinger's writing, however, is finally the "we" of the total society, the "we" of the state. This is because, in his view, the great domestic threat is the anti-democratic influence of the corporation, of "the business plutocracy." "The corporation began to impersonalize the economic order," wrote Schlesinger.

> Impersonality produced an irresponsibility which was chilling the lifeblood of society. The state consequently had to expand its authority in order to preserve the ties which hold society together. The history of governmental intervention has been the history of the growing ineffectiveness of the private conscience as a means of social

control. The only alternative is the growth of the public conscience, whose natural expression is the democratic government.[17]

There, in succinct form, is the nub of the dispute. The choice, we would contend, is not between the private conscience and the public conscience expressed by the state. The private conscience, as Schlesinger also wanted to say in part, is not private in the sense of being deracinated, torn from its roots. It is not "arrogantly" individualistic. Private conscience too is communal; it is shaped by the myriad communities from which we learn to "put the world together" in an order that is responsive to our understanding of right and wrong. As for "the public conscience," it is a categorical fallacy. It harks back to Rousseau's mythology of a "general will" of which the state is the expression. "The Public" does not have a conscience. "The People" does not have a conscience. Only persons and persons-in-community have consciences.

Schlesinger's enthusiasm for the triumph of "the affirmative state" is not widely shared today, neither on the right nor on the left. It is not merely that there is a groundswell of opposition to "big government" or an anti-modernist passion for decentralization in obedience to the axiom that "small is beautiful." It is all that, but it is not merely that. It is rather that there is a growing awareness of the limits of the political, a recognition that most of the things that matter most are attended to in communities that are not government and should not be governmentalized. This awareness is what some critics describe as a "retribalization" or "reprivatization" of American life. But "tribe" used in this way is simply a pejorative for community. And, far from this being a process of reprivatization, it is an expansion of our understanding of what is public. We are no longer content to let "public" be synonymous with "government." Thus, for example, in education the distinction is not between public schools and private schools. It is rather between government schools and voluntary schools, or "schools of choice."[18] All schools that advance a public interest and meet the needs of their relevant publics are public schools.

Jefferson, Jackson, Lippmann, Dewey, Schlesinger, and a host of others strove to articulate democracy as a credal cause. The last chapter of *The Vital Center* is titled "Freedom: A Fighting Faith." But finally it is a faith in which freedom is the end as well as the means. It is a faith devoid of transcendent purpose that can speak to the question of what freedom is *for*. This is, of necessity, a religious question. The truly "positive" state that presumes to address this question becomes the state-as-church. The Marxists are right: the political freedom of liberal democracy is essentially a "negative" freedom (freedom *from*). If we are not to succumb to totalitarianism, the positive meaning of freedom must be addressed in a manner, and through institutions, beyond the competence of what is ordinarily meant by politics or the government. The public square is the stage of many actors, not all of whom are following the same script. It is very confusing. It is democratic.

Historically, the churches in America have been leading actors in voicing the positive side of freedom's question. The purpose of Christianity in America, it is said somewhat scornfully, was to establish "The Righteous Empire."[19] In the nineteenth century there was the hope to construct "a complete Christian commonwealth." The mainline churches, as they are called, have retired such rhetoric in recent decades. Many of their members, joined by today's moral majoritarians, want to pick it up again. Those who retired the idea tended to share the liberal assumption that the tasks of moral definition could and should be taken over by "the public conscience" expressed through the state. In the frequently uncritical affirmation of "the secular city," it was thought a triumph that the churches could step back from what had been a transitional role in the public square. Now it is recognized, however, that man has not "come of age" in the way that many thought. We still need, we more urgently need, the critical tutelage of traditions that refuse to leave "man on his own."

Negative freedom is dangerous to ourselves and others if it is negative freedom alone. As Murray argued, it is not only dangerous but it is "impossible." It is most dangerous *because* it is impossible. That is, its very attempt invites the termination of the democratic freedom in the name of which the attempt is made. The question is not *whether* the questions of positive freedom will be addressed. The question is *by whom*—by what reasonings, what traditions, what institutions, what authorities—they will be addressed. If they are to be addressed democratically in a way that gives reasonable assurance of a democratic future, we must work toward an understanding of the public square that is both more comprehensive and more complex. Along the way to such an understanding, we must listen with critical sympathy to those who are speaking the very new-old language of Christian America.

CHAPTER SIX

DENYING
WHO WE ARE

MOST PEOPLE WHO HAVE PAID MUCH ATTENTION TO THE phenomenon called democracy allow that its historical roots are somehow related to biblical religion. Most, but not all. Some textbook tellings of democracy's story attribute the whole idea to classical Greece. In this version, the influence of Christianity was entirely negative. Religion as the enemy of democratic freedom is epitomized, it is said, in the Inquisition. The classic period and our modern era of enlightenment are the opposite of everything represented by the Inquisition. Those who tell the story this way overlook the fact that in three hundred years the Inquisition had fewer victims than were killed any given afternoon during the years of Stalin's purges and Hitler's concentration camps. Nonetheless, it is asserted that the modern era is uniquely friendly to democratic freedom.

Christianity, it is said, was responsible for the unrelieved darkness of the Middle Ages. The darkness was only broken by the dawning of the Renaissance in the fourteenth and fifteenth centuries. The following paraphrase of Alexander Pope on Newton rings true in many minds still today:

> Europe and Europe's mind lay hid in night;
> God said, "Renascence be!," and all was light.

As Robert Nisbet has persuasively argued, however, the Renaissance was hostile to the idea of historical progress, an idea that makes it possible to view democracy as an achievement to be defended and built upon. Renaissance thinkers rediscovered the classical deposit, to be sure, but what they revived was, for the most part, those elements that understood history in dismally cyclical terms. Nisbet writes, "Renaissance thinkers, from the fifteenth-century humanists in Italy to Francis Bacon, tended overwhelmingly to see history not as something unilinear in its flow, as continuous and cumulative, but as a multiplicity of recurrences, of cyclical ups and downs, all of them the consequence of the fixed elements in human nature: evil and good."[1]

This dismal view of history going around in circles is at a far remove from the actual sources of modern democracy. Those sources are found for instance in Christian feudalism's understanding of mutual rights that lord and servant were bound to respect; in the seventeenth century in the

Cromwellian revolution's vivid reinterpretation of the biblical understanding of the Spirit's speaking through dissenting voices; in the Puritan vision of America as a providential creation of new beginnings; in Roger Williams and the growth toward institutionalizing religious tolerance; in the constituting fathers' belief now emblazoned on every U.S. dollar bill, "Novus Ordo Seclorum," a new order for the ages. The American experiment, which, more than any other, has been normative for the world's thinking about democracy, is not only derived from religiously grounded belief, it continues to depend upon such belief. In his first year as vice president under the new constitution, John Adams said: "We have no government armed with power capable of contending with human passions unbridled by morality and religion. Our constitution was made only for a moral and a religious people. It is wholly inadequate for the government of any other."[2]

The contention that the American enterprise is derived from religious belief is widely, although not universally, acknowledged. Among secular historians and social theorists, however, that acknowledgment is typically accompanied by the observation that a new and different grounding is now necessary, for in a "secular society" religion cannot provide the cohesion required. The assertion that we have "moved beyond" the possibility of a religious grounding of democracy says more about those who make the assertion than it does about American society. Americans, as a people, are as religious, probably more religious, than they have ever been. Despite "new religions" and the attention focused on cults, their religious allegiances are identifiably Judeo-Christian. Dissent from a broadly defined religious orthodoxy is perhaps more marginal today than it was in the heyday of eighteenth-century deism. The militantly antireligious campaign of, for example, a Thomas Paine would likely have little influence today.

It might be argued that such overt hostility to religion is no longer in good taste because it is no longer necessary. Rather than attacking religion, cultural elites quietly assume its irrelevance. It is stated with smug certitude that any public appeal to religion is an effort to turn back the clock. Sometimes the statement that ours is now a secular time is made with a sigh of relief or with gratitude for liberation from alleged religious oppression. Sometimes it is said with regret, joined to a nostalgia-tinged longing for inspirations now irretrievably lost. Contemporary writers such as Robert Nisbet and Daniel Bell suggest that the democratic center can hold only if there is something like a religious revival, but they tend to be not very hopeful about that happening. The discussion of religion's demise in "secular America" is, whether joined to cheers or lamentations, a discussion carried on within a relatively small elite. All the while, the people who are the society have gone along assuming that of course morality, public and private, is derived from religion.[3] Most are mildly puzzled and a minority is outraged when told in textbooks and television that ours is a secular society.

Among the outraged the suspicion grows that there is some kind of conspiracy afoot. It is said that certain elites declare things to be the way they want things to be. They declare the demise, or at least the decline, of religion because it is required for the kind of emancipation they seek. They declare the nuclear family to be moribund because the family is seen as repressive. They declare the dwindling of familial care for the elderly because they desire to have that responsibility assumed by the government. The list of desires disguised as declarations of fact is very long. Meanwhile, however, the great majority of Americans, heedless of the wisdom imparted by their presumed betters, continue to go to church, to rate the "traditional" family as among life's highest goods, and to care for one another in myriad ways that elude the graphs of social planners. The instance of care for the elderly is instructive. We are told there is a "crisis" calling for massive governmental intervention in supplying nursing homes and other support facilities. In fact, however, close to ninety-five percent of the over-sixty-five population care for themselves or live with their children, and they seem to want it that way.[4]

I served as presidential appointee on the ill-fated White House Conference on Families. One of the most aggressive forces in the confusions which embroiled that venture was a cluster of activist homosexual organizations. They, in alliance with some feminists, were instrumental in having the name of the conference changed: from White House Conference on the Family to White House Conference on Fam*ilies*. The plural was critical because, they asserted, the sixties and seventies had witnessed a revolution in "alternative life-styles" and alternative ways of defining what constitutes a family. In a public hearing in New York City a gay activist spokesman, a medical doctor, was urging that the Conference recommend changes in law that would reflect the putative revolution in the way Americans live. He agreed that the government's legitimate interest in the family was not in regulating sexual relationships but in protecting children and other dependents. In the ensuing exchange we explored the nature and extent of the revolution, which called for a major overhaul of family law. Stipulating for the sake of the exchange that ten percent of the population, more male than female, is dominantly homosexual in inclination, it was allowed that there are about 25 million "homosexuals" in America. How many of those who are homosexual in orientation are exclusively and actively homosexual in practice? The doctor said his organization estimated the number to be twenty percent, thus arriving at the figure of five million "gays." Since one-night stands could not qualify as a "family unit," it was agreed that there should be a "longevity test" for such qualification, say of five years living together. While lacking precise statistics, the doctor's "informed guess" was that about five percent of homosexual couples

had lived together for five years or more. Of these 125,000 "married couples" how many would have a child or elderly dependent in their care?
Again, he thought about five percent, meaning 6,250 homosexual "families" of legitimate interest to government policy. The doctor's figures may
be greatly inflated, but, even if they are accurate, in a society of more than
230 million people the revolution he and others declare is an almost imperceptible ripple. A few thousand or a few hundred people are very important and, for the sake of children and dependents, public policy must
take them into account. But that a national commission should spend
millions of dollars recommending the overhaul of family law in America
on the basis of such "revolutions" is, not to put too fine a point on it,
absurd. Yet it is but one in a long list of absurdities by which desire is
disguised as declaration of fact.

For better and for worse, traditional values are very much alive in
America. Again, they are alive not only in observance but also in the
hypocrisy of the tribute that vice pays to virtue. Some who view all tradition as oppressive earnestly desire that such values should die. Toward
that end, they propagate "the fact" of their demise. These influential few
are the ones referred to by the moral majoritarians as the "secular humanist conspiracy." Some of the morally enraged have even come up with
fanciful figures to the effect that there are precisely 287 secular humanist
leaders in the conspiracy, which dominates politics, the media, the universities, and the liberal churches. However many there are who actively
promote a revolutionary reevaluation of values, there are many more who
quietly assimilate the dogmas of secularism. Among those dogmas, few
have been so widely assimilated as the proposition that ours is a secular
society. Even if it is acknowledged that historically our values were religiously based, it is alleged that that is a thing of the past. Religion may
endure and be indulged in privacy, but it is no longer available for the
reconstruction of a public ethic.

Those of us who received the grace of working with Martin Luther
King, Jr., know how profoundly his life and work were empowered by
religious faith. J. Edgar Hoover, among others, did his best to impugn the
morality of Dr. King's personal behavior, but that in no way invalidates
the intensity of Dr. King's faith, by reference to which he himself acknowledged his sins and weaknesses.[5] The point at hand has to do with a small
but significant event following Dr. King's assassination, April 4, 1968.
There was an ecumenical memorial service here in Harlem, with numerous religious, political, and cultural dignitaries in attendance. The service
was reported on television news that evening. The announcer, standing
before St. Charles Borromeo church where the service was held, spoke in
solemn tones: "And so today there was a memorial service for the slain
civil rights leader, Dr. Martin Luther King, Jr. It was a religious service,

and it is fitting that it should be, for, after all, Dr. King was the son of a minister."

How explain this astonishing blindness to the religious motive and meaning of Dr. King's ministry? The announcer was speaking out of a habit of mind that was no doubt quite unconscious. The habit of mind is that religion must be kept at one remove from the public square, that matters of *public* significance must be sanitized of religious particularity. It regularly occurred that the klieg lights for the television cameras would be turned off during Dr. King's speeches when he dwelt on the religious and moral-philosophical basis of the movement for racial justice. They would be turned on again when the subject touched upon confrontational politics. In a luncheon conversation Dr. King once remarked, "They aren't interested in the *why* of what we're doing, only in the *what* of what we're doing, and because they don't understand the why they cannot really understand the what."

The misunderstanding of Dr. King is not an isolated instance but is symptomatic of the way our world is interpreted by prestige communicators and other elites. These interpreters are not the masterminds of a secular humanist conspiracy but victims of a secularizing mythology of which they are hardly aware. It might be argued that the klieg lights go off and on according to what is and what is not "news." But the judgment of what is news is itself reflective of prior judgments. News is defined as politics, scandal, and tragic spectacle. News is, not incidentally, big business. Advertisers require a crowd, a crowd requires entertainment, and entertainment means score-card politics, corruption's exposure of moral pretension, and blood and tears served up at six o'clock. As hard-core pornographic films contain a mandatory "cum shot," so the evening news includes a mandatory "sob shot." "And how did you feel when you learned that your three little children were killed in the fire?" She felt terrible. Sob. Cut.

Even in its efforts at more serious analysis—60-second "commentaries" designed to provide historical and philosophical perspective—religion is seldom permitted to impinge unless it bears directly upon politics or scandal. It is not that excitement and confrontation, even much entertainment, cannot be found in the world of religion. It is rather, as media executives explain, that religion is a can of worms with so many competing and sectarian views that it poses a nightmare in view of a "fairness doctrine" that requires the balanced presentation of views. This and other reasons are given for largely ignoring the largest single network of voluntary associationalism in American life. Were the mythical Man from Mars to watch television news and read the prestige press for many months, he would likely be quite oblivious to the role of religion in this society. He certainly would not know that, next to family and work, the things that Americans do most are in the world called religion. Only a few decades ago major American newspapers started having "religion writers." Before that, it was assumed that general reporters would report on religion as part of the "normal reality" that qualified as news. Not long ago, metropolitan dailies reported Sunday sermons from major pulpits of the city. No longer. Some might say that the development of "religion reporting" as a specialty reflects an upgrading of attention paid religion. More accurately, I believe, it represents a sidelining of religion.[6] It is not that fewer people are going to church now than was the case fifty years ago. The opposite is true. It may be that sermons are not as interesting, but there is no reason to assume that. What has happened in recent decades is a redefinition of what constitutes "the real world." Under the current guardians of public perceptions, religion only shows up on the screen when it impinges upon a real world defined apart from religion. The reason is that we have all agreed, have we not?, that ours is a secular society.

The point is not to excoriate the mandarins of the media. In truth, they do a remarkably effective job of providing the entertainment that keeps their business going. The point is that the widespread exclusion of religiously grounded values and beliefs is at the heart of the outrage and alienation (to use a much overworked term) of millions of Americans. They do not recognize *their* experience of America in the picture of America purveyed by cultural and communications elites. At the heart of this nonrecognition—which results in everything from puzzlement to crusading fever—is the absence of religion. At one level, it can be said that the prevailing situation is extremely nondemocratic. At another level, more closely related to sociological theory, it must be said that the situation cannot be sustained. The emptiness of the public square will be filled by a state-promulgated civil religion, which poses a threat of totalitarianism, as discussed in the last chapter. Or the emptiness will continue until the public square is finally invaded by one or another existing belief system, whether of the left or the right. MacIntyre is right: in the absence of a public ethic, politics becomes civil war carried on by other means. In a civil war it is possible that one side should win and others lose. The broken conversation between religion and the business of the *polis* must be reestablished. The several possible, perhaps inevitable, alternatives to such a renewed conversation would severely diminish the possibility of America becoming the democracy that it professes to be.

Again, it is important to caution ourselves against the crisis-mongering of neophyliacs who would tell us that these problems came into being only yesterday. The role of religion and the democratization of public values have been problematic from the beginning of the American experiment. Thomas Jefferson was hardly a conventionally religious person. Unlike many of those who signed the Declaration of Independence, he thought one of its central purposes was to free people from "monkish ignorance and superstition." Monkish ignorance and superstition, in his view, is what is ordinarily meant by Christian orthodoxy. Jefferson thought his "Bill for Establishing Religious Freedom" in Virginia one of the three greatest acheivements of his life. The same Jefferson, however, had no illusions that democracy had resolved the religious question by establishing "the separation of church and state." Consider, for example, his well-known reflection on the immorality of slavery:

> And can the liberties of a nation be thought secure when we have removed their only firm basis, a conviction in the minds of the people that these liberties are the gift of God? That they are not to be violated but with his wrath? Indeed I tremble for my country when I reflect that God is just; that his justice cannot sleep forever; that considering numbers, nature and natural means only, a revolution of the wheel of fortune, an exchange of situation is among the possible events; that it may become probable by supernatural interference! The Almighty has no attribute which can take side with us in such a contest.

In short, Jefferson understood that the naked public square is a very dangerous place. No constitution or written law is strong enough to defend rights under attack. Their "only firm basis" is in their being perceived as transcendent gift. At the same time, the denial of such rights, as they were denied by slavery, cannot be sustained without invoking the dreadful judgment that follows upon the defiance of that moral basis.

Jefferson's understanding of the unstated religious foundation of this democracy has been seconded frequently by the Supreme Court. A perduring problem has been, and continues to be, how to state the unstated. In other words, the goal is to acknowledge the "only firm basis" of democracy without running into the difficulties of a government establishment of a particular way of expressing that religious basis. Again, the careful balancing and nuancing that is required is evident in *Zorach v. Clauson* (1952) in which the court declared, "We are a religious people whose institutions presuppose a Supreme Being." This is a statement not of establishment but of acknowledgment. Determined secularists sometimes dismiss the *Zorach* decision as something of a quirk in American judicial history. Such a dismissal is made easier because the decision was written by Justice William Douglas who, like Jefferson, was ostentatiously nonreligious, at least in conventional terms. The statement in *Zorach*, however, was not an idiosyncratic aside. It was accompanied by reasoned explanation that bears a closer look:

> We are a religious people whose institutions presuppose a Supreme Being. We guarantee the freedom to worship as one chooses. We make room for as wide a variety of beliefs and creeds as the spiritual needs of man deem necessary. We sponsor an attitude on the part of government that shows no partiality to any one group and lets each flourish according to the zeal of its adherents and the appeal of its dogma. When the state encourages religious instruction or cooperates

100

with religious authorities by adjusting the schedule of public events [such as "released time" in schools] to sectarian needs, it follows the best of our traditions. For it then respects the religious nature of our people and accommodates the public service to their spiritual needs. To hold that it may not would be to find in the Constitution a requirement that the government show a callous indifference to religious groups. That would be preferring those who believe in no religion over those who do believe.

A little over ten years later, in 1963, *Abington* came before the court. The quarrel then had to do with Pennsylvania's practice of Bible reading in government schools. Justice Clark wrote for the majority and attempted, as is required, to demonstrate that the decision was in agreement with prior court pronouncements. Quoting from an earlier finding, he acknowledged that "the history of man is inseparable from the history of religion." He observes that many of the founding fathers believed in God and cited other instances in which the state continues to recognize religion. The conclusion:

> It can be truly said therefore, that today, as in the beginning, our national life reflects a religious people who, in the words of Madison, are "earnestly praying, as . . . in duty bound, that the Supreme Lawgiver of the Universe . . . guide them into every measure which may be worthy of his [blessing]."

Scholars have pointed out, however, that there is a significant shift from Zorach to Abington. In the second there is no affirmation that our institutions presuppose a Supreme Being. Nor is it said, as it was said in Zorach and earlier statements, that people do in fact have religious needs that the state must respect. Nor is there admission of the need for public encouragement of religion. As Professor Glen Thurow writes, "All that is recognized [in Abington] is that our people do in fact participate in religious observances. . . . The Court does not say whether it is good or bad that our national life reflects a religious people."[7] Abington is also curious in that it introduces a distinction between religious observance and religious freedom: "This is not to say, however, that religion has been so identified with our history and government that religious freedom is not likewise as strongly imbedded in our public and private life." This is curious because, historically, religious freedom was thought to be in the service of religious practice. Religious freedom was not primarily freedom *from* religion—although the freedom to espouse no religion or even to oppose all religion was carefully protected—but freedom to exercise religion in whatever way a person deems fit. In Abington, however, religious freedom is set over against religious observance. Again Thurow: "Religion and the policy of freedom of religion are no longer seen as having a common root in recognition of presumed spiritual needs and institutional dependency on a Supreme Being. There is not one tradition, but two."[8]

Abington set asunder what had been a unified tradition, as articulated in Zorach and innumerable other statements from our legal and political history. To their credit, some of the other justices recognized the ominous implications of Abington. When "religious freedom" is set over against religious observance it tends to become the same thing as secularism. If, in addition to that, the burden of constitutional guarantees are put on the side of this version of religious freedom, the state's alleged neutrality to religion easily slides into hostility. Justice Steward said as much in his dissenting opinion: "And a refusal to permit religious exercises thus is seen, not as the realization of state neutrality, but rather as the establishment of a religion of secularism, or at the least, as government support of the beliefs of those who think that religious exercises shall be conducted only in private."

Although agreeing with the decision, Justices Goldberg and Harlan also had grave misgivings: "But unilateral devotion to the concept of neutrality can lead to invocation or approval of results which partake not simply of that noninterference and noninvolvement with the religious which the Constitution commands, but of a brooding and pervasive devotion to the secular and a passive, or even active, hostility to the religious." In their reservations, the justices edge up to the insight that the naked public square cannot remain truly naked. The need for an overarching meaning, for a moral legitimation, will not go undenied. What is called neutrality toward religion is an invitation for a substitute religion. That substitute will be constructed from reasoning that is compatible with "a brooding and pervasive devotion to the secular."

While the 1952 decision is more satisfactory than that of 1963, Professor Thurow is correct, I believe, in arguing that both miss the public character of religion and of religiously based values. Thurow's point is worth quoting at some length:

> Justice Douglas asserts that our institutions presuppose a Supreme Being, but he discusses only the accommodation of *private* desires and needs. *Neither opinion raises directly the question of the public good involved.* As under the theory of *laissez faire* in economics, the theory of the Court is that it is the function of government to allow or facilitate and to harmonize the private religious or irreligious desires of individual citizens, without any explicit consideration of the public good. But we may wonder whether the conflicting private desires of citizens can be harmonized for the public good without considering what the public good as a whole requires.[9] (emphasis added)

This supposed neutrality to religion is a novelty, a break with the one tradition of the republic. Along with many other students of the subject, Thurow points to Abraham Lincoln as the exemplar of that tradition. He underscores the dialectic between the Gettysburg Address, with its affirmation of "government of the people, by the people and for the people," and the Second Inaugural, which concludes with the majestic declaration: "Yet, if God wills that it [the war] continue, until all the wealth piled by the bond-man's two hundred and fifty years of unrequited toil shall be sunk, and until every drop of blood drawn with the lash, shall be paid by another drawn with the sword, as was said three thousand years ago, so still it must be said, 'the judgments of the Lord, are true and righteous altogether.' " Before the tradition was split and religious freedom was set against religion, it was understood that reference to the transcendent was a public reference by which public purpose was defined and judged. To be sure, that way of speaking of God in public lingers on in presidential Thanksgiving Day proclamations and in inaugural ceremonies. But such references are thought to be no more than elements of a vapid and residual "civil religion." When in 1968 Robert Bellah brought this "civil religion" to the attention of academics, it occasioned considerable astonishment. So quickly and so deeply had the dogma of "secular America" taken hold, at least among the elites who define what America is about.

As in the media, then, so also in the courts and centers of higher learning it is more or less taken for granted that ours is a secular society. When religion insists upon intruding itself into public space with an aggressive force that cannot be denied, it is either grudgingly acknowledged or alarums are raised about the impending return of the Middle Ages. Then the proposition becomes more explicit: if ours is not a secular society, it *should* be. Unless overwhelmingly countered by the evidence, the tendency is for that desire to be presented as fact. For an event to be *legitimately* public, it must be secular. If it is touched by religion, that is to be viewed as a private and somewhat idiosyncratic factor. Dr. King was a legitimate public figure, despite the fact that he "was the son of a minister." One "happens to be" religious, but it is not a factor that warrants public consideration. Public consideration of the religious beliefs of others is an invasion of privacy. The public assertion of one's own beliefs is an imposition upon carefully sterilized space. John Murray Cuddihy has brilliantly analyzed the private—"I happen to be a Catholic"—nature of religious association and belief. It is, says Cuddihy, a modern version of civility in which we agree not to lay uncomfortably ultimate burdens upon others. His book is aptly titled *No Offense;* the point being that our highest religious duty is not to offend those who might be offended by the idea of religious duty.[10] There is much that is necessary and even admirable in this understanding of civility. But, as noted earlier, civility is vacuous when separated from the *civitas* of shared values. More than being vacuous, it is untenable; it inevitably results in the construction of values that are hostile to those values that might have given offense in the first place.

The democratic vitalities of America are today being stirred by those who were not consulted when it was decided that this is a secular society. It should not surprise us that many people are upset by the present stirrings. Nor should we think that such people are necessarily hostile to religion. Many are privately devout. But they have been nurtured on the formula: public = secular. Other committed believers have gone further, declaring that secularity is in fact the modern expression of Christianity. Thus for a period of time we heard much about "secular" and "religionless" Christianity. Such expressions seem as dated now as does the "death of God" debate. The arguments advanced under these phrases were little understood by most Christians and were easily parodied by believers and nonbelievers alike. Those who advocated "religionless Christianity," for example, were making a very serious proposal. To put it too simply, it was a proposal that the religious community internalize, as it were, what had already presumably happened in the public square. Religion, in this view, could not only live with thoroughly secularized public reality but should embrace it. More than that, religion should see in this secularizing of the world the model for its own transformation. Only in what Max Weber called "the disenchanted garden"—the world stripped of transcendent meanings—does "mature" belief become possible.

Such ways of thinking about how to be Christian in the modern world should not be dismissed lightly. We take note of them here, however, only to underscore that the proponents of the naked public square also include Christians of good faith. But they were heard and are heard by only a minuscule elite of American Christians. That does not mean they are wrong; only that they are largely ineffectual with respect to the democratic expression of religion in American life. Almost the entirety of the religious communities in America does not understand that elite's difficulties in being religious in the modern world. It is not that these many believers are stupid, although, as with others, no doubt many are. It is rather that they have a different view of the modern world and, in many instances, of what it means to be religious. Many of them accept the secular divorce of public and private and are content to be religious on their own time, as it were. Many others, however, are not prepared to make that compromise. They insist upon what Thurow calls the "one tradition" of religion that is both private and public, and they, mistakenly, identify their form of religion as *the* religion of the tradition. They know nothing of Lincoln's agonized ponderings over the ambiguous purposes of the Almighty. They take from Jefferson, Madison, Adams, Lincoln, and others all the references to "God" and fill such references with the content of their own fundamentalist notions of public righteousness and apocalyptic Bible prophecy. In reconstructing the "one tradition," they grievously distort it, thus encouraging their opponents to become yet more insistent that the tradition be split.

These moral majoritarians of all kinds come to the public square not with the political religion of the republic but with the revivalist politics of the camp meeting. Revivalism's script is to be enacted in the public theater. Confession of sin, repentance, decision, walking the sawdust trail—all is transferred to political campaign and ballot box. Revivalist politics is also not new in American life. It is usually populist in nature and can erupt on the political right or left. In the early morning hours of the 1972 Democratic National Convention in Miami, George McGovern accepted the presidential nomination in a ringing speech that catalogued America's iniquities, her wanderings from the path of righteousness. Again and again he cried out, "Come home, America!" Condemnation, contrition, turning, and returning—such are the elements in what the theologians call the *ordo salutis*, the steps of salvation, whether for persons or nations.

Today's moral majoritarians have a different catalogue of iniquities and a different understanding of the "home" to which we are to return. However different the list of particulars, the appeal is similar to McGovern's. It is similar to Jimmy Carter's promise of 1976 to provide a government as good as the American people. Personal and public morality are conflated; individual and societal salvation are joined. The dikes of secular dogma are cracked by the stirrings of incorrigibly religious popular sentiment. Revivalist politics in its several varieties is hostile to other ways of thinking about politics.

It is hostile to the school of "Christian realism" represented most forcefully in our century by Reinhold Niebuhr. Not for the revivalists is Niebuhr's distinction between "moral man and immoral society." Revivalists have little use for Hobbes' view of society as a jungle in which human animals struggle for survival and advantage. Indeed, in contrast to their religious teachings, the revivalists sometimes seem to lack a sense of the radicality of sin. When dealing with the corruptions of society, it is sometimes suggested that everything is to be blamed on the evil influences of secular humanism. As some secular liberals believe man to be innocent and perfectible, if only the injuries of inequality and ignorance can be remedied, so moral majoritarians come close to suggesting that innate human righteousness would flourish in the absence of the decadence purveyed by television and other elite-controlled institutions.

Revivalist politics also has little use for notions of "social contract" in which disinterested and traditionless individuals strike a deal and call it justice. They are not about to discuss morality behind John Rawls' "veil of ignorance." Far from being anonymous individuals calculating their interests without reference to their own identities or placements in history, they wish to proclaim universal truths derived from and grounded in their most particular experience of the absolute. For them, justice is defined by a righteousness not of human devising; it is participation in a transcendent good. Above all, revivalist politics is incompatible with any "scientific" view of politics. Interests are not to be rationally harmonized through enlightened planning. Politics, like history itself, is the arena in which is enacted the drama of the conflict between good and evil. The revivalists are also the enemies of every form of determinism: nothing is inevitable except the final triumph of God's purposes.

Revivalist politics is the politics of high idealism, of undoubted confidence in the capacity of the human will to enlist on the side of righteousness. It is combative, inclined more to battle than compromise. At different times and at different points on the political spectrum, it erupts in the form of populism. Revivalist politics is very much at home in the raucous process we call democracy. It is the politics of "nonetheless." Despite the dismal, indeed lurid, descriptions of prevailing wickedness— *nonetheless* God will turn America around and make it the launching pad for world evangelism and cosmic fulfillment. On the one hand, it appeals to hoary precedent, patriotically dressing itself in American traditionalism. On the other, it calls for commitment to the utterly new thing that God will do.

The political expression of this religiously empowered "nonetheless" is not limited to moral majoritarians, of course. It is endemic to politicized religion of all sorts, and perhaps to Christianity itself. Today's proponents of various liberation theologies call for commitment to create "the new man in the new society," despite the awareness that the course they pursue has resulted in totalitarian misery for millions in this century. "Nonetheless, we rely upon the divine promise to do something new," it is answered. Jürgen Moltmann, who has his own problems with liberation theologies, takes this "nonetheless" even further, defying not only political experience but the entirety of what is known about the world: "The expectation of what is to come on the ground of the resurrection of Christ, must then turn all reality that can be experienced and all real experience into an experience that is provisional and a reality that does not yet contain within it what is held in prospect for it."[11] If taken seriously, and Moltmann is a very serious theologian indeed, this is an extraordinary statement. The posture of Christian hope is one that has let go of *experience itself.* Such language can no doubt induce an attitude of hopefulness, but it is unclear as to what the content of such hope might be. What can we hope for that is not, at least in a provisional way, contained in what is known? The "nonetheless" of revivalist politics is mild compared to assertions such as Moltmann's. However peculiar some moral majoritarian readings of texts and history may be, at least there are referents of continuity in the Bible, the American faith, and contemporary experience. In truth, for all the talk about the genuinely new thing that God is doing, the outcome hoped for in the end time is a world suspiciously like that of a certain Baptist congregation in Lynchburg, Virginia.

It is clear that revivalist politics is a democratic stirring against conventional notions about a secular society. It is not clear how this phenomenon relates to other democratic stirrings. At the same time that it calls itself conservative, it insists upon its difference from the rose-arbored English cottage conservatism that is the more familiar protest against modernity. It speaks dismissively of the conservative "northeastern-establishment" and flirts with the rhetoric of populism. In populist fashion, moral majoritarians attempt to market and coordinate discontents for political purpose. Societal discontents are spread all over the political and cultural map, however. They do not lend themselves to easy coordination. Populism finds its cohering theme in attributing the cause of discontents to "them." Since the sixties, language about "the people" has gravitated from the left to the right. The moral majoritarians now invoke the authority of "the people" against the elites. The result is very close to Niebuhr's description of what happens when "the children of light" are pitted against "the children of darkness." In addition, the leaders of revivalist politics fall back upon a presumed core constituency among self-identified fundamentalists. All of this creates problems, even contradictions, in the thinking of the leadership.

When Moral Majority, the organization, appeared, it insisted that it was not a religious effort. It declared itself to be reaching out to everybody, including nonfundamentalist Christians, Jews, and even nonbelievers. "The only thing that matters is that we agree on the issues," said Jerry Falwell. But herein lies a tension, if not a contradiction. While contending against "secular America," the distinction made between religious belief and public policy issues begins to sound very much like the distinction between sacred and secular. Here is an interesting development that may be more the result of intuition than of calculated purpose: the organizational instruments for the public intervention of religiously based values are themselves described as secular. At one level, it may be merely a matter of expanding the potential audience beyond the religiously committed. At another, perhaps intuitive level, however, there is the understanding that particularist religious beliefs must somehow be "translated" into more general terms in order to be admitted to the public arena.

As is evident also in the Supreme Court's wrestling with the question over the years, there is confusion about what is the publicly admissible content level of religion. The debate is not entirely dissimilar to debates in the Food and Drug Administration about other ingredients. With respect to religion, government regulators may despair of defining the ingredient qualitatively and therefore resort to the quantitative. Thus, for example, the Internal Revenue Service forbids churches to devote a "substantial" amount of their resources to direct political interventions. Most churches prudently restrain themselves from forcing the question of what is meant by substantial. In fact, they usually do not agree with the government's attempted sharp distinction between the political and religious, since they view their political interventions as part of their religious mission. Nonetheless, everybody, including groups such as Moral Majority, know that terms such as "religion" and "politics" must have *some* discrete meaning.

Even some who do not subscribe to the notion of the naked public square believe that religion *qua* religion does not really belong there. Naked religion, so to speak, is an intrusion even upon the democratically attuned public square. In order to be admitted, religion must be related to a discourse that is genuinely public in nature.

How much explicit religion is permissible is undecided. According to militant secularists, political advocacy that is even slightly tainted by religious motivation must be excluded. According to religious activists, any intervention that falls short of governmental establishment of particularist religious belief should be admitted. The floating consensus is somewhere between "taint" and "establishment." Groups that are so manifestly religiously motivated as Moral Majority must make the most extravagant profession of their openness to nonbelievers in order to distance themselves from the prospect of the "establishment" that, in the eyes of their critics, they so clearly threaten. They want it understood that supporters need not pledge themselves to the "five fundamentals" of the true faith. Swallowing hard, they declare they are ready to work even with people who do not believe in God. This effort to be inclusive is not without its problems. It may play into the hands of those who would draw a hard line between the religious and the secular. It is similar to fundamentalism's division between public policy and private faith, which we discussed earlier. That division tends to reinforce the secular prejudice that religion is essentially a source of private visions that are by definition foreign to public discourse. So also the attempt of religiously empowered political interventions to be entirely inclusive may blunt the sharpness of the challenge to the naked public square. In addition, it creates internal problems with respect to the real constituency of the movement.

The claim of being so inclusive is thought by some to come close to being a deceptive practice. There is the suspicion of being "used." Jews, for instance, have been divided and for the most part decidedly cool in response to the attentions of the moral majoritarians. Most Jews welcome fundamentalism's enthusiasm for the State of Israel but are understandably less positive about apocalyptic scenarios that call for the eventual conversion of Jews to Christ. Menachem Begin gave awards to leaders of the religious new right and made a fuss over them when they visited Israel, as they regularly do. To the objection of American Jews who are disturbed by this strange alliance, Begin is reported to have said, "What fundamentalists believe about the conversion of Jews is sometime in the future, maybe a thousand years from now. Israel needs all the friends it can get right now." However convenient such a particular convergence of interests may be, nobody has any illusions that Jews belong to the real constituency of, for example, Moral Majority.

Leaders may proclaim their desire to integrate fundamentalist doctrine with more inclusive beliefs and ideals, but integration, whether racial or doctrinal, has not been the strong suit of fundamentalism. Moreover, in bidding for a larger constituency, such movements may alienate the constituency that is the primary base of support and vision. It is not easy to operate in two quite distinct orbits; the one composed of the truly saved and the other of those who can be recruited for the work that is to be done before the truly saved are taken off in the rapture. The impression made is that the movement is divided into first class and second class sections. And, as noted, the two classes tend to fall along the old lines of sacred and secular. Those directing polemical fire at "secular humanism" may themselves be suspected of assuming a secular disguise. Between secular humanism and secular religionism, so to speak, secular humanism at least has the merit of seeming to be more straightforward. This is yet a further instance in which the religious new right is crippled and may be undone by internal conceptual confusions.

The core constituency of the moral majoritarians are people who make an undisguised identification between religious belief and public purpose. While funds and other resources for political intervention are presumably handled quite separately, there is an obvious constituency overlap with the audiences of fundamentalist journals and television programming. Indeed more than an overlap; this is the core constituency. According to researchers such as Hadden and Swann, that core constituency is much smaller than both friends and foes frequently claim.[12] Perhaps no more than two to four million Americans are in the "first class" section of the movement, and they are concentrated in the Southern states. The credibility of the much larger appeal claimed by the religious new right rests upon its ability to touch nerves of populist discontent that may have no direct connection with religious belief. That is, millions of Americans believe that "traditional values" should be revived and are religiously interested only to the degree that religion presumably serves such a revival.

The discontent of these millions beyond the core constituency is not primarily with the proposal that America is a secular society. In fact the idea of a secular society is linked to a practice of religious tolerance of which they approve. They tend to look askance at talk about "Christian America." Yet, with the core constituency, they share a resentment of what they see as the imposition of alien values upon American culture. The resentment is mixed with a vague awareness that somehow such value changes are related to religion. The Jerry Falwells believe they understand the workings of these connections. But it is not necessary that all their followers be convinced of their understanding. It is only necessary that the resentment should be legitimated and employed. A vague awareness of the connections between religion and the changes resented is sufficient in order to sustain the larger constituency's tolerance of a fundamentalist component that it might otherwise reject.

109

The starting point for understanding this widespread resentment of changes is to acknowledge that in fact there have been momentous changes. Unless one believes that change is self-legitimating, that change is a good in itself, it must be admitted that many of these changes are eminently disputable. Such changes touch frequently upon matters about which people are very passionate, both positively and negatively. They raise elementary questions of right and wrong, of justice, equality, and fairness. In short, these changes are value-laden. Consider some of the more obvious: prayer in public schools, abortion, welfare, the work ethic, sex education, job quotas, affirmative action, and the role of U.S. power in defending "the free world." On these and other questions a line—albeit sometimes a wiggly line—is drawn between liberals and conservatives. Some of the disagreements are over questions of fact—what is happening in the modern world and why. But, scratching the arguments over questions of fact, we quickly expose the underlying questions of values. It is less a matter of what *is* the world like and more a matter of what *ought* the world to be like.

The alliance between religion and the protest against perceived cultural directions is not accidental. That is, the protest could not have allied itself with some other institution, such as the university, or labor unions, or a political party. This is true because other institutions have narrower interests and lack a base in mass participation. But it is most importantly true because only religion must, by definition, insist upon moral truth that is transcendent, intersubjective, and therefore normative. True, science and the university that limits itself to scientific knowledge speak about normative truth; but, again by definition, scientific knowledge does not address the issue of moral purpose, not to mention the question of transcendent judgment.[13]

And so we return to the problems inherent in the notion of a secular society. Without a transcendent or religious point of reference, conflicts of values cannot be resolved; there can only be procedures for their temporary accommodation. Conflicts over values are viewed not as conflicts between contending truths but as conflicts between contending interests.[14] If one person believes that incest is wrong and should be outlawed while another person believes incest is essential for sexual liberation, the question in a thoroughly secularized society is how these conflicting "interests" might be accommodated. Since the person who practices incest can do so without denying the rights of the person who abhors incest, the accommodation will inevitably be skewed in favor of incest. Similarly, one person believes the government has an obligation to assist the poor through tax dollars while another denies that there is any such obligation. Since the "interests" of the first person cannot be accommodated without interfering with the "interests" of the second person (by imposing higher taxes), the accommodation will be skewed in favor of the second.

The secular reduction of moral discourse to a contest over interests is an essential part of MacIntyre's "politics as civil war carried on by other means." What the justices described as a "pervasive and brooding devotion to the secular" leads to the extreme forms of libertarianism that erupt from time to time on both the left and the right of the political spectrum. It is tenuously based upon the split in the one tradition by which historically our public life was held accountable to critical judgment. In a thoroughly secular society notions of what is morally excellent or morally base are not publicly admissible. That is, they are not admissible as moral judgment: they have public status only as they reflect the "interests" of those who hold them. That ours is not such a thoroughly secularized society is evident in the fact that undisguisedly moral judgments continue to play a very lively part in our moral discourse. Only when we are forced to talk about morality within the context of the formal polity, as, for example, in court cases, do we discover that the secular theory about our common life is frustrated by the moral and religious character of our common life.

In New York State a law has been passed forbidding the use of young children in the making of pornographic films. In order to protect it against challenges from extreme civil libertarians, it is specifically stated that the law is not based upon moral or religious reasons. The reasoning offered is that making pornographic films is injurious to the mental health of young children. Such are the results of what Philip Rieff described as "the therapeutic society." A secular polity requires that we profess more confidence in the "scientific" notions of psychiatry than in our moral judgment. In fact, while psychiatric and a host of other considerations might inform moral judgment, the law reflects the moral judgment of legislators who are responsive to the moral judgment of their constituencies. But they cannot admit that the law is based upon moral judgment. In a court challenge, expert psychiatric witnesses would no doubt be produced to testify that child pornography is perfectly healthy. Perhaps even a professional association of therapists might so testify, much as American psychiatrists in recent years "scientifically" determined that homosexuality is no longer an illness. Were that to happen, the legislature would have to resort to some other excuse in which to disguise its acting upon its moral judgment that child pornography is wrong.

Aristotle speaks of the impossibility of discussing virtue with people who are "handicapped by some incapacity for goodness." The notion of a secular society compels political actors to pretend to be more morally handicapped than they are. It might be argued that this is the price to be paid for a pluralistic society. The price is too high. What is meant by "pluralism" in such arguments is frequently indifference to normative truth, an agreement to count all opinions about morality as equal (equal "interests" to be accommodated) because we are agreed there is no truth by which judgment can be rendered. The result is the debasement of our public life by the exclusion of the idea—and consequently of the practice—of virtue.

A familiar statement from Aristotle is pertinent:

> Anything that we have to learn to do we learn by the actual doing of it: people become builders by building and instrumentalists by playing instruments. Similarly we become just by performing just acts, temperate by performing temperate ones, brave by performing brave ones. This view is supported by what happens in city-states. Legislators make their citizens good by habituation; this is the intention of every legislator, and those who do not carry it out fail of their object. This is what makes the difference between a good constitution and a bad one.[15]

It is only in recent years that the Constitution of the United States has been interpreted to mandate that legislators fail, or at least pretend to fail, in carrying out their object. As "by habituation" we pretend not to be concerned for the good, we become what we pretend to be. The intervention of religiously based values in public affairs is a protest against the pretense. Whether that intervention speaks to our obligation for the hungry of the world or to the necessity of protecting the unborn and other endangered humans in our own society, it is a call for us to assume the dignity of being moral actors. We are not merely atomistic individuals with interests to be accommodated but persons of reason and conviction whose humanity requires participation in the process of persuasion. From Aristotle through Jefferson, and up to the very recent past, politics was thought of as that process of persuading and being persuaded; a process engaged in by a community brought into being by its shared acknowledgment of the existence of truth beyond its certain grasp. It is not that the greats of Western political philosophy did not understand the importance of accommodation. Burke, reflecting on the American experience, observed: "All government—indeed, every human benefit and enjoyment, every virtue and prudent act—is founded on compromise and barter." Persuasion often reaches its limits. It is one thing for you to propose a compromise when you realize that you will not persuade your neighbor of your understanding of the truth. It is quite another to conclude that there is no question of truth involved. In the first instance you remain a moral actor, acting according to the virtue of prudence. In the second instance, it is merely a matter of ciphers with conflicting interests splitting the difference.

Were the battle against a cabal of "secular humanists," as some would have it, there would be reason for greater optimism. They could be exposed and driven from their positions of influence, perhaps. Our difficulty is greater than that. It is the pervasive influence of ideas about a secular society and a secular state, ideas that have insinuated themselves also into our religious thinking and that have been institutionalized in our politics.

The proposition that America is a secular society is contrary to sociological fact. The American people are more incorrigibly religious than ever before. The proposition is impossible in principle. The American experience is not self-legitimating; it requires what it has until recently possessed, some sense of transcendent meaning. And the proposition is politically unsustainable. There are simply too many people who are no longer prepared to pretend that we are not the kind of people we are.

Whatever he may have meant by it, and whatever he did with it, Jimmy Carter's intuition was democratically sound: the task is to provide government as good as are the American people. More precisely—since Americans are not necessarily more "good" in their behavior than others—a government responsive to the good to which most Americans aspire. Whatever our political persuasion, if we care about a democratic future, we have a deep stake in reconstructing a politics that was not begun by and cannot be sustained by the myth of secular America.

CHAPTER SEVEN

THE MORALITY OF COMPROMISE

IN A DEMOCRACY SOME ISSUES ARE BEST FUDGED. SOME QUEStions cannot be pursued relentlessly to their logical end, except at the price of imperiling public discourse. Restraint and compromise are not dirty words. What is true of democratic governance is, in fact, true of human community itself. Marriage and family life, cooperation in church and voluntary associations—all are possible only with a modicum of fudging. The fudging we have in mind need not be, indeed it must not be, deception. It is rather a readiness to patch things together that may not quite exactly fit, to live with a few loose ends not tucked in. Forgiving is not forgetting, to be sure, but in everyday life forgiving includes an element of fudging. And, in any community of significance, everyday life is impossible without forgiveness. Fudging is anathema to the fanatic. That is one reason it is so hard to live with fanatics. That is one reason why saints, who are often tinged by fanaticism, are more honored after they are safely dead.

People who compromise in accordance with the discipline of the democratic process know that they are compromising. That is, they do not tell themselves or others that it does not matter, that there was no principle at stake, that there was not a reasoning that had been stopped short of its logical end. In a similar way, to forgive someone is not the same thing as saying that it did not matter, that there was no offense. If there was no offense there can be no forgiveness. Compromise and forgiveness arise from the acknowledgment that we are imperfect creatures in an imperfect world. Democracy is the product not of a vision of perfection but of the knowledge of imperfection. In this view, compromise is not an immoral act, nor is it an amoral act. That is, the one who compromises does not step out of her role as a moral actor. To the contrary, the person who makes a compromise is making a moral judgment about what is to be done when moral judgments are in conflict.

The notion of compromise is morally odious to some Christians because they fail to make distinctions between the several communities of which we are all part. Their personal life, the life of the church, and the life of the society are all rolled into one. All are to be ruled by the righteousness prescribed by the Word of God. Compromise is therefore unfaithfulness to the divine will. In point of fact, our life together in families and in the church can hardly be sustained without a willingness to make adjustments between conflicting readings of the divine will. Especially between the church and the society, however, there is the significant difference that the church is mandated to be a kind of "signal community"—a model of how human life can be ordered by the redeeming grace of God. Because, in Chesterton's memorable words, America is a nation with the soul of a church, people have often thought of America too as a kind of signal community. America has been seen as a signal, a preview, a portent of the universal future of democratic freedom. In fact America has at times been that and may be that more fully in times ahead.

Yet, whatever the virtues of the American experiment, it is a society among other societies. It is part of the temporal order; it is in time as far short of the kingdom as is any other earthly kingdom. Its life is ordered primarily by power rather than by grace and love. And power—no matter how just or democratically limited—is by definition always "power over" others. There is important truth in the Reformation idea of the "two kingdoms." Frequently, however, that idea has been distorted into a rigid separation of the temporal order from Christian moral judgment. As a result of this divorce, it is thought that the sphere of law has nothing to do with the sphere of the gospel, the order of creation nothing to do with the order of redemption, the "world" nothing to do with the community of the redeemed, the state nothing to do with the church. The result of this is a theological construct that mirrors and reinforces the secular notion of the naked public square. Historically, in some places where a Lutheran notion of the "two kingdoms" prevailed, the consequence was predictable: the public square did not remain naked but was taken over by the state. In the period following the Reformation, German princes dominated the church and employed it in their rule over the entire society.[1] A later prince of darkness, Adolf Hitler, would more ambitiously seek to fill public space with religious meaning in a way that made necessary the displacement of the church. This is the doleful history that has, in many minds, entirely discredited the notion of two kingdoms.

As many scholars have urged, the two-kingdoms idea is better expressed in terms of the "twofold rule of God." This formulation underscores that it is the one God who rules over all reality, and his will is not divided. Yet, short of the consummation, he rules in a twofold manner. Even more precisely, in different spheres we experience and act upon his rule in different ways. "And Jesus called them to him and said to them, 'You know that those who are supposed to rule over the Gentiles lord it over them, and their great men exercise authority over them. But it shall not be so among you; but whoever would be great among you must be your servant, and whoever would be first among you must be slave of all' " (Mark 10:42-44). The society of believers is to live in contrast to the continuing societies of the world; until, one day, all the societies of the world are comprehended in the society of faith. Short of that time, however, we are to remember, first, that there are different societies differently ordered; second, that we are members of both societies; third, that the Lord is lord of all reality, as will be evident to all in the end time.

It can be argued that the "ideal society" would be a Christian society in which all of life is ordered in accordance with biblical teaching. This is in fact an argument that has been made many times in the history of the church. It emerged with the establishment of Christianity in the late Roman empire, with the Investiture Controversy of the eleventh century, with Calvin's grandly flawed experiment in Geneva, and is today espoused by some moral majoritarians. Until Vatican Council II vindicated the work of John Courtney Murray and others, official Roman Catholicism saw the ideal in a "Christian" society such as Franco Spain. Democratic pluralism, as in the United States, was, at best, a morally tolerable compromise. Today Christians are called to a clearer affirmation of democratic governance. At one level, Christians may recognize, along with other sensible people, that democracy is, in Churchill's words, the worst possible form of government, except for all the others that have been tried. At a higher level, however, Christians may see in democracy a development under divine guidance. Democracy is the appropriate form of governance in a fallen creation in which no person or institution, including the church, can infallibly speak for God. Democracy is the necessary expression of humility in which all persons and institutions are held accountable to transcendent purpose imperfectly discerned.

This is the understanding of democracy that makes it possible and imperative for Christians to endorse the "no establishment" and "free exercise" clauses of the First Amendment to the Constitution. The "separation of church and state," as Jefferson somewhat misleadingly termed it, is essential to check the pretensions of the church. More important, and more pertinent to the constitutional intent, it is necessary to check the pretensions of the state. The "no establishment" clause, it needs ever to be repeated, is in the service of the "free exercise" clause. The primary reason for the "no establishment" clause is not to prevent the church from taking over the state but to prevent the state from taking over the church. The church is the particular society within society that bears institutional witness to the transcendent purpose to which the society is held accountable. Historically, the church has sometimes been an overweening actor within the society, attempting to dominate the whole. Given the maddening diversity of churches that make up the church in America, that has seldom been a problem in American life. It is the other overweening actor, the state, that has posed the danger of trying to dominate the whole. This is more dangerously the case as people have come to equate the state with society itself.

Contrary to some conservative literature today, the problem of equating state and society is not a modern novelty. When in 1651 Louis XIV declared, "I am the state," it was a declaration also of his supremacy over the entire social order. The same issue had been joined earlier when in the eleventh century Pope Gregory VII had to bring Henry IV to his knees at Canossa. With dismal consequences for religion, Henry VIII got away with it in England in the sixteenth century. The difference in our century is that the state has demonstrated its ability to become an impersonal power backed by totalitarian theory and technique. Whether in Nazism or Communism, the formula is: "Everything in the state, nothing apart from the state." As suggested earlier, it is a dangerous naivete to think "it can't happen here."

The habit of mind that equates state and society is both fatal and insidious. It has insinuated itself also into the thinking of the churches. It is evident in the assumption that all public responsibilities are to be exercised by the government and that, for example, church programs of social welfare are only "temporary" expedients until the government can take them over. It is evident in the increasing litigiousness in which churches go to court to have the state rule on their internal affairs. Recently a family of parishioners in a Midwest Catholic church protested the parish council's plans for redecorating the church. They obtained a court ruling that the altar fell into the category of furnishings, to which the family had property rights because they had donated it. It is of some little symbolic significance when an altar is deemed to be no more than a piece of furniture. St. Paul cautioned Christians against going to court "before unbelievers" because it cast shame upon the church. ("Do you not know that we are to judge angels? How much more, matters pertaining to this life!" [I Cor. 6:3]). The same reason holds today, reinforced by the additional reason that resort to the courts of the state confirms the pretensions of the state. Already the state, through the Internal Revenue Service, presumes to define which activities of the churches are truly religious, and therefore tax exempt, and which are not. Already many churches have come to believe that tax exemption is a privilege granted by the state rather than a right inherent in the institution of religion. Already the idea is promoted that a tax exemption is in reality a "tax expenditure" by the government and therefore tax-exempt activities are subject to government control.[2]

This chapter started by saying that compromise is essential to democracy. The short excursus on the relationships between church, society, and state is aimed at illuminating what is meant by compromise. Theologically speaking, the understanding of compromise is based upon the distinction—but not separation!—between church and society. In this light, compromise is not so much something we do as it is something we acknowledge: we acknowledge that the ordering of the world short of the kingdom of God *is* compromised. One day every knee will bow and every tongue confess that Jesus Christ is Lord (Phil. 2:10-11). But that is not the case now. We cannot force it to be the case nor should we pretend that it is the case. Politically speaking, the understanding of compromise requires heightened vigilance toward the limitations of the state with respect to society and, most importantly, with respect to that part of society that is the church. Such vigilance is for the sake of the church and its mission, to be sure. But it is also for the sake of democracy itself. Religion is the singular institution that both keeps the state under transcendent judgment and affirms the divinely given nature of the rights of persons, especially of the most vulnerable, in society.

For some Christians, compromise will always seem to be, well, compromising. If one believes that God has revealed in detail his plan for the ordering of human life, there are several possibilities of action. One can put that plan into effect within the community that shares that belief. This has been attempted times beyond numbering in Christian history. The rich story of religious communalism in the American experience is evidence of the vitality of this sectarian option. The term "sectarian" in this connection is not pejorative. Those who have, in H. Richard Niebuhr's phrase, chosen "Christ against culture" have—whether or not they always intended to do so—contributed powerfully to the culture. They have provided an "alternative politics" or "counterculture" by which the society can be subjected to critical examination.

The word "counterculture" has in recent years been associated with various movements churning around radical politics, drugs, rock music, and the pursuit of "alternative life-styles," especially as the last touch upon sexual mores. That counterculture of more recent years was more a "dropping out" from the prevailing culture than it was a challenge to the culture. It must be admitted, however, that even dropping out or repudiation is a form of challenge. It must further be admitted that some proponents of the recent counterculture did see themselves as acting from foundational principles—political, economic, social—at variance with the pervasive assumptions in society. Closer to the sectarian option we have in mind, however, were the "Jesus People" of the late sixties and early seventies, especially those who tried to exemplify their beliefs in communes of conviction. But when we think of the venerable sectarian alternative we are even more likely to think of groups such as the Amish. Recognizing that they cannot live out what they believe to be the divine will in a world so severely compromised, they become a people apart. They need not engage in the compromises of a compromised public order. As the Mennonite theologian, John Howard Yoder, is fond of saying, "It is not the business of Christians to work out the ethical problems of Caesar."[3] In other words, those who engage themselves in the world of power politics no doubt have many ethical problems, but gospel answers are conditioned upon the abandonment of that world.

118

The sectarian option, seriously pursued, is one honorable alternative to the politics of compromise. In a time such as ours, when churches spinelessly acquiesce in cultural currents of all sorts, the witness of thoughtful sectarians is an urgently needed corrective. The Protestant ecumenical movement before World War II had as its slogan: "Let the church be the church!" That cry can be understood (although this is not how it was usually intended) as implying a certain recklessness, even indifference, toward the impact of the church on public life. It is the opposite of the anxious sniffing about for political influence or cultural respectability, or both, that is evident in the several churches today. As strange as it may seem, it may happen at times that the church is most influential when it is indifferent to exercising influence.

Most Christians, however, do not elect the sectarian model and are not likely to accept it unless it is forced upon them by a triumphant secularism that compels Christians to choose against participation in the public order. Those who, as it is said, favor the "ethics of responsibility" over the "ethics of perfection" enter upon the risks of participating in a compromised political order. In the absence of the best, they pursue the better. With respect to their deepest beliefs and the community that shares those beliefs, they are not prepared to compromise. That is, within the community of faith the ethic of self-sacrificing love and service is to be given full rein. But they are "realistic" about the world outside that community. They are ready to mix it up with "the Gentiles," fully aware that in the games of power politics they may end up with "dirty hands."

It is very easy to be cynical about this choice, a choice that is in fact made by most Christians. In *The Brothers Karamazov*, the Grand Inquisitor brilliantly argues against Jesus that willingness to exercise power over others is the perfection of self-sacrificing love. What is called ethical realism is sometimes no more than self-serving accommodationism. The ethics of responsibility becomes hard to distinguish from the ethics of expediency. That having been said, Christians nonetheless find themselves within the compromised orders of the world. Because they believe that Christian truth is not private truth but is public truth, there is the irrepressibly felt need to relate that truth to the several worlds in which we are involved. Not all Christians believe that the truth revealed contains answers adequate to the many questions about how our public life is to be ordered. Some of those who do believe there are such answers conclude that it is not possible to implement them in the public order and therefore, as we have seen, elect the sectarian course. Others who think they possess such a revealed design elect a different course.

One different course is sometimes described as "triumphalism." Triumphalism can take different forms. One form aims at making likeminded Christians of everyone in the society. Then everyone will recognize the revealed design for society and it can be implemented through democratic processes. Another triumphalism acknowledges that unanimity, even near-unanimity, will never be achieved. The aim then is to move in a theocratic direction that will replace democracy with "the rule of the righteous." A more tempered triumphalism accepts democratic forms (as the "least bad" of ways of government) but seeks to employ them to advance as much as possible "the Christian design" for society. Triumphalism may tolerate deviations from the divine design, but such toleration is always one of necessity and not of principle. Its attitude is suspiciously close to the pre-Vatican II Roman Catholic teaching that "error has no rights." The old qualifier that, while error has no rights, the person who is in error does have rights is a weak reed on which to rest democratic freedoms. The distinction between the error and the person who holds the error is an abstraction that does not bear up well in the give-and-take of politics, once governmental power is lined up on the side of "the truth."

An alternative to both sectarianism and triumphalism is to recognize that there is no coherent, detailed, revealed design for the social order. Or, to put it differently, whatever design there is points to the democratic protection of diversity. It is hard for morally earnest Christians who are concerned about the public order to accept this possibility. It is as hard for the moral majoritarians of the right as it is for the would-be moral majoritarians of the left. The yearning for government that reflects a coherent and compelling moral purpose is no respecter of political persuasion, but cuts across all partisan lines. It is often suggested that the choice is between such a coherent moral purpose, on the one hand, and absolute relativism, on the other. Were that the only choice, then the further choice would seem to be reduced to sectarianism or triumphalism. A principled commitment to democratic governance, however, offers a way out of this dilemma. Democracy is not to be equated with a laissez-faire morality in which "anything goes." In the understanding of democracy proposed here, the relativizers are relativized in two important ways. First, democratic government is premised upon the acknowledgment of transcendent truth to which the political order is held accountable. Second, democracy assumes the lively interaction among people who are acting from values that are, in most instances, grounded in specific religious belief.

With respect to the first condition, the acknowledgment of the transcendent is a question of principle and not simply of historical accident. In other words, it is not enough to stipulate that the American democratic experiment began with a sense of accountability to "Nature and Nature's God." That sense of accountability must be sustained, and in order to be sustained it must be regularly and formally articulated. Democracy cannot survive without such a limiting challenge to the imperiousness of the political. One reason it cannot survive is that, without an understanding of transcendently grounded rights, all rights are then subject to be overridden either by abstract principles or by raw majoritarianism. The danger of rights being overridden by abstractions is the danger posed by a "secular" approach that is typically utilitarian in its calculation of interests. In that approach, as we have seen, all values and all truth claims are reduced to the status of individualistic "interests." The danger of rights being overridden by raw majoritarianism is sometimes posed by morally earnest religionists who would pursue relentlessly the logic of this being a Christian nation.

In *The Spirit of Democratic Capitalism*, Michael Novak writes that in a democratic society the sense of transcendent accountability must be marked by a "reverential emptiness" at the heart of the social order: "Indeed, without certain conceptions of history, nature, person, community, and the limited state, the very notion of 'human rights' makes little sense. Respect for the transcendence of God and for full freedom of conscience—respect for the common human wandering in darkness—is better served, however, even in Christian and Jewish terms, by the reverential emptiness at the heart of pluralism than by a socially imposed vision of the good."[4]

Novak is writing against the left, but what he says applies also to the moral majoritarianism usually identified as being on the right:

> Theologically speaking, the free market and the liberal polity follow from liberty of conscience. Yet those religious persons who prefer the public enforcement of virtue find obvious attractions in socialism. What censorship is to free speech, the command economy is to the free market. What an established religion is to a traditional society, a collective moral vision publicly imposed is to a socialist society. There will not be wanting Christian, Jewish, and secular socialists to whom a socialist society promises methods of suffusing their views throughout every activity which no free society affords them.[5]

While agreeing with much of Novak's argument, one must raise a serious question about the "emptiness" at the heart of the public order. Such emptiness is very close to the idea of the naked public square. Novak speaks of virtue being "socially imposed," of its "public enforcement." But the democratic interplay of substantive moral discourse need not be coercive. The "religion of the republic" so compellingly described by Sidney Mead, for example, is premised upon a democratic movement from coercion to persuasion.[6] Democratic persuasion, not emptiness, is the alternative to coercion. The sense of transcendence that in its beginning and to this day marks the American experiment in democracy is not contentless. Both historically and in present sociological fact, it is religiously specific, it refers to the Judeo-Christian tradition. The acknowledgment of this reality is in the most particular interest of the considerable number of Americans who do not subscribe to that tradition in any conscious manner. And that is because it is precisely by the authority of that tradition that the rights to dissent are protected.

Needless to say, there are many believers who do not understand that democracy and the dissent essential to democracy are mandated by biblical faith. It seems to them that, if the Christian faith is the absolute and universal truth, then all ought to subscribe to it and public life ought to be ordered according to that truth. This universal mission should be carried out by persuasion, if possible, and (although few would put it so bluntly) by coercion, if necessary. To those who think in this way, talk about democracy and diversity as part of the divine intent seems to undercut the universal mission of the church. This, as we have seen, is a perennial problem in Christian thinking. Romans 9–11 reflect St. Paul's wrestling with this question as it was posed by the nonconversion of most of the Jewish people. His conclusion then was that it is perhaps part of the sacred design that living Judaism should remain until the end time as corrective witness and embodied memory, illuminating the grace of God that is also manifest in the Body of Christ, the church. This does not mean that Christians should not seek earnestly to share the gospel with all people, including Jews. It does suggest that diversity in belief is inherent in, and not accidental to, the divine purpose. That some do not believe is not necessarily evidence of the failure of the church or the failure of the gospel. It is evidence that the entirety of God's purpose is not limited to our programs, including our programs of evangelism.

The democratic sense of transcendent accountability is also a check upon the pretensions of the church. The sense of accountability must be cultivated within the community of believers before believers are able to cultivate it in the public order. The basic lesson, which Christians must learn again and again, is that the church is not the kingdom of God. As a nineteenth-century historian wryly observed, "Jesus came proclaiming the Kingdom of God, but what appeared was the church." The disappointment was understandable. The disappointment is not to be denied, however. It is rather to be recalled daily as a truth that should inform the whole of the church's life. If the church is the same thing as the kingdom of God, we have no reason to "seek first the kingdom," for the church is undoubtedly already here.

I have often, only half-jokingly, suggested that, if one post-New Testament writing is to be added to the biblical canon, it should be Dostoyevsky's aforementioned "Legend of the Grand Inquisitor." In that legend is the dismal working out of the logic that equates church and kingdom. The grand inquisitors of our day, whether of the left or the right, are as impatient as was Dostoveysky's with the limitation of their authority. Talk about Christian America will continue to frighten many sensible people until Christians make clear that they welcome and cultivate such limitation of their authority. People will continue to seek in secularity their safety from religious tyranny until Christians believably propose that there is greater safety under a sacred canopy that brings all institutions and belief systems, and most particularly religion, under judgment. The

122

canopy is that to which Judeo-Christian religion points. Religion bears witness to it but our religion is not to be equated with it. On the other hand, the canopy is a canopy, it is not mere "emptiness." It is generally describable in terms of the promises and judgments revealed in the biblical story. It is not Hinduism or Taoism. Historically and in present democratic judgment, it is the biblical story. That story is not yet over; the kingdom promise has not yet been consummated. It may be over in a matter of a few years or a few months, as some teachers of "Bible prophecy" claim. Or we may be the "early Christians," making our appearance in the first act of a drama that is to be unfolded over millennia beyond our imagining. Whatever our notion of the eschatological schedule, the important truth is that we act in a sense of provisionality and historical modesty. Only as the church, in its own teaching and life, cultivates this sense of provisionality and modesty will religion seem less threatening to those who would now bar it from the public square.

Unfortunately, there are those who insist upon what they think of as a full-blooded and aggressive version of the Christian mission. In their view, all talk about provisionality and modesty is suspect. It seems to suggest a weak-kneed accommodationism that is prepared to settle for less than the triumph of the truth. Such a view is understandable in light of the fact that most Christians and most churches do seem all too ready to settle for the world as it is. But our argument is that provisionality and modesty are required by rigorous fidelity to the gospel. What passes as a full-blooded and aggressive assertion of the truth is a denial of the greater truth. It is an assertion of *our form* of the truth, a substitution of our absolute for the absolute promised in the kingdom, an equation of our programs with the purposes of God.

The alternative to this false absolutism is not to say that nobody knows the truth. In a world of fashionable relativism, Christians must risk the embarrassment of saying that they do indeed know the most important truth—that truth regarding the personal and cosmic salvation promised in the revelation of God in Christ. But to know the truth is not the same thing as claiming to *have* the truth in the sense of mastering or possessing it. We can even allow for those who claim that, in grasping the Bible, they "possess" the infallible, inerrant, absolute Truth of God. But even they must allow that—in terms of intellectual understanding, trust, and moral obedience—they fall short of the truth. We are subject to the truth we possess, and therefore do not possess it in the sense of mastery. In addition to this inadequate apprehension of the truth to which we witness, the very content of the message points beyond our ability to apprehend perfectly, it points to that which is not yet part of historically available experience, it points to the coming kingdom of God. In this light, modesty and provisionality are not the result of weak-kneed accommodationism but are required by fidelity to the claims of the gospel.

Working tirelessly to share the truth we do know, we submit our-selves humbly, even joyfully, to the truth to which the truth we do know points—the truth that is beyond the mastery of our ways of knowing. What we might call cognitive modesty—an awareness of the limitations of our knowing—is the way of obedience to the One who *is* the Way, the Truth, and the Life. He has not yet made his triumphant appearance in earthly rule over all things. Christians, if they are faithful, seek no triumph that is not his. When this is understood and communicated, "the cultured despisers of religion" need no longer see the sacred canopy as an instrument of closure or coercion. Rather it can be seen for what it is: the transcendent truth that both legitimates and makes necessary the cultivation of democratic diversity. Then it will be seen that secularism's denial or attempted dismantling of the canopy removes what is finally the only moral check upon people who would repress those who do not subscribe to *their* truth.

Democratic compromise, then, is not to cave in to those who claim that all truth is relative. As we have urged, the relativizers are relativized by the assertion of democratic governance premised upon an acknowledgment of transcendent truth to which the political order is held accountable. The origin of the word "compromise" is instructive at this point. It is derived from *compromittere*, which means to promise mutually to abide by the decision of an arbiter. Compromise, then, is not a defeat or the striking of a deal so much as it is an act of trust, the offering up of a conflict to the Arbiter Absolute. Here too the phrase "under God" takes on new meaning for the democratic process.

To be engaged in a process of compromise is to be engaged as a moral actor. To put it differently, compromise is not the abandonment of morality but is itself a moral act. This does not mean, of course, that all compromises are moral in the sense of being the morally right thing to do. It does mean that, having set aside the sectarian and triumphalist alternatives, one acts with moral responsibility in an arena that requires compromise. One cannot, for instance, legislate everything that one's own conscience or the rules of a religious community might demand. Within the context of healthy democratic contention, a compromise is not the abandonment of religious duty but is the fulfillment of a religious duty. It is such a fulfillment, that is, if one believes that Christianity has a stake in advancing democratic governance. The suggestion here is that we do have such a stake—in terms of the fulfillment of the church's mission, and in terms of faithful witness to the transcendent truth that makes democracy both necessary and possible. The triumph of a moral claim at the price of destroying the democratic process is, to that extent, a moral defeat. There is, in other words, a moral duty to keep the political order open to the future. Democracy is the defense against premature closure. Of course democracy is unsatisfactory. All orders short of the kingdom of

124

God are unsatisfactory. The discontents of democracy—its provisionality and incompleteness—are the signs of political health. The hunger for a truly satisfying way of putting the world in order is laudable. But that is a hunger for the kingdom of God, and it is dangerously misplaced when it is invested in the political arena.

One enters the democratic arena, then, as a moral actor. This must be insisted upon against those who view compromise as the antithesis of moral behavior. It must also be insisted upon against those who claim that moral judgment must be set aside before entering the public square. The first error is more common among Christians and others of high moral purpose. The second error is implicit, and sometimes explicit, in pervasive attitudes about ours being a secular society. In this second error, people are thought of as anonymous, deracinated ciphers seeking their own interests and striking a deal where it is in their interest to accommodate their interests to the interests of others. In this view, the assertion of a moral claim is an intrusion upon public space, a violation of the democratic rules. The assertion of a moral claim is an "imposition" upon a presumably value-free process.

Morally serious people, however, cannot divide themselves so neatly. Democracy does not require and cannot survive such a schizophrenic demand. Although she may not speak in the political arena in the same way she speaks in the church, the moral political actor is the same person in both situations. Her moral judgment is not an intrusion upon the otherwise amoral public space. For example, the person who argues that it is morally necessary to protect unborn life and the person who argues for unlimited right to abortion are both making moral arguments. We do not have here an instance of moral judgment *versus* value-free secular reason. We have rather an instance of *moralities in conflict.* The notion of moralities in conflict is utterly essential to remedying the problems posed by the naked public square. Those who want to bring religiously based values to bear in public discourse have an obligation to "translate" those values into terms that are as accessible as possible to those who do not share the same religious grounding. They also have the obligation, however, to expose the myth of value-neutrality that is so often exploited by their opponents.

Politics is an inescapably moral enterprise. Those who participate in it are—whether they know it or not, whether they admit it or not—moral actors. The word "moral" here does not mean that what happens in politics is always morally approvable or in accord with what is right. It means only that the questions engaged are questions that have to do with what is right or wrong, good or evil. Whatever moral dignity politics may possess depends upon its being a process of contention and compromise among moral actors, not simply a process of accommodation among individuals in pursuit of their interests. The conflict in American public life today, then, is not a conflict between morality and secularism. It is a conflict of moralities in which one moral system calls itself secular and insists that the other do likewise as the price of admission to the public arena. That insistence is in fact a demand that the other side capitulate. By divesting ourselves of authoritative moral referents that are external to ourselves, such as religion proposes, we have acquiesced in the judgment that there is no moral appeal beyond the individualistic pursuit of interests.

I have referred to this view of the political actor as one that turns him into a cipher. It frequently happens in the modern world that another word for cipher is "citizen." (In some societies, "comrade.") V. S. Naipaul, that melancholy chronicler of third world disaster, tells about a French-speaking African dictatorship: "*Monsieur* and *madame* and *boy* had been officially outlawed; the President had decreed us all to be *citoyens* and *citoyennes*. He used the two words together in his speeches, again and again, like musical phrases."[7] It is indeed music to tyrannies of every sort when the particularities that constitute real persons can be abolished. Titles and forms of address reflect particular communities, enterprises, and loyalties that are a potential threat to political control. Mother, father, son, daughter, doctor, professor, pastor—all bespeak those mediating structures that give the isolated individual a choice of identities and leverage against the megastructures of society. In the name of making everyone equal, such distinctions are obliterated. The individual is to have only one identity and that identity is bestowed by the state. In Africa, for example, where tribal loyalties cross the colonially imposed boundaries of nations, the need for "nation building" is understandable. Sad to say, in most of Africa today "nation building" is a euphemism for dictatorship. Although in very different ways, the same dynamics are evident in American life. It is evident in the demand that one must enter the public square bearing only the identity of "citizen." Most particularly, identities tarred by the brush of religion must be left behind or disguised. In the public theater we are all to don the masks of anonymity.

Ciphers are not moral actors. In the theater of the anonymous we are spared the awkwardness of dealing with moral argument; we need only be able to count heads. The citizen is a statistic. Statistics do not have rights. Among statistics you cannot weigh arguments, you can only count opinions. Again it is Dostoyevsky who understood well the uses of depersonalization in order to live more comfortably with injustices. In *Crime and Punishment* the murderer Raskolnikov reflects on the suffering and death he sees all around him:

> Anyway, to hell with it! Let them [die]! That's how it should be, they say. It's essential, they say, that such a percentage should every year go—that way—to the devil—it's essential so that the others should be kept fresh and healthy and not be interfered with. A percentage! What fine words they use, to be sure! So soothing. Scientific. All you

have to do is say "percentage" and all your worries are over. Now, of course, if you used some other word—well, then perhaps it would make you feel a little uncomfortable.[8]

"If you used some other word"—like the word that is the name of some insistently particular person. A person with fears and dreams, and with convictions about right and wrong. It is sticky, dealing with persons; with citizen-ciphers you can deal in percentages. It is, as Raskolnikov says, so scientific. Scientific rationalism in public affairs is, in Michael Oakeshotte's famed phrase, "like making politics as the crow flies." It has the attraction of getting directly to the point. It is an intellectual satisfaction. Unfortunately, it ignores the streets and alleys and byways where we discover the particularities of the people who constitute the meaning of politics.

In eighteenth-century Enlightenment Europe, Jews were presumably emancipated. They were given full citizenship. The only price required was that they divest themselves of their identity *as Jews*. They had full rights as citizens, but could make no claims as Jews. What the state gives, however, the state can take away. Until it was too late many "emancipated" German Jews put their trust in the naked public square: "After all, we are German citizens." Yale's Alexander Bickel perceived the fragility and perversity of the concept of "citizen." "When they freed themselves from subjection, the makers of the French Revolution called each other citizen, denoting their participation in the state; so the communists later called each other comrade, denoting their common allegiance to an ideology, a movement."[9] The American founders, however, had a different idea. "The Preamble speaks of 'We the people of the United States,' not, as it might have, of we the citizens of the United States at the time of the formation of this union. And the Bill of Rights throughout defines the rights of people, not of citizens."

"It remains true," writes Bickel, "that the original Constitution presented the edifying picture of a government that bestowed rights on people and persons, and held itself out as bound by certain standards of conduct in its relations with people and persons, not with some legal construct called citizen." We would only add the important caveat that this constitutional government did not "bestow" rights on people but acknowledged the prior rights that are theirs. But the essential point is that government is "bound," is accountable to that which is not its own creation. Bickel notes that the idea of citizenship came to prominence in the infamous *Dred Scott* decision of 1857. The ruling was that "that unfortunate race" of Negroes "had no rights which the white man was bound to respect." And why? Because they were not citizens. "This," says Bickel, "was the first authoritative definition of citizenship in American law." He goes on to observe, "It has always been easier, it always will be easier, to think of someone as a noncitizen than to decide that he is a non-person, which is the point of the *Dred Scott* case." In the 1973 *Roe v. Wade* decision on abortion the court bit the bullet and did what is not easy to do, declaring that the unborn are nonpersons. In 1982 an Indiana court, adhering to *Roe v. Wade*, declared that "Infant Doe" of Bloomington, a handicapped child already born, was a nonperson and the court therefore permitted the child's parents to order the hospital to starve the baby to death.

The fatal move is in the elevation of the concept of citizen. The concept of citizen is then conflated with, and finally swallows, the reality of persons. That fatal move was made in *Dred Scott* and has since been carried much further. In 1957, Chief Justice Earl Warren wrote: "Citizenship *is* man's basic right for it is nothing less than the right to have rights. Remove this priceless possession and . . . his very existence is at the sufferance of the state within whose borders he happens to be." Bickel comments as an aside, "As if our government were in the habit of beheading people for not being citizens!" Against Warren's logic we must insist, both theologically and constitutionally, that people have "the right to have rights" *as people*. With Bickel we contend that "citizenship is a legal construct, an abstraction, a theory. . . . It is by such thinking, as in Rousseau's *The Social Contract*, that the claims of liberty may be readily translated into the postulates of oppression." The concept of citizenship "subsumes important obligations and functions of the individual which have other sources—moral, political, and traditional—sources more complex than the simple contractarian notion of citizenship."

One enters the public square, then, not as an anonymous citizen but as a person shaped by "other sources" that are neither defined by nor subservient to the public square. The public square is not a secular and morally sterilized space but a space for conversation, contention, and compromise among moral actors. Compromise is not mere fudging, then. It is not morally compromising. Within a universe compromised by fallen humanity, compromise is an exercise of moral responsibility by persons who accept responsibility for sustaining the exercise that is called democracy.

CHAPTER EIGHT

Private Morality, Public Virtue

IT IS A PERVERSE MINDSET THAT INSISTS THAT THE RELATION-
ship between church and state must always be one of conflict and confrontation. Life is problematic enough without picking fights. Yet Christians of uneasy conscience are sometimes led to act as though they cannot
be true Christians unless persecuted by the state; the hostility of Caesar
becomes the measure of one's friendship with Christ. In the long reaches
of Christian history and, sad to say, in large parts of the world today
persecution need not be contrived. In societies such as ours, which place
no formal liabilities upon being Christian, the contriving of persecution
can only trivialize the very real persecution of Christians elsewhere.
Achieving "victim status" is not the purity test for the true Christianity.
It is a sorry thing if a Christian adolescent has not had romantic dreams
about enduring a martyr's death. It is a sorrier thing if he continues to
indulge such dreams in adulthood. We sing stirring songs of discipleship:

> A glorious band, the chosen few,
> On whom the Spirit came,
> Twelve valiant saints; their hope they knew
> And mocked the cross and flame.
> They met the tyrant's brandished steel,
> The lion's gory mane;
> They bowed their necks the death to feel
> —Who follows in their train?

And then we get in the station wagon and go home for Sunday dinner and
football.

There is not necessarily anything wrong with that. Not necessarily.
To the contrary, there may be reason to give thanks for the nonincompat-
ibility of Christian discipleship and Superbowl CLXII. Our society contains strong elements of contempt for Christian values, and religion that
too insistently presses upon the public arena may encounter a degree of
open hostility. But lions of gory mane are not in prospect. Even if, as some
fear, we were by domestic madness or external force to succumb to a form
of totalitarianism, it would likely be marked by a measure of tolerance for
the expression of religion, within bounds. In view of all this, then, a case

can be made for leaving well enough alone. Why press points of tension and conflict between church and state when, all things considered, we have it so very good?

In truth, in relations between church and state, models of complementarity and cooperation are to be favored over conflict. At the same time, tensions are inherent in the relationship, and tensions will inevitably, from time to time, erupt in conflict. Perhaps we should not say that it is inevitable. There is the alternative of the theocratic model, in which the state succumbs to the church. And there is the alternative of erastianism, in which the church succumbs to the state. If we reject these alternatives, however, endemic tension and episodic conflict are inevitable. Many formulas have been offered for containing such tension and conflict. One current formula is that the relationship between church and state should follow the model of "functional interaction and institutional separation."[1]

The problem, of course, is that neither is prepared to remain within its institutional boundaries. Government, if it is to be sustainable, engages beliefs and loyalties of an ultimate sort that can properly be called religious. As the impulse of the modern state is to define all public space as governmental space, so the consequence is a tendency toward "civil religion." Religion, on the other hand, if it represents a comprehensive belief system, speaks to the human condition in all its aspects, including the right ordering (the government) of public life. In short, government does not have a monopoly on government, nor religion a monopoly on religion. Each sphere of activity, however, finds expression in institutions that tend to claim such a monopoly. Thus each institution is, in the eyes of the other, constantly bursting its bounds. Therein is the foundation of the open-ended argument between church and state. Open-ended, that is, so long as a society professes to be democratic.

In discussing church and state it is necessary to maintain the institutional focus. Otherwise we end up talking about everything, and thus about nothing. For example, to the educator all of human life may fall under the rubric of education. To those professionally concerned with public health, there is nothing outside the infinitely expandable category of health. (Little wonder that a Department of Health, Education and Welfare aroused the suspicions of conservatives who thought the title implied government control over the totality of life.) So also to the conscientiously religious, there is nothing that is not religious. Just as politics can become an idol, so religion can become an idol. This happens when what is institutionally identifiable as religion is permitted to gobble up all other human activities, denying them their proper autonomy in the created order. Today we witness a strange convergence of idolatrous propensities. This is evident when Christians assert that all significant questions are finally political questions. It happens when political goals are incorporated within

130

and equated with what Christianity means by salvation. It matters little whether the political goal be liberation through class struggle or the victory of freedom through the defeat of Communism.

Psychiatrists such as Robert Coles and Thomas Szasz have reminded us of the ways in which psychotherapy has become a comprehensive religious vision for many in the modern world. Equally comprehensive is the vision of "the new man in the new society" proposed by some Marxist thinkers. The felt need for some conceptual construct that can "get it all together" is perfectly understandable. The world is so confusedly in pieces and, in the words of perhaps the most cited poem of the century, "the center does not hold." Christians should nonetheless resist all temptations to get it all together before God has gotten it altogether in the coming of his kingdom. There is nothing wrong with viewing the world through a particular and partial prism. Indeed we have no choice but to do that. What we call reality is "constructed" in large part by our experience, interests, and commitments.[2] This is borne out in very obvious and mundane ways. A mortician, dentist, and prostitute walking through the same crowd will likely "see" quite different realities. As I say, that is obvious and not very problematic, except perhaps to the persons immediately involved. But in modern society we have presumed to differentiate, even to segregate, less functionally specific interests. Comprehensive categories such as health, education, and economics can be expanded to include almost everything. Especially is this true of religion and politics.

Despite the sprawl of some categories, we do think that, when need arises, we can specify what we want to talk about. We might, for instance, agree at some level of abstraction that all of life is education. But when we speak in public about education we mean those institutions—schools, teaching professions, curricula—that constitute education as distinct from economics or entertainment. Both religion and politics, however, are less easily defined and contained. Religion (*religare*—to bind) deals with the ultimate meanings and obligations in the whole of life. Politics, especially modern politics, tends to assume that "government" and "society" are interchangeable terms. Thus religion and politics contend for dominance over the same territory. Both are political in the sense of being engaged in a struggle for power. Both are religious in the sense of making a total claim upon life. (Some theological abstractions to the contrary, Christianity *as religion* is engaged in the struggle for power, despite its message being centered in the powerlessness of the cross.)

The contention between religion and politics (resulting in politics-as-religion and in religion-as-politics) takes many forms. One form of perennial contention is over specific issues of public policy: prayer in the schools, certification of Christian schools, abortion, tax exemption, and the like. There is a prior territory of contention, however. It is from this contention that specific controversies arise and are given their shape. That prior territory in contention might, quite generally, be called culture. Religion and politics are today engaged in a struggle over culture definition and culture formation. Admittedly, culture is a notoriously slippery term. For our immediate purposes we can employ the definition offered by sociologist Clifford Geertz. Culture, says Geertz, is "an historically transmitted pattern of meanings embodied in symbols, a system of inherited conceptions expressed in symbolic forms by means of which men communicate, perpetuate and develop their knowledge about and attitudes toward life."[3] Culture is "historically transmitted" and "inherited," but it is also undergoing constant change. In a living culture, the legacy is always being retranslated and redefined.

Put alongside Geertz's definition of culture his definition of religion. Religion, he writes, is "a system of symbols which acts to establish powerful, pervasive, and long-lasting moods and motivations . . . by formulating conceptions of a general order of existence and clothing those conceptions with such an aura of factuality that the moods and motivations seem uniquely realistic."[4] The Christian believer should not be disturbed that Geertz's is such a very "human" definition of religion. That is his business as sociologist. The believer—and, for all I know, Clifford Geertz himself—would want to insist that religion, at least Christianity, is about God, revelation, creation, redemption, and the promise of ultimate vindication. The theological and sociological views are not mutually exclusive. God's revelation in Christ is, in sociological language, the "system of symbols" by which Christians construct a world that is "uniquely realistic." As Christians, we want immediately to add that it is uniquely realistic because it is uniquely real, that is to say, uniquely true. But that assertion is beyond the competence of social science either to affirm or deny.

The crucial point here is to note the similarity between Geertz's definition of culture and his definition of religion. They are so similar that we may be tempted to accuse Geertz of a lack of conceptual clarity. But it is likely he and others do not propose a sharper distinction between religion and culture because a sharper distinction would be false to the facts. Clearly, there is a necessary unclarity; there is a very broad overlap between religion and culture. Religion would appear to be the ground or the depth-level of culture. Or, as it has sometimes been proposed, religion is the heart of culture and culture is the form of religion. On this view, then, politics is a function of culture and culture, in turn, is reflective of (if not a function of) religion.

Religion and politics meet at many points but most critically they meet at the point of culture-formation. A kind of "realist" argument can be made that politics is only the process of getting and keeping power. But a realism that excludes from consideration the force of culture (including religiously grounded morality) has properly been described as crackpot re-

132

alism. Were politics only the quest for personal and institutional power, there would be little contest between church and state. The state would win hands down, for it alone has the distinct advantage of being able to call in the police. As the regime in Poland, to cite but one example, should understand, power that is exercised in contradiction to culture is very fragile. It depends overwhelmingly, sometimes exclusively, upon coercion. It is not legitimate power; that is, it is not morally legitimated. It may have sounded realistic at the time but in truth it was extraordinarily naive of Stalin to ask, "How many divisions does the pope have?"

Objections are raised to the line of argument advanced so far. It is suggested, for example, that the idea that religion and politics are competing forces in the shaping of culture is now outdated. It used to be that way, it is said, and still is that way in primitive societies. But the great achievement of modern democratic societies is to clearly differentiate, if not to separate, the several spheres of societal action. Culture, including religion, is one sphere; government is another, and economics is yet another. In primitive societies there is one central authority. Some kind of priest-king presides over the whole of society, including its economic activities. In modern democratic society, the economic differentiation is represented by the free market of democratic capitalism, and the distinction between priest and king is assured by the separation of church and state. So the objection is stated, and there is considerable merit to it.

As an "ideal type" this tripartite distinction can be affirmed against the monistic hungers of those who strive to devise a social order that "gets it all together." Not only is it an ideal type, but this model is to a large extent in fact characteristic of advanced democratic societies. In such societies government is forced to be relatively modest and even self-limiting. The state is seen as the pragmatic broker between countervailing interests; it is not the generator or promulgator of values. On this view, the state does not presume to address ultimate issues nor to claim transcendent authority for its decisions. It is a classically liberal view and is highly unsatisfactory to those who want politics to deal not only with procedural questions but also with the substantive questions of justice, the common good, and even transcendent destiny. In recent decades it has been noted frequently that young people—but not only young people—want politics to provide a compelling moral vision. To which classical liberals (now sometimes called neo-conservatives) respond that that is precisely what government is not supposed to do. Providing moral vision, they insist, is a dangerous departure from the competence of government.

This approach contains important truth, I believe. The generation and promulgation of moral visions is primarily the business of other institutions in society, not of the government. Nonetheless, the theory is, like all theories, limited in application. We are more familiar with the questions raised about the distinction between economics and government than we are with the questions that need to be raised about the distinction between government and culture. It is commonly understood, for instance, that ours is not a pure free-market capitalist society. We use terms such as "welfare capitalism" or "mixed economy" to describe the actual state of affairs. Some bemoan and others cheer the departures from the strict separation of market and state. Those who defend government intervention in the market do so on both pragmatic and moral grounds. Pragmatically, it is said to be necessary to the successful functioning of the economy; morally, it is said to be necessary to assuring that the economy functions to the benefit also of the disadvantaged.

The debate about economics and government is familiar and the torrent of literature it has produced shows no signs of abating. That is not true of the relationship between culture and government. There is a literature, not terribly well known, on the totalitarian impulse, usually written from a conservative slant and cautioning against the dangers of government's presuming to exercise total control over the society. In addition, theologians and some social scientists are at home with the discussion of "civil religion," the ways in which government places a transcendent or quasi-transcendent halo around itself. But, in general, we are more familiar with the debate about government and economics than about government and culture because we suppose we know more about economics. Dollars and cents, inflation and unemployment are presented in neat and measurable terms. The same cannot be done with "historically transmitted patterns of meaning by which societies perpetuate and communicate their knowledge and attitudes toward life." Upon closer examination we may be inclined to believe that, compared to economics, theology takes on the appearance of being an exact science. But that is not the popular view of things. Economics and politics are the patois of newspapers and newscasts, and we assume their intelligibility. The attention given culture in the media is largely limited to the arts (those activities we call "cultural") and entertainment.

The ideal type of the tripartite design of society is, as we have seen, confused by the interaction between government and economics. It is at least equally confused by the interaction between government and culture. Insofar as politics deals with purely instrumental and procedural issues, a kind of commonsensical "muddling through" will do. Fortunately, most political issues are, despite the high moral rhetoric in which they are debated, at that instrumental level. It is a question of what will work in order to achieve agreed-upon ends. But, as we have seen, substantive questions erupt from time to time; the ends as well as the means come into question. Basic questions are posed, demanding basic answers as to what we believe about justice, about personal rights and communal obligations, and even about who is included in the network of societal protections.

According to liberal democratic theory such questions should erupt very rarely, if at all. In *Federalist No. 10,* James Madison wrote on the dangers of "factions" that might press first-principle questions beyond the limit of the polity to deal with them. He was especially wary of factions attached to some religious cause. It seems he might have had today's moral majoritarians in mind. He was somewhat sanguine, however, in view of the disparate and separated nature of the confederacy. His reasons for confidence are not so convincing in today's America:

> The influence of factious leaders may kindle a flame within their particular States, but will be unable to spread a general conflagration through the other States. A religious sect may degenerate into a political faction in a part of the Confederacy; but the variety of sects dispersed over the entire face of it must secure the national councils against any danger from that source. . . . [A faction] will be less apt to pervade the whole body of the Union than a particular member of it; in the same proportion as such a malady is more likely to taint a particular county or district, than an entire State.

Today's mass communications, taking their cues from a very few prestige organs, would seem to have changed all that. The factious first-principle questions can still be muted, however. This is the case because, despite certain conspiracy theories about media mandarins, there is not a consciously imposed party line on all issues of moment. There is not such a party line excluding the eruption of ultimacies because, as discussed earlier, the communications media are concerned about advertising markets, and thus about public affairs as entertainment. This evening's news about controversy over the meaning of life will surely be eclipsed by tomorrow's about the fiscal and sexual peccadillos of some Washington official. Thus sustained attention to factious absolutes is precluded and the polity is protected from an overload of meaning.

In the tradition of Enlightenment liberalism espoused by Madison, there are several stratagems aimed at keeping public space clear of metaphysical debate about ultimacies. One stratagem is to redefine all questions about values in terms of contests of "interests." As William Sullivan puts it in *Reconstructing Public Philosophy*: "The effect was to dissolve values into power, specifically, power to augment and foster the individual's passion-driven will."[5] Behind this dissolution of the force of value questions is the assumption that the base unit, indeed the only unit, in society is the individual. Individuals are driven by passions—avoiding pain and seeking comfort—and enter into a contract that aims at the adjudication of conflicts between individual passions. Apart from power struggle, the only court of appeal is a notion of "reason" that is severely truncated. That is, "reason" is defined as being limited to what, in the modern world, is called science. Science is limited to those realities that can be empirically observed, measured, and predicted under controlled circumstances. But, of course, life is not a laboratory; most of the things that we believe really matter—love, community, honor, purpose in life—are not subject to scientific measure and control.

But surely the founders such as Madison and Hamilton were aware of the limitations of the formal liberalism they propounded. They knew there was another tradition that spoke of "republican virtues" and thought it very much the business of government to cultivate such virtues. Sullivan describes that other tradition:

> Compared to the instrumental cast of liberal thought, with its affinity for mechanical metaphors of social life, the republican tradition has seen politics as essentially the application of prudence, an understanding that relies on a sense of practical reason missing from the liberal ideal of rationality. Civic republican thought derives from the political philosophy of classical antiquity, was developed by the medieval Christian concern for individual dignity and universal participation, and received new impetus through the Renaissance and developments surrounding the new states of early modern Europe. *As a tradition, it differs strongly from liberalism in its emphasis on the values of politics as moral cultivation of responsible selves.*[6] (emphasis added)

Also, the tradition of republican virtue recognizes the rule of culture and the fact that culture is composed not just of individuals but of communities. These communities are the bearers of values and truth claims that impinge upon the political process. "Instrumental liberalism," with its mechanistic view of politics, is not unaware of this impingement, but it views it as a disagreeable factor that is to be kept to an absolute minimum, if it cannot be eliminated entirely. Especially when it comes to religion, there are ultra-strict separationists who are determined to eliminate the impingement. More moderate instrumentalists, however, have realized that an absolute divorce of government from the operative values of the people would lead to an impossible legitimation crisis. They are therefore prepared to make some accommodation.

Once again, Sullivan puts it well:

> The peculiarity of the development of liberalism in America gives a unique texture to American liberal political thought. Because liberal ideas of politics became significant during the same revolutionary struggle against an identified despotism that also brought civic republicanism to the fore, liberalism in America has to absorb into its outlook a number of republican concerns. In addition, the unique religious climate of America meant that biblical religious language and organizations played an early role which reinforced rather than opposed the emerging political culture, so that American liberalism, unlike European forms, has not usually been hostile to religious teaching and practice. *Still, religious language on the national political level has frequently served as a substitute for explicit republican language, diluting republicanism's coherence as an alternative to liberalism.*[7] (emphasis added)

136

Three observations are in order, then, First, we are dealing with a style of liberalism that, in its "pure" form, has neither need nor use for religion. The perdurance and pervasiveness of religion is an embarrassment. It cannot be coherently included but it can be, to the degree necessary, accommodated. To try to eliminate it would be exceedingly imprudent. Such accommodation, while a practical necessity, is a theoretical embarrassment. It mightily confuses the machine-like design of the political process. Second, more moderate souls among instrumental liberals share the commonsensical intuition that vast dimensions of human life cannot be accounted for within the terms of power struggle or of a truncated rationalism. Whether willingly or reluctantly, they therefore adopt a rather modest notion of the competence of government. The concerns of those vast dimensions will be taken care of elsewhere—in churches, families, voluntary associations, and the like. There is much that is attractive in this approach. Its terrible flaw, however, is that it draws an unsustainable line between public and private. What is public and therefore the appropriate concern of government is limited to what can be fitted into a mechanistic political process. All the other business of society is taken care of "elsewhere." Those realities most important to our lives— belief, purpose, truth claims—have no place in the public square.

The third observation is that the most culturally influential religious forces in American life have tended to support a view of liberalism in which religion can impinge upon, but never really belong in, public space. By supporting liberal doctrine in theory, these religious forces would seem to be working for their own exclusion from the public square. At the same time, however, they want to be "politically relevant." The ironic result is that they exercise their political influence by reinforcing the parties that would reduce or eliminate the influence of religion. With the exception of issues related to tax exemption—which almost all religious institutions jealously guard—the public program of many mainline churches is hardly distinguishable from the program of the American Civil Liberties Union for the elimination of religious influence from American public life.

I am far from convinced of the spiritual imperative of classroom prayer in public schools, but there is no disputing the fact that its elimination was a further step in the "secularizing" of public institutions. Its elimination is generally supported by mainline churches. The same churches oppose the legal protection of the unborn because that would be an "imposition of religion" upon public policy. They also generally agree that education, at least at the elementary and secondary levels, is an exclusive preserve of government, and therefore government support must be limited to government schools. On issues related to the "rights" of children and adolescents, they generally come down on the side of an individualistic notion of privacy, as opposed to the norms of familial and

137

communal authority. In the tradition of republican virtue, politics is the cultivation of a community of morally responsible persons. In that view of politics, the churches would presumably have much to say. Many of our churches today, however, have aligned themselves with the view of politics as the individualistic contest of passions, tempered only by scientific reason. In that view of politics the churches have little or nothing to say. In its public interventions today, mainline Protestant religion is typically advancing a view of politics and society in which religion has no right to intervene.

The divorce of the state from the culture, and from the religion that is at the heart of the culture, is both old and new. As we have seen, such a divorce is theoretically mandated by a strictly instrumental view of politics embraced by some of the founders. At that time, and during most of our history, that view lived in tension with a more inclusive view of politics that comprehended the importance of public virtue. While the strict instrumental view prevailed in the constitutional structuring of the American polity, the strict instrumentalists did not try to impose their view strictly. In our more recent history they have tried, and, remarkably enough, they have had the wholehearted cooperation of religious forces that, in theory, one would expect to oppose their purposes. The strict instrumentalists are the "secular humanists" of fundamentalist propaganda. Because the far right tends to be as addicted to conspiracy theories as is the far left, the moral majoritarians have little patience with the idea that liberal religion's cooperation with "secular humanism" is another instance of what Reinhold Niebuhr called "the ironies of American history." In their view that cooperation is quite conscious and by design, a case of pseudo-Christians deliberately subverting "Christian America."

We earlier took note of statements of John Adams and others to the effect that a notion of limited government, such as ours, assumes that the business of values and culture is being taken care of "elsewhere." Throughout most of our history, the proposition that ours is a nation "under God" (although formally stated only in 1954), or that this is in some significant sense a Christian society, provided the background to the formal polity. It was the set, as it were, for the political stage. Today that background consensus cannot be taken for granted; indeed, it is increasingly and explicitly challenged. In the absence of such a set, however, the political actors play upon a naked stage. In this event, the action has lost its context, not only in the sense of a background but also of a continuing story or purpose that bestows meaning upon the action. Our public life becomes impromptu theater. Individual actors bump into one another, "inventing" their selves and their stories, restrained only by procedural rules about how much damage can be done to those one bumps up against. In the absence of a religio-cultural story line, the political action is forced back upon itself, it must declare itself self-legitimating. But politics is not an end in itself; it is not, except for some politics junkies, a game played for its own sake.

The strict separation of culture and state has been celebrated by historians such as Daniel Boorstin as "the genius of American politics." It is called pragmatism and it has a powerful appeal to people of a practical bent. Hannah Arendt, among others, has perceptively criticized this understanding of the political:

> This bias, as a matter of fact, is neither anti-theoretical as such nor specific to an American "frame of mind." The hostility between philosophy and politics, barely covered up by a philosophy of politics, has been the curse of Western statecraft as well as of the Western tradition of philosophy ever since the men of action and the men of thought parted company—that is, ever since Socrates' death. The ancient conflict is relevant only in the strictly secular realm and therefore played a minor role during the long centuries when religion and religious concerns dominated the political sphere; but it was only natural that it should have assumed renewed importance during the birth and rebirth of an authentically political realm, that is, in the course of modern revolutions.[8]

Critics such as Arendt recognized a part of the dilemma: the "ancient conflict" between thought and action, belief and pragmatism, culture and statecraft. This conflict is not addressed by our prevailing political theories today. Arendt, like Alasdair MacIntyre later, believed that linkages could be restored by revitalizing something like classical Greek philosophy in the modern political arena. Among those who urge such a restoration, the assumption often is that there is a necessary connection between "the strictly secular realm" and the "authentically political realm." It is suggested that you can't have one without the other; in fact, strictly secular and authentically political may be the same thing. Of the two main sources of Western civilization—the classical and the Judeo-Christian—the classical is thought to be compatible with a strictly secular understanding of politics. In any case, it is assumed that "the long centuries of religious dominance" are decisively in the past.

Contrary to the dogmas of secular Enlightenment, however, religion has neither withered away nor can it successfully be confined to the private spheres of life. The social scientists who until recently argued that there is a necessary connection between modernization and increased secularization have in many instances done an about-face. The social hypothesis could not withstand the social fact. If "the men of action and the men of thought" are to be reconciled, it will have to be in working toward a new synthesis that reappropriates the biblical as well as the classical tradition. This is the case if only because such a synthesis must be supported democratically in order to be viewed as morally legitimate. Again, the democratic reality, even, if you will, the raw demographic reality, is that most Americans derive their values and visions from the biblical tradition.

Aristotle's beliefs about the ultimate good do not carry the weight of St. Paul's. Both Aristotle and Paul, when addressing ultimacies, are religious. Restoring the linkage with Athenian ultimacies is no more compatible with maintaining politics as a "strictly secular realm" than is restoring the linkage with biblical ultimacies. This truth is obscured by secular intellectuals who are primarily concerned with the theocratic threat and are obviously more comfortable with Aristotle's religion than with Paul's. One reason for this greater comfort is that intellectuals have a monopoly on the interpretation of classical belief systems. The exegesis of Aristotle and Plato is reserved to the academy, whereas the exegesis of the Bible is a mass industry employing millions of professional and part-time believers. Choosing classical religion over biblical religion protects public philosophy as an aristocratic enterprise. It does not threaten the monopoly of the certified keepers and definers of the sacred cultural symbols. For the same reason, however, it cannot provide a public philosophy that is democratically legitimate.

The revived interest in "public virtue" today is often described as a conservative or "neo-conservative" phenomenon. That is accurate, in part. There has been understandable reaction to the lethal liberationisms that reached their frenzied apex in the late sixties and early seventies. Drugs, cults, mass sex murders, the explosion in divorce, teen-age pregnancies, and abortion—all these have, in the eyes of conservatives, vindicated their warnings about the consequences of cultural decadence. But those who think of themselves as liberals have also been shaken by the unmistakable evidence of the fragility of the social bond. How can the most vulnerable— minorities, the handicapped, the aged—be protected if there is no moral consensus about what is right and just, if we no longer affirm the virtues of fairness and caring. For liberal reasons, therefore, there is an appreciative reexamination of conservative premises about politics and society.

It is more widely recognized that a bare-bones constitutional polity, based on individualism and self-interest, assumes that there are other spheres of activity and other institutions for the cultivation of the virtue that makes it possible for such a polity to work. These activities and institutions must be included in our notion of what is public. For most of our history, mainline Protestant religion did attend to the cultivation of individual and communal virtue, and to maintaining a sense of national purpose, even of destiny. Only in its ruthlessly secularized version did the American polity appear as a procedural skeleton devoid of substantive beliefs about personal and public good.

The historical fact cannot be exhausted by the instrumental theory. Chesterton's observation that America is a nation with the soul of a church underscores the fact that Americans are a people on purpose and by purpose. In most other major nations, the people were prior to the polity. America, however, has been fabricated, in the precise sense of that term, by ideas and beliefs. Religion provided the "sacred canopy" (Berger) under which that deliberate construction took place. For this reason Tocqueville could confidently assert that religion is America's "first political institution." The founders' talk about "Nature and Nature's God" was a lowest common denominator form of ecumenism aimed at comprehending a diversity of beliefs, but it was not just rhetorical fluff. A limited, individualistic, and procedure-based polity was only plausible because so much else was already in place, so to speak. The values and virtues that the polity assumed were chiefly the business of religion. But there was no "separation" in the sense that term has assumed today. There was the liveliest interaction among the several players in the public arena. Indeed, the First Amendment of the federal Constitution did not prohibit established churches in the several states, and some persisted for decades after the Constitution's adoption. There was, in short, an expansive understanding of what was "public" in American life. The American polity did not assume that what was "authentically political" must be "strictly secular."

Some of those who deplore the decline of the public role of religion accuse militant secularists of engineering that decline. No doubt there have been and there are dogmatic secularists who have engaged in a veritable crusade to expunge the symbols and substance of religion from the public square. These religionists, however, seldom recognize the degree to which they have collaborated in their enemy's crusade. Stanley Hauerwas perceptively describes the consequences when believers succumb to secularism's dictum that religion be limited to the private sphere:

> Yet the very theory that has formed our public rhetoric and institutions gives no sufficient public basis for the development [of a virtuous] people. It was assumed that in making "morality" a matter of the "private sphere"—that is, what we do with our freedom—it could still be sustained and have an indirect public impact. But we know this has not been the case: *our "private" morality has increasingly followed the form of our public life.* People feel their only public duty is to follow their own interests as far as possible, limited only by the rule that we do not unfairly limit others' freedom. As a result we have found it increasingly necessary to substitute procedures and competition for the absence of public virtues. The bureaucracies in our lives are not simply the result of the complexities of an industrialized society, but a requirement of a social order individualistically organized.[9] (emphasis added)

Religion has followed the form of the polity. This is a critical reversal of affairs. The constitutional polity was not intended to bear the burden of cultivating virtue. Indeed virtue was outside the sphere of the polity, but not outside the sphere of what is public. The force of virtue was thought to be both prior to and reinforcing of the polity. The polity presupposed a culture of virtue; it was not intended to replace it and it could not create a new one in its place. The fateful mistake was to take the description of the polity for a description of the society. As Hauerwas argues, the churches also succumbed to that mistake. Instead of religion sustaining communities of virtue that could inform public discourse, it acquiesced in being relegated to the private sphere where it did a thriving business in "meeting the needs" of individuals for spiritual and other satisfactions. And when religion does—as biblical religion must—address public issues, it too often does so in a way that accepts the framing of the question without reference to anything specifically religious. It is pleased to be admitted as a guest to the public debate and takes care to behave by the rules prescribed by the host. This perhaps unconscious collaboration with secularism's agenda was reflected in the 1960s slogan of some ecumenical agencies, "The world sets the agenda for the church."

The churches, then, cannot stand aloof from the gathering legitimation crisis in our public life. They are in large part responsible for it. In addition to their responsibility—both in terms of blame and potential contribution to the remedy—they have a strong self-interest to protect. Very basic notions of religious freedom depend upon an understanding of religion as the bearer of transcendent truth to which the nation is accountable. Otherwise, the church is but one institution among many, indeed one corporation among many. Were that view to prevail, the consequences are far-reaching. An obvious consequence is that tax exemption would then become what some already claim it is, a "tax subsidy." What the government subsidizes the government should control. Another consequence is what might be called the deinstitutionalizing of religious truth claims. That sounds like a fine and liberating thing, until we recognize that it really means the reduction of all moral claims to individualistic passion. Then indeed every question of value is dissolved into a question of power.

A corollary of this is that, when the value-bearing institutions no longer have public status, they are reduced to public (read governmental) control. An extreme instance of this occurred a decade ago when Episcopalians were debating the ordination of women. Some who favored the change went to court in order to have the government rule that the denial of ordination to women was an illegal violation of civil rights. The effort did not succeed, but the implications of its possible success are stunning to contemplate. When an institution that is voluntary in membership cannot define the conditions of belonging, that institution in fact ceases to exist. Legal measures that aim at imposing individualistic rules of fair play are usually seen as threatening to authoritarian groups that impose various loyalty tests upon their members. But doctrinally latitudinarian bodies are equally threatened, for they too have internal tests of membership, even if those tests have more to do with procedure than with belief.

Hauerwas is certainly correct: "Our 'private' morality has increasingly followed the form of our public life." The religion that was the premise of the public polity increasingly imitates and is thereby dissolved into the polity it once supported and informed. When this happens the church is no longer able to contribute to the reconstruction of a public philosophy. Then the field is left to others: those who would reestablish a moral basis for a public ethic from the Aristotelian heritage, and those who would rehabilitate the notion of a social contract based on individual interests alone. There are many contenders for the job of asserting the public philosophy, including some who abhor the notion of public philosophy itself. That is, there are those who are still convinced that all that is needed is a more rational fine-tuning of politics as a "strictly secular realm," hoping that religiously tainted invasions of the realm can be definitively defeated.

CHAPTER NINE

THE PURLOINED
AUTHORITY OF THE STATE

RELIGION IS INCORRIGIBLY INTERVENTIONIST. JUDEO-CHRIS-
tian religion with its universalistic claims to truth relates to the totality of things. Christ is Lord of all or he is Lord not at all, as we have
already noted. To those outside the community of faith, and to many
within it, claims such as this seem to pose a threat of a different totalitarianism. In this view the totalitarian threat of the modern state is sub-
ordinated to an appreciation of the state's power to check the ambitions
of religion. Jacob Burckhardt, the great nineteenth-century Swiss historian,
saw the state, religion, and culture as "the three great powers."[1] He had
no difficulty in specifying the historical periods in which state and religion,
or both in collusion, attempted to exercise total control over the society.
For him, culture was the realm of freedom, of spontaneity. Culture encompassed "all social intercourse, technologies, arts, literatures, and sciences." "It is," he wrote, "the realm of the variable, free, not necessarily
universal, of all that cannot lay claim to compulsive authority."

Our earlier discussion of culture is dramatically different from Burckhardt's. It is perhaps peculiarly attuned to the American experience. As a
result, as we noted in Geertz's definitions of culture and religion, religion
in America can be perceived as part of that cultural "realm of freedom."
Thanks to the logic inherent in the First Amendment, religion "cannot lay
claim to compulsive authority" in America. Religion cannot call in the
police to enforce its truth claims. Although not writing from a specifically
American perspective, sociologist Thomas Luckmann analyzes what he
calls "invisible religion" in modern culture.[2] According to Luckmann, religion increasingly retreats into the private, purely elective, dimensions of
personal life and life in small communities. It loses entirely its public
character, not to mention its "claim to compulsive authority." The mem-
ories of Christendom may provide an aura around cultural discourse, but
religion is no longer able to intervene in the public arena; as a matter of
private taste, of individual choice about how best to meet metaphysical
needs, it is not a proper consideration in the process of ordering public life.

Many radical civil libertarians today are still influenced by Burckhardt's nineteenth-century view of religion. In their view the threat of the
reimposition of Christendom is a lively reason for fear. For understandable
reasons, many of this viewpoint are Jewish. As a rabbi friend once re-

marked, "When I hear the term 'Christian America,' I see barbed wire." Also within the Christian communities, there are those who fear the return of Christendom. This is especially true of those who have come out from a fundamentalist background. We witness what might be termed "the syndrome of the narrow escape." By this I refer to those who come from a religious experience, often Southern, that they viewed as anti-intellectual and oppressive. Having escaped from the religious farm, so to speak, they have found liberation in the city of more cosmopolitan discourse. They are often in leadership positions in the academic and bureaucratic worlds of religion. As with the radical libertarians, they take alarm at any hint of religiously grounded moral majoritarianism. They are not at all sure that, if it could, religion would not "lay claim to compulsive authority." For them, the naked public square is essential to assuring the realm of freedom.

Our understanding of the role of religion in American life (and, we would argue, the constitutional understanding) is neither that of those who fear the return of an oppressive Christendom nor that of those who suggest that religion is dissolved entirely into the categories of culture and the meeting of private needs. Our understanding is closer to that of Adams, Tocqueville, Lincoln, and a host of others who understood religiously based values as the points of reference for public moral discourse. In saying this, the suspicion is raised that one wants to go back to an earlier era in American life, and it is thought to be axiomatic that "you can't go home again." The question must at least be raised, however, whether our time is in fact so distant or so different from that of, say, the mid-nineteenth century in America. We are indeed a more pluralistic society in the sense of including people of various national, racial, and cultural experiences. The immigration policies of the United States assure that this pluralism will be even more magnified in the future. (While we think of the "great era" of immigration as the late nineteenth and early twentieth century, it should be noted that more immigrants entered America in the 1970s than in any other decade of American history.) Despite this much-discussed pluralism, however, over ninety percent of the American people say they believe in God and think the Judeo-Christian tradition is somehow morally normative for personal and public life. Not as much has changed as those who have a vested interest in proclaiming changes would suggest. Much is made of the influx of people from the Orient and of the influence of Eastern religions among some young Americans of Western background. This emphasis is pronounced in the writing of sociologists working in the Bay Area of San Francisco.[3]

The attraction of Eastern cults among the young seems to be on the decline in the 1980s. In addition, those attracted tend to sectarian patterns of withdrawal and are therefore largely irrelevant to the *public* ethos. The *polis* of chief concern to them is typically that of the small community under the leadership of a guru of their choice. As to those with whom

145

Eastern religion is indigenous, no lines of moral confrontation have been drawn against the prevailing Judeo-Christian ethos. Whether that is yet to come or whether it is in the nature of, say, Buddhism not to draw such lines is a subject that would carry us beyond the scope of the present discussion. Here we would only observe that such lines have not been drawn and contend, further, that the religious freedom of those outside the Judeo-Christian consensus is best protected by grounding such freedom in that consensus.

In recent decades, "pluralism" has become something of a buzzword. It is variously employed. Often it is used to argue that no normative ethic, even of the vaguest and most tentative sort, can be "imposed" in our public life. In practice this means that public policy decisions reflect a surrender of the normal to the abnormal, of the dominant to the deviant. Indeed it is of more than passing interest that terms such as abnormal or deviant have been largely exorcised from polite vocabulary among the elites in American life. The displacement of the constitutive by the marginal is not so much the result of perverse decision makers as it is the inevitable consequence of a polity and legal system in which the advantage of initiative lies with the offended. Terms such as "minorities" and "the marginal" have a high moral status in our society. Ironically, this too is deeply rooted in the Judeo-Christian tradition. Biblical justice is obsessively concerned with life along the fault lines of society, with the "orphans and widows and fatherless children." Special attention must be paid "the stranger within thy gates." When such mandates to benevolence are legalistically codified, however, the claims of those who deviate from the moral consensus constitute a powerful leverage against the consensus that gives moral status to the claims in the first place. Thus it is asserted that one who deviates has the "right" not to be affected, at least in public, by the beliefs, symbols, and rules of the majority culture. The annual legal actions against Christmas trees in public places, while apparently a small issue, reflect this skewing of the public ethos.

There is further irony: the dignity and honor of dissent disappears with the disappearance of a public norm that alone can give meaning to dissent. In the absence of such norm, everybody is a dissident and nobody is a dissident. The result, not surprisingly, is pervasive dissension. Every rule (nomos) is, as Peter Berger has observed, a private nomos.[4] As a consequence, we have noted, every value judgment is merely the assertion of a private "interest." At a level that brings this home to the outrage of many Americans, the protection of an "alternative life-style" such as homosexuality turns heterosexual marriage into just another "alternative life-style." In this way, the Judeo-Christian ethic, when legalistically implemented, works against itself; the morally mandated respect for the marginal assures that the center cannot hold. In this process of Christianity's undoing of itself, some, also some Christians, see a progress of secularization of which they approve. This too is part of what was celebrated as "secular Christianity" a decade and more ago. Most Christians, however, were not persuaded that the fulfillment of the church's public mission should be the church's going out of public business.

What is frequently meant by pluralism today is a legalized secular distortion of Judeo-Christian concern for the marginal. The result is often ludicrous and meets with almost no public approbation. The "free exercise of religion" becomes the legally protected right of the dissident to freedom from religion's exercise. For example, lawyers challenge a judge who is a Mormon from presiding at a trial dealing with sex discrimination. He might be influenced by his religion. For example, legal restrictions on the government funding of abortions is declared unconstitutional because Catholic legislators were likely influenced by their religious beliefs. For example, after-school meetings on school property can deal with any subject—political, philosophical, sexual, social—except religion. In short, the public exercise of religion is prohibited as an "establishment" of religion.

From time to time, this extraordinary situation results in a decision that is widely recognized as ludicrous. Then thoughtful people draw back, saying, "Really now, this is going too far!" While reactions to the ludicrous may be relatively rare, however, the ludicrousness is in the logic, and it has become pervasive in legal and political thinking about religion in American life. The supposed right to be untouched by the religio-cultural consensus is highlighted in *Lubbock Independent School District v. Lubbock Civil Liberties Union* (1983). The public school in Lubbock, Texas, permitted students to gather for prayer and Bible study on school property after school hours. The Civil Liberties Union took its umbrage to court, and won. Such religious meetings, the court said, might give to "the impressionable student" the impression that "the state has placed its imprimatur on a particular religious creed." The court went on to explain itself in what Elliott Wright, a student of church-state relations, calls "a classic statement of judicial overkill." The court wrote:

> An adolescent may perceive "voluntary" school prayer in a different light if he were to see the captain of the school's football team, the student body president, or the leading actress in a dramatic production participating in communal prayer meetings in the "captive audience" setting of a school. . . . Misconceptions over the appropriate roles of church and state learned during one's school years may never be corrected.

Wright comments: "Maybe the captain of the public school football team should be prohibited from all communal prayer in the 'captive audience' settings of small towns and urban neighborhoods. Do courts think students relate only at school?"[5] *Lubbock* is an instance of the ludicrous that evoked public outrage and legislative efforts at remedy. But again, the ludicrousness is in the logic, and the court was being quite logical. The

football captain's public status is a public benefit bestowed by his participation in a public (government) institution. Therefore he should perhaps
not be permitted to pray in public anywhere, lest the government's role
in his status and consequent influence be construed as the establishment
of religion. He may publicly espouse atheism and be quite public about
having sexual relations with the girls, or boys, in his class. These are
matters of constitutionally protected belief and life-style. But he may not
pray or evangelize. Is this absurd? Of course it is, but it is not very far from
the logic that has moved us incrementally from government encouragement of religion (although not of any one religion), to government neutrality toward religion, to government hostility to religion. We are arriving
at the point where the privileged status of religion, which was clearly the
intention of the First Amendment, is becoming the most particular hand-
icap of religion. Examples such as those cited suggest that we may already
have arrived at that point. Are these examples extreme and distortions of
public policy with respect to religion? One might think so from the expressions of outrage and rush to legislative remedy that they evoke. I think it
more reasonable, however, to view them not as distortions but as moments
of truth and candor with respect to the logic of one powerful stream of
legal thought (or thoughtlessness) about religion.

Pluralism is a jealous god. When pluralism is established as dogma,
there is no room for other dogmas. The assertion of other points of reference in moral discourse becomes, by definition, a violation of pluralism.
Pluralism, relativity, secularization—all come to be much of a piece. There
seems to be no place to stand from which it is possible to "relativize the
relativizers." A host of earnest philosophers try to establish a normative
ethic on grounds purely rational. They fictionalize a "disinterested observer" or "impartial spectator" who can make judgments that are truly
objective, and therefore true. But their disinterested observers do not agree
with one another. In an earlier time, an Aristotle could assume that a good
man is one who recognizes and practices what is good. It seemed self-
evident then, but no longer. In *The Theory of Moral Sentiments*—a book
as unread as his also unread, but frequently cited, *The Wealth of Nations*—
Adam Smith argued that the more we understand our natural moral judgments the more we have reason to trust them. He was not even prepared
to allow that there is such a thing as a "moral sense." Whatever is meant
by moral sense, said he, is at best the composite of sentiments that intu-
itively recognize and act upon the difference between courage and cow-
ardice, honesty and fraud, good and evil.[6] Again, it seems very simple but
is today dismissed as simplistic.

Despite the dismissal, however, most of us live every day according
to moral sentiments, without spending much time on their logic or au-
thorizations. We witness a son who routinely abuses his aged mother and,
without consulting the law or books of moral philosophy, we *know* that

148

is wrong. If pressed on why we think it wrong, however, we could likely provide reasons that we think should hold up to public scrutiny. Among other reasons and maybe foremost among them, most Americans would likely invoke biblical injunctions about the honor due parents. But, according to current doctrine, that reason is not publicly admissible. Until recently, the law would not have had much to say about this case, so long as it is contained within the limits of physical damage to the mother. Now, however, she might bring suit for psychological damage or similar cause. The son is not at a loss either, for surely he has a rich store of injuries, psychic and otherwise, accumulating from malpractice in potty training up to last week's gratuitous insult. So here we are in court— whether literally or just in conversation about the circumstance—and our "moral sentiments" are left far behind. As the law extends its reach ever further into the interstices of interpersonal behavior and disposition, it ever more rigorously excludes from consideration those moral sentiments by which alone our life together is tamed and ordered. And never is the exclusion more rigorous than when those sentiments are "tainted" by religion.

In speaking about moral sentiments—that is, ideas and feelings about virtue—we are not dealing with something that is necessarily nonrational, irrational, or subrational. On the contrary, moral notions that make some public claim and therefore have a bearing upon others must be supported by public reasons. If everybody in the community concerned has sworn allegiance, as it were, to a common authority, then it is usually sufficient to invoke that authority with respect to any question in dispute. In a pluralistic society, properly understood, there are different authorities in play. This creates an inescapably difficult situation. One facile way out of it is to say that, since people subscribe to different authorities, no authority or authorities will be recognized. This is the way proposed by anti-authoritarians who say that only what can be demonstrated by reason should have a claim upon public attention. The problem, of course, is that there is little agreement about what is reasonable, the "disinterested observers" of the moral philosophers' contrivance are forever quarreling with one another. A fall-back position when this problem is encountered is the claim that we are only mutually pledged to uphold the law. But what the law says is a changeable thing, so fickle as to make "moral sentiments" appear by comparison to be anchored in rock. Especially is this the case if we accept a currently common notion that the law is whatever the courts say the law is. Then our pledged allegiance is to a vacuous process and to its institutional machinery. For a morally serious person, such a pledge must be sharply qualified, for to be anywhere near ultimately committed to a process and its machinery is tantamount to idolatry.

In arguing for a renewed respect for moral sentiments and their democratic expression in the public arena, one is aware that moral sentiments are not unchangeable. In some instances the change is for the better. For example, fifty years ago most white Americans had no moral sentiment that viewed as odious racial slurs against black people. While perhaps most Americans today still harbor elements of racism, they also understand, at least when challenged, that racist attitudes, language, and behavior are somehow wrong. From slavery to the present day, the decline of overt racism is perhaps the most continuous single improvement in the public ethos of America. It must also be acknowledged that, insofar as that improvement has been brought about by law, it has been based upon a determined emphasis upon the individual and his rights, precisely the emphasis that has been so debilitating in other aspects of our public life.

The legal logic that was undoubtedly required in advancing race relations—with its insistence upon individualism and accompanying notions such as that of privacy—has spilled over into other spheres of law and public policy. Those who emphasize the singularity of black-white relations in the American experience are trying to build a dam against the spillover. Otherwise, a smooth continuum is established from the civil rights movement to the sundry liberationisms agitating our public life today. With respect to racial justice, law intervened in order to protect blacks from the majority moral sentiment or lack thereof. The legal precedents set in order to remedy racial injustice, however, are now exploited by every borderline person or group in order to establish their claim of immunity from prevailing moral sentiment. It is also noteworthy that the claim for racial justice was made, as discussed earlier in connection with Dr. King, in the name of biblical ethics and constitutional law. The legal triumph of racial justice (as distinct from its triumph in everyday life) was due to a convergence of legal development and a more honest articulation of the Judeo-Christian ethic. However long and arduous the process, this was an instance of the democratic process at its best.

Movements today that employ the anti-discrimination provisions won in the racial struggle see themselves as a continuation of that struggle. But the convergence between law and the democratic ethos is lacking. In fact, as often as not, the effort is to use the law in order to confront and overturn the base of moral consensus. This is notably evident in some of the more radical movements aimed at erasing all sexual distinctions, creating an androgynous society, and liberating children from their "captivity" to the "oppressive structure" that is the family.[7] And this is most evident in the perverse libertarianism that insists, in principle, upon the naked public square. Here again, we see the irony that the very legal redress which was made possible, in the case of racial justice, by its convergence with democratic moral sentiment is employed in order to nullify the morality by which it came into being. The result is that law is made to stand on its own, as it were; in isolation from, even in hostility to, the morality that can alone make law legitimate. As in philosophy fact is divorced from value, so law becomes sheer fact. The law is the law is the law. If one is trying to win a case in a courtroom, it may be sufficient to know the bare fact of the law, but that is not sufficient to maintain the regard for law that is required in a democratic society.

We have noted the changeability of moral sentiments. In some cases, as with race in America, the change is for the better. Some other changes range from the doubtful to the disastrous. Adam Smith, for instance, confidently asserts that anyone who understands virtue would find abortion and infanticide to be utterly abhorrent. In light of today's widespread tolerance of both, the words of Pope are pertinent:

> Vice is a monster of so frightful mien,
> As to be hated needs but to be seen;
> Yet seen too oft, familiar with her face,
> We first endure, then pity, then embrace.

The monstrous becomes habitual, and we cannot afford but to be on friendly terms with our habits. Today perfectly respectable, indeed distinguished, persons propose in public the doing of what earlier was thought unthinkable. That nuclear strategy should be based upon the indiscriminate mass destruction of civilian populations; that babies should be examined until five days after birth and be eliminated if found defective; that "triage" solutions should be implemented, checking population growth by the starvation of millions who have least chance of survival in any case; that children of aged parents should be authorized, with medical agreement, to administer a lethal pill to aged parents, thus allowing them to "die with dignity."

One must be careful not to be alarmist about these developments. Most of these horrors have not yet been adopted as policy. And, while it is possible to argue that the legitimating logic for other monstrosities is contained in, for example, the *Roe v. Wade* decision on abortion, it does not follow that, finding ourselves on a slippery slope, we must slide to the bottom. As mentioned earlier in the Lubbock school case, there are instances so ludicrous that outrage finds political expression leading to remedy. But, like the Beast slouching toward Bethlehem, the legal logic continues apace. It is hard to argue, and I have no reason to believe it the case, that people are "less moral" today than in the past. Indeed, as we have seen, there are instances of what might be called moral progress. It is the fact that "hard cases" that test our morality seem to be coming at us with greater frequency. Some of these cases have to do with death and dying, such as the Karen Ann Quinlan case of the late seventies.[8] There will undoubtedly be many more of that genre. But those hard cases hardly seem hard compared with the stunning ethical complexities posed by genetic engineering, cloning, and the computerization of life forms that throw into question the distinctiveness of the human.[9]

This, then, is the burden of our historical moment—to be facing moral dilemmas of unprecedented complexity at a time when we are inclined to throw away compass and map and to scuttle the ship. In our public life we are feverishly engaged in moral disarmament when the battle for what it means to be human, for the *humanum*, has not yet reached its peak. We cannot rely upon law alone. The great atrocities of our century were all perpetrated with the color of law, from Hitler to Stalin to Mao. As, for that matter, was the atrocity of slavery in our own history. The law is a friendly fellow, amenable to our wishes, plastic in the hands of the powerful. Nor can we rely upon moral sentiment alone, for as it can in rare instances move from vice to virtue it does more frequently move from abhorrence to the embrace of wickedness.

What is required is law combined with moral sentiment that is rooted in a tradition of belief. Moral sentiment that is not grounded, institutionalized, and transmitted in a living tradition is always subject to becoming mere sentimentality. Such living traditions cannot be created *ex nihilo*. Rousseau tried that with his "civil religion"; as philosophers such as John Rawls still try it with their elegant contrivances to establish a public ethic. More powerfully in our time, various forms of Marxist-Leninism have attempted to provide that religio-cultural order of meaning, as in the Soviet Union and China. The collapse of that effort and the pervasive *anomie* or orderlessness that followed the collapse are well described by observers as different as Hedrick Smith, Fox Butterfield, and Solzhenitsyn.[10] In such societies it is the still living traditions of religion that provide meaning for a dissident minority and leverage against the formal "religion" of the social order.

Perhaps the apparently inexorable logic that would divorce law from religiously grounded morality is in fact inexorable. Perhaps it cannot be arrested. Perhaps this is the price to be paid for secular liberation from religious authoritarianism—a liberation from which we have all benefited in myriad ways. Perhaps it has fallen to us to pay the piper for all his merry tunes along the way to modernity. Freedom, as they say, does not come cheap. Perhaps this is the meaning of Psalm 81:11–12: "And yet my people did not hear my voice, and Israel would not obey me. So I gave them over to the stubbornness of their hearts, to follow their own devices." *To follow their own devices.* In his loving anger, God corrects, scourges, and afflicts. But if it could ever be that divine love and anger are exhausted, then comes the most awesome judgment: "I gave them over to their own devices." God need not invent new punishments to fit hell with horror; hell is man abandoned, man on his own.

But why entertain this prospect of such an ominous ending to the course on which we are embarked? Because, contrary to the sometimes blithe confidence of moral majoritarian leadership, it may not be possible to "turn America around." If that is so and if, as it is commonly assumed, America is, for better and for worse, the "lead society" of world-historical change, then the human prospect is very grim. But it may be that God's grace is such that what has been done by human beings can be undone by human beings. A mid-course correction, not unlike repentance, may be possible. And so we may be rescued from *anomie* and brought again into the sphere of the possibility of salvation, under the no doubt angry judgment of God. I say mid-course correction because I do not share the conceit of many secularists and religionists alike that ours is the climactic moment of history's story. Our moment may be that, of course, but there is no compelling reason to believe it is so. For the secularist it is a conceit unalloyed; he cannot think of himself but as the apex of all that has gone before. His vanity is such that he can imagine no worthy successor or—and this is but a different form of vanity—he exaggerates his villainy so as to think it certain that he will destroy the world. The religionist's conceit is alloyed by belief in imminent supernatural interventions that will, according to Bible prophecy, drop the curtain on this the final act. A more modest and a much more helpful understanding of our moment is to see humanity itself as described by Dante: "In the middle of the journey of our life I came to myself within a dark wood where the straight way was lost."

It may seem that I have wandered into a homily on matters cosmic, and maybe I have. But such is the enormity of the questions engaged. If law and polity are divorced from moral judgment, then the apocalypse proclaimed by Nietzsche and his imitators is upon us; the slide has begun and it is irreversible; all things are permitted and, given the fertility of our imaginations and technological powers, all things will be done. It is not apocalyptic but simply descriptive to observe that when all things are permitted, when no wickedness is forbidden in order that excellence be exalted, then the end has come. When in our public life no legal prohibition can be articulated with the force of transcendent authority, then there are no rules rooted in ultimacies that can protect the poor, the powerless, and the marginal, as indeed there are now no rules protecting the unborn and only fragile inhibitions surrounding the aged and defective.

The end, having arrived, may be slow in getting it over with. We can stumble about in the dark wood for some time. We can even talk about the law, even about the majesty of the law, all the time knowing that we are speaking only of what John Noonan calls "the masks of the law."[11] The law was thought to be the mask of the lawgiver, the expressed truth of truth's source, but the giver and source have long since departed, or so it is thought, and we are left only with the masks. The credulous are eager to be deceived by the manipulation of the masks, and those in the know have vested interests in continuing the game, but our heart is not in it. We have not the will or the means to resist others who, neither credulous nor interested in the common weal, demand that the masks be played to their purpose. The ignorant who are deceived and the knowing who be-

153

nignly deceive (perhaps also themselves) are no match for the knowing who acknowledge no morality but power. As the twilight of the gods fades into night, the time of these knowing ones has come around at last.

Yet we may mistake the dark wood for the night. The way may not be lost altogether. In this society millions of people insist that they still see the gods behind the masks. And because this society is marked by a semblance of democracy, these millions may have their way. Certainly they can and they have made their impact felt in electoral politics. Legislatures rumble with metaphysical discontents. Beliefs are smuggled into bills, in the hope that the courts will not discern their moral intent. The love that dare not speak its name is not the love that Oscar Wilde had in mind. It is the love for, the sense of allegiance to, transcendent truth that has been ruled out of order in this pluralistic society. The courts, accompanied and prodded by libertarian vigilantes, patrol the borders of the public square on the watch for impermissible motives. With squint-eyed suspiciousness they examine whether that moment of classroom silence might not be construed as an invitation to pray. Among regulators, legislators, and judges themselves, the religiously observant are suspect. They cannot be counted on to manipulate the masks in accordance with our precedents if they believe the masks represent reality not under our control. They are, in sum, dangerous people who, if not kept in close check, can blow the whole game. And then what would we have, here in the dark wood, having lost the way?

Those who claim to see the gods behind the masks claim also to see a way out of the dark wood. Indeed they feel they have been quite abruptly and ungraciously pulled into the dark wood by leaders who seemed to have their minds set on losing the way in the first place. A way out is in mending the rupture between public policy and moral sentiment. But, as we have argued, the only moral sentiment of public effect is the sentiment that is embodied in and reinforced by living tradition. There are no a-religious moral traditions of public, or at least of democratic, force in American life. This is not to say that morality must be embodied in religion nor that the whole of religion is morality. It is to say that, among the American people, religion and morality are conjoined.

At the beginning of this chapter we cited Burckhardt on "the three great powers" of state, religion, and culture. With the effective disestablishment of the coercive power of religion, such as Burckhardt had in mind, religion has become part of culture. So close is the union that, as we have seen, they are sometimes indistinguishable. Religion in our popular life is the morality-bearing part of culture, and in that sense the heart of culture. Needless to say, there are other ways of describing our culture and, in fact, those who write and speak about culture are often inclined to ignore the role of religion. Our focus is not upon those other ways, however, but upon the popular culture, as befits an essay on religion and

154

democracy. Another essay might be given to more systematically making the case that those other ways of thinking about culture are also religious in character, despite the blindspot that many cultural analysts betray with respect to religion.

Our problems, then, stem in large part from the philosophical and legal effort to isolate and exclude the religious dimension of culture. Instead of the three great powers of Burckhardt, we now have the two great powers of state and culture. But of the two only the state can, in his words, "lay claim to compulsive authority." Certain institutions that we might ordinarily be inclined to think of as belonging to the culture also lay claim to compulsive authority, notably the institutions of education. This is the case, however, because the state has either taken over or extended its influence into such institutions. The state by no means has the societal field to itself. Within the culture are, for example, those powerful instruments we call the communications media. But, from the viewpoint of those who desire a neatly unitary social order, the most problematic "loose cannon" on the deck is religion. That is because, of all the institutions in society, only religion can invoke against the state a transcendent authority and have its invocation seconded by "the people" to whom a democratic state is presumably accountable. For the state to be secured from such challenge, religion must be redefined as a private, emphatically *not* public, phenomenon. In addition, because truly value-less existence is impossible for persons or societies, the state must displace religion as the generator and bearer of values. Therefore it must screen out of public discourse and decision-making those values too closely associated with religion, lest public recognition be given to a source of moral authority other than the state itself. To put it differently: in the eyes of the state the dangerous child today is not the child who points out that the emperor has no clothes but the child who sees that the emperor's garments of moral authority have been stolen from the religion he has sent into exile from the public square.

CHAPTER TEN

CHRISTENDOM RECONSIDERED

HOW STRANGE IS THIS HISTORICAL MOMENT IN WHICH TALK about the public role of religion is thought to be conservative. Stranger still that "liberal" forces believing in the promise, if not the inevitability, of moral progress are most eager to consign religion to "the dustbin of history." The strangeness can of course be tempered in part by reference to historical experience. As we have noted, the wars of religion of the sixteenth and seventeenth centuries have left an indelible mark upon Western political thought and practice. From that experience we presumably learned that particularist religion is an impossibly divisive dynamic, destroying the foundations of the *polis* it would control. Still in the nineteenth century, profound thinkers such as Burckhardt were operating from the memory of religion's ambition and ability to dominate. He was also keenly suspicious of the modern state and its ambitions, and therefore he placed his hope in culture, the realm of freedom.

Our historical moment is not new in the sense of being unlinked from the preceding centuries. But it is different, and a critical part of the difference is that, at least in formal theory and polity, religion has been removed from its role of either informing or threatening the polity and culture. And, again theoretically, the culture has been largely subsumed into the state. The realm of freedom, to the extent it exists, is the realm of privacy, outside the perimeters of public policy, philosophy, and practice.

Put so starkly, the above description may be misleading. It may suggest that we have arrived at a situation that is in some respects far from unattractive, namely a world of privacy and freedom secured from political controls. Unless one believes that all reality is finally political—that only what is political has significance and "meaning"—the idea of a secure world of freedom in privacy may seem to be a worthy advance. As it happens, however, many people have come to believe precisely that: only what is political is important and deserving of notice. This bias is reinforced by the communications media, which helps to assure that only what is political *gets* noticed. The bias became quite explicit in varieties of radicalisms in the sixties. Then it was more boldly asserted but now it is still powerfully implicit that "the personal is political." The significant life must be *publicly* significant. The only life that counts is the life that is politically "problematicized." Remember, for instance, the influential essay by Jerry Farber, *The Student as Nigger* (1969), whose title tells the story.[1] Or consider a young radical in the late sixties who was on trial in West Germany. He announced (with no apparent reference to the legal proceedings at hand): "I have orgasm difficulties and I want the public to take cognizance of this fact." The incident may seem bizarre but it may be argued that it is paradigmatic of the problematicizing and politicizing of the private sphere.[2]

Thus we are returned to an earlier observation that the naked public square cannot remain naked. When the value-bearing institutions of religion and culture are excluded, the value-laden concerns of human life flow back into the square under the banner of politics. It is much like trying to sweep a puddle of water on an uneven basement floor; the water immediately flows back into the space you had cleared. Or, in more apt imagery, the seven devils replace the first. Mussolini first embraced the totalitarian formula: "Everything within the state, nothing outside the state, nothing against the state." The implicitly totalitarian logic espoused by many non-totalitarians leads to the same consequence. If the state ordering of society is to exclude those institutions that generate and bear values, then that state must be prepared to assume the burden of meeting the human yearning for a life that is not value-less. The totalitarian, whether Fascist or Communist, welcomes that burden. Certain varieties of democratic liberalism are unprepared for, and severely embarrassed by, a naked public square that refuses to stay naked. But, if what is significant is defined by what is political, the political must be prepared to deal with orgasm problems, and myriad other problems of lesser and greater interest.

The impression should not be left that the exclusion of other institutional actors, such as religion, from the public arena is entirely the work of an elite that is indifferent to the democratic ideas and practices of "the people." But what Richard Hofstadter observed a long time ago is still largely the case:

> Intellectuals in the twentieth century have . . . found themselves engaged in incompatible efforts; they have tried to be good and believing citizens of a democratic society and at the same time to resist the vulgarization of culture which that society constantly produces. It is rare for an American intellectual to confront candidly the unresolvable conflict between the elite character of his own class and his democratic aspirations.[3]

Against populist lines of argument, however, it must be noted that there has been a kind of democratic acquiescence in the directions pointed by the intellectuals. Certainly most Americans have not agreed that religion is among the "vulgarizations" to be removed from the field demarcated as public. They have been quite eager, however, to permit concerns once thought to be private to be transmogrified as political. This is evident in the growing litigiousness of the American people, in which issues erupt-

ing in the interstices of interpersonal relations increasingly find their way
to court. Even what were once deemed to be internal disputes within
religious bodies are offered up for political adjudication. The instance cited
earlier, of a court ruling on a church altar in terms of property rights over
furniture, is the religious analogy of the state's taking public note of our
young radical's orgasm problem.

Democratic acquiescence in the pan-politicizing of life is also evident
precisely in those religious enterprises that are most insistent that religion
is essentially a private sphere based entirely on private authority. Here one
thinks of those fundamentalist and experiential forms of religion that are
self-consciously divorced from public reason. It is supremely and disas-
trously ironic that those fundamentalist forces which are most insistent that
religiously grounded values should have a stronger bearing upon public life
are also most insistent that those values are not subject to public discourse
and debate. This latter insistence only reinforces the prejudice among otherwise thoughtful citizens that religion is an irrational or subrational "vul-
garization" that dare not be allowed to impinge upon the realm of the
"authentically political."

By grounding religious values in essentially private and subjective
sources, certain species of religion make all but inevitable the religiously
sterilized public life that they then so vigorously protest. Democratic governance rightly resists the formation of public policy on the basis of private
reasons. The unhappy result is that government and religion, agreeing that
religiously grounded values are essentially private, and having no other
democratically recognized tradition of values from which to draw, conclude that values as such are outside the province of the authentically
political and thus end up dealing with values in terms of individualistic
"interests." This is an "unhappy result" because it is not what any of the
parties want, except for the very few who consciously embrace the totalitarian prospect or, for whatever reason, desire the delegitimation of democratic governance.

As mentioned earlier, the assertion of the public face of religion is
often thought to be a conservative concern. In part this perception is correct. Religion is by definition a conservatizing institution in society, trans-
mitting the tradition by which rights and wrongs, truths and falsehoods,
are to be measured. Even when religion is "radical," as in current forms
of liberation theology, it draws upon hoary tradition in order to legitimate
the changes it demands. Thus, sometimes amusingly, it is demanded that
the modern economic order be recast in conformity with the practices of
the primitive nomadic world of Old Testament Israel. But, however implausible the specifics proposed, even the most radicalized uses of religion
depend upon the continued suasion of the tradition. In this sense the assertion of the public character of religion is inescapably conservative. It

may be conservatism against itself, but the premise is conservative nonetheless.

At the same time, the public character of religion is an essential liberal premise, essential at least to the American version of liberal democracy. The historian of American democracy, Clinton Rossiter, sums up the argument of *The Federalist*:

> No happiness without liberty; no liberty without self-government; no self-government without constitutionalism; no constitutionalism without morality—and none of these great goods without order and stability.[4]

One may dispute Rossiter's ordering of "these great goods," but the point is a valid one. The notion of liberty (from which, at least originally, the meaning of liberalism) assumes that there are several actors in our understanding of the polity—from "morality" to the "self" of self-government. When these actors are reduced to one, then government, while theoretically excluding the other actors, in fact absorbs them. When "self" seeks to be defined by government, "self-government" becomes a tautology, for there is no self there apart from government. Similarly, the exclusion (but, in fact, absorption) of value-bearing religious traditions makes such concepts as "good government" or "just government" meaningless, for there is no measure of goodness or justness apart from government.

This is not the point at which we have arrived in American life. At least not in practice. Ours is still in many respects a lively, even a raucous, democracy. There are still many institutional actors not within the state but outside the state and even against the state. But *in our ways of thinking* we are closer to the totalitarian conclusion than we may wish to think. This is not simply true of political theorists who, in Hofstadter's terms, have not been able to square their thinking with their democratic aspirations. It is also true in the insinuation of these ways of thinking into the courts. In 1983 the Supreme Court, terminating tax exemption to a fundamentalist school that engaged in the odious practice of racial discrimination, embraced a logic that has for years been only a nightmare suffered by students of church-state relations. That logic is that religion, as such, has no constitutional standing. In this case, for instance, the court ruled that the operative term in the rationale for tax exemption is "charitable," and charitable is, in turn, defined by conformity to "settled public policy." The court has now accepted the argument that tax exemption is not only a privilege bestowed by the state (rather than a right as many constitutional scholars contend) but that that privilege is in fact a "subsidy" proffered by the state. A subsidy is, of course, a tax expenditure and tax expenditures are subject to governmental control. The issue of tax exemption is important in itself, and in the debate over tax exemption religion should not be intimidated by the claim that its concern is self-serving. At stake is the equation of "society" with "government." At stake is whether there is any sphere of life that is not political as the government (which claims a monopoly on the political) defines that term.[5]

If tax exemption is in fact tax expenditure, does this not assume that everything belongs to the government? Even putting the question sounds extreme, but consider the logic. If what a person or institution does not pay in taxation is in fact exempt by grace of the government, it would seem to follow that everything could be claimed by the government, were it so inclined. Of course that would be economically disastrous and is not likely to happen. The likely, indeed the present problem, is in the claim that what is not taxed is a government subsidy or expenditure. Say a person now pays thirty percent of her income in taxes. She then says that she has seventy percent which is "my own." Not so, according the legal logic that is gaining ascendancy. That seventy percent is exempted by grace of the state. It is given to you as a subsidy, a state expenditure, for doing the various things you do with that money. Since the state is expending that money, however, surely it follows that the state has an interest, nay an obligation, to be concerned about how you use it. In clothing and feeding your children, in paying the mortgage and buying a boat, you are an agent of the state. Of course this sounds outrageous, and the courts have not spelled out the implications of the logic so baldly. It is a dubious comfort that they may not have thought through the implications. It is the line of reasoning that must be of concern to those who believe that ideas have consequences. Lending credibility to the more doleful reading of current decisions on tax philosophy is the court's apparent absorption of the constitutional category of religion into the category of "charitable activity," and its further assertion that what qualifies as charitable is to be defined by government policy.

Nothing that is said here should be misconstrued as implying that jurists and intellectuals possessed by monistic hungers are engaged in a conspiracy to destroy institutional pluralism in the name of advancing individualistic pluralism under the auspices of the state. That may in fact be what is happening. To the extent it is happening, I suspect it is less by design or decision than it is by drift. While the secular humanist conspiracy of moral majority fantasies is not entirely a fabrication, as an explanatory device it distorts much more than it explains. I find much more plausible the explanations offered by William Sullivan and others: the vision of the American founders had a kind of built-in flexibility. Because the state did not hog all the public space available, it was assumed that other institutions, such as religion, would be taking care of the value-generating and value-transmitting needs of the society. Not only the institutions of religion but also the other mediating structures, notably the family, were "in place." The idea of the government devising a "family policy" would have been quite alien to their thinking, and the possibility of a "religion policy" was explicitly precluded by the First Amendment.

The founders were concerned in their designing with the formal polity itself, on the assumption that government is a necessary instrument within society, not absorptive of the society.

This variegated view of society—of "natural society" as Burke and others would have it—was part of their taken-for-granted reality. Well, perhaps not entirely taken for granted, for some of them did later draw lessons from the quasi-totalitarian tendencies of the French Revolution. But in the American context such tendencies were held in check by the other institutional actors in society's orderings. The American system did not look very neat, indeed it didn't look much like a "system" at all. It had about it a kind of make-do, muddling through appearance. But making do is what many have meant by American pragmatism. Not the more thorough philosophical pragmatism of a William James, to be sure, but a rough commonsensical way of getting along by refusing to be distracted by problems that they suspected, perhaps rightly, were irresolvable. To put it briefly, in theory and practice the founders were not inclined to borrow trouble. Or, as it is said by some today, "If it ain't broke, don't fix it."

It is noteworthy that First Amendment questions related to the free exercise and establishment of religion hardly appear in our jurisprudential history until well into this century. There was that embarrassing incident with the Mormons who thought they should have more than one wife, but that was settled by reference to the then self-evident moral consensus of the American people. (It is of some little interest to speculate on how that question would be or should be resolved today.) Church-state relations become problematicized relatively late in our history, and overwhelmingly in connection with conflicts related to education. This is not simply because the common school movement represented a major governmental expansion into a sphere previously outside the state's purview. That expansion was not legally problematic until it became official doctrine that there is no moral consensus in American life, that ours is a secular society. It was then thought that the Protestant-dominated values which had been advanced by the government school constituted an instance of the bootlegging of religion. The courts became ever more determined that such bootlegging must be stopped. The drift under discussion may in this respect be viewed as a new prohibition movement. As we are endlessly reminded by critics today, however, the prohibition of brand-name religion did not mean there was no religion in the educational public square. The brand-name products were replaced by no-name products to which some have given the name "the religion of secular humanism," but others of us view as a cramped secularism that is not humanistic enough.

There are no doubt many dynamics that have brought us to our present pass. Conspiracies aside, there is the dynamic of religious accommodation to a secularizing course that was believed to reflect the work of God in history. In addition, sociologists such as Max Weber described long

161

ago the dynamics inherent in modernization itself—dynamics leading to rationalization of social relationships and functions, to suspicion of the inherited in favor of the elected, to displacement of the "natural" by the humanly designed (that the author is a modern man is reflected by his compulsion to put "natural" in quotation marks, lest a reader think him so benighted as to assume agreement that anything might be natural.) In short, the modernist impulse is to turn any situation into a system. Those who resist such efforts are to be dismissed as anti-intellectual or even as irrational. In this view the public assertion of religious claims or values is an instance of "mystification," and it is the mission (note the religious overtones) of modernity to demystify reality.

But a rational "system" cannot contain religion. At least it cannot contain authentic religion in the Judeo-Christian tradition. It can perhaps contain, even give birth to, a "civil religion" of social utility but, as discussed earlier, any formal effort to assert an explicit civil religion would no doubt be met by overwhelming democratic resistance. What is happening is that, due to the influence of the social systematicians, we are increasingly living at two levels of the definition of reality, and they are quite out of synch with one another. At one level of political and jurisprudential theory, religion is not so much challenged, not to mention overtly persecuted, as it is defined into non-existence. At another level of everyday sociology, as it were, American society is more determinedly religious than ever before. In order to sustain their construction of reality, the courts and many theorists must avert their eyes from the vulgar fact of religious America. The other side of this is that millions of Americans, who don't "just happen" to be religious, find the official construction of reality to be implausible and increasingly oppressive.

In the seventies a growing number of thoughtful observers began to sense the existence of these incompatible constructions of reality and began to suspect that the situation, defying systematic synthesis, could not and maybe should not be sustained. Daniel Bell analyzed "the cultural contradictions of capitalism." Writers beyond number explored the insurgency of born-again Christianity and of the religious new right. One social critic puts it well: "Occasionally an almost anthropological detachment pervades characterizations of the Christian revival, as when in the middle seventies critics and journalists tried to explain Jimmy Carter's born again experience to each other and to their incredulous educated audiences as if it were as alien to American culture as a Balinese cockfight."[6]

The seemingly distant event of the collapse of the Shah of Iran had an enormous impact. Media attention was riveted, for a time, upon "militant Islam." Combined with a perception of the apparently growing power of Middle East oil nations, the suspicion formed that this may be the shape of things to come. This time the journalist returned to report, "I have seen the future, and it is very religious." One observer, pondering the new aggressiveness of Islam and the increasing vitalities of Christianity in Africa, combined with the "Jewish factor" posed by Israel in the Middle East, was led to wonder whether we in the very modern West are not the ones who are out of step with history:

> My guess is that the reaction against these [developments in Africa and the Middle East] will, one day, drive Western Christians too to recover their identity. But it will not be an identity of ifs and buts and mutual understanding. It will be confident, born again, bloody-minded. Our descendants will look back with curiosity on our bizarre age, a brief by-way of western history, in which people did not believe much and, what little it was, were quite ready to allow that other people might think differently. God's house will still have many mansions, and they will still be full of some saints, countless sinners, and a good many soldiers drawn from both.[7]

The editorial writer for *The Economist* may be right in thinking our descendants will look back with curiosity on our bizarre age. One hopes, however, that what they will think bizarre is not our religious tolerance but our effort to secure tolerance apart from its grounding in religion, indeed to secure tolerance by denying the reality of religion. This denial is too high a price to pay for the intellectual satisfaction of thinking we have turned our situation into a system. Even the minority whose hungers can be satisfied by nothing less than the systematic must realize it is too high a price to pay. If they persist and prevail, they will make it certain that the community of saints and sinners will also produce the soldiers. The call to arms is already being sounded by figures such as Francis Schaeffer and John Whitehead. They've had enough, they say, and they aren't going to take it anymore.[8]

To some the possibility of wars of religion in the modern world seems preposterous. But then, some of them are people to whom the possibility of religion seems preposterous. It is worth noting, however, that the militant Islam of Iran or the on-and-off wars between Christians and Muslims in Chad are only events "in the modern world" by our way of keeping time. In another view, these are events taking place in the premodern world and, at least in Iran, in explicit resistance against modernity. And yet, it is not so unthinkable that people should be willing to kill and be killed for religion. Certainly they have been willing to kill for much less noble reasons, also in the modern world. Whether, were it to happen in our society, such conflict should be viewed as postmodern or as a regression to premodernity, it is possible that our politics could become, to paraphrase MacIntyre, civil war carried on by means of civil war. Needless to say, we all have a deep interest in avoiding that unhappy outcome.

It is conceivable that it could be avoided by yet more determined efforts to displace the institutions and values of religion from our public life. After all, a large part of the religious enterprise is content to be confined to the private sphere. And, even were it sharply restricted in activities that we now consider private, Christians have historically demonstrated great aptitude in accommodating religion's claims to the requirements of the moment. In this vision of warfare avoided, it might be assumed that the current insurgency of the religious right is a last gasp of the culturally backward, a futile defiance of the inevitable.

This way of avoiding wars of religion, however, is hardly desirable. The triumph of the secularist option would, for all the reasons detailed earlier, do grave, perhaps fatal, damage to the American experiment in democratic governance. And it would do grave damage to religion. With respect to religion, the damage would be grave, but not lethal, at least not in the case of the church. It would not be lethal, that is, if the New Testament is right in saying that even the powers of hell cannot prevail against the church (Matthew 16). Yet, strange though it may seem, not all Christians are agreed that the collapse of democratic governance or even the triumph of totalitarianism would be bad for the church. One hears it said that the church in societies such as America has it "too good," it has become soft and too accustomed to its comforts. At the same time, almost envious looks are cast at the church in situations of persecution, such as in Eastern Europe and the Soviet Union. Perhaps, it is suggested, a century or two under totalitarian rule might mean the renewal of true Christian devotion.

We only note this line of thinking in passing. It is not entirely without merit. The "success" of the church in our society is in many respects conducive to a superficial and flaccid Christianity. The courageous witness of churches under persecution is indeed to be reverenced and lifted up for emulation. As in times past, the blood of the martyrs can be the seed of renewal but those who therefore want to be martyred are to be discouraged now, as they had to be discouraged in the early centuries of the church's persecution. Even more perverse are those who would volunteer countless others for martyrdom. In truth, those who think "a little totalitarianism might not be a bad thing for the church" reflect an aspect of the superficiality of American culture that they deplore. The romanticizing of persecution is only possible for those who have not taken the measure of history's horror, who have not read their church history nor their Solzhenitsyn. In any case, the present argument favors the intuition that there is a convergence, maybe even a providential convergence, between the vitality of the church and the advance of democratic governance. It is not a necessary convergence in the sense of being inevitable nor in the sense of precluding other imaginable futures for both religion and politics. Far from being inevitable, democracy with its religious foundations and functions seems, within the longer reach of historical perspective, to be a fragile and imperiled artifice. But from the viewpoint of general human well-being (securing what Rossiter calls "these great goods") and, most specifically, of religious freedom, democracy is an experiment well worth protecting and moving toward the fuller realization of its promise.

This, then, is the assumption that undergirds the claim that, for the sake of church and state, we must move beyond patterns of antagonism and warfare. The "victory" either of the forces of secularism or of the forces promoting an uncomplicated view of Christian America would be disastrous. To say that church and state must move beyond antagonism and warfare does not mean that all tensions can be or should be resolved. The vitality and integrity of democratic governance, as well as the vitality and integrity of religion, require that there be tensions. The state must be supported and judged by the transcendent truth that the church proclaims, and the church must be checked in her propensity to exercise in "the city of man" a political power that is not rightly hers.

The necessary tension, however, requires that church and state both be engaged as strong and mutually recognized institutional actors. In terms of institutional power, the church is, as we have seen, no match for the state. A critical part of our problem today is that the state increasingly uses its power to undercut the institutional role of religion and to withdraw recognition from religion as a significant actor within the democratic process. This is evident, for example, in the erosion of the First Amendment guarantees and the constitutional status of religion. If religion is not the strong institutional actor that democracy requires, however, the blame is not to be placed only upon those who are hostile or indifferent to the role of religion. At least equal responsibility rests with religious leadership—at all points on the political spectrum—that is not alert to the singularity and urgency of our historical moment. An important chapter of church history is now being written in America. Given America's role, for better and for worse, as "lead society" in world-historical change, the ramifications of what is happening here and now are beyond our powers to estimate. The issues in which we are engaged are, *mutatis mutandis*, the issues that engaged Paul, Augustine, Constantine, Innocent III, Calvin, Cromwell, and Edwards, among others. It is not too much to say that future generations will judge us harshly if our neglect of the church-state problematic leads to the failure of democracy by default. With that in mind, the remainder of this chapter considers the ways in which believers in the biblical promise have in the past related to the powers of this world and how that story illuminates our present dangers and responsibilities.

In the biblical tradition, the one model of more or less pure theocracy is the leadership of Moses over the children of Israel. Moses was intermediary between Yahweh and his people; through him the law was revealed and, obviously, it recognized no distinction between sacred and secular spheres. While the priestly leadership beginning with Aaron was to embody and perpetuate a similarly comprehensive authority, the history of Israel is in large part a story of the dissolution and fragmentation of governing authority. Judges and, later, kings were challenged by prophetic voices who laid claim both to direct revelation and to a more authentic reading of the law. In the so-called intertestamental period rabbinical authority was enhanced as foreign occupations made impossible a unified governance that would include the totality of life, including what we today call the spiritual and secular. The fissure created by foreign rule, however, intensified the futuristic hope for a messianic age in which the kingdom of David would be reestablished through divine intervention. The State of Israel today, which is formally not a secular state, is still embroiled in conflicting Jewish views of how the divine rule is manifested in human society. For many Zionists, the State of Israel is itself a kind of theophany and fulfillment of divine promise. For others, such as the very orthodox Hassidic leaders, the State of Israel is an act of presumption, a premature effort to force the hand of the Holy One before he is ready to usher in the messianic age.

Many Jews in America, and many in Israel who are not sympathetic to the religious parties here, are embarrassed by the ways in which the State of Israel is theologized in a manner that sets it apart from the consensus of secular modernity. For them Israel is a practical imperative, a place of haven and in-gathering for the victims of the Holocaust and a necessary instrument for the preservation of Jewish peoplehood. They are especially uneasy when Israeli leaders embrace the enthusiastic support of fundamentalist Christians in America who have their own version of Israel's role in the apocalyptic fulfillment of history. Yet even secularized Jews are hesitant to dispense entirely with the sacral aura that surrounds the State of Israel. There is a painful awareness of the fragility of Israel; its survival must not depend entirely upon military might in uncertain alliance with the United States, nor upon the world's even more uncertain remembering of the lessons to be drawn from the Holocaust.

Thus Israel, both in the past and the present, represents one important way of institutionalizing the relationship between sacred and profane. The importance of what Christians call the Old Testament is hardly limited to the State of Israel. As we have seen, there are also resurgences of militant Islam in which the same stories and the same sense of chosenness serve as the foundation of governmental legitimacy. (Countries such as Iran are sometimes described as "clerocracies," but the rule of the clergy rests upon their being the authoritative interpreters of the will of Allah, and thus these systems fit in the general category of theocracy.) There are related dynamics in South Africa. In the heated polemics of our day there are many caricatures produced about the religio-political justifications of apartheid; nonetheless South Africa is a notable instance of a society in which moral ultimacies are very near the surface of political debate and power.[9] In ways similar to an earlier period in American public thought, an analogy is drawn between the Boers' "errand into the wilderness" and

Israel's exodus experience. That analogy supports a still strong sense of "covenant" and providential purpose among the ruling groups of a society that is very much on the defensive and desperately seeking to bring its evolving polity into harmony with ideas of moral legitimacy more widely recognized in today's world. (Whether that evolution—sometimes described as "violent evolution"—will outpace the forces of revolution is a question beyond the scope of this chapter.)

As religion itself might be understood as a symbolic defiance of death and chaos, so it is among embattled peoples that the biblical story of Israel is most avidly embraced for protection and direction. This is markedly true of black religion in America. Both traditionally and in some more current "radicalized" forms, black preaching and worship give prominence to the judges, prophets, and other heroes of the Old Testament, with a focused emphasis upon the exodus experience. The identification with Israel's captivity and liberation can serve any political purpose, of course. As it is employed by Afrikaners and their black opponents in South Africa, so elsewhere Christians on opposite sides of the barricades quote the same biblical stories against one another.

Gustavo Gutiérrez, the Peruvian godfather of contemporary liberation theologies that appropriate Marxist analysis and (sometimes) revolutionary strategy, declares: "The Exodus is the long march towards the promised land in which Israel can establish a society free from misery and alienation. . . . It is in this event that the dislocation introduced by sin is resolved and justice and injustice, oppression and liberation are determined."[10] Strikingly similar is the use of Israel as a metaphor by conservative religious forces in this country. Of course their understanding of what constitutes liberation and oppression is rather different. It is also noteworthy that their emphasis is less upon the exodus itself and more upon Israel's difficulties in surviving and maintaining its spiritual integrity in the postexilic periods. Speaking of the United States, Jerry Falwell asserts: "But we have the promise in Psalm 33:12, which declares, 'Blessed is the nation whose God is the LORD.' When a nation's ways please the Lord, that nation is blessed with supernatural help."[11] In the political rhetoric of the religious right, probably no passage is quoted so frequently as Proverbs 14:3-4—"Righteousness exalteth a nation, but sin is a reproach to any people."

The use of biblical Israel as a metaphor is strongly protested today by Christian and Jewish leaders. Israel, they rightly note, is not a historical idea to be exploited but refers rather to the flesh-and-blood reality of living Judaism. Biblical Israel has in fact not played a strong role as a metaphor in the more catholic tradition of thinking about church and state. To be sure, the church has styled itself "the New Israel," but beginning with the New Testament church that had little to do with politics and everything to do with being heirs to the spiritual promises made to Abraham, Isaac,

167

and Jacob, whom Christians viewed as their fathers in the continuing covenant.

The decisive change for the first Christians was, quite simply and scandalously, Jesus. He came announcing not only that the kingdom of God was at hand but that, at least for those who received him, the kingdom had already arrived (Luke 9:21). The kingdom was present and yet still to come. Herein lies the notorious "now" and "not yet" character of Christian thinking about the rule of God and all its relation to earthly government. As though to compound the confusion, Jesus spoke frequently about the changes that the coming of the kingdom would bring about in the real world—what we call social, political, and economic changes. At the same time, however, he declared, "My kingdom is not of this world" (John 18:36). There is no doubt that the earliest Christian community believed that the final events of history were imminent—the return of Jesus in glory, the end of all existing worldly orders, the culmination of history, the definitive establishment of the rule of God over all things. There is a vast literature on New Testament expectations and how they shaped early Christian attitudes toward society and government. We recall Wilhelm Dilthey: "Jesus came announcing the Kingdom of God, but what appeared was the church."[12] The disappointment was and is understandable.

Christians have responded to this disappointment with the claim that the truth of the kingdom's coming is not dependent upon a timetable, so to speak. The ultimate fulfillment of the promise has been postponed indefinitely, but those who live with Christ as their Lord know now a preview or prolepsis of that fulfillment. As to existing political orders, Paul taught in Romans 13 that even an odious regime such as that of the Roman empire exists for limited but legitimate purposes and derives its authority from God. "Therefore he who resists the authorities resists what God has appointed, and those who resist will incur judgment." Worldly government was limited in purpose ("He is the servant of God to execute his wrath on the wrongdoer") but, more important, limited in time ("Besides this you know what hour it is, how it is full time now for you to wake from sleep. For salvation is nearer to us now than when we first believed; the night is far gone, the day is at hand"). Engagement in politics, as we understand that phrase today, was not an option for Paul or for those to whom he wrote. That was precluded by the nature of the empire itself, a distinctly predemocratic enterprise, and by the fact that Christianity was based in a subject people. In addition, even if such engagement had been possible, it would hardly make sense to devote much energy to fiddling with the improvement of a temporary order that would at any moment be succeeded by the perfect rule of Christ.

In today's religious situation, some Christians who favor aggressive participation in the political order are embarrassed by Romans 13. They emphasize the "historical conditionedness" of Paul's admonitions and in-

168

sist, quite correctly, that Romans 13 be kept in tension with other passages such as Revelation 13 that put the political powers in a somewhat different light. The empire is also "the Beast" with which Christ and those who belong to him are engaged in a struggle to the death. Other Christians, who are suspicious of political engagements (and sometimes, although not always, are also those who approve of the social order in which they find themselves), cite Romans 13 as the final word on government: "Let every person *be subject* to the governing authorities."

The debate over Romans 13 and related passages is very old. What is more than a new wrinkle today is the arrival on the political scene of groups that claim to be very conservative religiously and politically. They believe strongly in authority, indeed are often viewed as authoritarian. Everyone should be subject to the "the powers that be," and, in order to restore that kind of authority, they are vigorously contending against the way the society is presently ordered. They are rebels for the sake of authority. The oppression they resent is the permissiveness that others call · liberation. Further, like Paul, they speak incessantly of the imminent end of the world. Their interpretation of "Bible prophecy" makes clear that Christ is coming any day now. Far from this dampening their interest in politics, however, that interest is powerfully intensified. The reason why American must be "turned around," also politically, is that it is the "launching pad" for the evangelization of the world. At least according to some interpretations, the evangelization of the world is, in turn, a precondition for the return of Christ in glory. Among these groups, then, the experience of living under what they view as an oppressive regime and the belief in an imminent end to history lead not to political passivity but to increased activism in battles as varied as that against pornography and for a larger defense budget.

As with the Old Testament, so partisans of the political left and right invoke the New Testament in justification of their political choices. The consensus of biblical scholarship suggests that there is little in the way of political doctrine, and certainly nothing like a blueprint, to be found in the New Testament. The electrifying belief that the Absolute, that God himself, was revealed in Jesus the Christ and that the church, the Body of Christ, is the community in which union with the Absolute is possible—this was preoccupation enough for the early Christians. To be sure, throughout Christian history there have been those who contend that not only the gospel about Jesus but the moral teachings of Jesus provide a kind of blueprint for daily behavior, including behavior in the political realm. This view is given radical expression today also by those who stand in the venerable "left-wing" tradition of the sixteenth-century Reformation. On this view, according to John Howard Yoder, "the ministry and the claims of Jesus are best understood as presenting to men not the avoidance of political options, but one particular social-political-ethical option."[13] Key to this approach is a rigorous pacifism that denies the legitimacy of the powers of coercion that are common to all earthly political orders. This understanding of *the* New Testament ethic is frankly admitted to be "sectarian." It is not willing to postpone the "now" in light of the "not yet." It is provocatively and sometimes persuasively expressed in Christian history through religious orders, utopian communities, and individual prophetic leaders. But by the second century it was already clear that most Christians—or at least the Christians who would shape the majority future of the church—had no intention of belonging to a sect. Since the appearance of the church was certain, while that of the kingdom was partial and ambiguous, they would make the most of the church.

Common to all views of the state that can lay claim to being Christian is the assertion that Jesus Christ is Lord. Christian statements about the state are, in the first instance, statements about God who has revealed himself in Jesus. God is the power over all things; Christian reflection on other powers is aimed at relating (both conceptually and in practice) such powers to the absolute power who is God. When Jesus says in Mark 12 that one should render to Caesar what is Caesar's and to God what is God's, he is not suggesting a division of reality between the jurisdictions, so to speak, of God and Caesar. The claims of the kingdom that he proclaims and embodies encompass all of reality. Caesar's role is a temporary one until the claims of the kingdom are finally consummated. We have already noted this time factor, this eschatological expectation, in Paul's statements in Romans 13. The continued existence of the state is for a time; while "ordained" by God, it is by no means representative of that right ordering of the universe with which alone Christians can be content, and to which alone they can render unqualified obedience. In I Corinthians 6 Paul makes clear that Christians should as much as possible steer clear of Caesar's jurisdiction and should not, for example, take their disputes to the secular courts. Caesar is not in on the mystery of what God is doing in Christ: "None of the rulers of this world understood the wisdom of God; for if they had understood it they would not have crucified the Lord of glory" (I Cor. 2:8). Sometimes the state is worse than ignorant, making claims to a lordship that belongs to God alone. Then the state, as for example Nero's state, becomes "the beast from the abyss" (Revelation 13).

The state must be related to what Christians assert about God. That relationship is not one of divided jurisdictions or functions. It is a relationship of time, a question of an unfolding story. In this understanding, Christians are people ahead of their time in the sense that they now proclaim by faith what will one day be revealed to the sight of all. It is God's final intention that "at the name of Jesus every knee should bow, in heaven and on earth and under the earth, and every tongue confess that Jesus Christ is Lord, to the glory of God the Father" (Phil. 2:11). In Romans 13, Paul refers to the powers that be as *exousia,* a term normally reserved for angelic powers. There is ambivalence in the New Testament treatment of the many mysterious powers in the universe. Sometimes it is suggested that all these powers have already been vanquished by Christ (Col. 1:16-17; 2:15), while at other times the final conquest is in the future (I Cor. 15:25; Heb. 10:13). The angelic powers are of course both powers of good and powers of evil, Satan being the leader of the latter. In Revelation the question of the conquest is answered in terms of a temporary *binding* of Satan. The late New Testament scholar Oscar Cullmann sums up the ambivalence and the confident hope of Christians with respect to the *exousia*:

> The decisive victory over the powers has already been achieved; they have been brought into subjection and stand in the service of Christ. But, to use a figure of speech, the rope with which they are bound can be lengthened, so that these powers are able even now to attempt to emancipate themselves. But then their demonic nature becomes visible. As long as they remain in bondage to Christ, however, they stand in God's order. . . . Only when they try to free themselves from the subjection which has already been realized, and become "totalitarian," to use this modern word, only then do they demand what belongs to God. Therefore they must finally be conquered yet again, at the end of days, although the issue has already been decided.[14]

Since the one whom they acknowledge as Lord was executed by the state for political offenses, it would seem unlikely that Christians could ever view the state as anything but the enemy. At the heart of the Christian message, however, are the imperatives toward forgiveness and reconciliation and, more important, a robust belief in the sovereignty of God that is prone to work ironies beyond human imagining. Also, with the passing of time there were understandably different readings and expectations with respect to what God might be doing in history. Less edifying, there was an eagerness to be accepted and even a desire for power in a world ruled by the powers that be and that apparently would be for some time to come. In addition, unrelenting animosity toward the state ran into a very practical problem when the clear command to evangelize resulted in the conversion of those who *are* the state. Origen (d. 254), the brilliant albeit marginally orthodox Alexandrian theologian, was among the first to propose a systematic synthesis of the rule of Christ and the rule of the state. Components of his proposal are still basic to the understanding of the Eastern churches and are evident, for example, in the rationale of the Orthodox Church's relationship to the regime in the Soviet Union.

Eusebius (d. 340), commonly called the first church historian, perceived a providential convergence between the history of Christianity and that of the Roman empire. He recognized the emperor Constantine as the man chosen by God to establish the church on a firm foundation for its mission to the world, hand in hand with the empire. Constantine saw himself as divine instrument and, according to Eusebius, told a meeting of bishops, "You are bishops whose jurisdiction is within the church. But

I also am a bishop, ordained by God to oversee those outside the church."[15] Among Christians in the West today, "Constantinianism" is an almost universally negative term. It implies "triumphalism," another bad term, and represents the church's selling out its distinctive mission in order to obtain a secular place in "the establishment." The possibility should not be dismissed, however, that Constantinianism was an appropriate and faithful response to the church's understanding of its mission in that historical moment. Without "Constantinianism," it is quite possible that most of us would not be Christians today. In any event, it cannot be assumed lightly that today's formal dichotomy of politics and Christian truth claims reflects a greater fidelity to the gospel.

For Western Christians, however, the influence of the great Augustine (d. 340) has eclipsed that of Origen. For Augustine, the City of God had little in common with the City of Man. The political power had a limited positive value in that it provided a degree of provisional peace, but Christian eyes were to be fixed firmly on the promised New Order. The provisionality of worldly powers was dramatically underscored for Augustine by the collapse of the Roman *imperium* in his lifetime. Eusebius' vision of a providential convergence between church and empire under the lordship of Christ was in ruins. That vision would be revived from time to time in Christian history, not least of all in the American experience, but its later versions would always have to do battle with Augustine.

Augustine stood within the tradition of Jewish and Christian apocalyptic. Hope was to be focused not upon the rise and fall of empires but upon the coming kingdom of God. Those who now live in believing anticipation of the kingdom's coming constitute the *civitas Dei,* the City of God. From the beginning, from Adam, there have been these two cities, the one made up of those who resist and the other of those who welcome the promised kingdom. In the resurrection, believers of all previous times will be raised to receive their reward. Like Paul, Augustine acknowledged the temporary legitimacy of the secular powers. Unlike many who have invoked Augustine, Augustine himself did not urge passivity and withdrawal from the political task. Indeed Christians were to be actively involved in pursuing the limited peace and justice presently possible. But, at the same time, their citizenship is in the City of God and, in contrast with that splendor, the other city often appears as no better than a *civitas diaboli,* a city of the devil.

Subsequent Christian thinking about church and state has been in the shadow—or, as some would have it, the light—of Augustine. In the "Christendoms" to come his influence would be reflected in the assumed differentiation between the spiritual and the secular. One form of the institutional consequences of that differentiation was earlier expressed by Pope Gelasius I when addressing the emperor Anastasius: "There are two, O noble emperor, by whom this world is principally ruled—the holy authority of the bishops and the royal authority. Of these two the priestly power is more weighty in that at the judgment it must give account to God for these kings who rule mankind."[16] The preeminence claimed for the bishops was more moral than political. In this sense it was accepted in principle by emperors in the West. "Nevertheless," writes Wolfhart Pannenberg, "the emperors in the West as in the East understood themselves as the successors of Christ, that is, as earthly representatives of the heavenly royal power of Christ, while for them the pope was only the vicar of Peter."[17]

In the contentions between popes and emperors a near-fatal distinction became normative, that between *potestas spiritualis* and *potestas saecularis*. In truth, some such distinction between the spiritual and secular may be inevitable. As mentioned earlier, in dealing with the *institutions* of church and state it is necessary to designate functionally specific differences. But in the Middle Ages and even more today the distinction between sacred and secular is somewhat artificial. It does not accord with the church's comprehensive definition of its mission. Nor can it accommodate the drive of the modern state to include within its mandate an ever expanding notion of its power in order to fulfill that mandate. Further, the sacred/secular dichotomy does not agree with our understanding of the ways in which even quotidian "secular" politics derives its legitimacy from a larger world of meaning that can only be described as sacred.

But it would be a mistake to make too much of the difference between our time and that of earlier Christendoms. While institutional forms of both church and state have changed dramatically, the core questions are strikingly similar. The "investiture controversy" of the eleventh and twelfth centuries was over the right claimed by emperors to "invest" bishops and abbots with ring and staff and to receive their pledge of loyalty prior to their consecration by church authorities. That is not too different from the practice of some governments today that license those religious institutions they find acceptable and persecute those who do not cooperate with the government's "ministry for religious affairs." There are even troubling similarities with our own government's growing propensity to decide which activities will and which will not qualify as "religious" in connection with tax policy. Although differently vested, the investiture controversy keeps coming back.

Our current problems are, then, on a historical continuum. The history is not one of good guys versus bad guys. It is a history of embroilment in the nettlesome conceptual problems attendant upon institutionalizing different dimensions of social reality (especially when one of those institutions, religion, claims suprasocial purpose and authority). One theologian who acknowledges the importance of a theonomous society—a society that acknowledges accountability to transcendent truth—nonetheless expresses sympathy for the emperors in centuries past: "It seems that at that time, the independence of the emperor from the pope was conceivable only at the price of a total secularization and through restricting the church to spiritual concerns."[18] So today there are many who would argue that secularization is not the result of a program pursued by militant secularists hostile to religion. It is rather the unavoidable consequence if the state is to prevent the church from denying it room to fulfill its legitimate functions.

Not so much today, but in earlier discussions of these questions it was common to attribute the modern "liberation" of politics to the influence of the sixteenth-century Reformation. As discussed earlier, Luther in particular developed a rough doctrine of "two kingdoms" that seemed to grant autonomy to the secular realm. Many Christians, far from being grateful to Luther, have accused him and his doctrines of being the cause of the evangelical church's political passivity, notably in the face of Hitler's totalitarianism. Other scholars, more sympathetic to Luther, point out that the two-kingdoms doctrine was very rough indeed, that it did not separate the two kingdoms but merely tried to illuminate the twofold nature of the rule of the one God over all things, sacred and secular. In fact Luther did not hesitate to remonstrate with the princes again and again, and in terms firmly claiming the authority of the Word of God. It was nonetheless of the greatest long-term significance that the Reformation sundered the religious function from its institutional base in the papacy. Since the sixteenth-century schism—for which, Lutherans believe, Rome bears the primary responsibility—the power of the state was undoubtedly enhanced by the institutional fragmentation of the church. The role of religion in culture-formation was floating loose, as it were, and the institution of the church was at a disadvantage in trying to seize that role. Certainly there was no longer any possibility of the church exercising a monopoly on the *potestas spiritualis.*

True, the old distinction was still maintained by some churches, notably the Roman Catholic until Vatican Council II. In some places, such as Spain under Franco, the monopoly had a degree of believability, but generally the claim to monopoly ran counter both to sociological fact and, increasingly, to ecclesiological doctrine. In theory and fact the Roman Catholic Church is swimming after the flotsam of *potestas spiritualis,* much as are other religious institutions in the modern world. Only a great ecumenical advance that would once again institutionally "center" the religious dynamic could change the fragmentation of moral authority in the modern world. And that *should* only happen in a way that includes structural barriers against the church's temptation to exercise a monopoly over such authority. Such a barrier would be a thoroughly internalized Christian understanding of the continuing importance and theological status of living Judaism. Such a firm understanding can by no means be assumed today. Believable assurances are also required that such a "centered" moral authority would not compete with the state for monopoly control over culture but would befriend cultural endeavors in their resistance to imperialisms, whether political or religious. But these are questions that will become more pressing when the envisioned ecumenical advance is more imminent than it appears to be today.

Returning to the history of our question, the impact of the Reformation was hardly limited to Luther. Figures of the "Radical Reformation" such as Thomas Münzer launched ill-fated experiments in theocratic revolutionism. And then there was what we earlier described as Calvin's grandly flawed experiment in Geneva. More than any other figure of the period, Calvin systematically tried to reorder, both conceptually and practically, the institutional relationship of sacred and secular. It is no accident, as the Marxists say, that Calvin much more than Luther is relentlessly attacked in secularist readings of history. He posed and he poses a very real alternative to the way in which first-principle questions about religion and society have been publicly addressed in the last two centuries. The textbooks of a century shadowed by Auschwitz and the Gulag Archipelago villainize Calvin for the execution of Michael Servetus. He is given prominent place in the gallery of humanity's horrors in the hope that thoughtful people will be discouraged from considering anew the alternatives he explored. Yet today some of the most provocative and rigorous thought about religion and society is being done by those who call themselves Calvinists, especially by those who identify with the Calvinist "revisionism" of Abraham Kuyper (d. 1920), the Dutch theologian and political leader.[19]

The wars of religion following the Reformation ripped apart the civil fabric of Europe and precluded the possibility of any religious alternative being given a fair hearing or a chance to evolve. That fratricide provided powerful ammunition for those Enlightenment figures who would soon be insisting that religion and its inherent divisiveness must be exorcised from the public square. It may be that only now, surrounded as we are by so many signs of the collapse of the two-hundred-year ideological hegemony of the secular Enlightenment, can alternatives—including those derived from the continuing vitalities of Christian history—be given serious consideration. Of course it may also be too late. It may be that, despite a new centering of religious influence, and despite the collapse of the plausibility of the secular Enlightenment, the institutional dynamics of the modern state are such that the hoped-for avenue of reconstruction, not yet certainly discovered, has already been closed.

In briefest compass, then, we have surveyed some patterns and possibilities in relating church and state. Cooperation and complementarity have been pursued at times, but the essential tension is always there. All orders short of the promised kingdom of God run into the comprehensive claims of the community that understands itself to be living now under the rule that will be. We have in this chapter emphasized the institutional nature of the conflict, recognizing that neither government nor church has a monopoly upon discrete social functions. The state in particular cannot be "strictly secular" and still be deemed morally legitimate. Of the

possible traditions of moral legitimation in Western history, only the biblical tradition is democratically supportable in this society. The biblical
story is about the coming of the kingdom. Within that story, both church
and state are provisional actors. But, because it is the bearer of the story,
the role of the church is "the more weighty," as Pope Gelasius and John
Adams would agree.

Today "the great story" is no longer heard in the public square. The
minority that claims not to believe the story, and the still smaller minority
that abhors its being told, may feel liberated, but an oppressive silence has
fallen over the public square. The people do not know why they are there
or, more important, why they ought to be doing what the laws and procedures say they should be doing. In the academic corners of the square
a few story-tellers keep alive the tales of Athens, speaking of ultimacies
that can give new meaning to "authentic politics." In other corners of the
square, revolutionary noises are made by those who preach that God, if he
has not died, has at least abdicated in favor of Man as the master of his
own destiny; the kingdom of God is replaced by a tattered nineteenth-
century dream of the kingdom of unalienated freedom that is ours for the
taking.

Silence, antique tales, utopian dreams in the public square; but mainly
silence. Yet surrounding the square, pressing to get in, jostling the officials
who patrol its borders, threatening to invade, are those who sing the songs
not of Athens nor of Havana but of Jerusalem. They say they represent the
future, and at the same time they say they represent the American past.
Most insistently, they say they represent the majority of us. And, to an
extent, for better and for worse, their claims are true. The defenses against
them, to keep them and their story out, are very unsure. It may be that
the only alternative to civil war is to engage them in civil discourse. For
that to happen, our definition of civil discourse cannot exclude what they
want to talk about. They want to talk about God in public. Given the
choice, many of us might prefer to talk about the politics of orgasm. But
these invaders of the public square insist that they are not interested in
the "problematicizing" and "politicizing" of their private interests. They
are not asking for favors, they do not look to this present establishment
to bestow "meaning" upon their lives. They would enter the public square
in order to challenge the meaning-bestowing powers of those who preside
over the public square. They are, in the name of religion's truth, challenging the modern state. If they persist, if they refine their purpose in a manner reassuring to the legitimate interests of others, if they refuse to be
pacified by lesser benefits that the state can offer—then these despised
moral majoritarians may turn out to be the first wave of the democratic
renewal of the twenty-first century. They might even rehabilitate the idea
of Christendom. But there are so many ifs.

CHAPTER ELEVEN

INVOKING THE
NIGHTMARES WE FEAR

O F COURSE IT WOULD BE AN IRONY OF THE FIRST CLASS WERE the moral majoritarians to turn out to be the instrument of democratic renewal. Were this to happen, it would not be because they bring to our political life a more convincing and coherent theory of democratic governance. They do not have such a theory and therefore they cannot contribute it. Their most obvious contribution is a heightened level of suspiciousness and resentment. That will likely continue to be the case for some time to come. This is not to deny that there is an evolving intellectual sophistication among some leaders of the religious new right that emerged in the late seventies. Such evolution is evident, sometimes dramatically so, but it is hardly typical of that movement. To the contrary, in both rhetoric and substance, that movement is still marked (and marred) by the language of its initial phase: a language that recklessly and indiscriminately assaults almost the entirety of our recent intellectual history as a conspiracy of secular humanism.

Moral majoritarianism's potential contribution to democratic renewal, then, will, if it is fulfilled, be largely inadvertent. The renewal of democratic governance is not what many partisans of moral majoritarianism think they are about. Indeed, for many of them, the idea of democracy itself is suspect. In their literature one discovers still strong traces of an older conservative Republicanism that harps on the theme that America is not really a democracy at all but a republic. More commonly, one finds that the suspicion of the democratic idea is derived from fundamentalist readings of Scripture that suggest alternative ways of ordering society, ways that imply one or another form of theocracy. The irony I am suggesting, then, is that the moral majoritarian phenomenon may be an instrument of renewing the very democratic idea that it so largely despises.

Whether or not this happens probably depends less upon the moral majoritarians than upon our response to them. It requires an exercise of critical distance and sense of irony that is not easy to maintain in the midst of heated partisan polemics. But this challenge is not entirely new, although it has seldom been met successfully when it has come up in the past. Indeed the failure to meet this challenge in the past has been a major factor in producing the cultural polarizations of our present and immediate future. The philosopher John Dewey saw in the 1920s the destructive

177

antitheses that were building. He was especially concerned about the way in which intellectuals and those who today are called "the new class" despised and dismissed the masses represented by, for example, William Jennings Bryan. In a 1922 article in *The New Republic* Dewey warned that Bryan and his followers should not be derided as mere obscurantists because Bryan "is a typical democratic figure—there is no gainsaying that proposition." Of course he was mediocre, but "democracy by nature puts a premium on mediocrity." Bryan speaks, he said, for some of the best and most essential elements in American society:

> ... the church-going classes, those who have come under the influence of evangelical Christianity. These people form the backbone of philanthropic social interest, of social reform through political action, of pacifism, of popular education. They embody and express the spirit of kindly good will towards classes which are at an economic disadvantage and towards other nations, especially when the latter show any disposition towards a republican form of government. The Middle West, the prairie country, has been the centre of active social philanthropy and political progressivism because it is the chief home of this folk ... believing in education and better opportunities for its own children. ... it has been the element responsive to appeals for the square deal and more nearly equal opportunities for all. ... It followed Lincoln in the abolition of slavery and it followed Roosevelt in his denunciation of "bad" corporations and aggregations of wealth. ... It has been the middle in every sense of the word and of every movement.[1]

Admittedly, Dewey's description of the "church-going classes" of his day would seem to bear little resemblance to the moral majoritarians of today. Yet I would suggest that what came to be called "Middle America" in the Nixon years is not too different from the world Dewey spoke of. If today its expression seems reactionary, anti-democratic, and mean-spirited, that is because it is exploited by leaders of such negative dispositions. In a similar way, many decent Americans gave the benefit of the doubt to a Joseph McCarthy because many more respectable leaders in liberal politics, academe, and religion evidenced nothing but contempt for deep popular doubts about the directions of U.S. policies. One need not be an enthusiastic populist to note that elite contempt for popular sensibilities has, again and again, played into the hands of leaders who are not above exploiting the consequent popular resentments. When that happens, of course, the elites feel that they are vindicated in their initial contempt, failing to recognize that they have played a critical role in producing the result that they interpret as their vindication. In other words, the problematic addressed by Dewey (and, as noted earlier, by Richard Hofstadter) is of long standing. If it is true that attitudes surrounding the "monkey trial" of 1925 froze the cultural divides in American life, then it is not too much to say that we are today reaping the consequences of our failure to heed warnings such as that issued by John Dewey in 1922. As a result, the benign moral majority of the "church-going classes" has in large part turned sour.

Unlike Dewey's moral majoritarians, those of our day seem inclined to reactionary rather than progressive attitudes. But so much depends upon how we define "progressive," especially as that idea relates to religion and religiously based values in our public life. The crucial meeting ground of moral majoritarians—those of 1922 and those of today—is in protest against the modernist divorce of "value" and "fact." It may seem like a truism to say that values are related to beliefs, but it cannot be taken for granted in a cultural and intellectual climate in which judgments of fact have been separated from judgments of value. Statements of fact are presumably based upon rational, intersubjective evidence. They are objective. They are public. They invoke the category of "truth." And they do that because they are subject to public verification and falsification.

It is worth reminding ourselves of how very fundamental this divorce is in modernity's construction of reality (in doing so we keep in mind that religion, knowingly or not, has collaborated in this divorce by removing religious truth claims into the sphere of privacy and subjectivism, away from the perils of public scrutiny). We think we know what we mean by a statement of fact. If I assert that the Empire State Building is in St. Louis, the statement can readily be falsified by the production of evidence that is convincing to every person we deem reasonable. Those who do not recognize the evidence are finally ruled out of the community of rational discourse. The situation is very different, however, when it comes to assertions of value or what we call moral judgments. If I say it is better to live in New York than in St. Louis, the statement does not invoke the categories of "true" and "false'" in the same way that the statement about the Empire State Building does. If you express agreement that it is indeed better to live in New York, you are not stating a fact about living in New York but only saying something about yourself; namely, that you are a person who would rather live in New York (or, more precisely, you are a person who *says* she would rather live in New York). Similarly with respect to moral judgments. If I say that you *ought* to do this or *ought not* to do that, I am really only expressing my preference; I would *prefer* that you do this or not do the other thing.

When I persist in making moral judgments in public, I am, as noted earlier, thought to be advancing not a truth but an "interest." In certain theories, then, the whole of democracy is but a process for the adjudication of such interests; it is impervious to moral judgment, as such. More than that, the process is fatally threatened by any statement of moral judgment that claims to possess a status by virtue of being derived from a source outside the formal political process itself. That is why religion-in-public is viewed by many as such a fundamental violation of the democratic process. As we have seen, those who hold this viewpoint can find some authority in the thinking of the constitutional founders. But those who held to such a religiously sanitized view of the polity then also assumed a severely limited sphere of governmental authority. With the expansion of the modern state, government inescapably encroaches upon spheres previously thought to be outside the authority of government. In sum: we cannot at the same time have government that is expansive, religiously sanitized, *and* democratic. We have expansive government and there is probably no changing of that reality. The modern state's inherent ambitions toward totalist claims can perhaps be checked and tempered, but there is no going back to the limited government of pristine republicanism. Given the expanded scope of government authority, we must make decisions critical to whether that government will continue to be democratic. The question is whether government can be both large and morally legitimate—as "legitimate" is defined by reference to the religiously based values of the people. This was not such a painful question in the thinking of the founders when government claimed only a modest portion of the public space. Today, and in almost any conceivable future, it is certain that the reach of government is far more ambitious. It is far from certain that such government is or will be perceived as morally legitimate by the criteria of democracy.

In everyday life, fact and value are not divorced. What people believe to be true and what people believe to be morally right are closely related. Although the relationship may not be clearly thought through, the mutual dependence of fact and value is assumed. Indeed this taken-for-granted nature of the relationship is essential to a viable society. Were we all, like professional ethicists, constantly and self-consciously fretting about the connection between fact and value, the society would be in severe crisis indeed. The sociology of the everyday reality, however, is not encompassed by current political theory. More than that, it is frequently contradicted. Values are commonly based upon the religious fact-claims, not only in the sense of where such values historically came from but also in contemporary consciousness. When asked why certain attitudes or behavior is right or wrong, the great majority of Americans answer that the Bible or the church or religious teaching says it is so. This is an embarrassment to prevailing theories of politics and society. For instance, far from having entered into a "social contract" for the adjudication of interests, Americans are closer to thinking of themselves as accountable in some "covenantal" manner to divine purpose and judgment.[2]

There is considerable wisdom in theories that limit the idea of democracy to the purely procedural. Such wisdom is evident, however, only when it is recognized that these theories are of limited explanatory utility with respect to what actually happens in society. Our difficulty is that we have mistaken these limited theoretical constructs as literal and exhaustive explanations. This is notably evident in legal definitions of what is "public" which violate the personal and institutional behavior of "the public" that is the American people. A self-consciously limited and "pragmatic" theory of democracy attempts, wisely, to avoid or mute conflicts over religiously grounded ultimacies. In this approach it is recognized that democratic governance cannot readily accommodate first-principle questions. Practical arrangements are threatened by an "overload" of transcendence. In view of this, it is hoped that most conflicts can be resolved, or at least temporarily defused, by accommodations which rest upon a moral consensus that is, for the most part, deliberately unarticulated. Somewhat vague notions such as "fairness" and "decency" will ordinarily do the job in arriving at public decisions that will be recognized as legitimate, at least for the time being. As for those who do not recognize the legitimacy of such decisions, it is assumed that they will get their turn at bat, so to speak, and have a chance to modify the decisions in ways more amenable to their desires.

In democratic procedure every governmental decision produces unhappiness as well as satisfactions. It is possible that the unhappiness outweighs the satisfactions, since on questions of great moment those who "lose" may feel more violated than those who "win" feel vindicated. Vindication tends to be a brief satisfaction, while the sense of being violated goes on and on. Since they tend to manufacture resentments, there is wisdom in the bias that favors limiting the number of government decisions. Nonetheless, the form of governance is tolerable so long as it is assumed that there will always be another inning, another election, another appeal, another case to be tested. In this practical approach there are no final winners or final losers, and everybody understands that she will get her way only part of the time. This, in short, is one somewhat complacent orthodoxy about the nature of democracy. Now the complacency is shattered because a very large number of Americans who feel they have for a long time been on the losing end have come to believe that the winners are trying to deny them their innings. They believe that their case has not simply failed to carry the day in political procedure but it has now been declared invalid in principle. Because they do not understand or are impatient with the theory that divorces religious value from governmental fact, they declare their intent to overwhelm the opposition (whom they view as "the enemy") by sheer force of majoritarian might. Those who hold a pragmatic and provisional view of the democratic process, and who also recognize its fragility, are understandably alarmed.

A distinction might be suggested between "questions" and "issues." Our polity is not designed to ask and answer questions, especially not first-principle questions. It is designed to handle issues. A question comes to *public* attention when it is presented in the form of an issue. An issue is a dispute about a social arrangement and becomes a public issue when it impinges upon arrangements that fall into the category of public policy.

Similarly, a distinction might be made between a statement of moral truth and a value judgment. Value judgments are made by individuals and different value judgments can be negotiated by individuals. In this sense, values do reflect personal preferences, for individuals make the evaluation by which something is of value or not. We have procedures for making adjustments between different and even conflicting evaluations. A statement of moral truth is much more inconvenient to the political process. We do not have procedures for dealing with truths, for truths are presumably objective and universal and not amenable to negotiation. Therefore, in order not to stretch democratic polity beyond the breaking point, questions are to be treated as issues and truths are to be treated as values.

To a very large extent, this pragmatic understanding of democratic procedure "works." But from time to time the polity is confronted by issues which cannot conceal the questions that generated them. Slavery was such an issue, undoubtedly the most traumatic in American history to date. The question was whether those of African descent belong to the community of persons who possess rights that we are bound to respect. The Dred Scott decision of 1857 tried to handle the issue by answering the question one way. The Civil War reversed that decision. In the abortion debate today, as we have seen, "pro-life" advocates insist that the question is essentially the same as that posed by slavery. Do the unborn, who in the absence of lethal intervention indisputably would be citizens, have rights that we are bound to respect? The questions posed in the abortion debate are fundamental and it is therefore understandable that courts and legislatures might prefer that the issue—and, along with the issue, the questions—would go away. Obviously, the attempt to resolve the issue without addressing the questions (for example, *Roe v. Wade* of 1973) has not produced a stable resolution. The "pro-choice" advocates have no choice but to hope either that the issue will go away or that the public discussion of it can be limited to the procedural question of who has the right to make the decision about having an abortion. Brigitte and Peter Berger, among others, have made an honorable effort to propose a "middle ground" in the abortion debate. But, given the "pro-life" perception of what is at stake, they recognize the difficulty in achieving a compromise. "In view of this perception of the issue by large numbers of Americans, the accusation by [the "pro-choice" side] that these people are engaged in 'single issue politics' missed the point entirely: Given this perception, what single issue could be more important than a million murders per year?"[3]

Slavery and abortion are exceptions in that politically potent advocates insisted upon pressing the questions behind the issues, and the questions are not amenable to answer by compromise. Refusing to compromise, such advocates are viewed as agitators and bear the onus of being undemocratic, for compromise is the democratic thing to do. Basic questions break through other issues too, however, putting our procedures to the test. Issues about moral formation in public schools raise elementary questions about the rights of parents and about the role of education in the transmission of values. Quota systems in education and employment, aimed at rectifying past wrongs against minorities, engage foundational questions about fairness, justice, guilt, and reparation. Immigration policies and the treatment of aliens in our midst involve rudimentary beliefs about the moral status of national sovereignty and privilege. Law and convention are not self-justifying: Why should a child born on one side of the U.S.–Mexican border have access to opportunities and benefits that are denied to another child born two miles farther south? Increasingly, taken-for-granted assumptions are not being taken for granted. The list of issues is long. Scratch almost any political or legal issue of moment and we are faced by moral questions begging to be answered. Because we are better at handling issues than at answering questions, the general rule is not to scratch.

The people described by Dewey in 1922 assumed a congruence between issue and question. With allowances made for "high-brow" deviants in places like New York, it was thought that a moral consensus could be counted on. Many of Dewey's people have become the moral majoritarians of today because they believe that in the course of the last half-century "the deviants" have taken over. It is not that "bohemian" dissent is no longer tolerated; it is rather that, in the absence of a consensus from which to dissent, "bohemia" is no longer possible. It is possible that the most controversial dissent today is dissent from the proposition that there is or, more precisely, that there *should be* no normative consensus. As in our domestic life this question has broken out of its packaging as a series of "issues," so also the role of America in the world has become highly problematic. In a way unprecedented in our modern history, the American experiment itself has become a question. True, the experiment was launched as a question (thus its being called an experiment), but in the Puritan and constitutional periods, as in the nineteenth century of evangelical confidence, it was thought that the question was emphatically answered by the American fact. The American experiment was vindicated by the American experience. Today experiences both domestic and global challenge not only the success but also the desirability of the experiment. We are a long way from the confidence of the eighteenth and nineteenth centuries; in fact we are a long way from the 1950s' confidence in "the American Way of Life" and its promise for the world.[4]

Not long ago there was a secure consensus that American interests in the world were congruent with—indeed essential to—such worthy goals as spreading prosperity, advancing democracy, and defending the free world. Today the morality of America's role in the world is by no means self-evident. To many Americans it is not evident at all. It is commonly suggested that the Vietnam War was the turning point, and there is no doubt some truth in that. War is a testing of a society. Obviously it is a testing of military and economic strength and of political leadership. More profoundly, it is a testing of the legitimacy of a social order, or at least of that order's perceived legitimacy. The question is posed whether the survival of a society or the expansion of its influence justifies killing and the risk of being killed. War dramatically raises the stakes in the contentions over social legitimation.

I say there is "some truth" to the belief that Vietnam fundamentally changed popular perceptions of America's role in the world. Caution is in order. People at all points on the political spectrum may greatly overestimate the influence of "the Vietnam syndrome." Some new military conflict, supported by popular persuasion that vital interests and honorable purposes make the conflict necessary, could very quickly overwhelm the memory of Vietnam. This may not be a happy prospect, but it would be a great mistake to think "the lessons of Vietnam" are permanent (or even, as we shall see, that there is a stable agreement on what in fact are "the lessons of Vietnam"). One recalls the stunning rapidity with which intellectual and religious leadership abandoned its proclaimed pacifist convictions upon the beginning of World War II. Nor would it require a world war of that magnitude (which could indeed be "the war to end wars"—and most everything else) to effect such a sea change in current attitudes toward American power in the world. One suspects that a determined *and successful* military expedition in, say, Central America could have that effect. We have only to recall the seemingly inordinate impact of Britain's Falklands exercise in 1982. Seemingly inordinate, I say, because what had some of the appearances of a comic opera episode so powerfully transformed the British public's perception of its place in the world. Few would doubt, for example, that, had the Falklands enterprise ended in disaster, Margaret Thatcher would have been retired in ignominy. Such are the contingencies, both serendipitous and tragic, that caution us against excessive certainty in analyzing trends and attitudes.

Keeping that caution in mind, it appears today that different sectors of the American population worry about the moral legitimacy of American society and its place in the world in quite different ways. Many who believe that the governance of our domestic life is corrupted, decadent, and thoroughly illegitimate are nonetheless convinced that American power in the world has a mission that is not only legitimate but divinely mandated. At the same time, many who approve of the "liberating" directions of the domestic order have the most grave misgivings about America's role in international affairs. Frequently the latter group subscribes to an isolationist view of world affairs and evidences enthusiasm for reducing America's global influence. (As observers have noted, "isolationist" and "internationalist" views tend to shift back and forth between right and left in American life.) Critics of the current "isolationists" accuse them of

184

being anti-American, a criticism that is understandably resented. Yet the debates about American influence in the world, especially military influence, do engage questions about the legitimacy of the American experiment itself.

To the extent these debates are shaped by the Vietnam experience, it is imperative to examine briefly the range of thought and feeling about that "moment of truth." For many Americans, Vietnam was a war that we could have "won" had we the nerve for it. But, they claim, a minority of Americans, chiefly those of the "new class" that mints and markets ideas, succeeded in undermining national confidence and smoothed the way for abject defeat. In this line of thinking there are remnants of the *machismo* view of war. In a nuclear age, many thoughtful people believe, such a view of war steps over the border into the absurd. Nonetheless, the Vietnam War, fought by unconventional yet "conventional" means, did bring to the surface conflicting views of a most comprehensive nature. The story of Vietnam is told and its "lessons" are drawn to quite opposite ends. But the lessons drawn are exceedingly moral in tone and substance, and, opposite conclusions aside, each party to the debate is convinced that Vietnam exposed something fundamentally wrong with America.

American attitudes toward the Vietnam War can be divided into four categories. The first category is not so much a formed attitude as an inclination to "go along" with government policy. If, with respect to foreign affairs, we distinguish between an "attentive" and an "inattentive" public, one may safely assume that most Americans were more or less inattentive to Vietnam. This is not necessarily a fault, for there are a great many things in life claiming our attention more urgently than foreign policy questions over which we have little control. Popular readiness to give the government the benefit of the doubt, even though that gift can be grievously misplaced, is generally thought to be a mark of a viable society. It is noteworthy that, until the bitter ending with the collapse of Saigon in 1975, polls indicated that a majority of Americans supported the U.S. intervention in Indochina. That is noteworthy, but it is not decisive for understanding the ways in which Vietnam reflected and formed attitudes toward America's role in the world.

More important in this connection are the arguments and attitudes that mark "the attentive public." First, there were those who believed and who continue to believe that the Vietnam War was a just and necessary exercise of American power in defense of the free world. Second is the view that, however just the original intention, the war was doomed by Washington's mistakes and mendacities, which undercut domestic support for the effort. In this camp were "realists" such as Reinhold Niebuhr and Hans Morgenthau who opposed U.S. policies because they were convinced that those policies were in conflict with the legitimate interests and responsibilities of American world power. A third view among the attentive public came to be described as the "radicalized" view. For those in this group, Vietnam was not a mistake but a manifestation of an awful truth; it was not the distortion but the revelation of the real meaning of America's role in the contemporary world.

For some years one of the most frequently quoted lines was that of the comic strip character Pogo, "We have met the enemy and he is us." Napalm, defoliants, carpet bombings, and tiger cage prisons were depicted in ways that almost secondarily said something about what was happening to people in a faraway land. Primarily they said something about us, about what we had become as Americans and about what America had become to the world. This view represented a dramatic reversal. Some decades ago an isolationist sentiment that favored American withdrawal from the world was premised upon the belief that America was too good for the world, that our experiment in liberty would be poisoned by entanglements with others. Now the "new isolationism" was advanced upon the argument that America is bad for the world, especially for the third world of the poor. Once Americans fought to make the world safe for democracy; now it is suggested that democracy (at least the American version of democracy) is not safe for the world.

Even the "inattentive" among Dewey's people were badly shaken, not so much by the Vietnam War as by the debate over that war. Public debate became highly moralistic in a way that further confused the meaning of public morality. That is, both supporters and opponents of government policy were emphatic in saying that Vietnam was "a moral issue." Politicians declared that Vietnam was not a political issue but a moral issue, leaving the distinction between the political and moral painfully unclear. It was as though, by declaring something to be a moral issue, political judgment was superseded or suspended. A moral issue, as we noted earlier, turns out to be a political issue on which we turn up the volume. It is as though a political issue becomes a moral issue by virtue of the intensity of tone with which it is debated. Intensity demonstrates that one is not merely declaring a policy preference but a passionately held—that is, moral—preference. One result of the Vietnam debate is that it tended to increase the separation between the political and the moral. That is, by setting moral judgment against political judgment, the possibility of political morality was reduced. Political morality—from Aristotle through Machiavelli to John Courtney Murray—assumes normative truth by which political discourse and action are to be guided and judged. A moral statement in the public arena is not simply high decibel politics but an application of a shared sense of the true and the good to a political exigency. Without such a consensus, moral claims cannot help but seem to be intrusive and disruptive in our political life.

Whatever one thinks about the rights and wrongs of the Vietnam War (this writer was strongly and publicly opposed to U.S. policy), the debate over that war did little to heal the rupture between fact and value, truth and morality. On the contrary, that divide was deepened. On all sides, moralisms overwhelmed morality. Moralism in this connection means high decibel partisanship that employs the language of morality in a cause that is itself exempted from moral judgment. The credibility of "moral judgment" in the public arena was further eroded after the fall of Saigon, when many opponents of the war refused to bring such judgment to bear upon Hanoi's regime of brutal and massive oppression. But that is another story and would take us beyond the scope of the present argument.[5]

After Vietnam it was said that Americans suffered from "moral fatigue." Our public life, some said, had been subjected to an overload of moral challenge. Yet about that time we elected a president, Jimmy Carter, who was powerfully prone to the public use of the language of morality. And a little later the phenomenon of moral majoritarianism broke into our common life. It may be that both came along at just the wrong time, at a time when opinion makers had decided they had had their fill of morality in public. If so, it may further be that there was an element of the self-serving in the suggestion by those of liberal views that we observe a moratorium on morality in public. After all, they had already had their moral crusades.

The two formative moral crusades in our recent history have been for civil rights and against the Vietnam War. Both movements succeeded in gaining their chief point. The United States did withdraw from Indochina and, however ambiguous the actual success in race relations, the official policy is conformed to the initial goals of the civil rights movement. Today's moral crusaders were, for the most part, not involved in the earlier crusades. In fact they were often on the other side in both. Almost all leaders of the religious new right now admit that they were wrong on race relations, although some feel called upon to qualify that admission by referring to the questionable tactics and moral failings of civil rights leaders. On the Vietnam War, however, there is little sign of penitence. From that loss in the moral sweepstakes they have concluded only that America should never again fight a war that it is not determined to win. The lesson they draw from Vietnam is the need for renewed struggle against those who draw the contrary lessons from Vietnam.

The language of morality is an unreliable ally. It too has no permanent friends, only permanent interests. Its inherent logic has a troublesome habit of cutting in all directions. In Dewey's day and ours, most Americans are inclined to think that the interests of morality and of America are, if not allied, at least in happy convergence. Despite the sustained assault upon any such notion, the thought persists that America is something like a "theonomous" society. The idea of theonomy is associated with Paul Tillich, an eminently liberal theologian of great influence in our recent past.[6] Until the modern era, Tillich wrote, culture and society had been

187

heteronomous, ruled from the outside, as it were. Heteronomy is the authoritarian pattern in which law is an external imposition. Tribal chieftains, kings who claimed to rule by divine right, an authoritarian church—these were the old heteronomous patterns for the ordering of societies. With the modern era and the new birth of the democratic idea, heteronomy gave way to autonomy, to self-rule. Tillich limned the ways in which an entirely autonomous society and culture is finally dehumanizing and not sustainable. Freedom without meaning creates a longing for a new authority, thus preparing the way for a return to heteronomy. A theonomous culture, on the other hand, is one in which religious and cultural aspirations toward the transcendent are given public expression. Theonomy is not theocracy. Theocracy is in fact a form of heteronomy in which an institution, namely religion, claims to embody and authoritatively articulate absolute truth. Theocracy is a false theonomy, an act of historical closure, and therefore a form of idolatry.

Although the language may not be familiar, the "church-going classes" of America are sympathetic to the idea of America as a theonomous culture. This does not mean they are moral majoritarians. In fact many of them find themselves in strange alliance with the champions of secular autonomy in opposition to what they perceive as the theocratic threat of heteronomy posed by the religious new right. Fearing a religiously oppressive public square, they find themselves supporting a naked public square, when what they really want is a theonomous public square. A theonomous culture suggests a "sacred canopy" that legitimates a social order. Because religious rightists appear to propose not a canopy but a straitjacket, many Christians and Jews find themselves in a defensive posture that, sometimes inadvertently, reinforces those who equate theonomy with theocracy, and oppose both. Thus the religious right solidifies its opposition. When it lumps together liberal Christians and militant secularists it is attacking a coalition that is in large part of its own creation. This is a very human propensity, to invoke the nightmares that we fear. It is the error against which Dewey cautioned the cultural leaders of the 1920s. If people are portrayed as barbarians, they may feel obliged to behave in barbaric ways. If we are capable of living up to high expectations, we are equally capable of living down to the expectations of those who have declared themselves our enemies. The American experiment is today being rudely tried by militants both rude and respectable who are busily creating the enemy they claim to fear.

CHAPTER TWELVE

A PROPOSITION ON TRIAL

JOHN COURTNEY MURRAY SPOKE OF THIS DEMOCRATIC EX-periment as "the American proposition." Until he was soundly vindi-cated by the Second Vatican Council, Murray's was a distinctly minority voice in the Catholic Church. Viewed as suspect by the religious official-dom, he was for long periods forbidden to publish his views, especially as these touched on church-state relations. Murray's understanding of dem-ocratic governance as a "proposition" is similar to the concept of "the American experiment." Neither a proposition nor an experiment can be taken for granted. A proposition must be proposed, again and again. An experiment must be sustained by careful observation and nurture. A prop-osition-experiment is a possibility set forth and explored.

Both terms, proposition and experiment, are subject to misunder-standing if we think of propositions as something appropriate to classroom discourse or experiments as conducted in a laboratory. There is nothing closeted or aseptic about our subject. Above all, unlike an ordinary sci-entific experiment, this one is not a "controlled experiment." It is of the very essence of an experiment in democracy that it not be controlled. Were it a controlled experiment, it would not be an experiment in democracy. In scholarship and writing we strive to achieve a degree of scientific-like "distance" from our subject. The pitfall in this effort is that we may con-fuse our manner of study with the subject studied. There is nothing cool, distanced, and disinterested about the democratic experiment. It is a stage crowded and confused with actors contending and cooperating in inter-actions of truths, passions, and interests that defy our certain discernment. It is exceedingly unsatisfactory to ideologues of the right and of the left who want the political order to be orderly, who are morally and intellec-tually offended by social arrangements that do not "make sense." It must be admitted that democracy is, among other things, a matter of taste. Some do not have the stomach for its enprincipled disorderliness, its frustrating determination to remain always "unfinished." Its mediocrity, vulgarity, and stridency repulse those of more refined sensibilities. Its propensity for producing surprises is a scandal and bother to those whose job it is to offer systematic explanations that package reality in forms amenable to plan-ning and prediction. The packaging is forever coming undone, much to the chagrin of the systematizers, and to the equal delight of irreverent democrats who knew all along that the future could not be known.

The resurgence of biblical religion in our public life is one of those things that, according to sophisticated explanations of the world, simply should not be happening. It was not in the future we had anticipated. This is very embarrassing. It requires that we confess we were wrong about the future. Or, less awkward, we can dismiss it as only a momentary deviation from the course we had projected, which remains essentially on track. This religious rash is just that, an irritant which portends no serious threat to the secular future we know to be inevitable. Those who share this viewpoint frequently take the tack that, while residual religion may break out in public from time to time, it is not really the future at all; it is a regression to the past, a nostalgic spasm of attempted return to a world irretrievably lost. No matter that it is happening today, and today is the future that yesterday we thought we knew. No matter that it may be happening into the unforeseen reaches of the future; it is still not the future but the past. The idea that what happens in the future is not the future is a curious notion that apparently poses no great problems to people who are otherwise thought to be quite rational.

Again, the proposal here is that politics is most importantly a function of culture, and at the heart of culture is religion, whether or not it is called by that name. Increasingly now it is being called by that name. Not only is it being called religion in the sense of some vague religion-in-general or "civil religion," but it is being called Judeo-Christian, biblical religion. No-name religion does not pose such a serious threat to conventional wisdoms about modernity. The public sphere can tolerantly accommodate the limited play of beliefs perhaps once derived from particularist religion but now made safe by the solvent of secularity. It is brand-name religion that is illegitimate in public. Its normative traditions and truth claims—above all, the embodiment of those traditions and claims in institutions that demand recognition as public actors—cannot be accommodated. The secular wisdom can put up with religion that is private, individualistic, subjective. Such religion is an idiosyncrasy in which almost any number can indulge without impinging upon "the authentically political." Students of the subject have noted that the historic enemies of democratic disorderliness, such as Hitler and Stalin, make their most determined assaults not against religious belief as such but against the institutions of religion.[1] It is the institutions that must be constrained or destroyed in order to make thoroughly secular sense of the social order. This is a point sometimes lost upon folk who speak disparagingly of "institutional religion."

As we have seen, those inclined to a "scientific" or "rational" ordering of society tend to believe that the future is on their side by virtue of a more or less inevitable process of evolutionary progress. The emergence of public religion is therefore viewed as a throwback to prerational tribalism, a momentary fall from evolutionary grace. Phenomena such as the religious new right are depicted as efforts to take us back to a real or imagined past and, if there is one thing on which all right-thinking people agree, it is that "you can't go home again." Change is the only constant. In truth, the idea of the forward movement of history is deeply rooted in Western and, most specifically, biblical thought. History has a purpose, an end, a *telos*; God is not going around in circles, he is not repeating himself.

If it is accurate to say that American democracy is in the midst of a legitimation crisis, then the challenges producing the crisis are not manufactured from nothing, *ex nihilo*. It is the stuff of the past—the traditions of alternative vision, the remembered glimpse of roads not taken, and the experience of roads abandoned—that makes possible the criticism of the present and the anticipation of futures quite different. The remembrance of things past does not contradict the idea of the forward, even linear, movement of history. Rather, it locates the continuum by which such movement is defined. An alternative approach would consign the past to an Orwellian "memory hole." Its invocation, except for antiquarian purposes, must be proscribed. Those who insist upon invoking the past in order to call the present to judgment must be derided as fanatics, irrationalists, destroyers of the world order. The past is, by definition, finished and therefore can have no part in the future.

Jacob Burckhardt speaks with special wisdom on the nature of crisis in historical change:

> Crises and even their accompanying fanaticisms are . . . to be regarded as genuine signs of vitality. The crisis itself is an expedient of nature, like a fever, and the fanaticisms are signs that there still exist for men things they prize more than life and property. . . . All spiritual growth takes place by leaps and bounds, both in the individual and, as here, in the community. The crisis is to be regarded as a new nexus of growth. Crises clear the ground of a host of institutions from which life has long since departed, and which, given their historical privilege, could not have been swept away in any other fashion. . . . Crises also abolish the cumulative dread of "disturbance" and clear the way for strong personalities.[2]

To be sure, in Burckhardt's view, the historically privileged church was one of those institutional forms to be cleared away. In nineteenth-century Europe it seemed to him that "morality, as far as it can, tries to stand on its own feet apart from religion." Religion, in order to retain its privileges, is "apt to lean upon morality as its own daughter." But, he wrote, "the artificial assertion of Christianity in the interests of good behavior has always been utterly useless." He thought it likely that "on the whole, men do their duty today far more from a sense of honor and an actual sense of duty in the restricted sense of the word than from religious motives." At the same time, however, Burckhardt had a powerfully realistic (some would say pessimistic) understanding of human nature and of the fragility of ideas such as honor: "We may well wonder how long the sense of honor will hold as 'the last mighty dam' against the general deluge."[3] An ingredient of the crisis today is that a politically potent and determined sector of the public believes that the dam has broken and the deluge is upon us.

Perhaps our crisis, which could be a "new nexus of growth," brings together the democratic impulse—often antireligious in its original expressions—with a reappropriation of religious tradition. Ranke, that other great nineteenth-century historian, wrote: "There is no political idea which has had so profound an influence in the course of the last few centuries as that of the sovereignty of the people. At times repressed and acting only on opinion, then breaking out again, openly confessed, never realized and perpetually intervening, it is the eternal ferment of the modern world."[4] While fundamentalists and most evangelicals have little use for the idea of the sovereignty of the people, at the practical level it is upon the sovereignty of a religious people that they count in the effort to "turn America around." The democratic idea, which played so large a part in clearing the societal ground of religion, on the assumption that morality could stand on its own feet, is now the instrument of what may turn out to be a restoration of religion. That restoration can take antidemocratic forms, as in versions of the theocratic impulse, or it can, at long last, provide a secure grounding of the democratic idea in religious belief. After centuries of warfare, democracy can serve religion and can be served in turn by a popular religious legitimation that it lacked heretofore. This could be the emerging shape of the "new nexus of growth" produced by the current crisis.

But is not the very idea of "restoration" a regression to the past? Not necessarily. Burckhardt once more, reflecting on restorations, also religious restorations, in history: "Their greatness lies in the effort they evoke, in the power to realize a cherished ideal, which is not the actual past, but its image transfigured by memory. The result is necessarily somewhat strange, since it is established in a changed world."[5] The invocation of the past cannot be discredited as "false consciousness" simply because it can be demonstrated that the past never was the way it is described by those who invoke it. The invocation may be the more effective by virtue of the past being an "image transfigured by memory." We can debate whether we are in a period such as that described by Burckhardt, but all can agree that what is happening is "somewhat strange." If we are witnessing a restoration of religion in public, it is not an instance of going in circles, for it is happening in a "changed world." It is new. It may be the transfigured past that is our future.

If we can speak of the American character, there is nothing so typical of that character as its orientation to the future. I suspect this is still the case, despite elite devotions to ideas such as entropy, zero-growth, and "the end of progress." In any event, to the extent that it is still the case, the effectiveness of a movement requires that it be perceived as being oriented to the future. This is one reason why the opponents of public religion work so relentlessly to portray it as nostalgia and regression. Yet in our own lives, in very practical ways, we know the progressive interplay between past and future. We all make different decisions at different times, sometimes deciding to do again what once we decided to stop doing. At twenty I may decide to be a teacher, at thirty I decide to be a lawyer, only to discover at fifty that I was right in the first place and go back to teaching. I may not regret the years of lawyering at all, and at fifty being a teacher is quite different from being a teacher at twenty.

So, *mutatis mutandis,* in societies. There can be midcourse corrections, as there can also be midcourse distortions. For example, after a "sexual revolution" in which erotic restraint was widely denigrated, it is not impossible that chastity might be restored as a culturally approved norm. After a period in which the family was denigrated as an institution of oppression and birth rates fell, we are seeing signs of a cultural rehabilitation of the family led by opinion-leaders of quite diverse prejudices.[6] If there is merit to the metaphor of the swinging pendulum, such developments should not be entirely surprising. (Admittedly, while the swinging pendulum may keep the clock going, the metaphor does not do justice to the workings of history, which are hardly clocklike.) It is basic to our experience that we change our minds in changing circumstances. We do not always change our minds because we have learned from our mistakes. Santayana's axiom—"Those who cannot remember the past are condemned to repeat it"—is only partially correct. Because each moment of history is genuinely new, we do not simply replicate the past. We do change and make changes: sometimes making mistakes similar to those made before, sometimes making quite novel mistakes, and sometimes doing what appears to be enduringly right.

History is contingent. The unthinkable becomes routine, the inevitable turns out to be illusion. Nobody is an authority on the future, and those who trust alleged authorities will likely end up looking very foolish. Societies once governed by dictators become democratic and then return to dictatorship. Policies aimed at racial justice advance and then recede and then, one hopes, advance again. A bishop friend who is known for his advocacy of controversial positions says his rule of thumb when uncertain about which course to choose is "Go with the future." Had he lived in Germany in 1932 and followed that rule of thumb he would have been a spirited supporter of Adolf Hitler. There is no "future" to guide our present decisions. There are only possible futures that we can strive to advance or resist. More precisely, there is no "future" until it happens, and then it is fleetingly the present on the way to becoming the past. Yet we persist in trying to dismiss proposals labeled as conservative because, we confidently proclaim, they are not of the future but of the past. Interestingly, people who are thoroughly irreverent toward the rules of the past are frequently religious in their devotion to the rules of the present. They are supposedly superior to the past simply by virtue of being of the present and therefore closer in time to the future. With respect to the ordering of society, almost everybody wants some rules from Sinai, the difference being whether we locate our Sinai in the specific past or in the speculative future. The commandments of the future are easier, of course, because we can make them up to our liking. And when our ways of ordering reality have been invalidated by speculative futures that have become specific pasts, they are still valid in our sight because they are of "the future." Thus are put into motion the ever receding horizons of utopias religious and secular, in endless flight from the perils of falsification.

In their thinking about the future that they have chosen because they believe it is willed by God, moral majoritarians reveal tensions and perhaps contradictions. On the one hand theirs is a highly voluntarist, as distinct from determinist, view of history. History is malleable to great men and great visions; America and, with America, the world can be turned around; each person is called now to make the decision that will be decisive for time and eternity. At the same time, there is the fundamentalist belief in "dispensations" by which the future is precisely determined by "Bible prophecy." Their literature is replete with prophecy of the most remarkable precision, right down to Andropov's rise and fall as head of the Soviet Union, and to the discovery of dioxin poisoning in a small town in Missouri. All happens according to scriptural plan. Simultaneously, then, everything is up to us and nothing is up to us. In a matter of years or even of months, the whole drama of history will be wrapped up when Jesus returns to "rapture" his saints to himself. This belief in the imminent end of the world can lead to a sense either of urgency or of resignation. The language of fundamentalist engagement in social change reflects the oscillation between that urgency and that resignation. To be sure, there is a similar dynamic in any Christian view of the "now" and "not yet" of history's fulfillment. But fundamentalists, like many of their secular opponents, express a greater certitude about "the future."

In other ways too, the moral majoritarian vision is notably similar to that of its opponents. The "good life" with which God blesses believers is in many respects what thorough secularists would think of as the good life. True, there are very significant differences in personal and familial ethics (although relatively little emphasis is put on divorce, perhaps because many fundamentalist leaders and their followers are divorced). But "success" as defined by Cadillacs, swimming pools, and luxury vacations is apparently no respecter of belief systems. There is a verbal difference in that what most Americans call "making it" these preachers term "blessings." Even their enthusiasms about sexual fulfillment need not take second place to those promoted in the erotic magazines of the wicked world. Absolutely everything goes better with God and, within the bond of marriage, apparently anything goes. So also, this species of moral majoritarianism is second to none in its confidence about "the future."

Some critics espy the religious internalizing of secular values also in fundamentalism's rapturous embrace of the latest technology. Especially is this true in communications. The equipment and operations of some of the large evangelistic enterprises are said to be the envy of the major television networks. Preachers flash about the country in private jets, alternately perusing the latest catalog of electronic gadgetry and preparing the next sermon on the urgency of returning to an old-fashioned America. They are not above peddling the past in order to fund the future, but it is the future that really matters. The program may be called, for instance, "The Old Time Gospel Hour," which sounds safely nostalgic until it becomes apparent that the old-time gospel preached is all about tomorrow's headlines. Advanced technology, they say, is providentially provided for the task of this historic moment. Our Lord would have used a Lear jet and St. Paul would have exploited the advantages of computerized direct mail, if they had had the technology. Statements such as these suggest that the problem is not that these leaders are stuck in the past and lacking any sense of the future. The problem is that there is no texture, no particularity, in their understanding of time and times. Nothing really has happened, nothing really has changed. History is flattened out, as it were. The view is the opposite of that of a neophiliac culture in which everything is new, unprecedented, revolutionary, and much more complex than you think. Given this flattened view of history, there is no conceptual obstacle to, for example, "restoring the Holy Bible as the basic law of the land." The only obstacle is posed by those who are the declared enemies of Bible truth.

There is no doubt that in some areas of social policy this sector of politicized religion does want to go back, to rescind developments of the last several decades. Welfare policies, prayer in government schools, pornography, abortion—these are all questions on which it is believed that grievous mistakes were made. But it is not, they say, a matter of going back to the way things were. The analogy commonly employed is that of a journey. It all depends on what you set out to do. Your purpose, for instance, may be to drive from San Francisco to New York—or, better, from Orange County to Lynchburg, Virginia. If somewhere in Kansas you discover that you took the wrong turn and are headed for North Dakota, finding your way back to the right route is not an instance of regression but of advance. In finding your way you might go back to where you took the wrong turn or, more likely, you would look for another way to your destination that would not require wasting time by retracing your steps.

However you redirect yourself to where you wanted to go, in doing so you are moving forward and not backward.

The analogy can be criticized as simplistic, of course, To begin with, it assumes that American history, even world history, has a purpose similar to one's purpose in taking a trip. Today, getting any agreement on whether America has a purpose, or on what that purpose might be, or even on whether it makes any sense to ask the question, is, to say the least, highly problematic. Politicized fundamentalism thinks it knows what that purpose is. It is to evangelize the world in preparation for the fulfillment of biblical prophecy. Toward that end, America must be economically, militarily, and morally powerful in the defense of freedom. In alliance with Israel, God's chosen instrument, it must be ready for the final battle between good and evil.

By shrewdly drawing on themes of national purpose, the religious new right greatly expands its audience beyond the believers in fundamentalist specifics. Figures as religiously maverick as Jefferson, Lincoln, and John F. Kennedy can be invoked in support of an American vocation. The religious new right is also shrewd in recognizing a potent heritage of patriotic rhetoric and sentiment that has been made available to it by default. That is, many leaders of other institutions have retired such rhetoric, either because they are embarrassed by it or simply because they no longer believe it is true. Until not so long ago mainline Protestant churches talked about America as a Christian nation with a special destiny, but that seems like a long time ago. Immigrant groups, such as Roman Catholics and Lutherans, were never really at home with that patriotic language. Jews, for obvious reasons, had problems with it. There are the Mormons, of course. They have their own somewhat fundamentalist vision of America's destiny—a vision that in recent years has been employed to good effect in recruitment efforts—but to most Americans the Mormons seem even more eccentric than the Old Time Gospel Hour. Thus the band of the religious new right is left with an almost clear field on which to play the marching tunes of patriotic purpose and national destiny.

The American proposition and its experiment are grotesquely vulgarized in this exploitation of patriotic sentiment. And it is easy to demonstrate that the telling of the American story is often ludicrously distorted. These observations, while accurate, are somewhat beside the point. The point is that, as noted earlier in connection with the ministry of Martin Luther King, Jr., no people willingly moves into the future unless accompanied by the past. Critics can rail against the abuse of "the mystic chords of memory," but they gain nothing unless they play those chords to better ends. A great advantage lies with those who can invoke a sense of continuity and rightness. A syndicated political columnist recently criticized President Reagan for creating "a climate of righteousness in the country." From the context it was obvious that she meant self-righteousness, and I asked her if that were not the case. "Yes, I suppose you are right," she responded, "but to me righteousness and self-righteousness mean the same thing." The inability to use moral language in public is not shared by the religious new right and the millions to whom it appeals. As most of us have become stumbling and tongue-tied in trying to speak of good and evil in the public arena, a vacuum has been created that invites the vulgarized moralism of others.

It is not simply among the Yahoos and uneducated that there is a yearning for a public language of moral purpose. The yearning is increasingly manifest also among influential writers on the left of the political spectrum. Among the things that seem a long time ago are confident statements about the "new world" we have entered in which moral sentiments can be left behind. In 1929 as thoughtful a soul as Walter Lippmann hailed the new order of reason: "This is an original and tremendous fact in human experience: that a whole civilization should be dependent upon technology, that this technology should be dependent upon pure science, and that this pure science should be dependent upon a race of men who consciously refuse, as Mr. Bertrand Russell has said, to regard their 'own desires, tastes and interests as affording a key to the understanding of the world.' "[7] Original and tremendous it was, but its consequences are not welcomed by many today.

The protest against this morally sanitized scientific world takes many forms. In the 1960s the dominant forms were leftist. While not addressing himself primarily to public philosophy, Theodore Roszak's *The Making of a Counter Culture* protested precisely the society Lippmann thought so promising: ". . . that society in which those who govern justify themselves by appeal to technical experts who, in turn, justify themselves by appeal to scientific forms of knowledge. And beyond the authority of science there is no appeal."[8] In recent years others have followed in the steps of Ivan Illich and his colleagues in debunking the myths of expertise. Feminists have been prominent in challenging scientific expertise, which, they say, is but a disguise for patriarchal control. In myriad ways the limitations of science, the discontents of modernity, and the sterility of secularism have all been exposed to the popular consciousness. The alternatives espoused by what was called the counterculture were usually private or limited to small experimental communities, but their influence was widely disseminated through media attention. It was blithely assumed that the counterculture would serve social and political purposes favored by the left. It did that, no doubt, but it did not do only that. The "Jesus People" variation on counterculture themes was an early portent. Some intellectuals who helped discredit the assumptions by which the public square was morally denuded may not be pleased to think that their efforts contributed to preparing the way for purposes they view as socially and politically reactionary. But it seems unlikely that the moral majoritarians would have been able to recruit so many to their banner if there had not been a popular awareness that the doctrines of scientific secularism were in disrepute. And they would not have been able to storm the public square with such effect had its secular defenders been more confident of their own cause.

For purposes of neatness, historians sometimes divide epochs into centuries. At least that is done with more recent history. Dealing with distant time, we casually lump centuries and even millennia together. In part because we know less about them, in part because of a historical hubris that assumes that so much more, and so much more of importance, is happening in time that is closer to us. Thus the Mentor philosophy series of the New American Library treats the whole of the Middle Ages as The Age of Belief, the Renaissance as The Age of Adventure, the seventeenth century as The Age of Reason, the eighteenth as The Age of Enlightenment, the nineteenth as The Age of Ideology, and the twentieth as The Age of Analysis (which made a kind of sense in 1950, before the analytical philosophers went into decline). Were one to venture a very broad generalization, it seems more than possible that the era now drawing to a close might be called The Age of Modernity. Today we see, if not a revolt against modernity, at least a disillusionment with its key doctrines. Those doctrines are built upon a restrictive idea of science that assumes, in turn, a very truncated notion of rationality. What came to be called the religious new right in America may have, as I have suggested, kicked a tripwire alerting us to this massive cultural and political change. That may be the long-term significance of organized moral majoritarianism, far more significant than how many elections it has won or will win in the future.

Modernity, it will be remembered, comes from *modernus* and means "just now." Every age has been modern in the sense that every time is "just now" to those who are living it. Our time is peculiar in having constructed an ideology, indeed a cult, around being "just now." It is a vacuous religion devoted to the obvious, namely that we do not have the option of living our lives in the last century or in the next. But behind the modernity project is one important belief, the belief in progress. The idea of progress is easily confused with a collective egotism that assumes this time must be superior simply because it is, after all, *our* time. In *History of the Idea of Progress* Robert Nisbet argues that, perhaps for the first time in history, the intellectual leaders in Western culture no longer believe in progress. As evidence he cites Roszak and other ideologists of the counterculture now past. He notes the dour invocations of authoritarianism by writers such as economist Robert Heilbroner. A world of rising demands and declining resources, it is said, can no longer support the naive optimism that gave birth to the modernity project. Not so incidentally, the experiment called democracy is also a luxury that will likely have to go.

Distinguished theologians such as Langdon Gilkey of the University of Chicago offer religious ratification of the bad news.[9]

Nisbet traces the connections supporting the intuition that such a fundamental disillusionment may be underway, at least among certain cultural elites. In the 1960s Charles Reich (*The Greening of America*) declared that we are moving into a new consciousness, beyond the nature-dominating, technology-obsessed, scientific rationality of the past. Sociologists Peter and Brigitte Berger responded in a well-known essay that, to the extent Reich is right about what is happening in a certain sector of society, the result would likely be the "blueing of America." That is, if the educated and privileged children of the elite were in fact to be "greened" and were to drop out of the success patterns of American life, their places would readily be taken by the children of blue-collar workers and others who have not been in the mainstream of societal advantage. The graduates of Yahoo State will gladly take over from the graduates of Harvard if and when the latter cancel their reservations for the rooms at the top. In religious, cultural, and political terms, the religious new right may be viewed as a facet of the blueing of America.

Fundamentalists did not have to be told that their views were incompatible with the modernity project. That was made quite clear to them when in the 1920s they were drummed out of the worlds of prestige discourse in American life. Yet they did need others to explain to them why what they always suspected to be the case is true; namely, that the project is based upon assumptions that are specious even by the canons of reason. It is not simply that the modernity project contradicts the Bible. Fundamentalists always knew that about the varieties of "modernism." It is rather that, in addition to violating biblical truth, the project is unreasonable and dehumanizing. Francis Schaeffer is such an explainer, assuring fundamentalists and conservative evangelicals that they were "right from the start." His messages, offered under the theme of "What Ever Happened to the Human Race?", do not simply juxtapose biblical and modernist claims but argue the case that secular humanism is very bad for humanity. Underscoring this line is the enormous popularity in these circles of writers from more classic Christian traditions, such as C. S. Lewis and G. K. Chesterton. Jacques Ellul is appreciated for his debunking of the political illusions of modernity (but there is some ambivalence toward Ellul among people who are, after all, set upon using politics to establish righteousness—a distinctly un-Ellulian enterprise).

Here is a most unlikely company: Jerry Falwell, Tim LaHaye, Theodore Roszak, and Charles Reich. At the personal level there would likely be no love lost between the first pair and the second, but the intellectual companionship is in their common challenge to foundational notions of modernity: that public life can be constructed on the basis of scientific rationality apart from morality and religion, that the public square must be stripped of what Bertrand Russell described as "the desires, tastes, and interests" of real people. For figures such as Roszak and Reich, arriving at this position is a question of disillusionment. For Falwell and LaHaye it is a question of feeling confirmed in what they thought they always knew. In disposition and on substantive issues, the two pairs have little in common. The "new consciousness" of the counterculturalists is free, spontaneous, and in rebellion against every restrictive authority. The religious new right is sober, achievement-oriented, and unabashedly authoritarian.

In this maze of cultural interactions, the counterculturalists have served the moral majoritarians by whom they feel threatened. There is little doubt about which group has the more politically potent constituency. It may be that as many people smoke pot in America as read the Bible daily or send money to television evangelists. But it is the latter group that has the larger potential for being mobilized to "turn America around," in part because it has a more definite idea about the desired direction of the turning. It might be objected that the great majority of Americans belongs to neither group. The counterculture of the 1960s and early 1970s is a spent force: Who has thought of Charles Reich in the last five years? The objection has limited merit, I believe. Cultural formation is a subtle process, the ideas that shape a society are more a matter of the air we breathe than of the conscious decisions we make. The sundry radicalisms associated with the 1960s may be a spent force in that they cannot muster today the massive mobilizations of those years, but the distrust of science and technology, the animus toward narrow rationalisms, the intuition that the American experiment is finished, the suspicion that progress is an illusion—these motifs are pervasive among the "new class" of what has been the cultural elite.

The air of modernity has been breathed too often, it is used air. It is impossible to image today a burst of freshness for the "fighting faith" of secularism such as produced the *Humanist Manifesto* in 1933. In fact, we do not have to try to imagine it. It will be recalled that in 1973 some of the original signers organized *Humanist Manifesto II*. The list of 1973 signers indicated that, in attacking militant secular humanism, the religious new right is assaulting a vision from a geriatric ward. Observers have noted that the attack on secular humanism is, for the most part, a matter of beating a dead horse. There is truth in the observation. The more pertinent and indeed startling observation is that a world view that only thirty or forty years ago was embraced by a culturally formative leadership is today so lacking in partisan support. Today we condescendingly dismiss an ideology that not very long ago was believed to chart the way toward a certain and infinitely promising future. Walter Lippmann was a man of cautious, even conservative sensibilities, yet statements such as his quoted earlier now sound like wild fancy.

The religious new right, then, is shrewd in its polemic against secular humanism. In education, in law, in public policy and manners, the ideas of the secular humanist creed have had consequences. The signers of 1933 were persons of wide and powerful influence, exultant in their confidence of being the vanguard of "the future." Today's moral majoritarians do not need to invent, at least not entirely, the foil for their inveighing. They are shrewd also because the creed they attack, and with which they tar almost everything they oppose, today has few defenders. And in one respect that is too bad. For, however wrongheaded the secular humanists of yesteryear may have been on other scores, they did, for the most part, believe in the democratic idea.

This chapter started with John Courtney Murray and the American proposition-experiment. Thirty years ago Murray recognized that the democratic reality could not be sustained on narrow secular grounds. He saw that the anti-Catholicism of militant secularists such as Paul Blanshard was really aimed at driving religiously grounded values from the public arena, and he deplored the fact that too many mainline Protestants had internalized the reasonings of secularism that fit their own anti-Catholic bias. "In the presence of this enemy [the ideology of the Blanshards] I consider Catholic-Protestant polemic to be an irrelevance," Murray wrote. Anti-Catholicism was given "a philosophical armature which they call evolutionary scientific humanism. Other men more practical than [Blanshard] are endeavoring to give it political expression in what I should call 'our Holy Mother the State,' almighty (by democratic means, of course), creator of all things visible and invisible, even the dignity of man. Here, I think, is the enemy."[10] Such sentiments, less elegantly expressed, are today found among the religious new right.

There are significant differences between Murray and the moral majoritarians, however, and the differences are in more than style and erudition. Murray had a clear understanding of democracy, its virtues, strengths, and fragilities. Although organized majoritarianism employs "democratic means," in view of its subliminal theocratism it is not certain that it is committed to democratic ends. In addition, in challenging "the future" posed by what he calls evolutionary scientific humanism, Murray looked to the mainstream Protestant religious tradition as an essential ally. He may have been disappointed in that hope, but today's warriors against secularism do not even entertain the hope. In their view the liberal mainline is apostate and the enemy of true religion. It is now time to turn our attention more directly to that mainline, asking why the historic bearer of the idea of "Christian America" is so often perceived as friendly to the forces that would dismantle the religious legitimation it did so much to construct in advancing the democratic proposition-experiment.

CHAPTER THIRTEEN

THE CAPTIVITIES
OF THE MAINLINE

THE "MAINLINE" OR "MAINSTREAM" OF A PHENOMENON
would seem to be that reality which requires little explanation. It is
the normative, the obvious, the taken for granted. It is by reference to the
mainline that alternatives and deviations are explained. In this meaning
of the term it may be questioned whether "the mainline" is any longer
mainline religion in America. It is certainly not mainline in numerical
terms. Taken together, the memberships of Roman Catholic, Lutheran,
Orthodox, evangelical, and fundamentalist churches—all outside the usual
definition of "the Protestant mainline"—make up the great majority of
Christians in America. Beyond numbers, there is a growing body of literature suggesting that the mainline is also no longer "mainline" in terms
of religious vitalities or cultural influence. Unlike numbers, vitalities and
influence are harder to measure. Media attention is likely to skew our
perception of the continuing strength of the mainline, since the media of
course assume that "news" is the new and, frequently, the bizarre.

Before looking at the mainline *within* American religion, therefore,
we need to be reminded of the context of American life in which is revealed
the mainline character of religion itself. For better and for worse, America
has been, is, and almost certainly will continue to be a strikingly religious
society. Americans are not necessarily religious in the sense of being good
or upright, contrary to the religious new right that is fond of declaring,
"America is great because she is good; the day she stops being good she
will stop being great." In this connection we are rather using "religious"
in a descriptive, not an evaluative, sense. To say that America is religious
is simply to say that religion is everywhere and may be expected to erupt
in unexpected places and unexpected forms. When it is not erupting, it is
the quiet stream of assumptions that shadow and illumine the lives of
most Americans. The typically American "construction of reality" is closely
linked to loyalties and infidelities shaped by religious visions.

What we tend to take for granted (and therefore find it easier to
ignore) is often seen more clearly by visitors from other countries. This
has been notably true of the place of religion in American life. The nineteenth-century visitor most commonly cited in this connection is Alexis
De Tocqueville, but his observations were shared by a host of others. The
Austrian journalist Francis Grund wrote in 1837: "The religious habits of

the Americans form not only the basis of their private and public morals, but have become so thoroughly interwoven with their whole course of legislation that it would be impossible to change them without affecting the very essence of their government. ... With Argus-eyes does public opinion watch over the words and actions of individuals, and whatever may be their private sins, enforces at least a tribute to morality in public."[1]

Some have suggested that this situation has changed dramatically in recent years. Consider, for example, how Adlai Stevenson's divorce worked against his presidential aspirations, while thirty years later the most righteous-minded Americans overwhelmingly supported a divorced Ronald Reagan. The difference is exaggerated, I believe.

While attitudes toward divorce may also have changed, the significant difference was between bachelor Stevenson's sophisticated attitude toward traditional values and Reagan's manifest, almost cloyingly manifest, devotion to a very traditional marriage, albeit a second marriage, of long standing. The Argus-eyes are still alert, as is evident in public attitudes toward Senator Edward Kennedy's problems with marital and other personal values that Americans profess to revere. The alertness, almost to the point of fanaticism, is most evident in the uproar over Richard Nixon's "Watergate." To this day, leaders and publics in other nations express disbelief that a petty burglary and its accompanying lies could really have been the cause of such moral outrage and national turmoil. They should read their Tocqueville and Grund (in France, his native land, Tocqueville is almost totally unpublished and unread). Significantly, it was not the churches but the press that in full cry led the forces of moral indignation over Watergate. Jonathan Edwards had nothing on "investigate reporters" such as Woodward and Bernstein or the editorialists of the prestige papers. Here too Vilfredo Pareto's theory about "the circulation of elites" may be pertinent. When the incorrigible moralism of the American people is no longer articulated by the establishment churches, that expressive task "circulates" to the establishment media.

There is, then, this striking continuity of propensity for moral judgment. The occasions of outrage may change from time to time. Sixty years ago no national politician would be photographed with an alcoholic beverage in hand. Today it might be equally devastating to be caught tossing a candy wrapper in public space or pictured smoking a cigarette. In things big and little, the Argus-eyes are ever watchful. Jimmy Carter had it partly right: the people want a president as good as they think they are, or as good as they want to be. Popular respect for Mr. Carter's uprightness was finally matched only by impatience with what was thought to be his incompetence. In the last century Oscar Wilde, the Trollopes (mother and son), and Charles Dickens were all inclined to deplore American religious expressions as being in unspeakably bad taste, but they had no doubt that Americans were obsessed by religion. More recently, the English journalist

Martin Amis visited Jerry Falwell's Thomas Road Baptist Church and had to caution himself against "the vulgar British delight in deploring American vulgarities." What earlier visitors saw and contemporary visitors see is not seen by many American intellectuals and writers. They may be familiar with descriptions of "religious America" in the past, but it is assumed that they describe an America that is indeed past. (The only network television series depicting religion as a fact of everyday life are safely placed in the last century.) The last two decades in particular have seen an avalanche of books and articles definitively declaring America to be in a secular or post-Christian phase of its development—or of its decline, as others would have it.

What theorists such as Durkheim claimed is true of all societies is most manifestly true of America. Religion in some form seems to be required. There must be some ultimate value or truth which lays upon individuals and communities a claim that gives meaning to "duty." There must be some final sanction, both positive and negative, that hallows law. There must be a widely shared confidence that what we describe as "the real world" is in harmony with, or at least not in obvious conflict with, the way things really are. We recall the truth described by Clifford Geertz in "Religion as a Cultural System": "Sacred symbols function to synthesize a people's ethos—the tone, character, and quality of their life, its moral and aesthetic mood—and their world view—the picture they have of the way things in sheer actuality are, their most comprehensive ideas of order."[2] In perhaps the most ambitious (and frequently neglected) of his books, *The Homeless Mind*, Peter Berger and his colleagues make the argument that the question about modern society is not whether it will be religious or secular, but which religious symbols will provide "the sacred canopy" under which we mortals will dream our dreams and try to sort out the rights and wrongs of our confused existence.

The evidence of survey research overwhelmingly and consistently confirms the religiousness of the American people. This is the mainline American experience. And, despite the attention paid Eastern and other exotic cults, that religiousness defines itself with reference to the biblical traditions. One reason this mainline experience seems marginal to some observers is that the "what is happening now" of the communications media is highly politicized. What is "news" is for the most part what shows up or might show up in terms of shifts of political power. Martin E. Marty of the University of Chicago notes that during the American Bicentennial Year numerous polls of news reporters, and also of historians, ranked the most important events in American history. "Never did the First Great Awakening of the 1730s and 1740s show up in the one hundred top selections," writes Marty. Yet scholars of the colonial period suggest that this religious movement "was perhaps the most extensive intercolonial event; that it reached into virtually every kind of community and crossroads; that its effects were at first profoundly unsettling to the established order and then became creative elements in establishing a new order; and that indirect lines connect many of its impulses to those of the War of Independence and nation-building endeavors." The great student of Puritanism, Perry Miller, concluded that that awakening began "a new era, not merely of American Protestantism, but in the evolution of the American mind," that it was a watershed, a break with the Middle Ages, a turning point, a crisis.[3]

Is it, as some moral majoritarians argue, that there is a conspiracy, in the manner of Orwell's *1984*, to rewrite history? It is not so simple as that, Marty contends. The misperception of American life is in part because those who define the American reality—whether in high school textbooks or television documentaries—were educated by a historians' guild that operates on the assumption that ours is "a secular period and a pluralist society." "With the birth of the modern university and its accompanying division of labor, the study of religious history was edged into segregated seminaries and divinity schools. Especially with the rise of public tax-supported institutions the study of religion became problematic. Add to this the fact that many intellectuals were themselves in rebellion against what they experienced as repressive and limiting childhood religion, and it is easy to see why the study of awakenings did not draw notice the way charting of military conflicts or presidential elections did."[4]

Furthermore, the values of the university are universalistic. There is something not quite respectable about taking too seriously that which is "parochial," or, God forbid, "sectarian." Then too, in many cases those most interested in religious history might themselves be religiously committed, thus throwing into question whether their work is "objective" and "value-free." And, of course, there is the frequently affirmed dogma, dating from the secular Enlightenment, that religion is residual, backward, primitive, definitely of the past. Even historians do not want to give their lives to studying something that will be irrelevant to "the future." Finally, among the more politicized, there is the suspicion that religion is poor compensation for the lack of social justice; therefore to accent religion is to reinforce this traditional obstacle to the coming of the desired new order.

As we have seen throughout this essay, there is also a very legitimate fear of the divisive force of religion in public. Historically, it is based on the remembrance of the religious wars of the sixteenth and seventeenth centuries, but that remembrance has been refreshed by bloodlettings in the modern era. There has not been the same intellectual response, however, to the much greater bloodlettings of determinedly secularized politics. Hitler, Stalin, Mao, and sundry revolutionisms in the third world have not led us to think that politics should be allowed to simply go away—as much, at times, as we might wish it would. To ignore the role of religion in the ongoing story of America is deliberately to blind ourselves to reality. A much-respected film critic in New York is said to have exclaimed the morning after Nixon's crushing defeat of McGovern in 1972: "I simply don't believe it. How could it happen? I don't know anybody who voted for Nixon!" A similarly refined insulation from reality is evident in the attitudes toward religion assumed by many who bear responsibility for informing the national consciousness. It is said that this situation is changing, and one hopes that is the case. But it has not changed fast enough to prevent prestige opinion from being caught by surprise by the religious new right, or from expressing astonishment at the "revolutionary politics" in establishment churches. Above all, it has not changed far enough to motivate secular opinion makers to examine religious America on its own merits, quite apart from its immediate impact upon the political scoresheets that make up "the news."

All the same, one must sympathize in part with the reluctance of reporters and social analysts to examine seriously the American religious situation. The situation is so maddeningly complex. The temptation is to assume that there are Protestants, Catholics, and Jews, and let it go at that, with marginal notes on various cults and occasional spasms of anxiety about those Protestants who call themselves evangelicals or fundamentalists. Who except religion specialists has time to go into greater detail? As church historian Philip Schaff observed in 1854, "the United States is a motley sampler of all church history." Historian Sydney Ahlstrom notes that by the 1920s "virtually every surviving heresy and schism in Christian history had its representatives in America."[5] In addition to all the divisions of the past, America has been astonishingly fecund in producing its own schisms and heresies, each of which is to some Americans the true faith. With more than 400,000 local churches and literally hundreds of denominations, it is little wonder that some sensible people hesitate to begin an exploration through the mazeways of American religion.

Add to size and complexity the sheer volatility of American religion. It is always changing. One historian notes that the more he studies American religion the less confident he is that he understands it. He quotes Hannah Arendt who wrote in *Between Past and Future* about a world that, lacking authority and stability, is transforming itself "with ever-increasing rapidity from one shape into another, as though we were living and struggling with a Protean universe where everything at any moment can become almost anything else."[6] Establishments decline, outsiders make a bid to become insiders, the outside is redefined as the inside, and the issues that divide and unite lap back and forth over the reefs of denominational and ideological alignment.

Instead of doing an inventory of religious groups and their belief systems, it may be possible to produce some sort of "map" of American religion on the basis of behavior patterns.[7] It is suggested that on this map would be six basic groupings of religious behavior: the mainline, evangelicalism and fundamentalism, pentecostal-charismatic religion, the new religions, ethnic religion, and civil religion. By "new religions" is meant the non-Christian and non-Jewish groupings, often Eastern, that have grown up, and sometimes died, in the various subcultures of American life during recent decades. They are new, of course, only in the sense of being new in America. "Ethnic religion" focuses on black, Chicano, eastern European, and other groupings in which religion is a chief, sometimes the chief, support and expression of ethnic identity. Denominationally speaking, these may range from Armenian Orthodox to independent pentecostal churches. "Civil religion," as we have noted, usually does not call itself a religion but is that cluster of beliefs and symbols which Geertz describes as defining a society to itself.

The subject of these pages has been mainly the mix of evangelical/fundamentalist religion. Other actors are very much in play. Roman Catholics and Lutherans, for example, are in some ways mainline, to a significant extent ethnic, and also shaped by what are broadly termed "evangelical" leanings. (Although vigorously denied by its leaders, there are undoubted elements in Missouri Synod Lutheranism of what can properly be called fundamentalism.) While keeping the many actors in play, the fundamentalist/evangelical reality is critically defined by its relationship to the Protestant mainline. This is historically the case in that the bulk of evangelical/fundamentalist religion went into exile from the mainline (before it was called the mainline and all Protestants styled themselves "evangelicals"). It is also the case strategically, in that the militancy of these "outsiders" is today directed at displacing the mainline as the establishment, culture-defining religious force in American life. To understand the insurgency, then, we must examine what it is surging against, so to speak, and why its leaders believe that this is their moment in the religious, cultural, and political sun.

Mainline religion is the channel of continuity, the mainline, of American religious experience since the seventeenth century. Here are located the churches that many Americans view as "standard brand" religion—Presbyterian, Methodist, Episcopalian, Congregationalist. If one wanted to physically locate the mainline, to actually walk up to the door and push the bell, one would go to 475 Riverside Drive in New York City. This is the headquarters of the National Council of the Churches of Christ in the U.S.A. (more commonly called the National Council of Churches or just "NCC"). The NCC was organized in 1950 but has its roots in cooperative Protestant work going back much further than that. With more than thirty member churches, it is no longer exclusively Protestant. It includes some Eastern Orthodox churches, although the Orthodox, who count more than five million adherents in America, are perennially nervous about their tenuous association with the mainline.[8] The NCC does not include Catholics, most Lutherans, nor the Southern Baptist Convention, the largest single Protestant denomination (all of these participate, however, in some NCC-related programs). And, of course, the NCC is unqualifiedly the enemy in the eyes of millions of other evangelicals, fundamentalists, and pentecostals.

If one were to go further and try to locate "the mainline of the mainline," she would look to the Consultation on Church Union. COCU, as it is called, emerged from the 1960 "Blake-Pike Proposal" (Eugene Carson Blake and the late James Pike) that Protestant denominations should form one church that would be both "evangelical and catholic." Starting with the United Presbyterian and Protestant Episcopal churches, the United Methodists, United Church of Christ, and Disciples of Christ were also in on the ground floor. Three black denominations, all Methodist, are now participating in COCU, which has a total of ten churches still working, as it is said, "in quest of a Church of Christ Uniting." The basic premise is that these churches are similar enough in belief and in practice that there is no reason why, in principle, they should be separated and every reason why they should be together. Fundamentalists and many evangelicals readily agree. Like George Wallace on politics, they assert that "there isn't a dime's worth of difference" between these churches anyway. Efforts such as COCU, in which many have invested high ecumenical hopes, appear to the opposition as little more than attempted consolidations of spiritual and institutional bankrupts.

Perhaps the first thing to be said about the American mainline churches, however, is that they are very American. They are confident that they belong here and, at least until recently, confident that God had put them here for a purpose. They are the historic bearers of the idea of "Christian America." One of the leading theological voices of the nineteenth century, Horace Bushnell, spoke for the assured consensus: "The wilderness shall bud and blossom as the rose before us; and we will not cease, till a christian nation throws up its temples of worship on every hill and plain; till knowledge, virtue, and religion, blending their dignity and their healthful power, have filled our great country with a manly and happy race of people, and the bands of a complete christian commonwealth are seen to span the continent."[9] God had a hand in America's beginnings and was guiding it to the fulfillment of his appointed purpose. Other nations might be a people by tribal circumstance or historical accident, but America is a people by purpose and on purpose. America is "the redeemer nation" that has broken with the decadence of the "Old World" and carries the promise of humanity's future.[10]

America's story was, in this view, replete with evidences that this is a chosen people. Historian William McLoughlin suggests that the continuity of signs is almost unbroken until as little as three decades ago: "The success of the British colonists against then pagan Indians and their Catholic Spanish and French allies prior to 1776 . . . our successful revolution against British tyranny, our rapid expansion to the Pacific, our rise to industrial power, our triumphal role in the great European wars, and our assumption of global power after World War II added further conviction that we were indeed God's chosen people."[11] And, if America was a Christian nation, its Christianity was definitely Protestant. The whole providential story rested on the ideological assumption that Protestants had replaced Catholics after the sixteenth-century Reformation, just as Christians had replaced Jews after the inauguration of the church. The nativism, anti-Catholicism, and anti-Semitism that marked reactions to the massive immigrations of the late nineteenth and early twentieth centuries were not led by redneck or working-class bigots (although many of them subscribed) but by the elite custodians of America's cultural identity. (Not so incidentally, Francis Schaeffer, John Whitehead, and others who want to talk about Christian America today also frequently suggest an exclusively Protestant and implicitly anti-Catholic version of God's providential workings.)

A little more than a century ago the president of Amherst College could say that the nation had achieved a sense of "the true American union, that sort of union which makes every patriot a Christian and every Christian a patriot."[12] Today such a sentiment at most college commencements would be challenged vigorously and, at state institutions, would likely be declared unconstitutional. Given the mix of the American population, it would also be ludicrously inaccurate. Similar sentiments are proclaimed today by those who believe that the linkage between providence and patriotism still has a powerful hold upon the American popular mind (although care is taken to say "Judeo-Christian" rather than just "Christian"). In the last century, such Protestant sentiments were in no way associated with conservative or right-wing politics. The Social Gospel movement that engaged mainline religion at the end of the century was in many ways what today would be described as politically "left" or even "radical." In fact its proponents frequently described it in those terms then. But its leaders had little doubt about the moral superiority of America, its system and its people. The Social Gospel proponents were eager to convert and "Americanize" the newly arrived immigrant hordes. Much of the "radical" activism of that period was focused on goals such as "character formation" and other notions that are today thought to be distinctly conservative.[13]

Advocates of the Social Gospel generally supported the Spanish-American War and thought Teddy Roosevelt's imperialism quite bully. To advance American fortunes was to advance American values and was therefore very much in the interest of the less privileged peoples of the world. It should not be thought that this represented unqualified chauvinism. It placed a very heavy responsibility upon Americans. Washington Gladden, one of the prophets of the movement, put it this way, "If we want the nations of the earth to understand Christianity, we have got to have a Christianized nation to show them."[14] By "Christianize" the Social

Gospel proponents did not just mean that people should accept Jesus as their personal Lord and Savior, as contemporary evangelists put it. Rather, Christianization and civilization were almost synonymous in their minds.

"The real question is," declared Gladden, "what Christianity is able to do for the civilization of a people." Gladden and his colleagues were not intimidated by the moral claims of what we today call the third world. "The keen-witted Orientals, to whom we are making our appeal, the Japanese, the Chinamen, the Hindus, the Turks, understand this perfectly." What they understood is that their religious and cultural values were up against Christianity in a "fair test." "The religions of the world are forced by the contacts and collisions of world politics into a struggle for existence; the evolutionary processes are sifting them; and we shall see the survival of the fittest—that religion which best meets the deepest needs of human nature." Gladden was not in suspense about the outcome: "Doubtless each will make some contribution to that synthesis of faith which the ages are working out, but none of us doubts which one of them will stamp its character most strongly upon the final result."[15] It is worth noting that the economic advantages enjoyed by the rich Western nations, and most particularly by America, did not invalidate the fairness of "the test." On the contrary, economic success was itself one of the confirmations of the superiority of the Christian world.

In addition to the amazing confidence in the American way, what is significant about statements of which Gladden's is typical is the proposed relationship between utility and truth. Note how the merit of religions is measured: that religion which "best meets the deepest needs of human nature" will be declared true. The deepest needs meant are included in the wondrous package called civilization—an end to barbarity, economic security, education, and other benefits that would make "them" more like "us." Classical orthodoxy had declared that the deepest need of human beings is for a saving relationship with God through Christ in the fellowship of his church. In that view, while there might be attendant blessings upon becoming Christian, the truth of the gospel cannot be proven or disproven by the social benefits Christianity might advance.

We earlier took note of Burckhardt's skepticism toward the claims of a failing religion that religion is essential to morality. The Social Gospel movement was, among other things, making a much more ambitious claim. The truth claims of Christianity were to be made vulnerable to the historical testing of the American way. It is worth pondering whether this extravagant assertion reflects religious confidence in decline or in ascendancy. That is, the shift of religious claims to grounds of social benefit might reflect an earlier abandonment of more traditional grounds for the validation of religious belief. In any case, with the Social Gospel movement it was proposed that America and the gospel would rise or fall together. It will not escape the reader's attention that the "liberal" Social

Gospel movement, which was "building the kingdom of God on earth," is in this important respect not unlike the politicized fundamentalism of our time. Both tend to suggest that the truth of Christianity is contingent upon historical events, although the Social Gospel was candid in saying so, while many fundamentalists would be scandalized to recognize that that is in fact what they are suggesting. Nonetheless, historical events—especially those related to American-Soviet conflict and the role of Israel—are essential to the Second Coming and, therefore, to the truth they preach. For all the differences, the Social Gospel and the religious new right are similar in their assertion that Christians have an ultimate stake, a salvific stake, in what happens in and to America.

Lyman Abbott was a leading editor of the Social Gospel period and he needed no infallible Bible to shore up his confidence that "it is the function of the Anglo-Saxon race to confer these gifts of civilization, through law, commerce, and education, on the uncivilized people of the world." Already at the beginning of this century there were minority voices warning about the dangers of "American imperialism." Abbott and those for whom he spoke in mainline Protestantism were not moved: "It is said that we have no right to go to a land occupied by a barbaric people and interfere with their life. It is said that if they prefer barbarism they have a right to remain barbarians. I deny the right of a barbaric people to retain possession of any quarter of the globe. What I have already said I reaffirm: barbarism has no rights which civilization is bound to respect. Barbarians have rights which civilized people are bound to respect, but they have no right to their barbarism."[16]

The bullish doctrines of the Social Gospel movement only made more explicit the marriage between Christianity and America that had earlier been assumed. In the centennial year of 1876 the Methodist bishops praised the nation in these terms: "Here the human spirit of Christianity has been signally exemplified. . . . Here have been added the visible agencies by which the world shall be subjugated to Christ a free, great, and enlightened nation, and a Church vital with the missionary spirit of its Lord."[17] Robert Handy perceptively notes that in such statements "the nation itself as bearer of civilization was elevated as an agency of the subjugation of the world to Christ!"[18] The mission of the church is identified with the mission of America—more accurately it is defined by the mission of America. Historian Winthrop Hudson has suggested that already by the time of Lincoln the expected order of things had been reversed; instead of the church ministering to the nation, the nation was ministering to the church. "The ideals, the convictions, the language, the customs, the institutions of society were so shot through with Christian presuppositions that the culture itself nurtured and nourished the Christian faith."[19] The marriage between mainline Protestantism and the American experiment—entered with such rapturous abandon and sustained through so many trials—would be exceedingly bitter in its divorce.

If there is one group that is the mainline of the mainline, it is almost certainly the Methodists. In 1947 an editorial in *Life* magazine described the Methodist Church: "In many ways it is our most characteristic church. It is short on theology, long on good works, brilliantly organized, primarily middle-class, frequently bigoted, incurably optimistic, zealously mission-ary, and touchingly confident of the essential goodness of the man next door."[20] That is not the Methodism that one would see in, for example, the social pronouncements of the United Methodist Church today. And perhaps just as well. Yet the 1947 description might still be accurate for countless Methodists and their local churches. United Methodism, along with some other mainline groups, is numerically declining, aging, and mainly female. Within it today are individuals and groups who contend that decline is related to the "liberal" and "radical" directions of church leadership.[21] Their complaint has old, if not entirely venerable, precedent in Methodism. In 1866 the Methodist bishops of the South protested that "a large proportion, if not a majority of Northern Methodists have become incurably radical. They teach for doctrine the commandments of men. They preach another Gospel. They have incorporated social dogmas and political tests in their Church creeds."[22] In the "fair test" between aboli-tionists and those who thought slavery not the proper business of the church, America once again came through, vindicating and sealing with a sea of blood the convictions of the "progressive" party.

But the issues then and now are not finally amenable to the categories of liberal versus conservative, left versus right. The heart of the matter is a tortuous ambivalence about the connection between Christianity and culture. Recall the incident of the Lutheran theologian from Germany who spent the day with a group of Methodist ministers discussing various world and domestic problems. "It was very strange and very touching," he said. "They kept talking about what 'we' had failed to do, how 'we' should repent, and how 'we' must set things right. It was puzzling because most of the time I couldn't tell who they meant by 'we'. Did they mean we Methodists, or we the Christian church, or we Americans? But I finally saw that the 'we' is interchangeable. Methodist, Christian, American—they are all the same thing!"

Therein lies both the strength and weakness of the mindset of main-line Protestantism. When it is great to be an American it is great to be a Christian. But, having been privileged to stand with the captain at the helm for so long, even at times taking a turn at the wheel, the mainline nonetheless has mixed feelings about going down with the American ship. And, if one believes that the impending disaster is due to the captain's folly and could be avoided, one might decide to join the less privileged in mutiny.

CHAPTER FOURTEEN

FOR THE WORLD
AGAINST THE WORLD

WHEN DID THINGS BEGIN TO FALL APART? THE QUESTION IS subject to many answers. The theologian's first impulse might be to refer to our original parents who thought it would be splendid to be like gods. The question itself assumes that things have fallen apart and, within the context of this essay, that the reference is to something more recent than the Garden of Eden. Paul Johnson begins his history of "modern times" with a sentence of bracing panache: "The modern world began on 29 May 1919 when photographs of a solar eclipse, taken on the island of Principe off West Africa and at Sobral in Brazil, confirmed the truth of a new theory of the universe."[1] The new theory then was Einstein's on relativity. In the minds of many cultural historians that marked the end of all certitudes. Yeats' intuition that the center cannot hold was confirmed by the knowledge that the center *does not hold.* In the world of religion, the battles over "modernism" had been associated with Darwin, evolution, and biblical authority. But among the "modernists" there was still high confidence in the happy convergence of cosmic forces making for progress, as evidenced in the Social Gospel movement. The traditionalists—some of whom identified with the innovation called fundamentalism—thought such confidence a poor substitute for Christian faith. Whether Christian faith produced that liberal confidence or was displaced by it, it was not to last very long.

Scientific theories about the uncertainties of reality's ordering broke upon the world in conjunction with the massive disillusionments following World War I. It was a war that was not supposed to happen in the first place. At the beginning of 1914 Andrew Carnegie financed the establishment of the Church Peace Union (now the Council on Religion and International Affairs). The purpose, he wrote the trustees in February 1914, is "the abolition of war." He acknowledged that some people might think this goal idealistic but, as one schooled in the real world of finance and power, he assured the trustees the goal would be achieved much sooner than some expected, for already, he said, our imperial cousins in Great Britain and Germany had joined hands with us "in the sacred bonds of commerce," making war unthinkable. He therefore adjured the trustees that, when the goal of abolishing war is achieved, they should give the remaining monies to "the deserving poor." In August of that year the world blew up, and the deserving poor are still waiting.

The dismal aftermath of "the war to end wars" had a corrosive impact also in American religion that is almost beyond measurement. Some historians have contended that the period of mainline religion from 1890 to 1920 represented another Great Awakening. It was the period that witnessed the bold construction of a synthesis between Christian faith and the modern world, according to this view. To the extent such a synthesis was effected, the match was of doubtful benefit to Christian faith. Seldom has there been such quick and painful confirmation of the adage that he who marries the spirit of his time will soon be a widower. Rather than speaking of a marriage between mainline religion and the American experience, we might think of it as a *ménage à trois*. The key participants were Protestant Christianity, civilization, and America. Protestant Christianity produced civilization, and America carried the promise of both.

The disillusionments following the Great War did not take everyone entirely by surprise. Already by the mid-nineteenth century there were dissenters who raised questions about the trinity of Protestantism, civilization, and America. They doubted that the connections among these three were either necessary or real. Beginning with the 1840s, the left wing of Unitarianism produced a transcendentalist movement that had little patience with Protestant doctrine and its cultural self-assurance. Thoreau's *Walden*, Hawthorne's *The Scarlet Letter*, Melville's *Moby Dick*, and Whitman's *Leaves of Grass* all challenged the frequently smug certitudes of established Protestantism. Writes one historian, "They represented what may have been the first successful post-Protestant generation in the United States. From then on, the intellectual and academic communities were increasingly divorced from Christian sources. After them, those who fashioned or controlled the symbols of community for the nation were free to ignore the Protestant context."[2] This intellectual divorce evident in the literary world had its counterpart in "the division of the one moral tradition" in politics and law, as discussed in Chapter Six.

It is perhaps too much to say that these cultural leaders could ignore the Protestant context, for it was still the context within which they thought and wrote. But now the context is no longer normative; it is less the norm than the foil for their thought. Nonetheless, "After their era, people have always been surprised to see expressions of loyalty to orthodox Christianity in the literary community. A schism was occurring in the national soul and psyche."[3] Ralph Waldo Emerson, among others, realized that this change was not all to the good. As a leader of the "liberation movement" from oppressive orthodoxy, he was troubled about what came next. With some regret, he remembered "that old religion which, in the childhood of most of us, still dwelt like a sabbath morning in the country of New England, teaching privation, self-denial and sorrow! . . . What is to replace for us the piety of that race? We cannot have theirs; it glides away from us day by day. . . . A new disease has fallen on the life of man. . . . our torment is Unbelief, the Uncertainty as to what we ought to do; the distrust of the value of what we do. . . . Our religion assumes the negative form of rejection."[4] How now, and by whom, would the sacred symbols of the American experiment be fashioned and forged? More than a century later the question is still awaiting an answer.

Mainline Protestantism was catholic in the sense of inclusive. It did not exclude its children who threw into question its authority. It had lost its power or inclination to excommunicate. At the levels of intellect and high culture, it largely assimilated the doubts about its truth. By the end of the nineteenth century, mainline religious leaders were disinclined to insist upon their truths; they were eager, sometimes poignantly so, to assert their usefulness to the world, as others defined the world. Intellectually, they were inclined to accommodate; socially, they were eager to contribute. Accommodation was the fact and contribution was the hope. Historian Robert Handy observes, "In the earlier period, the priority of the religious vision was strongly and widely maintained; it was Christianity *and* civilization, Christianity as the best part of civilization, and its hope. In the latter part of the century, however, in most cases unconsciously, much of the real focus had shifted to the civilization itself, with Christianity and the churches finding their significance in relation to it."[5]

It has been said of mainline Protestantism today that it is embarrassed to make any religious statement that does not possess redeeming social merit. If true, the cause can be traced back to that "schism in the American soul." In the world of ideas and the shaping of culture, Protestantism felt it was no longer needed or wanted. Its hope, again, was to be of some use, to make a contribution, on terms set by others. William McLoughlin is among those who contend that 1890–1920 represents "The Third Great Awakening" in American religion and culture. (The First Great Awakening was in the early eighteenth century and the Second in the early nineteenth. Some observers suggest we are now experiencing another Great Awakening, whatever number it is to be assigned.)

"The prophets of the Third Great Awakening," writes McLoughlin, "had to undertake an enormous rescue operation to sustain the culture. They had to redefine and relocate God, provide means of access to him, and sacralize a new world view."[6] Perhaps that is what had to be done in view of evolutionary and other theories that appeared to undermine old certitudes. But it is not so clear that the "prophets" of that era either understood or attempted the task. Social Gospel proponents such as Walter Rauschenbusch and Washington Gladden were for the most part content to demonstrate the moral power of the churches to "Christianize" the social order, specifically to challenge "laissez-faire capitalism" with a "social" or "fraternal" reordering of the economic system. Toward the end of this "Great Awakening" popular preachers such as Harry Emerson Fosdick and a host of religious academics were preoccupied with "reconciling" religion and science in the hope of demonstrating the intellectual respectability of Christian faith. As McLoughlin notes, the "key concepts" in this movement were relativism, pragmatism, historicism, cultural organicism, and creative intelligence. All of these concepts, be it said, were important, and some had significant explanatory power. But none of them emerged from Christian sources and some of them were, at least in origin, explicitly hostile to religion.

This eager movement to accommodate and contribute became known as Liberal Protestantism. (Its opponents, and some of its participants, called it Modernism.) Kenneth Cauthen kindly defines Liberal Protestantism as "the attempt of men who were convinced of the truth of historic Christianity to adjust this ancient faith to the demands of the modern era."[7] Sixty years ago, and still today, there were other Christians who believed it to be less a matter of adjustment than of abdication of historic Christian claims. Most secular thinkers were quite indifferent to these religious efforts; others viewed them with amusement; yet others cheered on those Christians who were trying so hard to board the ship of the modern world of which they, the secular thinkers, were clearly now in charge. Clambering aboard an already sinking ship does not, in retrospect, have the appearance of a Great Awakening.

The "prophets" of what might more accurately be called the Great Accommodation were for the most part honorable, and often courageous, men. Yet they now appear to have been less prophets than pacifiers. They were prepared to accept nature's laws as promulgated by science, and to allow no exceptions for God. Their God was reliable, he would not embarrass anybody by challenging the "realities" determined by prestige opinion. As McLoughlin admits, "Religion under Liberal Protestantism . . . was bereft of its miraculous and transcendent quality. Only the Pentecostals and Holiness people held to this faith, and for them it was purely personal; it saved them from a real world that was doomed by its materialism."[8] There were and would be other voices raised to challenge the course of accommodation—intellectually astute and socially conscious voices calling themselves evangelicals. And, from the heart of Liberal Protestantism, a counterattack would be launched by "neoorthodoxy" under the American leadership of the Brothers Niebuhr, Reinhold and H. Richard. But, these dissents aside, mainline Protestantism assumed during this period the social, cultural, and intellectual posture that continues to this day.

The mainline churches would come to view themselves as moderate, tolerant, ecumenical, more disposed to dialogue than to confrontation. Still in the 1980s, however, they also wanted to see themselves as "prophetic" on selected social and political issues. "Consciousness raising" with respect to the "systemic victimization" of the poor would lead some

216

to endorse revolutionary violence in liberation struggles for justice. These more "radicalized" tones emerged intermittently in the NCC during the 1960s and 1970s, as they were similarly evident in other institutions, notably the universities. In church circles they continued long after student radicalisms had become the stuff of nostalgia. In part that is no doubt because student generations are very short while the careers of church bureaucrats can be very long. Also, churches fit the category of "soft institutions," and thus are subject to becoming a haven for refugees from radicalisms past. Radicalized forms of making a contribution to the modern world have been more persistent in the World Council of Churches. The WCC, while not organically related to the NCC, shares a world of free circulation of ideas and personnel.[9] Thoughtful observers such as Thomas Derr, writing for the WCC, acknowledge the conceptual and practical problems posed when such agencies hitch their fortunes to one highly politicized version of "the future."[10]

The picture of the mainline and of its agencies such as the NCC and the WCC does not lend itself to simple categories of conservative versus liberal. In American life, writes Marty, mainline Protestantism has been marked by "a decorous worldliness with which [its] popular preachers could christen the culture."[11] Christening culture is generally thought to be a conservative course. It is the course for which today's television preachers are criticized when it is said that they christen, indeed apotheosize, the American Way of Life. But there are different definitions of American culture, and perhaps conflicting cultures, and it depends on which is being christened. From the Great Accommodation of 1890–1920 on, mainline Protestantism has read "the signs of the times" and thrown in its lot with what is deemed to be liberal, progressive, avant-garde. It is therefore not surprising that, when the secular left-of-center definition of cultural change was "radicalized," mainline Protestantism followed suit. In the 1980s, when it is widely thought that culture and politics reflect a conservative trend, the mainline may again change course. But it is probably unfair to accuse the mainline of being no more than "trendy." It may be that its leaders have learned something from the cultural captivities of the past and are now prepared to be genuinely countercultural on principle. Or it may just be that the once "radicalized" functionaries of the several denominations and ecumenical agencies are either too entrenched or too weary for such a change of direction to happen.

Reading the signs of the times is as parlous as it is imperative. Jerry Falwell declares, "I can feel the wind of God blowing across the country and across the world. You can go with the wind or you can go against it. As for me, I'm moving with the wind of the Lord!"[12] We earlier referred to the very leftist Episcopalian bishop who says that he follows the rule of thumb, "When in doubt, go with the future." Both are reading the signs of the times, but obviously they are reading different signs or reading the same signs very differently. Both are engaged in the essentially conservative enterprise of christening the culture. Both are moving with and not against what they perceive to be the trend. Neither is prophetic.

This shifting with the wind—"trendiness," as some would have it—of mainline Protestantism has not been without its critics. In the period of cultural disillusionment after World War I, a strong critique by Francis P. Miller, Wilhelm Pauck, and H. Richard Niebuhr was titled *The Church Against the World*. Miller put it quite directly: "The plain fact is that the domestication of the Protestant community in the United States within the framework of the national culture has progressed as far as in any western land." Niebuhr asserted: "The church is imperiled not only by an external worldliness but by one that has established itself within the Christian camp. . . . The crisis of the church from this point of view is not the crisis of the church in the world, but of the world in the church."[13] Forty years later, in 1975, an ecumenical group of Christian thinkers issued a book of strikingly similar title, *Against the World for the World*, containing the "Hartford Appeal for Theological Affirmation."[14] The writers took to task both Protestants and Catholics, liberals and conservatives, for their "loss of the transcendent" as evident in their succumbing to the slogan, "the world sets the agenda for the church." (The apparently slight difference between the titles of the two books may be significant. Forty years later "the world" had attained such uncritical theological status that the suggestion of being against it had immediately to be modified by "for the world.")

The "mainline" is a many-splendored thing. As we have suggested, its story line is not smooth or unbroken. For example, from the 1930s through the late 1950s it was challenged by a formidable theological movement commonly termed "neoorthodoxy." This movement was scathingly critical of the cultural accommodationism and illusions of inevitable social improvement that had marked the dominant liberalism. In league with the European "crisis theology" of Karl Barth and Emil Brunner, neoorthodoxy grew out of the post-World War I disillusionment and the later need to abandon pacifist "sentimentality" in order to confront the embodiment of the demonic in Nazism. The emphasis was on "Christian realism," and Reinhold Niebuhr's best-known title, if not his best-read book, was *Moral Man and Immoral Society*. In it he emphasized that the individual ethics of biblical piety could not be transferred easily, if at all, to the conflictual relationships between interest groups and nations. Later, during the Vietnam years, "Christian realism" fell into disrepute among some, largely because the apologists for the war claimed to have realism, if not always Christian realism, on their side. This despite the fact that Reinhold Niebuhr had by the late sixties and near the end of his life turned strongly against U.S. policy in Indochina. (His critics quipped that Niebuhr turned out to be no Niebuhrian but, as discussed earlier, a minority strand of opposition to Vietnam was motivated by a "realistic" assessment of American interests and responsibilities.)

Almost nobody today comes right out in favor of cultural accommodation. Cultural accommodation, once expressly affirmed as the mission of mainline Protestantism, has become a term of opprobrium, just as that perfectly nice word, appeasement, came to mean something different by virtue of Neville Chamberlain's illusions about Hitler. Even the critics of cultural accommodation, however, can be coopted to serve a different cultural mood, which is to say, to serve cultural accommodation. Thus Jacques Ellul, the French jurist and lay theologian, has seen his critique of "technological society" employed to condemn free societies, despite his own condemnation of "false signs of the kingdom" embraced by varieties of religious radicalism. Thus also Karl Barth's assertion that the preacher should preach with the Bible in one hand and the daily newspaper in the other has been turned, according to one wag, into the revolutionary doctrine that "Christianity should be preached with the daily newspaper in one hand and a gun in the other, while standing on the Bible." The late Marxist, Herbert Marcuse, complained about a society that practiced "repressive tolerance," ingeniously assimilating its revolutionary critics. So also the critics of Protestantism's cultural accommodationism are accommodated within liberalism's commodious mansions. At least that has been the pattern in the past.

It is not clear today that the mainline either can, or is inclined to, assimilate its critics. The practice of cooptation requires a degree of confidence. It may be that in more recent years an influential and "radicalized" minority that establishment leaders view as extremists who can be tolerated have come to the conclusion that the mainline is, and should be, no longer mainline. In their view, the critics of their "progressive" views are not to be coopted but confronted. While still claiming the name "ecumenical," their disposition is toward the narrow, exclusive, and partisan. When the criticism is too strong to be confronted successfully, they assume the posture of the besieged. This reaction was evident in some mainline churches and in the NCC in face of "conservative" political victories at the end of the 1970s and mounting criticism of mainline leadership in the early 1980s. The besieged posture appears to be defensive, and it is. Yet when we hunker down we may also be acting upon the assurance that "the future" is on our side, that it is only a question of patiently and bravely waiting out the storm.

Among its more "radicalized" leadership, then, the current defensiveness of the mainline need not betray a lack of confidence. This sector of the leadership is in the minority, however, representing one "positive" interpretation of what are manifestly hard times for mainline Protestantism. The main line of the mainline story was confidence and hope regarding the Americanizing of Christianity and the Christianizing of America.

219

In its most ideological forms, today's "radicalized" interpretations evident in some liberation theologies are a matter of putting the best face on the collapse of that earlier confidence and hope; what cannot be transformed by cooperation must be overthrown by revolution. For the less ideological, which is the great majority of leaders and followers alike, the response is closer to what Handy describes as "religion's loss of confidence and morale."[15]

Whether one traces that loss to the cultural "schism in the American soul" or to Gladden's belief that the truth of Christianity would be proven by its social utility, or to a mix of these and other factors, in the 1980s the story of the mainline did not seem to be moving to a happy ending. Since the days of Bushnell there have been causes and crusades and revivals, but nowhere in the mainline today is there assurance that here in America would be established "the complete Christian commonwealth." Perhaps that is just as well. The need for culturally formative religion cannot be met today by a revival of mainline Protestant hegemony. We do well to remember, however, that the vision of today's moral majoritarians was in large part lifted from the mainline. Its notion of Christian America is not peculiarly fundamentalist and it is most certainly not "unAmerican." The estranged cousins have come back decked out in the family wardrobe. It is always embarrassing to be confronted by the ideals of our younger and more vital days.

1890–1920, liberalism's formative period, was not, then, the Third Great Awakening. For better or for worse, it was, in Handy's phrase, "the second disestablishment." The first disestablishment of the colonial churches was completed by 1830. Afterward, even those who had virulently opposed disestablishment came to see it as a blessing that liberated the juices of what would come to be admired as American voluntarism. After this second and informal disestablishment (no laws were passed to that specific effect), there was little cause for cheering. Mainline religion was no longer in the intellectual or cultural lead; indeed it was pathetically pleased if those who shaped the culture deigned to take note of religion at all. The mainline was left to sniff around for crumbs that fell from the tables of the cultural elite. Or, like an aged and somewhat eccentric aunt who shares the house, it was thanked for occasionally helping out with tasks defined and controlled by others. The great white tower of 475 Riverside Drive turned out to be not the capitol of the Protestant empire but a marginal service agency trying very hard to be helpful in other people's "progressive causes."

Of course there is nothing wrong in helping out with other people's progressive causes. But somebody has to decide which causes are to be helped. When causes are highly politicized, such decisions inevitably lead to political partisanship. To which it may be asked what is wrong with political partisanship. Was not the abolitionist movement against slavery politically partisan? So today many urge that the risks of partisanship must be taken in, for example, supporting revolutionary movements aimed at overthrowing apartheid in South Africa. Others (although not generally in the mainline churches) believe the risks of partisanship are mandated in defending the unborn and the handicapped from a society that ever more narrowly defines the community entitled to legal protection. Without a shared world of moral discourse that transcends the divisive issues at hand, however, partisanship slides into dehumanizing polarization.

In the nineteenth century the substantive questions behind the issue of slavery were articulated. There were shared points of reference that made moral discourse possible, even if that discourse finally failed and led to arbitrament by arms. It may be that, in view of the bloody costs, the existence of a shared world of moral discourse was small comfort. But it is no little thing that thoughtful antagonists could understand themselves to be moral actors. Whether we judge an action to be morally right or wrong, there is a gesture of respect in the judgment itself. The final obscenity is not war but the dehumanizing of war that reduces it to an animal fight over interests, particularly over that sleaziest of interests which the modern world mistakes for a moral value, survival. It is tragically possible that moral discourse gives way to mortal conflict. It is even more tragic when we come to believe that the cure for conflict is the abandonment of moral discourse. When that step is taken, human action, which is to say morally significant action, is displaced by animal behavior. When the public square is thoroughly desacralized, political action is, in every sense of the term, thoroughly demoralized.

The public framework of moral reference cannot sustain itself, it cannot stand on its own feet, so to speak. It needs to be attended to and articulated. This is the task not just of individuals but of institutions, most particularly the institutions of religion. During most of our history it has been the task attended to by mainline Protestantism. We have discussed the ways in which, in an earlier civil rights movement, Martin Luther King, Jr., invoked and employed that framework of moral reference. To their credit, the more consistent proponents of liberation theology in the mainline churches today recognize this need for a comprehensive and compelling moral vision. Unfortunately, the encompassing sense of purpose they propose, such as "getting America on the right side of the world revolution," brings them into alliance with forces that claim to believe that moral discourse is nothing more than an exercise in false consciousness. And unfortunately, the vision they propose implies the dismantling or destruction of the values and advantages most Americans cherish. Therefore, their surrogate for the traditional moral vision borne by mainline Protestantism is not likely to command popular support.

Most of the leadership of mainline Protestantism today, it may be safely assumed, identifies neither with the traditional vision nor with its current antitheses. There is what appears to be a middle ground. The idea is frequently touted that the whole concept of Christianity as a culture-forming force is pretentious and dangerous. The ambitions of that older Protestantism are dismissed as "triumphalism," of a piece with the cultural and political ambitions of pre-Vatican II Catholicism in, for example, Franco Spain. The alternative to triumphalism is a "servant church" which does not delude itself into thinking that it is the sole or even the chief instrument through which God is working. There is much that is attractive in this viewpoint. It refuses to equate the church with the kingdom of God, or to mistake our limitations for the limits of what Christ can do and is doing. There is also much that is attractive in the idea of cultural accommodation, despite its negative connotations. If cultural accommodation means respect for secular wisdoms and a determination to speak the gospel in a manner attuned to the particularities of a cultural moment, then cultural accommodation is of a piece with the Christian mission itself. And, as we have seen, there is much that is attractive in helping other people in their good causes, if we do not lose hold of the moral references by which we understand good and evil.

Mainline readers may think of Harvey Cox's *The Secular City* as a book from a long, long time ago. Among some moral majoritarian writers today, however, that 1965 volume is much quoted. John Whitehead and others quote it approvingly for Cox's sharp distinction between secularization and secular*ism*. Its much greater influence in the Protestant mainline is still evident, however. Cox, being a more thoughtful soul, has since been critical of some forms of liberationism and has written about the religiously borne transcendence that challenges the disenchantment of the modern world. But his greater and continuing influence is in the gravamen of *The Secular City*, that Christians should trust and supportively engage themselves in God's secular struggles and achievements. *The Secular City* was written in the glow of John F. Kennedy's Camelot, and of the aggiornamento of Pope John XXIII; it reflected a high point of liberal confidence—before black power turned nasty, before Vietnam, before acid rock, before Charles Manson, before Watergate, in short, before the secular city (or at least the American version of it) went sour.

Yet the basic argument still has wide sway: "The world sets the agenda for the church." Christian-Marxists (or, as some would prefer, Christians who "employ Marxist analysis") believe that axiom, and they have their own reading of what the world is up to. And more moderate mainliners seem to believe that, although they are more at home in their societies, trusting the elites of secular society to provide the terms of discourse, to produce the good causes to which the church hopes to be helpful. This description of affairs might be challenged by those who could point to numerous statements and resolutions from, e.g., the NCC which are critical of this secular society. But that says nothing more than that, when selected causes are declared to be good, opposing causes are declared to be bad. In the selection itself, the mainline very seldom dissents from left-of-center conventional wisdoms. Yet those critics of the mainline miss the main point when they focus on the "leftist" orientation of church pronouncements. It would be as troublesome—although exceedingly unlikely in view of the "new class" placement of mainline church leadership—were the pronouncements typically "rightist." The main point is that in making such pronouncements we do not believably articulate the framework of public moral reference by which all positions—right, left, or unlabeled—must be evaluated. To do that would be uncomfortably close to agreeing with the moral majoritarians that there is in fact an authoritative moral tradition to which public discourse should be held accountable. Rather, facing a selection of prepackaged positions, we make our choice and, because in some sense we are presuming to speak for the church, we try to remember to append a Bible passage or two. Secular opinion-leaders, if they take note at all, are at a loss to understand in what way such pronouncements are specifically religious or Christian, since they seem to do nothing more than to restate, in mode of argument and conclusion, one of several viewpoints already in public play.

The rather odd consequence is that those who do not claim any specific religious warrant for their views call upon religious leaders to be more significantly religious in advancing theirs. One of many instances is a *New York Times* editorial of June 1983. (This instance is additionally odd because the statement that occasioned the editorial was also subscribed by some moral majoritarian leaders, which is perhaps an indication of the price some of them might pay for "respectability.") Jeremy Rifkin had coordinated a statement signed by a broad range of Protestant, Catholic, and Jewish leaders calling for a ban on introducing inheritable traits into the human gene set.

The editorialist believes that the religious leaders are wrong "to utter so far-reaching a proscription on the basis of little argument." He thinks that, although it is not yet technologically possible, there would be considerable merit in altering the gene set of people who are especially prone to inheritable diseases such as sickle-cell anemia. The editorial disagrees with the religious leaders who contend that "no one has a right to decide for future generations which genes should be perserved and which replaced." The editorial reflects a particular irritation that the religious leaders' statement seems to add nothing to the debate since it arbitrarily picks out one possible direction of genetic research for condemnation.

"According to the book of Genesis," the editorial says, "man is made in God's image. Does that make it sacrilege for humans to change their own genetics? Most theologians do not interpret their faith so literally. In any case the religious petitioners, surprisingly, do not rest their case on theology. . . . Those now demanding a veto have acted at the persuasion of Jeremy Rifkin, director of the Foundation on Economic Trends and author of a new book of human genetic engineering. . . . If they really want a ban, they should state it in their own terms and words rather than letting Mr. Rifkin be their only spokesman. The issue deserves more than a slogan without a rationale."[16]

The incident of the statement and the editorial reaction to it is of interest in several respects. The statement indicates what the editorialists and others view as an antiscientific or, at least, antitechnology bias. The mainline leaders who signed it have in this instance, it might be suggested, gone over to the fundamentalist side with its traditional suspicion of "scientific progress." (A similar suspicion, even hostility, is evident in mainline rhetoric about space exploration.) We noted earlier the ways in which the "radical" counterculture with its animus toward modern technology prepared the way for a convergence between elite opinion and a traditional fundamentalist disposition. Also of interest is the editorial complaint that the religious leaders do not make their case on the basis of theological or ethical argument. To that complaint it could be answered that the editors of The New York Times would not recognize a theological argument if it fell like a stone tablet on their heads. It might also be pointed out that in the months prior to this editorial the paper had given extensive coverage to the Roman Catholic bishops' pastoral on nuclear warfare and paid little attention to the theological argumentation that it contained in abundance; the Times was chiefly interested in how the pastoral agreed or disagreed with the defense politics of the administration in Washington.

These points made, however, the editorial response is significant in what it says about mainline Protestant penchants in the issuing of social pronouncements. Here and elsewhere, the "progressive" wing of Christianity assumes a "prophetic" posture against what the world takes to be progress. At the same time the prophecy does not invoke distinctively religious claims, since such claims were muted or abandoned as a condition for religion's marriage with the world's agenda. The marriage, however, turns out to rest upon a one-way agreement. The world did not agree to having its agenda taken on by the church. In the "big world" of secular reality the other players do not understand the basis of religion's intervention in their games. If religion intervenes with truths that are otherwise being ignored, its intervention may be welcomed or resisted but at least the reason for the intervention would be clear. But when religion wants to intervene in the secular arena with secondhand claims that are already current there, and indeed originated there, it must not be surprised when its offer of help is declined, not always so politely, by those in charge of the world's agenda.

These then are some of the problems encountered by the idea of "the servant church." For the idea to be effective, the church must be clear about the service it has to render. It can in a modest way offer money, prestige, and some recruits for the causes that it believes signal God's work in the world. But such an approach means drawing upon declining capital.

The capital was created by a community of faith gathered by distinctive truth claims; it can only be replenished by proclamation and faith's response. This means recovering the metaphor of "the church militant," a metaphor almost entirely absent from mainline religious thought today. Against the world for the world; the church's significant contribution is to significantly challenge. The challenge is not significant when the church merely endorses existing positions that challenge other existing positions. Significant challenge means throwing all positions into question.

Only the church militant can be a servant church. Today talk about the church militant seems impossibly triumphalistic. Yet it is worth asking whether the current polemic against triumphalism is not the result of the failure of a different triumphalism. No doubt mainline Protestantism with its historic belief in the trinity of Christianity, America, and civilization believed itself to be on the road to triumph. Cultural accommodation was not simply a marriage of convenience, it was a marriage through which this trinity would conquer. That hope has been disappointed most severely. The image of the church militant does not propose another triumphalism, thus setting up the church for further disappointment. Ultimately, to be sure, we believe that the church will triumph in the sense of being vindicated in the coming kingdom of God. Because it has said Yes to that hope, the church must say No to all lesser hopes of influence. Precisely in the power of that Yes and No, however, lies its influence short of the final vindication. The church militant is marked by an "againstness" that is for the world. Using H. Richard Niebuhr's terms, it is an instance of "Christ transforming culture" by pointing the culture to a transformation that is beyond its own means to attain or even imagine.

The muting of Christian distinctiveness, the rejection of the idea of the church militant, the polemic against triumphalism, all are consequences of the collapse of the synthesis attempted by the Great Awakening of 1890–1920, an "awakening" that resulted in a second and thoroughly demoralizing disestablishment of mainline Protestantism. Current talk about the servant church smells of rationalization. It betrays a yearning to play in the big arena of the secular world, to be useful to somebody, somehow. If those in control of the dominant forces of our time do not want our help, then we will seek out the opposition to those forces and find our meaning in helping them to overthrow their oppressors. Thus we have moved from christening the culture of the strong to signing up with the revolutionary opposition to that culture, but in divorcing one party and marrying another we are a servant church to neither. The church, in biblical imagery, is the bride of Christ and its proper service is to proclaim the revolution of the coming kingdom, by which all existing establishments and revolutionary would-be establishments are brought under divine promise and judgment.

225

CHAPTER FIFTEEN

CLASS WARFARE AMONG THE SAINTS

WE HAVE CONSIDERED THE NINETEENTH-CENTURY PROT-estant vision of America as the complete Christian commonwealth. Today other visionaries speak of the coming "church of the catacombs." The first vision has not worked out. At least it has not worked out as mainline Protestantism had hoped and expected. Now others, such as the moral majoritarians, want to give it another try, or at least to try their version of the dream. The second vision, the church of the catacombs, is the antithesis of the first. It is not, I believe, very promising, being neither probable nor desirable. There are elements of nobility in both visions. It is too easy today to deride the sense of high confidence and responsibility in the religious thought of nineteenth-century America. From our perspective in the rubble of their dreams, their expectations appear ludicrous. But they did not seem ludicrous then. We, like them, are children of a particular time with its peculiar insights and illusions. To assume that we are wiser because we are later is, strangely enough, to subscribe to their illusion of chronological progressivism. One need not be a conservative to believe that our grandparents knew, in things that matter, as much or more than we.

In saying that our visions are conditioned, I do not suggest agreement with those who deny the possibility of universal truth. I do suggest that we should nurture a becoming modesty about the visions with which we have replaced the vision of "Christian America." Such a vision is that of the church of the catacombs, the persecuted church, the adversarial church, the church of the poor. Today we are awash in post-disestablishment language. It is a romantic language, much more so than the ambitious language about the complete Christian commonwealth. It is compensatory language, the language of failed dreams and failed dreamers. Since we are no longer confident of our assertions about what the church should be or do, we hope that persecution will define our mission for us. This is another side of letting the world set the agenda for the church. This time, however, it is not in triumphant collaboration with the world, as was the case in the nineteenth century or even in "the secular city" of the early sixties. This time the powers of the world will define our mission by their opposition to us. For example, at a recent conference an Anglican bishop was listening to a Russian emigré discuss the camaraderie among Christians

226

in the Soviet Union, the depth and intensity of their debates about the
meaning of life. "Ah," said the bishop in subsequent discussion, "that is
what I miss in all the fearful talk about what would happen if the Russians
took over. Totalitarianism might be the best thing that could happen to
the church here. At least we would learn what it means to be a Christian."
Persecution might indeed teach us much, in the same way that terminal
cancer has been known to build character. In the absence of so harsh a
teacher, it may be harder to learn what it means to be a Christian where
religion suffers chiefly from being ignored. The romanticism of catacomb
Christianity is the compensatory reaction of those who were once but are
no longer taken seriously at court.

The real church of the catacombs was made up of early Christians
gathered to celebrate the victory of Christ, which, they knew, had prevailed spiritually and would prevail historically over the principalities and
powers of evil. The "church of the catacombs" today, were it to happen,
would be more like a ragtag band of the disillusioned slinking off to lick
their wounds. The coming of the barbarians, as C. P. Cavafy observed,
would be some kind of solution. Short of their coming to remedy our
spiritual malaise, however, persecution as an elected option is difficult to
sustain and not terribly attractive. In part this is because the church headquarters of Nashville, Indianapolis, Madison Avenue, and Riverside Drive
make very improbable catacombs.

Not so long ago the fundamentalist and "separatist" groups were
accused of indulging the illusion that they could recreate ("repristinate")
the primitive church. The mainline, by contrast, was determined "to confront the problems of the modern world." Now, however inept their efforts,
we see fundamentalists assuming the posture of confrontation and confidently asserting the need to embrace the culture-forming tasks of recon-
necting American society to its Christian sources. The streams issuing
from "the social sources of denominationalism" (H. Richard Niebuhr) are
taking surprising twists and turns. In the process of the "circulation of
elites" (Pareto), streams previously distant are straining to find their way
into the hollows left by the disestablishment of the Protestant mainline.
The mainline, possessing neither energy nor rationale to make a bid for
reestablishment, is inclined to declare its defeat an achievement and its
increasing marginality a choice.

There are several ways of accommodating to disestablishment.
Adopting the posture of the persecuted remnant is one, identification with
the revolutionary avant-garde is another. As we have seen, these two postures are closely related. That is, if the remnant is seen as the agent of
revolutionary change, then this posture combines the possibility of being
simultaneously persecuted and a key collaborator in building "the future."
After failing in the effort to establish the complete Christian commonwealth, we can nonetheless engage in an equally ambitious project, the

establishment of "the new humanity in the new society." That this hoped-for result is not specifically Christian and may indeed be hostile to Christianity is no great problem; not if we have come to understand that God's work in the secular world may be against the church and its gospel. In that case, the only justified way for the church to be militant is in support of secular militancies, including those militancies that would, in Marxian terms, consign religion to the "dustbin of history."

Another and less radicalized way of accommodating to disestablishment is through consolidation of residual forces. Consolidation is not the whole rationale of the ecumenical movement but it is an important part of it. Here again there are apparent contradictions. On the one hand, ecumenical agencies such as the World Council of Churches speak about ecumenism in terms of solidarity with the revolutionary struggles in a post-Christian world. In this connection we encounter calls for "a partisan church" that deliberately divides Christians along lines of oppressor and oppressed. From a more conventional understanding of ecumenism, it seems that this form of the ecumenical movement must become more and more anti-ecumenical.

As Wolfhart Pannenberg has argued, there has been a reversal of the ecumenical slogan, "The unity of the church—the unity of humankind."[1] That is to say, it used to be thought that the unity of the church would provide a basis for unity within and between societies. The proponents of the partisan church, however, suggest the slogan ought to read, "The unity of humankind—the unity of the church." That is to say, through revolutionary struggle humankind must find its unity in the just social order; the unity of the church is discovered and established among those who support that struggle. Thus the "marks of the church" (those indicators by which we can tell what is church and what is not) are no longer gospel proclamation, sacraments, and discipleship but being on the right side of the liberationist project. Or, as advocates of this view insist, gospel, sacraments, and discipleship are understood, by virtue of revolutionary translation, in terms of the liberationist project.[2]

Within the same ecumenical movement, however, the themes of consolidation find more conventional expression. It is said that the failure of Christianity to be the culture-forming force that it ought to be is attributable to the division of the church. The ecumenical task, then, is to consolidate churchly resources in order to exercise greater clout in society. This regrouping is the prerequisite for another go at establishing the complete Christian commonwealth. The tension between the ecumenical movement as a consolidation of forces for societal reconstruction and the ecumenical movement as a gathering of partisans against existing societal structures has brought a debilitating incoherence into enterprises such as the World Council of Churches. Both versions, however, turn upon a political judgment about the social utility of the church. Neither is based in the originating ecumenical vision, "Let the church be the church!" Neither sees the unity of the church as the imperative, with the unity of human-kind as a desired consequence. For the proponents of a partisan church, the unity of the church is an abstraction, except as it is defined by the desired consequence. This assumes that we have a clearer understanding of what is meant by the just society than of what is meant by the church. The latter is given meaning by reference to the former.

Current confusions about and within the institutionalized ecumen-ical movement tend to obscure for us the enormous enthusiasm for ecu-menism that gripped mainline Protestantism only a few decades ago. In a 1959 book surveying the history of Christianity, Martin E. Marty con-cluded with a chapter on "The Great New Fact of Our Era"—the ecumen-ical movement.[3] In an ebullient (triumphalist?) spirit, Marty saw Christian unity, spearheaded by the World Council of Churches, leading to a con-solidation of spiritual resources to surmount the "catastrophe and disil-lusion and anxiety" of the modern world. Most important, there would be renewed confidence in the truth claims of Christianity: "Partly as an out-growth and partly as a constitutive factor of the Ecumenical Movement, and partly coincident with its rise, has come a profound theological re-covery that bids fair to make this the most theologically conscious era since the Reformation." Fast on the heels of that "bids fair" came secular theology, play theology, gay theology, feminist theology, and the death of God.

Of course Marty's "bids fair" was not a prediction, for historians who work in Clio's garden are not permitted predictions. And ten years later Marty was to write in a tempered tone about the ecumenical movement as consolidation: "The Protestant churches in the nineteenth century are usually pictured as having a centrifugal momentum. By their missionary activity, every move they made seemed to spin them out from a spiritual center through a competitive principle to divisions all over the world. In the twentieth century, their momentum has been centripetal: they noted the limits of their competition and division, experienced frustration in mission around the world, and began to draw back together in the ecu-menical, or Christian unity, movement."[4] This drawing back had about it the appearance of retrenchment and of a retreat that was not notably stra-tegic. From the sixties through the eighties there were many denomina-tional consolidations and much talk about "merger for mission," but little evidence of renewed vitality. Indeed it was observed that religious vitalities seemed more evident in those churches that still spoke of "missions" (centrifugal) rather than of "mission" (centripetal). The suspicion arose that there might be a causal connection between ecumenism and exhaustion.[5]

While it is commonly said that the ecumenical movement has lost its momentum, it would be more accurate to say that there is widespread disillusionment with the Protestant version of ecumenism represented by various councils of churches and, preeminently, by the World Council of Churches. (The WCC is an essentially mainline Protestant enterprise, although Orthodox churches are tenuously related. After a short courtship in the 1970s, the Vatican has increasingly distanced itself from the WCC.[6]) The chief activities and hopes of the ecumenical movement today are in "bilateral" relationships. There is, for example, significant progress in healing the millennium-old division between the West, centered in Rome, and the Eastern churches. There is both official and grass-roots enthusiasm for steps taken to "heal the breach of the sixteenth century" between Roman Catholics, Lutherans, and Anglicans. Other instances of ecumenical advance could be cited, and much of it is consciously aimed at presenting a less divisive Christian witness that could again help to shape "the symbol system" for the moral reconstruction of the modern world. What has changed dramatically is that the World Council of Churches, in which mainline Protestantism had made such a steep investment, is no longer the center of that ecumenical advance. Indeed the argument is increasingly made that the WCC, by its establishment of narrow sociopolitical tests, has become a hindrance to Christian unity—in North America, in Europe, and most particularly in the third world where only a small minority of the most vital Christian groups identify with the ecumenical establishment based in Geneva.

Sundry reform movements, the consolations of being the despised remnant, revolutionary rhetoric, ecumenical engagements—all these have from time to time given a momentary sense of momentum to some in the mainline. But Robert Handy is surely right in seeing that, for the mainline in the United States, all these pulsations are shadowed by a failed dream, the hope of "turning America into a Christian nation." As Handy writes, "Because that overarching dream was so often referred to in a rather generalized way, its fading has given many Protestants a sense of uneasiness and guilt without their really being able to say why."[7]

In this post-disestablishment uneasiness some themes from the past survive. There is, for instance, a more or less constant ambition to "Christianize" the social order, especially the economic order. The synonyms for "Christianize" today include terms such as justice, equality, and sustainability. But the ambition has not changed much from 1885 when Richard T. Ely, a prominent Social Gospel proponent, brought young economists together to form the American Economic Association. Ely's own works were read appreciatively by Theodore Roosevelt and Woodrow Wilson. His belief with respect to housing, labor, banks, monopolies, and a host of other economic problems was simply stated: "Government should interfere in all instances where its interference will tell for better health, better education, better morals [including, of course, prohibition of alcohol], greater comfort of the community."[8] It was the mission of the church to achieve this "Christianizing" of the economic order. The trouble with making this the mission of the church is that it could in fact be achieved. If that happens, what then is the mission of the church?

McLoughlin writes, "It could be argued that the Third Great Awakening [what we are calling the second disestablishment] was not completed until the majority of the Supreme Court, late in the 1930s . . . proceeded to endorse the kinds of New Deal legislation that previous decisions had declared unconstitutional."[9] The demoralization of the mainline is due in large part to the success of a too limited goal. Since the 1930s the social mission of mainline Protestantism has been to advance—albeit with "a sense of uneasiness and guilt"—the programs and fortunes of the left wing of the Democratic party. The canard about the Church of England being the Tory party at prayer now finds its counterpart in the Protestant mainline of this country. Among the leadership of mainline Protestantism—not necessarily the membership—the prayer is for the second coming of a George McGovern, assuming that FDR is no longer available.

We have had occasion to remark the importance of the 1980 presidential election. A church devoted to eternal verities would seem to have little reason to take much note of electoral returns, much less to refashion its mission in response to them. And there is no doubt that in the hundreds of thousands of local churches in America—including mainline Protestant churches—there is a constancy of mission, electoral season in and electoral season out. The situation is different, however, among those who hold portfolios for prophecy in the church-and-society offices of the several churches. The situation is different if one believes that, as a mainline bishop has explained to me, "The mission of the church is to build the kingdom of God on earth, and the means of the mission is politics." Then one must take electoral returns very seriously indeed, especially when, as was the case in 1980, they are thought to portend major change in the society.

In an issue immediately before the 1980 election, the editors of a national magazine published by the United Methodists reflected: "Sometimes, as a critical national election heats up, we long to shuck off our non-profit, tax-exempt status. It's hard to stay out of it, to remain editorially nonpartisan [sic], to avoid endorsing or denouncing any particular candidate."[10] Note that the inhibition against partisan endorsement has to do with tax exemption and not with principle. As one reads further, however, it becomes obvious that the editors are not so inhibited after all. If the issues are properly presented, the proper conclusions become self-evident. As Jerry Falwell of Moral Majority says, "We don't endorse candidates. We don't need to. The people are smart enough to draw the proper conclusions."[11]

The opening article in this particular, but typical, mainline magazine treats the proper relationship between church and government. "Here there is no confusion of role or identity. The political order is engaged and taken seriously. The mission of the church is independently defined by the church and the larger mission of God is thereby not placed into captivity by the limited mission of the state. The church is free to be the church." This robust assertion of apparent nonpartisanship is exercised, according to the magazine, by "the disassociation of 'God' with imperial power . . . and the re-identification of 'God' with the struggles for justice and love in the world." (Most Methodists, it should be noted in fairness, do not yet feel constrained to put God in quotation marks.) The article explains that "struggles for justice and love" mean waging the good fight against "racism and sexism," completing "Eleanor Roosevelt's vision of a United Nations," "building a new economic order that works to reduce unfairness, to extend justice, and to enhance the human community," and, in general, overcoming the "oppressive neo-colonialism" of the West's exploitation of the third world.

Lest the reader miss the voting booth implications of this vision of God's agenda in the world, the editors helpfully include an extensive section comparing the platforms of the Democrats, Republicans, and John Anderson (who, it may be remembered, ran as an independent) with the official "Social Principles" and policy statements of the United Methodist Church. The list of issues is long, including: human rights, health care, welfare reform, Equal Rights Amendment, gun control, arms control, abortion, the military draft, the United Nations, energy conservation, the death penalty, South Africa, and school busing. The conclusion is short and to the point: on issue after issue, it turns out that the United Methodist position is identical with or closer to the Democratic platform and almost always in clear conflict with the Republican. Where the church's position differs from that of the Democratic party, the difference would have been remedied had the planks pushed by the left wing of the party, and resisted by President Carter, been adopted.

This representative publication is not cited in order to impugn the motives of Methodist leadership or to question its right to take positions on controverted issues. Although it seems exceedingly implausible, it may in fact be the case that there is a happy convergence between God's purposes and the purposes of those on the left of the Democratic party. Publications such as this might be kept in mind, however, in evaluating the mainline complaint that activists on the right advance a narrow political agenda in the name of Christianity. It is not clear why it is condemnable to say that support for school prayer is *the* Christian position while it is laudable to make the same claim for supporting, say, the New International Economic Order. In any event, such is the sorry state of the legacy of Washington Gladden and other champions of the Great Accommodation. The formula of the church's contributing and accommodating to the good causes defined by others has resulted in mainline Protestantism's becoming, in large part, a haven for fugitive ideas from liberalisms past.

The mainline churches are not going to go out of business tomorrow or the decade after that. Admittedly, there are some who make very dour predictions. Based upon their survey research, Gallup and Poling assert, "The Presbyterian, Episcopalian, and United Church of Christ communions cannot long exist as viable church organizations nationally if the declines of the 1970s persist in the 1980s."[12] It is said that someone has figured out that, according to present trends, on July 17 in the Year 2020 the Episcopal Church will have one priest for every lay member. In fact, however, by 1983 statisticians reported that, while there were few signs of positive growth, the membership losses of mainline church had begun to decline. Again, it is well to remember that historical change is no respecter of graphs which extrapolate from patterns past and present. History, religious history in particular, is the story of surprises that nobody foretold and many knowledgeable people declared to be impossible.

Whatever may be the signs of demoralization and decline, the reality of mainline Protestantism is in local churches that are largely immune to the alarums and enthusiasms that seize executives at national headquarters. The signs are pertinent, however, in thinking about the role of the mainline in our public life. These institutions are, for the most part, living off their membership capital, so to speak. Unlike stocks or savings accounts, membership capital does not collect interest. It is the other kind of capital—stocks, bonds, endowments, etc.—that may institutionally sustain these churches for a long time to come. Many programs, including many that have little membership support, are financially shielded and removed from accountability. Because of accumulated resources in various forms, a national church body does not need to appeal for "the widow's mite" in order to sustain every program. For whatever purpose they were once given, mites of the past are subject to executive decisions of the present, and the widows need not be consulted.

The mainline churches can take little comfort, however, from data showing that they are being abandoned by substantial numbers of the faithful. Forty percent of American Protestants have changed denominations at some point in their lives.[13] But, according to Kirk Hadaway of the Southern Baptist Convention, the patterns of "switching" are very uneven. The "conservative" churches gain from switching but they also lose members rapidly, so that they need the most aggressive evangelism, "which they must continue if they are not to lose ground." Other churches, such as the Lutheran and Baptist, tend to hold on to their members better, mainly through strong catechesis of the young. Presbyterians, United Methodists, and Disciples of Christ, however, lose massively through switching and do not do a very good job of holding on to their children. The Episcopalians and the United Church of Christ come out ahead on switching. In many communities the Episcopal Church is still the beneficiary of upward social mobility. But both churches finally come out on the losing end because they suffer a hemorrhaging from their own ranks. Forty percent of the children of Episcopalians and forty-five percent of the children of Congregationalists (UCC) leave their churches. Hadaway's conclusion: "Since this switching occurs predominantly among younger members, it raises the possibility that the more liberal bodies are losing the very members that would normally be expected to produce the next generation of liberal Protestants."

The years since Dean Kelley's *Why Conservative Churches are Growing* have mightily confirmed his central argument. People expect, and rightly so, that religion be a "mediator of meaning," that churches be "meaning movements." By reference to transcendent truth, churches provide an ultimate definition of reality within which people can cope with the ecstatic, trivial, and tragic of their earthly sojourn. Liberal churches have downplayed these "traditional" functions of religion in favor of taking on the role of "change agents" for global transformations. Critics of Kelley have claimed that his call for "strictness" is an invitation to regress to fundamentalist obscurantism and withdrawal from worldly tasks. Kelley's argument, however, is not that the churches should abandon social involvement but that they should be much more selective and reflective in taking on issues. Clearer connections must be made with the specific warrants of Christian faith, and there should be a more modest acknowledgment of the church's limitations, of its role of assisting Christians in making decisions rather than telling them how to decide. "Strictness" does not mean repression but greater clarity about what it means to be a Presbyterian or a Methodist, or whatever. If there is no such clarity, with its attendant expectations, there is no communal identity and then churches become residual collections of sundry whatevers. Institutions that appear to stand for nothing may for a time be sustained by habit but they will not be renewed by commitment.

Kelley's outlook was not entirely bleak. "This process of decline can be delayed—though probably not reversed—by the exercise of 'strictness,' which is the consequence and evidence of the seriousness of meaning. Even from declining religious groups many people derive what meaning they have; for some it may be all they need. And from declining groups new movements spring, which may lend vitality to the old or may begin a new evolution or both."[14] The decline Kelley and others diagnosed in the late 1960s did not begin then. During the Eisenhower years there had been a much-celebrated "religious boom" that tended to distract attention from a deeper continuity in the troubles of mainline Protestantism. Writes Robert Handy, "The recovery [of the 1950s] did not run deep for it did not clearly recognize that what was missing was the former close identification with American civilization. Had it been able to see that, it might

234

have been able to face more fundamental questions, rather than trying to replace what historical circumstances had made irreplaceable."[15] Handy agrees with an "epitaph" written in 1960 by Edward A. Farley. As the boom subsided, he found that Christian faith or piety was not passing away, but "that one historical piety (Protestant piety) is passing off the scene. . . . As I look at the evidence, it seems to say that a certain historical form of Christian piety (Victorian Protestant piety) is going. Faith itself remains, searches for, and in part finds new forms—some idolatrous, some innocuous, and some seemingly genuine."[16]

Where the mainline churches were no longer the mediators of ultimate meaning, they at least had for a time a penultimate meaning in their close identification with the American experiment. It was an identification with a liberal version of America that climaxed in the New Deal. As the moral credibility and practical effectiveness of the liberal tradition became more uncertain, the confidence of these churches was also undercut. By the end of the 1960s Theodore Lowi (The End of Liberalism: Ideology, Policy, and the Crisis of Public Authority) analyzed the problem, which had been in the making for more than two decades.[17] The liberal tradition, he contended, had degenerated into "interest-group liberalism." That is, the basic and thoroughly pragmatic assumption was that society is composed of interest groups or "countervailing forces" that, if permitted free contention with one another, would somehow advance the common good. This was, Lowi argued, implausible in theory and refuted in practice.

At the deeper level of "moral legitimacy" interest-group liberalism directly affects the role of the churches that identified with it. "Liberal governments cannot achieve justice because their policies lack the *sine qua non* of justice—that quality without which a consideration of justice cannot even be initiated. Considerations of the justice in or achieved by an action cannot be made unless a deliberate and conscious attempt was made by the actor to derive his action from a general rule or moral principle governing such a class of acts. One can speak personally of good rules and bad rules, but a homily or a sentiment, like liberal legislation, is not a rule at all."[18] The resulting form of pragmatism, Lowi concludes, "is merely an appeal to let theory remain implicit."[19]

Such a pragmatism is fatal to the church's witness. If religion is supposed to do anything in the social order, surely it is to explicate those rules and general principles that should guide the shaping of our life together. That is not all that religion does, nor is it the most important thing it does, but it is the warrant for its participation in the public square. Without that authority to explicate moral referents, religious social witness becomes but a "homily or a sentiment," a moralistic gloss on the deals struck by contending forces quite apart from moral considerations. The naked public square does not tolerate explication of religiously grounded principle. Having accepted that intolerance (as the price of living in a "secular society"), churches are tempted to assume a different role, to take a hand in the striking of the deals. As "change agents" they must become partisan, they must be for some measures and therefore against others. As relatively weak players in the games of powers, they end up aligning themselves with and becoming captive to one or another set of countervailing forces. That is demeaning enough, but what is disastrous is that they stop being agents of truth-telling. Truth-telling and the quest for power are incompatible. All earthly power employs mendacity, some mendacities being justifiable and others not. For those set upon getting or keeping power—no matter how noble their ends—truth always means *effective* truth, truth relevant to the end pursued. In its extreme revolutionary form, the end itself is "the truth" and everything which advances that end is therefore true.

Protestants have traditionally believed that the church should not tell lies. In the past Protestants excoriated the Vatican for its "Jesuitical" compromises in playing the power games of the world. Today it is alleged that not much has changed in the case of those Jesuits who have adopted a "revolutionary morality" in support of diverse liberationist struggles in, for example, Latin America. Whatever may be the truth in such allegations, the new thing in recent years has been the mainline Protestant entry into the murky spheres whose denizens fancy themselves change agents in "the real world." There is wickedness in all this, but it is a wickedness more pitiable than impressive. Catholic liberationists in Latin America may feel repaid for their sins by having actually contributed to revolutionary change (whether or not such change finally benefits the poor in whose name it was wrought). But mainline Protestants have no such satisfaction. If, for instance, the World Council of Churches sends ten thousand or five hundred thousand dollars to one revolutionary movement or another, it has simply reduced by that relatively small amount the aid required from the movement's more substantial backers. The most that the donor gets out of it is feeling good and being thanked (maybe) for having helped. In exchange for the world one might consider the loss of his soul, but not in exchange for a politician's acknowledgment that one has been useful to his purposes.

In the world of interest-group liberalism, the church seeks to make itself interesting by backing one or another interest. It employs its moral language and speaks much about "compassion," "justice," and "community," but such terms are without specific content, at least no content that challenges the interests that are backed, certainly no content that challenges the power game itself. It is simply a matter of choosing sides, or, like the awkward boy in a game of sandlot baseball, hoping to be chosen by one side or another. Having been permitted to play, the church becomes the team moralizer, offering "homilies and sentiments" in support of its goals and against its opposition. But even that satisfaction is diminished, for, as both mainliners and moral majoritarians have discovered in these last years, factional moralizings from opposing sides tend to cancel one another out. And, of course, in the minds of the real players on the several teams it tends to confirm the suspicion that the moralists should not have been admitted to the game in the first place.

The literature of the religious new right is replete with horror stories about liberal Protestantism's support for communist and other subversive activities. Such literature greatly overrates the degree of ideological consistency or seriousness among the functionaries of mainline religion. High up on Riverside Drive they write memoranda about God's call for a new economic order to replace capitalist oppressions and at the end of the day they cross the bridge to New Jersey on their way to places like Ridgewood, Pennsauken, and Basking Ridge, attaché cases loaded with other people's memoranda to be read that night, and minds uneasy about the mortgage and the bill from the orthodontist. It is more Prufrock than Lenin. And yet the reality cannot be lightly dismissed.

They are the institutional bearers of a tradition of once great cultural force and therefore of power in the fuller sense of that term. The absence of that tradition from our public life is a major factor contributing to the vacuousness of public discourse. When the bearers have lost confidence in the tradition they bear, then that tradition must be ridiculed, lest it be suspected that it has in fact been betrayed. The trinity of Christianity–America–civilization may have been naive and discredited, but probably no more so than the current bureaucratized obeisance to the trinity of Christianity–third world–revolutionary justice. They may both be instances of backstopping Christian truth by demonstrating its utility to some other end, but at least the first version engaged American Christians "where they live" and resulted in more than memos for a revolution, the noise of prophetic assemblies, and pervasive feelings of failure and guilt.

"On balance and considering the alternatives, the influence of the United States is a force for good in the world." Asked for a Yes or No answer (always unfair of course), much of mainline leadership answers No and many others ask for time to think about it. There is nothing wrong with thinking about it, but those who hesitate too long, like those who promptly answer No, are not likely to play a part in redefining the American experiment. Dr. King's "whom you would change you must first love" is not the same thing as "love it or leave it." Quite the opposite, it suggests the critical patriotism that has frequently marked the engagement of the religious mainline in social reform, and may do so again. But one only works to reform that which seems worthy of reforming. Like a spurned lover, there is a variety of liberalism that has given up and withdrawn into bitterness. If America has rejected our vision and is turning conservative, let it. It deserves whatever it gets. Then some, taking the next step, say they are going over to, have already gone over to, the other side. At least in their own minds.

The quality of demoralization in the mainline is not significantly different from the same thing in, say, Americans for Democratic Action. As some social theorists might suggest, the shared perspective is closely related to shared membership in "the new class." Readers will have noted that we approach somewhat gingerly the question of class and its influence on how people view the world. As an explanatory device, class theory is too often used not to explain but to explain away the views of those with whom we disagree. This is notoriously the case among some Marxist theorists who in principle deny the existence of truth or objectivity that transcends or cuts across class lines. Opponents of Marxist thought take understandable delight in turning class theory on its head, so to speak, arguing that the views of those sympathetic to Marxian ideas can be explained by their belonging to the "new class" that has a vested interest in advancing socialist, or at least "statist," directions. Yet no discussion of the social views of the Protestant mainline leadership would be complete without reference to the inescapable fact that we are all conditioned by our social placement, which includes the economic placement called class.[20] Class is not the only factor but it is a major factor in helping us understand why the taken-for-granted views of mainline leaders are so different from the views of many whom they would lead and even more different from the views of evangelicals, moral majoritarians, and, it would seem, most Americans.

We have earlier noted other factors, such as the "narrow escape syndrome." The narrow escape syndrome is evident, for example, among church officials who have "made it" to New York headquarters. With remarkable frequency they have come from small towns and medium-sized cities in, for instance, the South and Southwest and were brought up in an evangelical-bordering-on-fundamentalist piety that they found oppressive. Having arrived in a cosmopolitan center, they feel theirs was a narrow escape and any suggestion that more attention should be paid to, for example, biblical authority smacks to them of the threat of authoritarianism, of being dragged back into the world of "the fundies" from which they are so tenuously liberated. As with class theory, reference to this syndrome does not discredit the views such people hold. Their views may be quite valid and are, in any event, to be argued with on their own merits. It is insufferably reductionistic to dismiss viewpoints simply because they have their source in recognizable sociological dynamics. At the same time, an understanding of those dynamics contributes to our understanding of why some viewpoints are pervasive in sectors of the society, such as the leadership of mainline Protestantism. (The objection that critics of the new class are themselves part of the new class is not terribly interesting. In every period of history there have been people who, for reasons that need not delay us here, are traitors to their class.)

The leadership of mainline Protestantism, then, is overwhelmingly composed of members of the new class. If that proposition is true, the conflict of ideas may be viewed as part of a class struggle. In this connection, "class" refers to two elites in American life. There is the old elite associated with the "business" ethic and enterprise. Then there is the new elite of people who make a living by minting and marketing the metaphors by which they think society should be ordered. It is a "knowledge elite" and its business is symbols, designing them and manipulating them. It is made up of people who are self-conscious about being well educated and "enlightened." Members of the new class certify one another's membership, usually by reference to educational or professional "qualifications." Not surprisingly, educators are prominent in the new class, as are media people, those in the "helping professions," and social planners of all sorts. The reader of this book probably belongs to the new class, as the author certainly does. Membership is no vice, and treason to the class is not necessarily a virtue, but deciding what to do about belonging begins with knowing that one belongs.

The older elite, the business class, may be on the wane in modern post-industrialist societies. Its capitalist and "bourgeois" values were based in the production and distribution of material goods. The new class produces and distributes symbolic goods—knowledge and enlightenment. It is indeed a class, also in the Marxist sense, since it is defined by its relationship to the means of production. It is also like other classes in that it is stratified within itself, develops its own subculture, and advances its own interests. Also like other classes, it cloaks its own interests in terms of the general welfare. This does not mean that its members are insincere. Not at all; they really do believe in the happy convergence of their interests and the common good. In the case of the religious new class there is a triple convergence of class interest, common good, and the will of God. It is a potent combination. When a business executive declares that what is good for General Motors is good for America, members of the knowledge class react with derision and indignation. The same people nod agreement or cheer at the proposition that the business of America is education. They may be right; they also have a deep stake in gaining popular assent to that proposition.

Not so incidentally, the new class is "statist" in orientation, it favors increased government intervention in all aspects of the society. This is because a very large part of the new class makes its living in the rapidly growing public sector. Others work in programs dependent on government subsidy. Numerous church programs are also financed by government. In fields of health and social services, for example, the church relationship of church-related programs becomes almost indiscernible as these enterprises become captive to the state's "secular purposes."[21] It is not surprising that officers in these programs favor expanded government expenditure in these areas. The point is not whether they are right or wrong in the policies they advocate, but only to note that their livelihoods depend upon such expenditures. Of course this situation includes an occasion for corruption of motive and practice. He who pays the piper. . . . Not only in government agencies but also in religious agencies, programs tend to be tailored to the availability of funding. It should come as no shock that in all new class enterprises people are usually devoted to the government programs to which their careers are linked.

Most of the political commotions of our time have a class component. To speak of interests may seem vulgar, as though everybody is engaged in a struggle of grubby selfishness. That is not our idea of how Christians should live. But to say there is a class component does not mean that self-interest is the only or even dominant motivation. It is to say that it is there and candor requires that we acknowledge its presence and possible influence. Class involves more than self-interest; there are also symbols of class *culture*. Peter Berger puts it this way:

> The symbols of class culture are important. They allow people to "sniff out" who belongs and who does not; they provide easily applied criteria of "soundness." Thus a young instructor applying for a job in an elite university is well advised to hide "unsound" views such as political allegiance to the right wing of the Republican party (perhaps even to the left wing), opposition to abortion or to other causes of the feminist movement, or a strong commitment to the virtues of the corporation. Conversely, a young business school graduate seeking a career with one of *Fortune* magazine's "500" had better not advertise his or her career in the new politics, or views associated with the environmentalist, antinuclear or consumer movements.[22]

There is a *Kulturkampf* also in American religion. Any update of "the social sources of denominationalism" would today have to take into account the class component as it helps us understand the dividing lines between and within the several churches. As a community of transcendent allegiance and ecumenical destiny, the church, we might all agree, should be able to resist slipping into class warfare. (We might all agree, that is, except for those who, on the global screen, call for a partisan church in solidarity with the revolutionary class of liberationist struggles.) In American religion, however, we are slipping into, indeed may already have arrived at, class warfare. The religious new right clearly identifies with the older business class. It is of a piece with all the discussion since the 1960s about "middle America," "the real America," "the not-so-silent majority," and so forth. Most Lutherans, Roman Catholics, and moderate evangelicals are also of the old class, unabashedly bourgeois in their sympathies and behavior. An aspect of old class culture is that it is not uncomfortable with the idea that religion and religiously grounded values should play a prominent role in the business of the public square.

This puts mainline religious leadership in a bind. It may be assumed that few of us in principle think that open-ended class warfare is to be desired. If warfare there must be, however, it may be tempting to think that the new class is the wave of "the future." Eventually those on the other side of the class divide will have to come over. Educational levels rise, as does growth in the knowledge industry and helping professions— all bullish indicators for new class stock. The barometers of "respectability" are all fixed in favor of the new class. Harvard is ours: if it invites Jerry Falwell to speak, it is only for an amusing distraction. Fundamentalist colleges with academic aspirations lust for a "real Ph.D." from, say, the Divinity School of the University of Chicago. Eventually, "they" will have to come to "us." Even the attention they receive in the media depends upon their defining themselves in relation to us. We decide what is "interesting" and newsworthy. We can at will "take them up" for a season and, when that becomes too boring, consign them again to the cultural hinterland from which they came.

What then is the bind for mainline religious leadership? First, there is at least a residual ecumenical conscience in these circles. Few are prepared to accept the claim that the theology of the church catholic as an inclusive and transcending community is nothing but false consciousness, that the reality is nothing more than class warfare. Second, the "barbarians" may not be susceptible to our civilizing and assimilating designs, and they may no longer be dismissable. With impressive numbers, energy, organization, and political influence they are determined to create their own criteria of "respectability," to so redefine upper mobility that one day—a decade or three from now—"we" will be going to "them." Third, the bind of mainline leadership is that it becomes increasingly clear that those whom they would lead are by no means certain in their allegiance to the new class. In fact, when class conflict is more clearly delineated and a choice is called for, it becomes more obvious that the "constituencies" in mainline churches are remarkably loyal to the values of the old class that they associate with the American way. Many have already made that clear by "voting with their feet" into other churches. Many more are being alienated by new class leaders who condemn them as "apathetic" or "unenlightened" because they do not share the leadership's enthusiasms.

Finally, however, the leadership is in a bind because it is engaged in a self-liquidating enterprise. That is, it finds itself allied with those cultural forces that are indifferent or hostile to religion in the public square. On no question of moment does mainline religious leadership dissent from the conventional wisdoms of the prestige media or academic worlds. There is one notable exception to that general proposition: mainline leadership does not in principle endorse the idea of the naked public square. But even here there is debilitating ambivalence. Mainline Protestantism is not prepared to say that this is *not* a secular society. Many of its leaders emphatically say that it is and that it should be. (The term "pluralistic" is often preferred to "secular," but this is much of a sameness. The point is that there are no religiously grounded referents which should be normative for public discourse and policy.) The thesis of the secularists is that religion is atavistic and/or must be rigorously confined to the private sphere of life. Religious leaders who agree with or are ambivalent about this thesis are obviously in no position to assert the relevance of religion in public affairs. If, at the same time, their primary understanding of religion's purpose is its advancement of social justice, they are caught in a contradiction that stymies, if it does not liquidate, the enterprise to which they are devoted.

There is a Catch-22 dimension in this. Consider again that *New York Times* editorial in response to a religious leadership statement on genetic research. The editorial complains that the religious leaders did not make their argument on religious grounds. Perhaps they did not because, in view of the variety of leaders involved, agreement on religious grounds would have been almost impossible to attain, whereas they could agree on the public policy conclusion. More pertinent to the point at hand, an argument on religious grounds would have been viewed as a "sectarian" intrusion on public space, an effort to "impose religious values" on others. In other words, the secularist argument wins both ways. If religionists want to speak in the public forum they should speak religiously, or else they have no right to say anything *qua religionists*. If they do speak religiously, on the other hand, they are guilty of a sectarian violation of pluralistically sanitized public space. The way out of the bind is to challenge the secularistic dogma head-on. The religious new right is doing that, clumsily. Liberal Protestantism, among others, ought to be doing it in a more sophisticated manner. But to date it appears to have neither the insight nor the inclination nor the nerve for such a challenge.

The heirs of the great culture-defining tradition of Puritanism seem puzzled. The descendants of those who during the constitutional period linked liberal democracy to Christian freedom seem no longer able to make the connections. They wear with embarrassment the tattered mantle of an earlier evangelicalism's ebullient faith in Christianity–America–civilization. There is, as Robert Handy notes, an air of uneasiness and guilt. The happy convergence on which mainline Protestantism counted has not worked out. By the end of the last century its leaders had pledged their lives, their fortunes, and their sacred honor to the enlightened leadership of the nation. But the pledge was not reciprocated. By the middle of this century the nation's cultural elite began to make it quite explicit: the complete Christian commonwealth was not on, at least not the "Christian" part; the "redeemer nation" would make it on its own without reference to the Redeemer. Mainline Protestantism was barely thanked for its help in bringing the society to the point of secular self-sufficiency. It had succeeded in making itself dispensable. It would be permitted to tag along on the continuing journey, to help out with odd jobs and, for old times' sake, to offer an invocation when appropriate, but it must not make a nuisance of itself.

Some mainline leaders find these terms unacceptably demeaning and have, at least in their minds and their rhetoric, joined the ranks of rebellion against the American enterprise. The great majority, however, see no alternative to accepting the terms laid down. Not if they are to maintain the alliances and associations to which they are accustomed. There is, after all, a price to be paid for being treated as a member of the establishment, even if the demand that one not make a public issue of being very religious seems a bit much at times. The alternative is to join with those Christians from the hinterland, and that will never do. In culture, in sensibilities, in interests of every kind, they are simply not of our class. The old class that has made it in America has become the new class. It is outrageously *declasse* of these country cousins to be invading our space with the noisy promotion of our discarded values and verities.

In vague uneasiness and guilt the new class closes ranks. In 1983 in Virginia the Christian Church (Disciples of Christ) met in 150th Annual Assembly. The assembly joined in the confession of sins: "We confess our guilt as one of the wealthiest countries in a world full of starving people, as citizens intent on order in a country full of desperation." Then, presumably describing themselves: "We are Americans blind with nationalistic pride, mad for revenge, because we ignore the existence of whole countries and refuse to accept borders of peace." They acknowledged not keeping faith with the generations that had gone before, "the dead who lived before us and whose dreams we betrayed, the dreams of 1789 and of 1917."[23] In these mainline sentiments we encounter again the confusion of the aggregated "we"—we Disciples, we Christians, we Americans, we human beings. The result is a miasma of guilty laceration. Not really self-laceration, to be sure, for the good Christians assembled likely do not think of *themselves* as "Americans blind with nationalistic pride, mad for revenge." The exercise is finally not a confession of sin but an exercise in self-righteous congratulation for being ever so morally superior to "them." Perhaps most poignant is that here was a gathering of Christian Americans who in specifying that ideal to which they aspire refer not to the great events of Christian or of American history but to the "dreams" of the French Revolution of 1789 and the Bolshevik takeover of 1917.

Other mainline leaders are not so completely alienated from the American experience. Their points of moral reference are still within that experience, if somewhat on the edges of it. In November 1980 the United Methodist bishops met in Houston and assessed the election in which Ronald Reagan came to the White House. A Bishop Nichols, then head of the council of bishops, observed, "We must interpret what has happened as a season of history. Perhaps the blame ought not be placed on all the vigor of the right, but maybe on the weakness of the 'saints' who somehow in their faltering leadership could not quite gain the confidence of the populace." A better day will come, he said, "if the people of faith will be strengthened by defeat and address themselves to the new agenda which is upon us."[24] He urged that the church should be "examining with greater care both our strengths and weaknesses." Apparently the self-examination did not extend to inquiring into whether the defeat of the Democratic party is to be equated with the defeat of the "saints" and "people of faith."

Another United Methodist bishop, soon to become President of the National Council of Churches, said of the 1980 election results: "People voted their self-interest instead of the social principles of the church. It looks like United Methodist with everybody else forsook their Christian idealism at the ballot box."[25] Two years later, when the NCC had been subjected to sustained public criticism for its narrow partisanship, the bishop declared: "It is my prayerful intention as the President of the National Council of Churches of Christ not to identify with political movements or economic systems, but to broaden the base of the ecumenical reality in this country and to be faithful to the gospel of Jesus Christ."[26] In view of the bishop's long-standing assertions about *the* Christian, or at least *the* Methodist, position in partisan politics and his praise for Cuba and sundry revolutionisms, the critics were understandably skeptical about this declaration of nonpartisanship.[27] While excoriating the political alliances of the religious new right, however, the bishop and many others seemed quite honestly unaware of their own captivity to a single slice of the political spectrum. In response to the public criticism, the bishop noted some of the good work that mainline churches do for the disadvantaged and urged that the critics "ought to be forced to stand in the presence of the world's hungry and oppressed and ask for forgiveness."[28] From the NCC and its several churches came a torrent of statements and press releases declaring that those who questioned established policies were really opposed to Christian concern for the poor. It seemed a strange way to "broaden the base of the ecumenical reality."

The illiberality of statements such as the above seems to escape those who make them. Indeed such crabbed statements of extraordinary insularity come readily to those who, one has no reason to doubt, sincerely believe themselves to be liberal and ecumenical. The style and substance distress conservatives for obvious reasons. Other critics are more relaxed, saying that it really doesn't matter since almost nobody in the churches or outside pays much attention to the radicalized pronouncements of "resolutionary Christianity." But this, I believe, is to miss the point. People should pay attention. Historically and potentially the contribution of mainline Protestantism is too important to be dismissed and discredited because of the styles of leadership that have prevailed in recent years. Those religious forces most opposed to the cultural and political directions of the mainline must recognize that they too lose when the mainline witness is dismissed and derided. The forces that gain from the discrediting of religious engagement in public life are those who insist upon the naked square—in order that they may have a public monopoly on the "mediating of meanings."

The flagship journal of liberalism, *New Republic,* offers this comment: "It is the thinking of many clerics and laymen that the church's sacred role in the world is to supplement the efforts of the Americans for Democratic Action and the Sierra Club. Small wonder that so many people are abandoning denominations like . . . the United Presbyterians and filling up the pews in the evangelical churches. The fundamentalists offer the faithful redemption and salvation, the Word made flesh, a cross at Golgotha. The mainstream churches offer a political agenda indistinguishable from Barry Commoner's."[29] (Barry Commoner was prominent in the 1970s as an ecologist and proponent of democratic socialism.) By the mid-1980s such derisory comments had become more frequent in the secular media. Journalists with a keen nose for blood sensed yet another establishment institution ripe for the kill. Mainline institutions that came under attack responded for the most part reactively, sometimes hunkering down, sometimes lashing out in all directions, almost always failing to distinguish between hostile critics and those critics eager to see restored the credibility of the mainline's public witness.[30]

The picture was not entirely bleak, however. Some institutions, such as the National Council, began to take steps to ensure greater accountability to the member churches. For too long heads of churches and of the council itself had been required to rally to the defense of programs and statements of units and subunits that had little if any authorization to act or speak for the council. Some critics complained that questions of structural accountability did not deal with the ideologically skewed directions of the council itself. Other thoughtful observers, perhaps reflecting greater confidence in the member churches and their memberships, hoped that, with a greater measure of democratic accountability, the ideological questions would take care of themselves. Attention to internal reforms was reinforced also by a new awareness that the council suddenly seemed dispensable. Some religious leaders called for a new and more inclusive ecumenical structure that—although this was not said publicly in so many words—would replace the National Council.

In the churches themselves surveys suggest that younger clergy have for some time been in the process of becoming more conservative, if conservative means a deeper interest in the integrity and distinctiveness of Christian doctrine and a declining inclination to let their ministries be defined by whatever is declared the progressive cause of the moment.[31] It may become apparent that the social action enthusiasms of recent years have become a middle-aged phenomenon led by people who yearn for a revival of some new version of "the movement" dating from the 1960s. At the same time, the categories of conservative and liberal, left and right, would be further confounded if these younger clergy let their passion for Christian depth and distinctiveness lead to a basic challenge of the secularist assumptions of the present social order. Such a challenge, in which Christian social engagement moves beyond serving as an appendage to causes charted by others, would in fact be a quite new form of radicalism.

In addition to these hopeful signs of change, there was in the mid-1980s a resurgence of expressed interest in evangelism. The increasing reference to evangelism was in part a response to evangelical criticism of the mainline and, perhaps in larger part, a reflection of concern about membership losses. While church leaders were trying to rescue evangelism from the rag bag of pious irrelevancies to which it had been consigned, it was not clear that "a renewed emphasis upon evangelism" would serve to remedy institutional ills. As Dean Kelley and others argued, a reversal of identity loss cannot be effected simply by willing it to happen. Evangelism requires an *evangel,* a gospel message that provides a strong and clear "meaning system." One evangelical observer of the mainline puts it this way: "Liberal Protestant churches themselves must be evangelized before their members will wholeheartedly evangelize others. *Evangelicals* can do evangelism because they have had an experience of God that they feel they *must* share with others—so powerful an experience that the zeal to witness comes almost naturally. Liberals, if they do not have a describable faith, simply cannot share it with others, despite the finest training programs designed by their denominational bureaucrats."[32]

This then, in brief compass, is a picture of mainline Protestantism in America as it moves, or drifts, into the twenty-first century. It is not a flattering picture, but I hope it is not unfair. Apart from the decline of the mainline it is not possible to explain the cultural and political influences of the religious new right. It is precisely the failure of "the ecumenical churches" to be truly ecumenical that also helps to explain their isolation from the vitalities of other communities now "coming of age" in America, such as the Roman Catholic and Lutheran. However severe the failings of the mainline, the nobility of its earlier vision should not be slighted. From the seventeenth century and well into the present century, it carried and articulated the moral tradition that made authentically political discourse possible. Nor should one forget the devotion of millions—perhaps a majority of mainline church people even today—who sense that vague "unease and guilt" about having somewhere taken a wrong turn and missed their mission. These millions believe deeply in the revelation of God's love in Christ, in the authority of Scripture and Christian doctrine, in the values of family and work and fairness, in the enduring promise of the American experiment. They hope their churches believe in these things too and are puzzled that they seem unable to proclaim it convincingly. Looking at the religious new right, they ask: "Why should these newcomers—these television vulgarians, these born-againers, these fundamentalists—be viewed as the champions of biblical truth and the American promise?" Why indeed.

CHAPTER SIXTEEN

LAW AND THE
EXPERIMENT RENEWED[1]

O UR QUESTIONS BRING US BACK TO LAW, WHAT IT IS AND what it is not. This is not surprising. Law speaks of what is authoritative in a society. Like travelers consulting a road map we consult the law. Or like players in a game consulting the rule book in order to settle a dispute. We usually look at the road map when we are lost and at the rule book when there is disagreement. With respect to the law, however, we are map makers as well as map followers; we ask not only what the rule is but also what the rule ought to be. In a democracy we participate in the drawing of the maps and the making of the rules. Or so it is said.

Some of the sharpest challenges to secularist ideology are being raised by Christian lawyers who believe that what is said about democratic governance is true, or should be true. Organizations such as the Council on Religion and Law and the Christian Legal Society involve legal minds from all sectors of American religion who are asking fundamental questions about the nature of law in our society and our world. Some of a fundamentalist persuasion believe that life must be ordered by law and that ultimately the basic law of the land should be that revealed in the Bible. Others, living by the gospel and more nuanced in their approach, ask only that the provisional structure that is human law should not oppose or disregard our understanding of what is human—including the ways in which that understanding is democratically informed by religious faith. But despite their differences, which are not unimportant, lawyers, ethicists, and other thoughtful believers have dared to approach contemporary law and ask, "By what authority?" The question has been met by the ominous secular silence of the naked public square. In law, where conflict compels us to try to articulate the meaning of the community to which we belong, it seems we have run out of meanings. In law, the movement from the authoritarian to the autonomous to the recognition of what is authoritative has become stuck in the autonomous. It is therefore not surprising that the questions which have preoccupied us in this book conclude with a reflection on the nature of law as it relates to religion and democracy in America.

The law is not like life. Therein lies its utility and even its majesty. The law is not like life. Therein lies its weakness and even its danger. To be sure, the law is part of life; it is part of that communal experience we call history, including this present moment. Law itself, as we shall emphasize, has a history. And yet, when we speak of "the law" we imply that it is something distinct from ordinary experience. It has a normative status by which we order, remedy, and judge the interactions that make up what we call "life."

Legal virtues are impartiality, rationality, objectivity, equality, consistency, and fairness. Such virtues have only limited applicability in the larger reality called life. Life is marked by preference and passion, by contingency and contradiction, by gradations of merit and success, by tragedy and serendipity, by fancy and whim. Most of all, life—in both endowments and opportunities—is unfair. Law that mirrored life would be no law at all. And life ruled by law alone is lethal.

Our understanding of law is subject to both distortions. Our society becomes ever more litigious as people seek securities and solutions in law. In part this is because lawyers encourage the extra business; in larger part it is because people have been taught and have come to believe that they are entitled to protection against the insecurities of existence. Thus, for example, the intimacies of marriage and friendship are increasingly subjected to the calculus of legal contract. Thus, to take a more bizarre example, some lawyers at a recent Congressional hearing on the regulation of religious cults proposed consumer protection laws against false or dangerous religious ideas. Contracts are designed to spare us the uncertainties of human relationships. The covenant of trust mutually pledged is, by comparison, precarious and arduous in its demand for constant renewal in love. The sensible person knows the difference between law and life. She knows that life is fully lived in the risks of decision and the insecurities of commitment beyond the call of contract. She knows that, in the things that really matter, the litigious life is no life at all.

If life, in all its mystery and diversity, cannot be ruled by law, neither can law be subjected entirely to the mysteries and diversities of life. The law is not merely an instrument for solving problems, a set of rules to be manipulated to advantage by the clever and powerful. Admittedly, the law may sometimes seem to be no more than that, but most of us persist in believing it should be more than that. To speak of "the law" in terms of awe and majesty may be no more than an exercise in false consciousness— as the Marxists say, an indulgence in mystification. After all, "the law" is patently a very human thing. Prick it, and does it not bend? Tickle it, and does it not accommodate? Wrong it, and does it not avenge? Like Shylock, the law is not a thing apart.

Or is it? Is it merely useful to think so, or is it true, that the law has its own integrity, its own logic, its own authority? While the law is clearly susceptible to our decisions, is there not another sense in which our decisions are accountable to the law? I do believe that is so. While it is a part of life, the law calls life to account. That is to say that the law possesses authority. Without such authority the law is merely a bundle of rules backed up by force; with such authority, the law is a power we are bound to acknowledge. Again, the word "bound" is important, coming as it does from *religare,* the root of religion.

Critical to any life worth living is the ordering of our loyalties— accepting responsibility for deciding by what we will be bound. The life without obligations that are freely accepted and faithfully observed is a life in bondage to chaos, a life without meaning. Freedom is found in obedience to the normative; all other liberations are just different ways of being lost. With greater and lesser degrees of reflection, we thus bind ourselves in friendship, in marriage, in vocation, and a host of other decisions. The obligation that we affirm most deeply, most daringly, and perhaps most desperately, that is our religion.

Our religion may be called a religion, such as Christianity or Islam, or it may be a variation of religion, such as atheism, or it may be a political program or humanitarian ideal or an aspiration to some excellence. It may be superficial or profound, a false god or true, but it is that by which we are bound and which bond we affirm, or at least want to affirm. Such a bond is not at our disposal; we do not possess it, and it is prior to our being possessed by it; to it we hold ourselves accountable because to it we are accountable. Having decided upon the ordering of our loyalties, our loyalties order us. After choosing our obligations, we discover they have chosen us. And Jesus said, "You have not chosen me but I have chosen you" (John 15:16). In theological argot it is like prevenient grace, the grace that is always a step ahead of us, turning our achievements into gifts, our discoveries into revelations, and our choices into the knowledge of being chosen.

Laws may be just or unjust, wise or foolish, but behind the laws is the law. It binds us before we embrace it, and indeed whether or not we embrace it. A lawyer may be an officer of the court, an agent of a particular law, and yet it is not mere hyperbole to say he is a *servant* of the law. So it is with all of us in relation to the law, when our choices encounter the socially articulated loyalties reflected in laws. In describing this attitude toward the law, we are dealing with what philosophers call "moral sentiments": shame, guilt, resentment, indignation, reciprocity, trust, mercy, and so forth. It can be argued that such sentiments are not truly universal and therefore cannot be made necessary to the foundation of law. And, to be sure, there may be people unacquainted with guilt or shame or pride, just as others may be incapable of love. But in our communal conversation about the meaning of law we should not give veto power to the handicapped. Musicians do not defer to the tone deaf, nor painters to the color blind. Moral sentiments may not be universally distributed, they certainly are not evenly distributed, but then, neither is anything else of value.

The contention here is that moral sentiments point to a prevenient reality. This is not first of all an argument from logic; namely, that there must be a reality prior and related to such sentiments. That argument can be made, but here I would appeal to our experience. Alfred Schutz, the pioneer of "sociology of knowledge," spoke of "Aha!" experiences. Such an experience is a moment in which we are surprised by the self-evident. It is seeing what we had not seen before but had been there all along; and, having seen it, it is impossible to imagine not having seen it. It promptly becomes a part of our "taken-for-granted reality" without which the world is inexplicable. Thus this latest step in discovery becomes the first step, the conclusion turns out to be the premise.

Moral sentiments are part of our experience. To deny their existence is the kind of solipsism that among sophomores passes for profundity. (Yet, as we shall note, they are ignored, if not denied, in much theory about law today.) And these sentiments—guilt, shame, gratitude, and the like—are inherently relational. That is, they do not exist in a vacuum, they do not stand on their own feet. The experience is related to something or someone beyond itself. Guilt is to have offended against an other and leads, or should lead, to saying you are sorry; gratitude likewise is to give thanks; resentment is to protest. The experience and the expression, the feeling and the language, are not two distinct things, as though one were the cause and the other the effect. No, the phenomenon we call guilt, or gratitude, or resentment, is itself relational. To experience it is to be related to what occasions it. Such relationships engage the *religare,* the network of binding of which our obligations are part.

At this point it may be suspected that we have smuggled God into the argument, and that rather clumsily. But that is not the case. At the appropriate point I will announce his entrance quite candidly. (Although we will then discover he has been here right along, he being the prime instance of the conclusion that turns out to be the premise.) At the moment I would only suggest that this network of binding to which we are related by moral sentiments is what we mean by the law. The law is more than the sum of its parts. There are laws, for example, against indiscriminate stealing. They are not adequately explained by reference to their utilitarian value, nor by the fact that all societies have had such laws. It is rather the case that there is, in Harold Berman's language, "an all-embracing moral reality, a purpose in the universe, which stealing offends."[2] We break a law, but we offend against the law.

Now offense suggests a personal event, one offends against someone. This does not prove, of course, that there is a someone who is offended. You may drop a cherished vase on the floor and say most sincerely to its shattered remains, "I'm sorry." We do that sort of thing all the time. We personalize, or anthropomorphize, inanimate objects. We do not really think for a moment that breaking the vase offended some great Master Vase that holds together the "vaseness" of the universe. Yet when we break a law, our feeling is not one of having offended against that law but of having offended The Law. This does not prove the existence of The Law, but I suggest it is our common experience and that its possible implications are deserving of careful thought.

To be sure, we can attempt to "explain"—meaning to explain away—this experience of having offended by employing psychological and other explanatory devices. What we mean by "the law" may be no more than a residual "father image" or the afterglow of flawed potty training. The trouble with such explanations is that they are reductionist and finally trivializing; they do not do justice to the relational character of our moral sentiments. The person who insists that my experience of a Mozart piano sonata is not an encounter with beauty but a neuro-chemical response to physical vibrations has said nothing of consequence about the experience; he has said a great deal about his own poverty, if not perversity, of mind. His explanation is not more reasonable, it is simply less interesting.

The suggestion, then, is that while the law is of necessity unlike life in important respects, it is rooted in life experience. The further suggestion is that that experience is relational, pointing to something other than itself. It is, in short, of enormous consequence that people have a sense of right and wrong. The experience of right and wrong, in turn, relates to a more universal rightness and wrongness, which is reflected in the law. The person who says the sense of right and wrong is meaningless is, if taken at face value, revealing a deplorable personal deficiency. In any event, he is saying something about himself. For those who know the reality of right and wrong, to ask what it "means" is meaningless. Of course one must ask what it means in the sense of what does it mean in this case or that. But the sense of right and wrong itself is the conclusion that turns out to be the premise of all other meanings. But what is to be done about the person who persists in challenging the reality of the experience of right and wrong? One should be patient of course, and, if one is a believer, one should pray for him. That some people lack a moral sense no more negates the existence of morality and what it implies than does the frequent lack of clear reasoning negate the existence of rationality. Again, in morality, as in music, the arts, the sciences, or anything else of importance, reasonable discourse should not be stymied by the veto power of the handicapped. If moral sentiments and the traditions that shape them are ruled out of court, so to speak, the result is law that makes the normal subservient to the pathological. Even if, as cannot be demonstrated, the normal is not numerically normal, the law by definition deals with that which is normative.

So far, however, we have spoken of the law in terms of personal and somewhat individual experience. The personal dimension is important because, however much our ideas may be socially constructed and conditioned, it is as individual persons that we give our yes or no to the moral sense that is the foundation of law. Yet the law is preeminently a social phenomenon. However we severally acknowledge that which is binding, it is together that we spell out those acknowledgments in the bonding that creates community. Law is by definition a public enterprise; it is trans-subjective. We can withhold our subjective assent from the reality to which our moral sense points, but we cannot, without abandoning the world of reasonable discourse, refuse to recognize the empirical fact of the law as it makes its appearance in every society. Nor can it be denied that—at least in Western societies, although I suspect the phenomenon is more universal—people distinguish between particular laws and that which they call "the law." It is the latter that partakes of a numinous, even a divine character that, like religion, is binding. In everyday language a person who protests what he thinks to be the unfairness or silliness of a particular rule is told, "But that's the law." He may with Mr. Bumble respond that "the law is a ass, a idiot." But it is with respect to "the law" that a particular law or system of laws is declared deficient. While particular rules may be deemed silly or unfair, it is acknowledged that they have an authority that, however wrong in particular application, is derived from "the law."

Those who call themselves "realists" in jurisprudence object that talk about the religious dimensions of law is obscurantist mystification. (Herbert Butterfield once remarked that, in law and other fields, "realism" is not a school of thought but simply a boast.) To the charge of obscurantism and mystification, it must be honestly answered that the origins and sustaining force of law are indeed obscure and mysterious. There is nothing more unrealistic, in the sense of being contrary to the evidence, than the proposal that laws are created or obeyed apart from a communal consensus about what is right and wrong. Nor can it be reasonably denied that that sense of right and wrong is inseparably connected to an awareness of prevenient obligation, whether or not that obligation is expressed in explicitly religious terms.

In light of this, then (and with a bow to Harold J. Berman who has done so much in our time to reconnect religion and law), permit me to take a try at a definition of law: Laws issue from and participate in "the law." The law is more than a body of rules; it is the historical, living process of people legislating, adjudicating, administering, and negotiating the allocation of rights and duties. Its purpose is to prevent harm, resolve conflicts, and create means of cooperation. Its premise, from which it derives its perceived legitimacy and therefore its authority, is that it strives to anticipate and give expression to what a people believes to be its collective destiny or ultimate meaning within a moral universe.

Of course talk about ultimate meanings makes many jurists and political theorists nervous. Law and the social sciences, like most intellectual enterprises in the modern world, aspire to the status of being "scientific" in the sense that the natural sciences are scientific. Nothing in this book

253

is intended to deny that this is in many ways an admirable and necessary aspiration. The scientific method, as it has been understood in the last two hundred years, is a monumentally important liberation from authoritarianism. Any reconstruction of public philosophy and its religious groundings must be an emphatically post-Enlightenment reconstruction. Only those who have internalized the contributions of the Enlightenment can move beyond its confinements. Scientific method makes everything subject to critical reason. Authoritarianism declared, "This is the law and it is to be obeyed because the king (or the church, or the Bible, or tribal custom) says so." And that was that. The law is the law is the law, and nobody is permitted to ask, "By what authority?" The king forbad the challenge because it was deemed impious and insurbordinate. Certain moderns forbid the challenge because it is deemed meaningless or irrelevant. But the point is that both proscribe what is precisely *the* question of critical reason: What is the foundation of the authority that law claims for itself?

That question cannot be answered within the terms of the law itself. That is to say, the law is not self-legitimating. To be sure, the question of legitimacy can be suppressed, but suppression is presumably the enemy of scientific inquiry. Once the question is asked, it must be answered by reference to something beyond law itself. "This law has a claim upon your observance because _____." Over the years legal philosophies have filled in the blank with many different answers. Although evasions and circumlocutions have been frequent, the "because" finally comes down to the question of right and wrong, of the good to be maximized and the evil to be minimized. Except, of course, for those who, bowing to the divine right of kings or to the positivism of existent fact, refuse to ask the question "By what authority?" Critical reason refuses to conform to the authoritarianism of pretentious kings and overweening facticity. Critical reason invokes the "oughtness" of things in order to bring the "isness" of things under judgment. Finally, whatever explanations might satisfy us personally, critical reason recognizes that the historical phenomenon of law is produced and sustained by the perception of a people that law is somehow correlated with the way things really are, or with the way things really should be.

It is commonly said that law has evolved from being organic to being technical. It no longer reflects the belief systems, customs, and traditions of the tribe, but has become a tool chest of complex instruments to be rationally applied for the achievement of specified personal and social purposes. To the extent that this transition does indeed represent a demystification of law, it is to be welcomed. To the extent, however, that it inhibits critical reason from venturing beyond the technical and utilitarian, it becomes a new mystification. The new authoritarianism may be worse than the first, and the new mystification worse than the first, because they claim for themselves the virtue of freedom. In Orwell's "New Speak," war is peace and slavery is freedom. The slavery that claims to be freedom is the most desperate form of slavery because it has subsumed into itself the idea of emancipation. Much social theory today is in bondage to a species of rationality that refuses to ask, or even forbids the asking of, the questions that get in the way of making law and politics an "exact science." The obsession with exactitude is inimical to what is called the human factor (an interesting term, implying that people are one factor among others to be taken into account). Human behavior is notoriously lacking in that prime scientific virtue, predictability. Whatever else law may be, it is a human enterprise in response to human behavior, and human behavior is stubbornly entangled with beliefs about right and wrong. Law that is recognized as legitimate is therefore related to—even organically related to, if you will—the larger universe of moral discourse that helps shape human behavior. In short, if law is not also a moral enterprise, it is without legitimacy or binding force.

An excessive emphasis upon law as technique is also demeaning to its professional practitioners, to lawyers, politicians, and social theorists. Lawyers, for instance, want to be viewed as something more than mechanics. To the extent that that desire reflects merely a search for status, it is just a piece of snobbery. After all, to be a mechanic—an automobile mechanic, for instance—is a perfectly honorable occupation and one can fulfill it without fretting about the metaphysics of transportation. But the thoughtful jurist or legislator is vaguely repulsed by the idea that his task is merely mechanical. The revulsion results from an intuition that is to be trusted. A priest who has great confidence in the mechanical, *ex opere operato*, effect of the sacraments may content himself with doing the technical job at hand, but that is hardly a worthy model of priesthood. So the lawyer and public officer have a quasi-priestly role, mediating between human conflicts and what is hoped is a moral universe. The law then becomes the agreed upon language of mediation. It is not so important that the lawyer who sees his task as purely mechanical demeans herself and her profession; more important is that such an approach demeans the human effort to sustain moral meaning in the universe.

If some theories would turn law into the technique of exact sciences, others take quite the opposite direction. They want to be relentlessly realistic about how law is made and applied; there is a tone of iconoclasm, even cynicism, in their exultation over the arbitrariness of law. To speak of principles or of morality is, in their view, ludicrously naive. Some who are of this temperament say laws are the instrument of class interests, the rules of convenience for the powerful. Others, less ideologically inclined, emphasize accident more than conspiracy. Law is an arbitrary game, and the lawyer is a skilled player of the game. In ancient times it was said that the law is what the king says it is. In our enlightened era it is declared

255

that the law is what the court says it is. No more and no less. The king and the court may be good or bad, they may have the counsel of wise men or of scoundrels, but if there is no appeal beyond king or court, the law is finally capricious. And capricious is the one thing that, by definition, law is not supposed to be. Capriciousness has always been the mark of tyranny. Law that issues from the whim of monarchs or the caprice of courts can command obedience only by the threat of coercion. It is the formula in which naked force displaces legitimate power.

Recall the earlier definition of law: The premise of law, from which it derives its perceived legitimacy and therefore authority, is that it strives to anticipate and give expression to what people believe to be their collective destiny or ultimate meaning within a moral universe. At this point theology enters the picture. The disciplined application of critical reason to the meaning of life is what is here meant by theology. Pursued relentlessly enough, the question of meaning is the question of God. Theology is the exploration into God; that is, the exploration of the ultimate or absolute meaning, the final source and purpose, of all reality. *Christian* theology works with the data of God's self-revelation in the life, death, resurrection, and promised return of Jesus whom we call the Christ. But there are ways of doing theology other than the Christian way. Much that is in fact theology, as that term is employed here, is not connected with any brand-name religion. But, in law or any other field, the search for ultimate meanings that provide morally binding legitimacy for an enterprise is a theological search.

To put it somewhat differently, theology is the disciplined reflection upon transcendent truth and value that gives significance, perhaps eternal significance, to our lives. It is important to underscore that, while theology may speak of the supernatural and of other worlds, its meaning is the meaning of *this* life, *this* world, *this* history of which we are part. At least Judeo-Christian theology, unlike that of some Eastern religions, is pledged to the ultimate significance of this ordinary stuff of history that makes up what we call reality. And, again in Christian theology, the ultimate meaning of anything is to be found in the end of that thing. As the meaning of an epoch of history is perceived at the end of the epoch, as the meaning of a life is perceived from the end of that life, so the meaning of all history is revealed—if the Christian gospel turns out to be true—in the end time of the consummation of history in the Messianic Age.

But now we may be getting ahead of ourselves. The Messianic Age is, after all, about as far as you can go, while this present moment is, to judge by the evidence, far short of that consummation devoutly to be wished. In this present moment we are witnessing in social philosophy and jurisprudence some signs of an incipient revival of theology, although, of course, it is not always called theology. But some thoughtful persons are addressing the legitimacy crisis of modern law by searching for transcendent meanings that can rescue law from the tyranny of the capricious. In Chapter Six we discussed briefly the work of John Rawls. His elegantly argued *A Theology of Justice* is probably the single most influential effort in recent intellectual history to establish a foundation of moral authority in political philosophy.[3] It is an important effort to establish principle over caprice and moral purpose over mechanical precedent.

It will be recalled that Rawls attempts to redeem the idea of social contract as the basis of law, asking how the terms of justice might be established in a normative way that transcends past and present disagreements about the meaning of justice. He argues that the meaning and terms of justice can be determined by rational persons seeking their own interests behind a "veil of ignorance." The veil of ignorance assures that these people do not know what their own placement in life might be. They do not know, in this social contract they are designing, who will be rich and who poor, who gifted and who disadvantaged, who the darling of fate and who life's loser. Therefore, it is argued, they will try to maximize the chances of each but also build in some hedging of their bets for the less fortunate. The result, he contends, will be as close an approximation of justice as we are likely to get.

Rawls' argument, to which the above can hardly do justice, has been much discussed, much celebrated, and much criticized. It is noted that Rawls assumes a rather narrow definition of the rational person, excluding the gambler and adventurer. It is pointed out that antecedent and abstract choices are qualitatively and substantively different from choices made in particular circumstances. It is objected that it is by no means obvious that people would choose equality as the chief goal; they might well prefer some other personal or social excellence. It is proposed that Rawls' "sense of fairness" would not necesarily be the controlling moral sentiment— that a sense of obligation, of altruism, or of achieving some collective purpose might well have priority. It is argued that, while Rawls' theory is on the surface relentlessly individualistic, it in fact destroys the individual by depriving him of all those personal particularities that are the essence of being an individual. There is considerable merit to the criticism that Rawls' theory of justice is in the final analysis a theory of ignorance and selfishness.

In Rawls' theory we have, I believe, an instance of a laudable intention miscarried. It is symptomatic of our problems in relating law to life, in democratizing the public square. Rawls' way of establishing a normative concept of justice contradicts almost every part of the definition of law offered earlier. Law, it was suggested, "is the historical, living process of people legislating, adjudicating, administering, and negotiating the allocation of rights and duties." But Rawls' people behind the veil are, in fact, non-persons. They have no history, no tradition, no vested interests, no self-knowledge, no loves, no hates, no fears, no dreams of transcendent purpose or duty. Living persons are distinguished by partiality, by passion, by particularity. Instead of re-linking life and law, Rawls subsumes life into a totally abstracted notion of justice that could not be further removed from the world in which the legitimacy of law must be renewed.

It is of paramount importance that there is no history behind the veil of ignorance. Like many other contemporary theorists, Rawls assumes a universe in which everything is, as it were, already in place. As Eliade, the great scholar of comparative religions, has noted, in this respect the "scientific" approach of the secular Enlightenment is similar to the "primitive" world views of ancient times. There is finally no real history, no real contingency, no real change; the world is either composed of static entities or what looks like change is simply a cyclical recurrence of the same old thing. The Judeo-Christian tradition, however, is premised upon the concept of real history, real change, happening in an incomplete universe that is still awaiting its promised fulfillment.

Despite the elegant and earnest abstractions posed by some theorists, there is no alternative to history. Only in history can we address the problems of history. Students of jurisprudence have noted that the idea of the "ongoingness" of law—the way it develops and grows incrementally and corrects itself—is dependent upon the Judeo-Christian understanding of history. Thus, in our earlier definition, it is suggested that law has an "anticipatory" quality; it reaches forward, so to speak, to embrace an excellence of "right order" that has not yet been actualized. Law is therefore always provisional, the "isness" never perfectly embodies the "oughtness," the "now" is at its best only a preview of the promised "not yet." (Here again we recognize the importance of the concept of the twofold kingdom, the kingdom of grace revealed in Jesus Christ and the kingdom of historical experience in a creation not yet fulfilled under the rule of that grace.)

The contrivance of a historyless idea of justice miscarries for all the reasons indicated. Also, and closely related to our concern for religion and democracy, such an idea will not serve because it is impossibly exotic. The legitimacy of law in a democratic society depends upon the popular recognition of the connections between law and what people think life is and ought to be. As for theories such as that proposed by Rawls, only a few thousand people can, or care to, read them—and even then there is little agreement on what to make of them. Thus the theorists' quest for universality becomes simply the parochialism of a few intellectuals. This is not meant to indict intellectuals as a class, nor to suggest that truths must be made easy and popular in order to be true. It is simply to underscore the limitations of theories of justice that cannot sustain a democratic consensus regarding the legitimacy of law. I believe that Rawls' theory fails a number of tests, as indicated above, but most pertinent to this essay, it fails the test of democratic legitimacy.

This is the cultural crisis—and therefore the political and legal crisis—of our society: the popularly accessible and vibrant belief systems and world views of our society are largely excluded from the public arena in which the decisions are made about how the society should be ordered. As we have seen, critics such as Daniel Bell conclude, with some reluctance, that the answer lies in a more public role for religion. What they conclude with reluctance is the gravamen of this book. Specifically with regard to law, there is nothing in store but a continuing and deepening crisis of legitimacy if courts persist in systematically ruling out of order the moral traditions in which Western law has developed and which bear, for the overwhelming majority of the American people, a living sense of right and wrong. The result, quite literally, is *the outlawing of the basis of law.* When the moral sentiments and the traditions that have given them shape and voice are ruled out of order, even the most solemn questions are "resolved" by mechanistic reduction to the lowest possible factor. Thus in *Roe v. Wade,* the questions of the meaning of human life and who belongs to the human community for which we accept common responsibility are reduced to the question of "privacy." Numerous constitutional scholars have challenged the Supreme Court's development of the "right to privacy." More immediately pertinent to our discussion is the similarity between "privacy" and life behind the "veil of ignorance." It is an instance of law against life, of individualism's assault upon the individual, of the eradication of the personal and communal bonds without which it is not possible to be an individual.

There is in store a continuing and deepening crisis of legitimacy unless a transcendent moral purpose is democratically asserted by which the state can be brought under critical judgment, unless it is made clear once again that the state is not the source but the servant of the law. As we have paraphrased Spinoza, transcendence abhors a vacuum. Recall John Courtney Murray's cautions about the invitation extended when there is a vacuum in the public space of law and politics. The vacuum will surely be filled, as has so tragically happened elsewhere, by the pretensions of the modern state. As the crisis of legitimacy deepens, it will lead—not next year, maybe not in twenty years, but all too soon—to totalitarianism or to insurrection. The insurrection may be on the way to totalitarianism or on the way to what is described as authoritarianism, but after a period of either it is difficult to envision the resumption of the democratic experiment. Already figures such as Francis Schaeffer call for a reconsideration of justifiable revolution, and a good many less sober than he are in full-throated support of rebellion. They are in curious alliance with those on the left who, with very different analysis and intent, assert that there is no way out apart from revolution.

Meanwhile, the "vital center" of liberal democratic faith is largely unattended. In the deepening night of "cultural contradictions," jurists and politicians go about their business of serving precedent and procedure, warding off the questions that break through "the issues" of the moment. Yet others who fancy their philosophical indifference makes them pragmatists count on continued material prosperity to give everybody a stake in holding at bay the legitimacy crisis which threatens a system that "works," more or less, to the benefit of all, more or less. The American proposition is no longer proposed. The democracy that began as an experiment has become at best a habit, a temporary condition, perhaps a luxury that can no longer be afforded. The barbarians look less like a threat and more like some kind of answer.

We will not be rescued by religion. Secularists who not long ago were celebrating the twilight of the gods now put their hopes in a great religious revival. There may be a great revival of religion; perhaps it is already underway. But it will not help if it is a religion of private benefit and blessing, offering what Bonhoeffer called "a god of the gaps," filling in and compensating for the discontents of modernity. And it will not help if it is religion that threatens to revive theocracy, whether of the left or of the right. That kind of religion led to the expulsion of religion from the public square in the first place. At his inauguration in 1978, Pope John Paul I refused to be crowned with the papal tiara, the vestigial symbol of the claim to temporal power. John Paul II followed his example, and so must all the churches set aside their tiaras, not even keeping them in the closet but destroying them altogether. It may seem unwarranted to us, but there are many secularists in this society (and many believers) who do most genuinely fear the church's ambitions to rule. Those fears must be put to rest if we are ever to achieve a more natural and fruitful relationship between church and state, between religion and the public square.

The religious revival that might help must be an ecumenical revival. The wars of religion once destroyed the basis of civil life and nobody who cares about authentic politics should want to run that risk again. There almost certainly will not be and there probably should not be one institutionally unified church. There can be a public and trustworthy expression of the fact that Christians are, in their differences, bound by one Lord, one faith, one baptism, one God and Father of us all. Among Christians this means that mainline Protestantism must reach out to the evangelical/fundamentalist insurgency by which it feels threatened. In the institutionalized ecumenical movement, as in the World Council of Churches, it means that the primacy of Faith and Order must be reasserted over and against those divisive forces that press for a politicized "partisan church."

There are also imperatives for evangelicals and fundamentalists who have lately come in from the cold of their sixty-year exile. Although the advantage lies with them in many ways, they must not come back as conquerors but as members of the family. If they have "come over to slay the Philistines," as some of them think, they will only drive into the enemy camp the great majority of Christians who do not belong there and do not want to be there. In that event, the moral majoritarians will never be more than a noisy protest movement; they will never "turn America around" as they say they want to, and they will never, as many others hope, contribute to the reconstruction of a public philosophy that is democratically responsive to the values of the American people.

For a revival of religion to help in leading us out of the dark night of cultural contradictions there must also be a profound security about the relationship between Christians and Jews. The rabbi who said that the words "Christian America" conjure for him the image of barbed wire is not irrational. The cosmetic change of talking about "Judeo-Christian" values is not enough. Not nearly enough. Nor is it enough to be enthusiastic about the indispensable role of the State of Israel in the playing out of Bible prophecy's apocalyptic scenarios. Nor is it enough to appreciate the continuing existence of Jews as some kind of "corrective" to the church. What is required is the secure establishment of Christianity's bond with living Judaism, a bonding in theology, piety, and practice that is strong enough to last for the duration—even if the duration be many millennia before the consummation of the Messianic Age. With St. Paul (Romans 9–11) we must ponder anew the divine mystery of living Judaism.

Many Jewish leaders today are coming to the conclusion that the naked public square is a very dangerous place. Where there are no transcendent sanctions, positive and negative, there is no final inhibition against evil, including the evil of anti-Semitism. For good reasons, Jews and others who are uneasy about the idea of "Christian America" will continue to prefer the naked square until it is manifest that Christians have internalized—as a matter of doctrine, even of dogma—reverence for democratic dissent. In Christian thought at present, the linkages between faith and democratic governance are tenuous. And, of course, we may not have the time required for these linkages to be securely fastened and sealed. It may also be that contemporary Christianity can no longer recall the faith that can renew the democratic vision to which that faith once gave birth.

There was once religion in America that attended to the experiment and proposed the proposition. At first it simply called itself Christianity, then evangelical Christianity, and then, much later, mainline Protestantism. It did a far from perfect job of attending to the experiment and proposing the proposition, as witness our present confusions. But it was the culture-defining elite in American religion. Thus we come back to Vilfredo Pareto's concept of "the circulation of elites." Social functions, he said, are performed by groups that, after a while, constitute themselves as elites. After a longer while, the elite (whether economic, military, governmental, or religious) becomes flabby or disillusioned and no longer performs the function by which it acquired its privileged social position. When that happens, the function is not simply neglected. No, some other group, usually a quite different group, moves in to displace the old elite. And so elite functions circulate from one group to another.

In America there are a number of religious groups that have not had their turn at the culture-forming tasks. The single largest grouping is the Roman Catholic Church, counting fifty million members. In many ways, this ought to be "the Catholic moment" in American life. By virtue of numbers, of a rich tradition of social and political theory, and of Vatican II's theological internalization of the democratic idea, Catholics are uniquely posed to propose the American proposition anew. Not least among their strengths is that in John Paul II we have a historic figure who is singularly persuasive about the ominous alternatives to the human freedom that democracy protects. The Catholic moment was not, as some say, in 1960 when John F. Kennedy was elected, in large part because he reassured the electorate that he was not a very serious Catholic. The Catholic moment is now. It may be missed, however.

If it is missed, some will say that it is because, just as a previously immigrant church "came of age" in America, it began to collapse within. I do not find that persuasive. The silly season is largely past in American Catholicism. Those who wanted to be freed from the disciplines of being Catholic have already elected their forms of liberation or lostness. Communally and institutionally, American Catholicism seems to have weathered the storm. But whether it will become a public force of culture-forming influence is quite a different question. It may become simply the largest among churches successfully attending to needs defined as "religious." In part this is because Catholic leaders are understandably put off by the implicit and sometimes explicit anti-Catholicism of the Protestant fundamentalists who are most exercised about the crises of secularism. They have no illusions about the good old days of Protestantism's "Righteous Empire" and are not likely to sign up for a crusade in which they might be among the targets. In larger part, the culture-forming tasks may not "circulate" to American Catholicism because those Catholics who are most concerned about the public role of religion often tend to be those Catholics who are most imitative of the failing Protestant mainline. For many, the style of the Protestant mainline still represents the respectability of having arrived in America. Then too, "the new class" and its struggle is no respecter of denominational lines. For these and other reasons, Catholicism may miss its moment, prematurely embracing the mainline's sense of guilt and unease, finding satisfactions in having failed at a task it never got around to attempting.

We cannot pass over Lutheranism. According to Gallup there are twenty million Americans who claim to be Lutheran, although the church jurisdictions count a little less than ten million. Some of the earlier and more Americanized Lutherans in the Eastern states feel themselves to be part of the Protestant mainline. Most do not, being sociologically and psychologically (and, although not always admitted, theologically) closer to Catholicism and its immigrant experience. Years ago historian Winthrop Hudson called Lutheranism "the sleeping giant" of American religion. At least with respect to religion in the public arena, the giant sleeps on. Especially in the upper Midwest, Lutherans still resemble the progressive "church-going classes" described by John Dewey in 1922. But Lutheranism as a tradition does not have a rich store of social theory. The specifically Lutheran contribution to democratic practice and thought is not notable. Several Lutheran futures can be envisioned. Some Lutherans have no difficulty in being viewed—indeed aspire to being viewed—as part of the mainline Protestant establishment. Others, particularly in the Missouri Synod, have strong sympathies with evangelical, even fundamentalist, worlds. Cutting across the Lutheran jurisdictions, however, is also a deep intuition that the Lutheran destiny is, as Lutheran beginnings were, with Catholicism. Were there ecumenical advance in the next decade or more toward "healing the breach of the sixteenth century" between Lutherans and Roman Catholics, the result could be a dramatically different future for both communions. But here again there is no one "future" and speculation bogs down in imponderables.

Sad to say, in connection with the present discussion it is almost possible to pass over the Orthodox quite completely. There are approximately as many Orthodox Christians in America as there are Jews. Their influence upon the general culture escapes detection. According to their theologians, such as Alexander Schmemann, John Meyendorff, and Thomas Hopko, Orthodoxy in America is uncertain about whether it is *the church* in America, an American denomination, or the Eastern Orthodox Church in Exile. Nationally and internationally, Orthodoxy's relationship to culture and to other Christians is very important and very complicated. But it is beyond doubt that Orthodoxy in America will not in the foreseeable future be a player in Pareto's circulations.

And so we are returned to the chief subject of our discussion—the religious new right, the moral majoritarians, the politicized religion that finds its home in worlds called evangelical and fundamentalist. As we have taken pains to make clear, not all evangelicals are involved in or sympathetic to moral majoritarianism. On the questions that have concerned us here, most evangelicals are indistinguishable from other Christians, be they mainline, Catholic, Lutheran, or whatever. That is because most Christians in all these groups have other things to worry about than the role of religion in society. Which is what one might expect, and what may be just as well. Among evangelicals who are so concerned, as we have had occasion to note, are scholars and activists of a Calvinist persuasion who are as distant from the moral majoritarians as they are from the secularists against whom both contend. Of the most militant majoritarians, often led by professed fundamentalists, we have perhaps said enough.

They are making the most aggressive bid to become the new culture-forming elite in American religion. This author's sympathies and skepticisms should be evident by now. I do not think they will succeed. I hope not. At the same time, I am confident they will not go away. They have kicked a tripwire alerting large sectors of the society to the absurdities and dangers of the naked public square. The most hopeful prospect is that, if we and they have the imagination to move beyond present polarizations, we will become partners in rearticulating the religious base of the democratic experiment.

Mainline, Jews, Catholics, Lutherans, Orthodox, Evangelicals, Fundamentalists—such religious taxonomy is of limited usefulness. He who said, "Behold I am doing a new thing. Do you not perceive it?" no doubt has other surprises in store. We can engage in denominational and confessional classifications as we will, but it may have little to do with where that new thing comes from, with where it is perhaps already stirring and on the edge of its public debut.

But the new thing we are looking for may not come at all. The naked public square may be the last phase of a failed experiment, a mistaken proposition. We have no divine promise that a nation so conceived and so dedicated will endure any longer than it has. Afterward, there will still be laws, of that we can be sure. And the history books, if history books are allowed then, will record this strange moment in which a society was in turmoil over the connections between laws and the law, between law and life. Then the turmoil will seem very distant, for then no dissent will be permitted from the claim that the law is the law is the law.

This dour prospect is not alarmist. Surely something like it is what those thoughtful people must mean when they say that the day of liberal democracy is past. It makes little difference whether the successor regime is of the right or of the left or unclassifiable. By whatever ideology the idea, this audacious democratic idea, would be declared discredited. By whom, where, under what circumstances, by what conception and what dedication could it ever be tried again? Yes, of course, life would go on and God's purposes will not be defeated, not ultimately. But the world would be a darker and colder place. That it can happen is evident to all but the naive and willfully blind. That it will happen seems probable, if we refuse to understand the newness, the fragility, the promise, and the demands of religion and democracy in America.

ENDNOTES

CHAPTER ONE

1. The bibliography on the religious new right is large and growing fast. Jerry Falwell's *Listen, America!* (Doubleday, 1980) sets forth basic program and rationale. For background understanding of the varieties and tensions within fundamentalism, George Marsden, *Fundamentalism and American Culture* (Oxford, 1980), is indispensable. Peggy Shriver, *The Bible Vote* (Pilgrim, 1981), contains a useful collection of responses to the phenomenon from various church groups. Gabriel Fackre, *The Religious Right and Christian Faith* (Eerdmans, 1982), is helpful in its effort to take seriously the belief system of the religious new right. Hadden and Swann, *Prime Time Preachers* (Addison, 1981), focuses on the communications aspect of the movement but contains insightful commentary on other dimensions. Alan Crawford, *Thunder on the Right* (Pantheon, 1980), is a strident polemic that includes background and personal sidelights. Tim LaHaye, *The Battle for the Mind* (Revell, 1980), reflects the movement's assault on "secular humanism" in its most relentless form. This brief sampler represents the range of analysis. Other important works appear elsewhere in these notes. As exhaustive a bibliography as was possible in 1983 was produced by Richard Pierard of the Department of History, Indiana State University, Terre Haute.

2. H. Edward Rowe, *Save America!* (Revell, 1976). Published when the religious new right had not come to wide public notice, this statement is remarkably suggestive of things that were to come.

3. Hadden and Swann, *Prime Time Preachers*, p. 60.

4. Robert Nisbet, *History of the Idea of Progress* (Basic, 1980).

5. Sacvan Bercovitch, *The Puritan Origins of the American Self* (Yale, 1975), p. 62.

6. The idea of theology as a "public" enterprise, as advanced here, is indebted to the work of David Tracy and, most particularly, of Wolfhart Pannenberg, who has for many years been a friend and collaborator in thinking about Christianity in the modern world.

7. See Marsden, *Fundamentalism*, especially pp. 199ff.

8. The notion of the authoritarian personality is associated with Theodor Adorno's study by that title (Harper, 1950).

9. Dean Kelley, *Why Conservative Churches Are Growing* (Harper, 1972), is a vital and prescient study of some of the religious dynamics that prepared the way for the subsequent political militancy.

CHAPTER TWO

1. There is a formidable literature on civil religion. The current state of the discussion is fairly represented in Robert Bellah and Phillip Hammond, *Varieties*

of Civil Religion (Harper, 1980). For the early development of my own thinking on this subject, see *Time toward Home* (Seabury, 1976).

2. Alasdair MacIntyre, *After Virtue* (Notre Dame, 1981), p. 236: ". . . modern politics cannot be a matter of genuine moral consensus. And it is not. Modern politics is civil war carried on by other means."

3. Diane Ravitch, *The Great School Wars* (Basic, 1974).

4. Rowe, *Save America!*, p. 42.

5. Ibid., p. 44.

6. Robert Handy, *Christian America: Protestant Hopes and Historical Realities* (Oxford, 1971).

7. Leo Pfeffer, *God, Caesar, and the Constitution* (Beacon, 1975), p. 97.

8. John T. Noonan, *A Private Choice* (Free Press, 1979).

9. James Tunstead Burtchaell, *Rachel Weeping* (Andrews and McMeel, 1982), especially pp. 239-87 on parallels between abortion and slavery.

10. For a suggestive discussion of the distinctions between "public" and "political," see Parker Palmer, *The Company of Strangers* (Crossroad, 1981).

11. Peter Berger and Richard John Neuhaus spell out the concept and some policy implications of "mediating structures" in *To Empower People* (American Enterprise Institute, 1977).

12. Daniel Bell, *The Cultural Contradictions of Capitalism* (Basic 1978).

13. Michael Novak discusses the antistatist views of some on the left in *The Spirit of Democratic Capitalism* (Simon and Schuster, 1982).

14. For a thoroughly negative but nonetheless informative evaluation of the phenomenon, see Peter Steinfels, *The Neo-Conservatives* (Simon and Schuster, 1979).

15. Abraham Joshua Heschel, *The Prophets* (Jewish Publication Society, 1962), p. 4.

16. Both Noonan *(A Private Choice)* and Burtchaell *(Rachel Weeping)* contain illuminating discussions of the ways in which survey research reveals and obscures popular attitudes on abortion.

CHAPTER THREE

1. Hadden and Swann *(Prime Time Preachers)* suggest that the audiences of the political evangelists are vastly overestimated and are in fact composed of the "already converted" who live largely in the South and Southwest.

2. *This World* (Summer 1982) contains the results of an extensive survey of theology and religion teachers conducted by the Roper Center. It is reasonable to speculate that the negative-to-ambivalent "leadership attitudes" toward popular values would have been more pronounced had the research isolated the variable of teachers of social ethics and policy.

3. Jeffrey K. Hadden, *The Gathering Storm in the Churches* (Doubleday, 1969).

4. The text of the NCC Governing Board statement is in Shriver, *Bible Vote.*

5. Burton Yale Pines, *Back to Basics* (Murrow, 1982), brings together a mighty host of "traditionalist" movements in order to portray as almost inevitable a surge of fundamental social change.

6. Samuel Hux in *Commonweal* (10 September 1982).

7. Searle quoted in Basil Mitchell, *Morality Religious and Secular* (Oxford, 1980), p. 4.

8. For other examples of "rating systems," see Pines, *Basics*, pp. 302ff.

9. Quoted in Religious News Service release, August 20, 1982.

10. McCarthy, Oppewal, Peterson, and Spykman, *Society, State, and Schools* (Eerdmans, 1981).

11. For data and argument regarding the religious basis of American values see *The Connecticut Mutual Life Report on American Values in the '80s: The Impact of Belief* (1981), John Crothers Pollock, director of research. See also the study of "Middletown," *All Faithful People*, by Theodore Caplow et al. (Wisconsin, 1983).

CHAPTER FOUR

1. For a statement on the credibility of a moral universe, written from a theologically unconventional viewpoint, see James M. Gustafson, *Ethics from a Theocentric Perspective* (Chicago, 1981).

2. The theological status of the idea of "election" or purpose in world-historical change is underscored in Wolfhart Pannenberg, *Human Nature, Election and History* (Westminster, 1977).

3. Robert Benne and Philip Hefner, *Defining America* (Fortress, 1974). Two Lutheran scholars discern the "distinctives" of the American experience, underscoring also the future orientation of the national ethos.

4. Gilbert C. Meilaender, *Friendship* (Notre Dame, 1981).

5. Ibid., p. 19.

6. See Peter Berger and Richard John Neuhaus, *Movement and Revolution* (Doubleday, 1969).

7. John Courtney Murray, *We Hold These Truths: Catholic Reflections on the American Proposition* (Sheed and Ward, 1960).

8. For a thoroughly revisionist telling of the Vietnam experience that is rigorously critical of the antiwar movement, see Norman Podhoretz, *Why We Were in Vietnam* (Simon and Schuster, 1982).

9. For details on personal statements, resolutions, and the like, see *A Time for Candor* (Institute on Religion and Democracy, 1983) and Ernest Lefever, *From Amsterdam to Nairobi* (Ethics and Public Policy Center, 1979).

10. Roper Survey in *This World*.

11. Aristotle, *Ethics* (Allen & Unwin, 1953), p. 65.

12. Ibid.

13. Meilaender, *Friendship*, p. 81.

14. Gustafson on "consent to being" (*Ethics*, pp. 201-03).

CHAPTER FIVE

1. David Lewis, *King: A Critical Biography* (Praeger, 1970), p. 228.

2. Quoted in Bellah and Hammond, *Civil Religion*, p. 156.

3. Ibid., p. 41.

4. John Courtney Murray, "The Church and Totalitarian Democracy," *Theological Studies* (December 1952), p. 531.

5. Murray, "Return to Tribalism," *Catholic Mind* (January 1962).

6. The phrase is from Peter Berger, *Rumor of Angels* (Doubleday, 1968).

7. MacIntyre, *After Virtue*, p. 245.

8. Reported in *Newsweek* (February 22, 1982).

9. *Forum Letter* (December 1982).

10. *The New York Times* (November 27, 1982).

11. "Christianity and Democracy," a statement of purpose drafted by Richard John Neuhaus and adopted by the Institute on Religion and Democracy, Washington, D.C.

12. For example, the symposium on the statement in *The Center Journal*.

13. Arthur Schlesinger, Jr., *The Vital Center* (Houghton Mifflin, 1962), p. 188.

14. Ibid., p. 254.

15. Ibid., p. 240.

16. Ibid., p. 248.

17. Ibid., p. 176.

18. Sugarman and Coon; also David Sealey.

19. Martin E. Marty, *Righteous Empire* (Dial Press, 1970).

CHAPTER SIX

1. Nisbet, *Idea of Progress*, p. 103.

2. Quoted in Stanley Hauerwas, *A Community of Character* (Notre Dame, 1981), p. 79.

3. For a strong statement on the persistence of religion and religious values, see Andrew Greeley, *Unsecular Man* (Schocken, 1972).

4. A thorough overview of the relevant literature is contained in Brigitte and Peter Berger, *The War over the Family* (Doubleday, 1983).

5. For a sensitive treatment of the public and personal life of Martin Luther King, Jr., see Stephen Oates, *Let the Trumpet Sound* (Harper, 1982).

6. I am indebted to Elliott Wright, himself a religion journalist, for clarifying my thinking about religion as a journalistic "specialty."

7. Glen E. Thurow, *Abraham Lincoln and American Political Religion* (State University of New York, 1976), p. 7.

8. Ibid., p. 8.

9. Ibid., p. 10.

10. John Murray Cuddihy, *No Offense* (Seabury, 1978).

11. Jürgen Moltmann, *Theology of Hope* (Harper, 1967), p. 180.

12. Hadden and Swann, *Prime Time Preachers*.

13. For an informed and provocative statement of the limitations of scientific methodology, see Huston Smith, *Beyond the Post-Modern Mind* (Crossroad, 1982).

14. The idea of values as interests is critiqued by Richard Stith, "A Critique of Fairness," *Valparaiso University Law Review* (Spring 1982).

15. Aristotle, *Ethics*, p. 92.

CHAPTER SEVEN

1. For an overview of "two-kingdoms" thought from a variety of mainly Lutheran perspectives, see Karl H. Hertz, *Two Kingdoms and One World: A Sourcebook in Christian Social Ethics* (Augsburg, 1976).

2. Dean Kelley, *Why Churches Should Not Pay Taxes* (Harper, 1977).

3. John Howard Yoder, *The Politics of Jesus* (Eerdmans, 1972).

4. Novak, *Democratic Capitalism*, p. 68.
5. Ibid., p. 112.
6. Sidney Mead, *The Lively Experiment* (Harper, 1963), pp. 16ff.
7. V. S. Naipaul, *A Bend in the River* (Vintage, 1980), p. 160.
8. Dostoyevsky, *Crime and Punishment* (Penguin, 1966), p. 69.
9. Alexander M. Bickel, *The Morality of Consent* (Yale, 1975), p. 34.

CHAPTER EIGHT

1. The formula on church-state relations is usually attributed to William Lazareth, director of Faith and Order of the World Council of Churches and formerly head of the church in society office of the Lutheran Church in America.
2. For the sociological assumptions underlying this section, see Peter Berger and Thomas Luckmann, *The Social Construction of Reality* (Doubleday, 1966).
3. Clifford Geertz, *The Interpretation of Cultures* (Basic, 1973), p. 89.
4. Ibid., p. 90.
5. William M. Sullivan, *Reconstructing Public Philosophy* (California, 1982), p. 19.
6. Ibid., p. 21.
7. Ibid., p. 21.
8. Hannah Arendt, *On Revolution* (Viking, 1963), p. 318.
9. Hauerwas, *Community of Character*, p. 79.

CHAPTER NINE

1. Jacob Burckhardt, *Reflections on History* (Liberty Classics, 1979), pp. 58-59.
2. Thomas Luckmann, *The Invisible Religion* (Macmillan, 1967).
3. Reflective of this tendency is Robert Bellah, *The Broken Covenant* (Seabury, 1975).
4. Peter Berger et al., *The Homeless Mind* (Random House, 1973).
5. Elliott Wright, "Does Free Exercise Stop at the Schoolhouse Door?" *Commonweal* (8 April 1983).
6. Adam Smith, *The Theory of Moral Sentiments* (Liberty Classics, 1969).
7. Allan Carlson, "Religion, the State and the Schools" (Rockford Institute, Illinois).
8. For the complexities of legal address to these issues see Richard K. Fenn, *Liturgies and Trials: The Secularization of Religious Language* (Pilgrim, 1982).
9. For a popular but scientifically informed treatment of these boundaries between human and other life, see the several works of Robert Jastrow, including *The Enchanted Loom* (Simon and Schuster, 1981) and *God and the Astronomers* (Norton, 1978).
10. For one aspect, see the finely limned *Solzhenitsyn: The Moral Vision* by Edward Ericson (Eerdmans, 1980).
11. The imagery is from John T. Noonan, *Persons and Masks of the Law* (Farrar, Straus & Giroux, 1976).

CHAPTER TEN

1. Peter Clecak, *The Quest: Dissent and Fulfillment in America* (Oxford, 1983), p. 105.
2. Brigitte and Peter Berger, *Family*, p. 5.
3. Quoted in Clecak, *The Quest*, p. 29.
4. Quoted in A. Worral, *Politikon* (December 1981).
5. In the spring of 1983 the Supreme Court handed down a number of important decisions regarding church-state relations. My own reading of these decisions, enhanced by discussions in connection with a research project sponsored by the National Conference of Christians and Jews, underscores the confusions in the present state of legal thought about religion. Two decisions on tax exemption routinely equated exemption with government subsidies or expenditures. In discussion, Professor Boris Bittker of Yale, a preeminent authority on tax law, suggests that this could mean a loosening of restrictions regarding "establishment of religion." That is, if tax exemption is equivalent to tax subsidy, tax subsidy could be given for clearly religious purposes since tax exemption always has been given. A question arises, however, as to which factor (subsidy or exemption) will define the other. To put it differently, if it is now the case that tax exemption is the same thing as tax subsidy, and since it has long been understood that subsidy cannot be given for religious purposes, it may follow that neither can exemptions be allowed for religion. There are other severe complications in these decisions. In disallowing tax exemption for Bob Jones University (because of its practice of racial discrimination) the court noted that the exemption had been given for "religious, educational and charitable" reasons. The court went on to say that "charitable" is the operative term and must be understood as activity that does not violate "settled public policy." This would seem to imply a downgrading or dismissal of the constitutional status of the category of "religion." The implications are far reaching indeed, indicating that religious exemption may now be defined as a *de facto* "charitable" exemption and the institutions receiving such exemption, namely churches, must act in accord with "settled public policy." A month after the Bob Jones decision, the court ruled on a long-standing Minnesota law that allowed tax credit for parents sending children to nongovernment schools, including religious schools. The majority held that such noncredit did not violate the three criteria by which constitutionally prohibited "establishment" must be measured: (1) the law must serve a secular purpose; (2) it must not directly advance or hinder the exercise of religion; and (3) it must not lead to excessive entanglement between religion and the state. (Catholic ethicist Charles Curran, among others, suggests that "secular purpose" should be stated as "political purpose," that is, as a purpose appropriate to the ordering of the polis [*Moral Theology: A Continuing Journey*].) While some welcomed the Minnesota decision for its move toward "neutrality" toward religion, others worried that it narrowed the constitutional category of "religion" excessively. Then, on July 5, the court ruled on a case from Nebraska which claimed that paying chaplains of state legislatures is in violation of the no-establishment clause. In upholding the practice of having chaplains on the legislature's payroll, Chief Justice Warren Burger noted that it was the practice in the Congress that wrote the First Amendment in the first place, and that it was not establishment nor a step toward establishment because "It is simply a tolerable acknowledgement of beliefs widely held among the people of this country." Writing in dissent, Justice William Brennan said it was "obvious" that "if the Court were to judge legislative prayer through the unsentimental eye of our settled doctrine, it would have to strike it down as

a clear violation of the establishment clause." As we have noted, the court "follows the election returns" and must have known that a ruling against legislative prayer would have been powerfully unpopular. With the continuing furor over prayer in government schools and related issues, the court, we may reasonably speculate, did not want to add this additional assault upon popular sensibilities. But I believe Justice Brennan is correct: an "unsentimental" (and unimaginative) observance of precedent would have had the decision going against legislative prayer also. The doleful fact is that the "settled doctrine" of the court is the naked public square. The "unsentimental" ruling that Brennan wanted might have contributed to the salutary, I believe, unsettling of that doctrine. Mid-1983 was, then, an extraordinarily busy jurisprudential period in church-state relations. With the exception of the Minnesota decision—the implications of which are still unclear—the decisions, separately and in combination, reinforce the thesis of the present book. Removing legislative prayer is, as indicated in the text, one of those "mopping up operations" that even extreme separationists tend to believe is not worth the political trouble. It does not make for enprincipled neatness, but it is, as the Chief Justice implies, a "tolerable" exception to what Brennan describes as "settled doctrine." It is tolerable because it is innocuous, and removing it might be viewed as a frontal attack on "beliefs widely held among the people of this country." Note the distance we have come from earlier court statements on religion in America, as Professor Glen Thurow and others have demonstrated (see discussion in text). The tax decisions, on the other hand, are exceedingly inauspicious. They would seem to constitute not steps but strides toward withdrawing constitutional recognition from religion and other independent actors in the public square.

6. Clecak, *The Quest,* p. 112.

7. *Economist* editorial (December 25, 1983).

8. Francis Schaeffer, *A Christian Manifesto* (Crossway, 1981); John W. Whitehead, *The Second American Revolution* (Cook, 1982).

9. See, for example, John de Gruchy, *The Church Struggle in South Africa* (Eerdmans, 1979).

10. Gustavo Gutiérrez, *A Theology of Liberation* (Orbis, 1973), p. 167. For a cogent critique of liberation theologies, written from a Niebuhrian perspective, see Dennis McCann, *Christian Realism and Liberation Theology* (Orbis, 1981).

11. Falwell, *Listen, America!,* p. 24.

12. For the current state of New Testament scholarly thought about the political factor in Jesus' ministry, see A. E. Harvey, *Jesus and the Constraints of History* (Westminster, 1982).

13. Yoder, *Politics,* p. 23.

14. Oscar Cullmann, *The State in the New Testament* (Scribner's, 1956), p. 69.

15. Quoted in Paul Johnson, *A History of Christianity* (Atheneum, 1976), p. 69.

16. Pannenberg, *Ethics* (Westminster, 1981), p. 119.

17. Ibid., p. 120.

18. Ibid., p. 121.

19. For a consideration of Kuyper's contemporary significance, see McCarthy et al., *Society.*

CHAPTER ELEVEN

1. Quoted in Paul Johnson, *Modern Times* (Harper, 1983), p. 209.

2. The concept of "covenant," in contrast to "contract," is developed in the author's *Time toward Home.*

3. Brigitte and Peter Berger, *Family,* p. 67.

4. For a comprehensive view of the operative value assumptions about America and its role in the world that prevailed until recently, see Allan Carlson in *This World* (Winter 1983 issue).

5. For the divisions among antiwar leaders following the collapse of Saigon, see James Finn, "War Among the Doves," *Worldview* (April 1976).

6. For a statement of these distinctions, see Paul Tillich, *The Protestant Era* (Chicago, 1948).

CHAPTER TWELVE

1. For an appreciation of the institutional dimensions of religion, see Herbert Richardson, *Toward an American Theology* (Harper, 1967).

2. Burckhardt, *Reflections on History,* p. 248.

3. Ibid., p. 206.

4. Quoted in Burckhardt, *Reflections,* p. 180.

5. Ibid., p. 154.

6. One thinks of such ideologically diverse figures as Christopher Lasch, Mary Jo Banes, Allan Carlson, and Brigitte and Peter Berger.

7. Quoted in Mitchell, *Morality Religious and Secular,* p. 26.

8. Theodore Roszak, *The Making of a Counter Culture* (Doubleday, 1969), p. 8.

9. Langdon Gilkey, *Reaping the Whirlwind* (Seabury, 1976).

10. Donald E. Pelotte, *John Courtney Murray: Theologian in Conflict* (Paulist, 1975), p. 19.

CHAPTER THIRTEEN

1. From the discussion of nineteenth-century visitors' impressions of America in Peter Conrad, *Imagining America* (Oxford, 1980).

2. Quoted in William G. McLoughlin, *Revivals, Awakenings, and Reform* (Chicago, 1978), p. 102.

3. Marty in McLoughlin, ibid., p. viii.

4. Ibid.

5. Sydney Ahlstrom, *A Religious History of the American People* (Yale, 1972), p. 4.

6. Quoted in Marty, *Righteous Empire,* p. 255.

7. This taxonomy is indebted to, but deviates from, that proposed by Martin E. Marty, *A Nation of Behavers* (Chicago, 1976).

8. These ambivalences are reflected in the still interesting essay by John Meyendorff, "The Significance of the Reformation in the History of Christendom," in Meyendorff, *Catholicism and the Orthodox* (Sheed and Ward, 1966).

9. Quoted in Handy, *Christian America,* p. 27.

10. The reference is to Ernest Lee Tuveson, *Redeemer Nation: The Idea of America's Millennial Role* (Chicago, 1968).

11. McLoughlin, *Revivals,* p. 3.

12. Ibid., p. 106.

13. James Q. Wilson of Harvard has drawn connections between the "character building" aspects of earlier social activism and the state of crime. See his "Crime and American Culture" (Ethics and Public Policy Center, Washington, D.C.).

14. Quoted in McLoughlin, *Revivals,* p. 178.

15. Ibid., p. 183.

16. Quoted in Handy, *Christian America,* p. 127.

17. Ibid., p. 111.

18. Ibid.

19. Ibid., p. 64.

20. In F. E. Mayer, *The Religious Bodies of America* (Concordia, 1954), p. 310.

21. See Ira Gallaway, *Drifted Astray* (Abingdon, 1983). This appeal to "return the church to witness and ministry" is written by a prominent United Methodist pastor who was one of the leaders of the Institute on Religion and Democracy, which was instrumental in focusing attention on what it viewed as the mainline's ideological distortions.

22. Handy, *Christian America,* p. 69.

CHAPTER FOURTEEN

1. Paul Johnson, *Modern Times,* p. 1.

2. Marty, *Righteous Empire,* p. 114.

3. Ibid., p. 41.

4. Ibid., p. 116.

5. Handy, *Christian America,* p. 110.

6. McLoughlin, *Revivals,* p. 152.

7. Quoted in McLoughlin, *Revivals,* p. 157.

8. Ibid., p. 156.

9. Lefever, *Amsterdam to Nairobi.* A much earlier critique of what he called the "church and society syndrome" was offered by the eminent ethicist Paul Ramsey of Princeton in *Who Speaks for the Church?* (Abingdon, 1967).

10. Thomas Sieger Derr, *Barriers to Ecumenism* (Orbis, 1983).

11. Marty, *Righteous Empire,* p. 234.

12. Jerry Falwell in an April 1981 meeting in Washington, D.C., observed by the author.

13. Quoted in *Righteous Empire,* p. 235.

14. Peter Berger and Richard John Neuhaus, eds., *Against the World for the World* (Seabury, 1976). At the time this title was chosen, the editors did not know, although Neuhaus should have known, about the earlier book of similar title.

15. Handy, *Christian America,* p. 203.

16. "Genes and Genesis," editorial in *New York Times* (11 June 1983).

CHAPTER FIFTEEN

1. *Christian Century* on World Council.

2. Among the most comprehensive and relentless statements of this position in

liberation theology is the five-volume *A Theology for the Artisans of a New Humanity* by Juan Luis Segundo (Orbis, 1973).

3. Martin E. Marty, *A Short History of Christianity* (Meridian, 1959), p. 352.

4. *Righteous Empire*, p. 244.

5. See Richard Hutcheson, *Mainline Churches and the Evangelicals* (John Knox, 1981).

6. Derr, *Barriers*.

7. Handy, *Christian America*, p. 213.

8. Quoted in McLoughlin, *Revivals*, p. 171.

9. Ibid., p. 170.

10. *engage/social action* (published by the Board of Church and Society of the United Methodist Church) (October 1980).

11. From interview with Jerry Falwell, April 1981.

12. George Gallup and David Poling, *The Search for America's Faith* (Abingdon, 1980), p. 10.

13. Kirk Hadaway analysis in the *1980 Yearbook of American and Canadian Churches*.

14. Kelley, *Conservative Churches*, p. 174.

15. Handy, *Christian America*, p. 221.

16. Ibid.

17. Theodore Lowi, *The End of Liberalism* (Norton, 1969).

18. Ibid., p. 290.

19. Ibid., p. 294.

20. Peter Berger, "The Class Struggle in American Religion," *The Christian Century* (February 25, 1981). It may be too much to speak of the "new class theory," and this is reflected in the question mark in the title of what is still the main theoretical address to the subject, *The New Class?* edited by B. Bruce-Briggs (Transaction, 1979).

21. The related church-state questions have received considerable attention in connection with domestic programs. Bruce Nichols is heading a research project titled "When Church and State Go Abroad" that examines the overseas aspects of these issues. The project is sponsored by the Council on Religion and International Affairs, is funded by the Lilly Endowment, and intends to publish its report in 1984.

22. Berger, "Class Struggle," *The Christian Century* (February 25, 1981).

23. "Peace: Not as the world gives . . . ," the program of the 150th Annual Assembly of the Christian Church (Disciples of Christ) in Virginia, May 20-22, 1983.

24. *United Methodist Newscope* (November 21, 1980).

25. Ibid.

26. "30 Minutes With Bishop Armstrong," an interview prepared by the Indianapolis office of United Methodist Bishop James Armstrong, June 1983.

27. See *Time for Candor*.

28. "30 Minutes."

29. "Washington Diarist," *The New Republic* (November 1, 1980).

30. While mainline leadership understandably protested what they viewed as the "distorted" impression conveyed by media attention to the councils and their

member churches in 1982 and 1983, no significant challenge was offered to the facts reported by the critics. While major media such as CBS News and *Time* magazine did their own extensive research, undoubtedly the most extensive investigative reporting was done by the *United Methodist Reporter*, which in its several editions reaches more than a million United Methodists. In April 1983, the paper put out a special reprint of its findings and recommendations. Over the vigorous objections of Bishop James Armstrong, the United Methodists appointed a committee to investigate the many questions that were raised. These developments had considerable influence also on other churches, as might be expected from United Methodism's centrality in the mainline establishments such as the National Council.

31. Gallup and Poling, *Search for America's Faith*, p. 139. On the change in theological "mood" toward a more classical, if not conservative, direction, see also Thomas Oden, *Agenda for Theology* (Harper, 1979).

32. Richard Quebedeaux, *The Worldly Evangelicals* (Harper, 1978), p. 140.

CHAPTER SIXTEEN

1. A large part of this chapter was delivered as a lecture at the centennial of the Law School of Valparaiso University in 1979.

2. Harold Berman, *The Interaction of Law and Religion* (Abingdon, 1974).

3. John Rawls, *A Theory of Justice* (Harvard, 1971).

INDEX OF NAMES